Finance for Development

Finance for Development
Latin America in Comparative Perspective

BARBARA STALLINGS
with
ROGERIO STUDART

BROOKINGS INSTITUTION PRESS
Washington, D.C.

UNITED NATIONS
Economic Commission for Latin America and the Caribbean

Finance for Development: Latin America in Comparative Perspective may be ordered from:
Brookings Institution Press, 1775 Massachusetts Avenue, N.W., Washington,
D.C. 20036, www.brookings.edu. Telephone: 800/537-5487 or 410/516-6956;
Fax: 410/516-6998; E-mail: hfscustserv@press.jhu.edu

Library of Congress Cataloging-in-Publication data
Stallings, Barbara.
  Finance for development : Latin America in comparative perspective /
Barbara Stallings, with Rogerio Studart.
      p.   cm.
  "United Nations. Economic Commission for Latin America and the Caribbean."
  Includes bibliographical references and index.
  ISBN-13: 978-0-8157-8085-4 (alk. paper)
  ISBN-10: 0-8157-8085-0 (alk. paper)
  1. Finance—Latin America. I. Studart, Rogério, 1961– II. United Nations.
Economic Commission for Latin America and the Caribbean. III. Title.
  HG185.L3S83 2006
  332.098—dc22   2005037073

9 8 7 6 5 4 3 2 1

The paper used in this publication meets minimum requirements of the
American National Standard for Information Sciences—Permanence of Paper for
Printed Library Materials: ANSI Z39.48-1992.

Typeset in Adobe Garamond

Composition by Peter Lindeman
Arlington, Virginia

Printed by R. R. Donnelley
Harrisonburg, Virginia

Contents

Acknowledgments

This book began five years ago when we were both working at the United Nations Economic Commission for Latin America and the Caribbean (ECLAC) in Santiago, Chile. Stallings was director of the Economic Development Division and Studart was an economic affairs officer. An earlier ECLAC project on economic reforms in the region had left an important gap—the role of the financial sector in the development process.[1] We set out to remedy the omission.

In the process, we incurred a great many debts that we would like to acknowledge. The Ford Foundation provided a generous grant, which made the research possible. We would like to thank the foundation for its support, in particular that of Anthony Romero and Manuel Montes, although both have now gone on to other jobs. We also want to thank ECLAC for its help in initiating the project and its support for the coedition of the English-language publication and the forthcoming Spanish translation. Particular mention goes to José Antonio Ocampo and José Luis Machinea, past and present executive secretaries; Alicia Bárcena, deputy executive secretary; João Carlos Ferraz, director of the Productive Development Division; and Laura López, director of publications.

In the course of the project, both of us changed institutions. Stallings is especially appreciative of the time given her to work on the book by the Watson Institute for International Studies at Brown University. Studart would like to

1. Stallings and Peres (2000), also published by Brookings.

thank his colleagues at the Inter-American Development Bank, especially Anita Fiore, although his duties there prevented him from taking the active role in the writing of the book that we had originally envisioned.

Parts of the manuscript were presented at various seminars, where we obtained useful feedback. Two seminars at ECLAC were particularly important: one early in the project, in December 2001, and the other at the end, in April 2005. In between, we received helpful comments through presentations at Tokyo University, Korea University, the World Institute for Development Economics Research (WIDER) in Helsinki, the Asian Development Bank Institute (ADBI) in Tokyo, the International Federation of Latin American and Caribbean Studies (FIEALC) in Osaka, an Inter-American Development Bank seminar in Beijing, and two Forum on Debt and Development (Fondad) seminars in Amsterdam and Seoul. We are also grateful to a number of people who read chapters of the manuscript or its earlier incarnations: Hubert Escaith, Ricardo Ffrench-Davis, Alicia García-Herrero, Celso Garrido, Ricardo Gottschalk, Stephany Griffith-Jones, Gunther Held, Sergio Kurczyn Bañuelos, Ross Levine, Sergio Luna Martínez, Robert McCauley, Heather Montgomery, Gonzalo Rivas, Sergio Schmukler, and Anthony Tillet.

Stallings would like to acknowledge the assistance of several people who facilitated research trips: Bernardo Kosacoff (Argentina), Guillermo Larraín (Chile), Eun Mee Kim (Korea), Mahani Zainal Abidin (Malaysia), Jorge Mattar (Mexico), and Yun Han Chu (Taiwan). She would also like to thank several institutions that hosted her: the Institute of Southeast Asian Studies in Singapore, the Institute of Social Science of the University of Tokyo, and the Research Department of the International Monetary Fund. Help with research and access to data were provided by Gabriela Clivio (for Chile), Celso Garrido (for Mexico), and Giovanni Stumpo (for Brazil). Eduardo Moncada at Brown University went well beyond the call of duty as a research assistant. Without all of this support, it would have been impossible to complete the book. Finally, in the production process, we benefited from the guidance of Robert Faherty, director of the Brookings Institution Press, and his excellent staff, including Janet Walker, Larry Converse, and Susan Woollen. Jennifer Hoover greatly improved the readability of the manuscript. To all of these individuals and institutions, we offer our gratitude. Of course, all remaining errors are our own responsibility.

BARBARA STALLINGS   ROGERIO STUDART
Providence, R.I.   *Washington, D.C.*

1

Finance for Development: Issues and Trends

Access to finance is a crucial determinant of the development process in emerging market economies. Although it may seem obvious now, this view was not always widely accepted. The tendency in development economics during most of the postwar era was to focus on the "real" sector of the economy—namely, industrialization, technology transfer, and the international exchange of goods—with the financial sector relegated to the sidelines. Insofar as finance formed part of the constellation of priority topics, it centered on international finance, in the form of foreign direct investment, bilateral and multilateral aid, and international commercial bank loans.

Over the last decade, a large body of literature has highlighted the role of the domestic financial system in developing economies. Three topics have been of particular interest. The first centers on financial crises: why they erupt, how to prevent them, and how to foster financial stability. A second topic is the link between finance and growth. While the long-standing debate on the causal relationship between finance and growth continues, the current empirical literature clearly argues that finance should be considered the independent variable—and thus of interest to policymakers. A third issue, much less studied than the other two, concerns access to finance. The questions researchers are asking include who can obtain finance, at what cost, and how access affects the potential of small and medium-sized firms to contribute to economic growth and a more equal distribution of income and wealth.

Recent interest in financial crises began with the Mexican debacle of 1994–95, which has been called the first financial crisis of the twenty-first century.[1] That is, it did not match the traditional pattern whereby crises were the result of loose macroeconomic policy or poor management of individual banks. New theoretical approaches were introduced, but it was not until the Asian crisis of 1997–98 that they attracted much attention. Among the new elements was a switch in focus from the behavior of the current account of the balance of payments to the capital account and from flows to stocks. Another dominant theme was the role of external factors, especially international capital flows, in causing problems for countries that had made major strides in liberalizing their economies in line with formulas promoted by the international financial institutions. Ironically, successful economies have turned out to be the most vulnerable.

Crises and stability are not the only concerns of experts and policymakers, however. Governmental authorities have two potentially contradictory roles to play in dealing with the financial sector. On the one hand, they must try to maintain the stability of the system as a whole. This requires establishing broad guidelines for the behavior of individual institutions, including limits on the amounts and types of credit that they can offer and requirements for capital and liquidity. On the other hand, today's governments are also expected to promote growth. In the financial realm, this involves providing incentives so that financial institutions will channel investment funds to productive enterprises. Since such loans embody varying types and amounts of risk, they must be balanced against the need for stability at both the micro- and macroeconomic levels.

Another role that governments are expected to play in modern economies is to correct market failures that may lead to gross distortions in the distribution of income and wealth. The tax system has traditionally been the instrument of choice for carrying out this task, but finance can be useful too. The trade-off mentioned above also comes into play here. If too much emphasis is put on stability, banks will not lend to productive enterprises in general and will certainly avoid dealing with more risky small and medium-sized firms (SMEs). Unwillingness on the part of banks to lend to SMEs is especially problematic since the capital markets and international finance are the exclusive domain of larger, more established firms. Access to finance for SMEs is relevant not only because of the effect on income distribution, but also for its important impact on job creation: in virtually all economies, SMEs are the major source of employment.

The trade-offs among stability, growth, and access exist in all countries, but they pose a particularly daunting challenge for developing nations. There are a number of reasons for the greater difficulty. The financial systems themselves are more fragile in developing countries, and governments lack the instruments and institutions, as well as the trained personnel, that are typically found in industrial nations. At the same time, high growth rates are more necessary in develop-

---

1. Camdessus (1995).

ing countries to begin to provide their populations with an adequate standard of living, and inequality is likely to be more prevalent. Finally, international attempts to provide help and guidance on financial issues may actually increase problems for developing countries, as has been argued with respect to the new guidelines established by the Bank for International Settlements (BIS).

The trend toward financial liberalization and international integration has further complicated the task of financial management for all, but again it has posed special problems for developing countries. As a result of liberalization, developing countries lost the instruments—however imperfect they were—that they had previously used to maintain financial stability. The transition to a more open system frequently took place so rapidly that substitutes could not be created in time; the industrial countries established strong systems of regulation and supervision over decades, not months. In addition, the small scale of most developing countries' financial systems made them particularly vulnerable to the large, volatile flows of international capital that have characterized the global markets in recent years. While these flows can help to relieve the foreign exchange constraint that has typically limited growth in developing countries, they can also undermine stability and result in major crises with profound implications for macroeconomic performance and serious negative effects on both growth and equity.

Finance within a New Development Model in Latin America

We examine these issues with respect to Latin America in the decade and a half beginning around 1990. This time frame is a critically important one for Latin America because it witnessed an acceleration of the move toward an open, market-based development model in place of one that relied heavily on the state and was semiclosed with respect to foreign trade and capital flows. The financial sector was a key part of the transformation, and it changed dramatically as a consequence.[2] Since most other economies, including those of East Asia, have also been moving toward greater reliance on the market in financial and nonfinancial areas, this time period increases the relevance of the book's findings beyond the Latin American region itself.

During most of the postwar period, Latin American countries followed some version of the so-called import-substitution industrialization (ISI) model. The ISI approach featured a dominant role of the state in the economy, including extensive regulation of prices, a high share of GDP made up of government expenditure, control of credit, regulation of labor markets, and direct ownership

2. This section is taken from Stallings and Peres (2000). That book includes an extensive review of the literature on economic reform in Latin America up to 2000. Notable works published since then include a new quantitative regional overview (Lora and Panizza, 2002) and several comparative country-oriented studies of the political economy of reform (for example, Snyder, 2001; Teichman, 2001; Weyland, 2002).

of key industries. At the same time, barriers limited Latin America's interactions with the rest of the world economy. Trade protection was pervasive through taxes on exports and high tariffs or quotas (or both) on imports. Financial integration was also restricted via controls on foreign exchange transactions by citizens, limits on foreign capital inflows and their sectoral destination, and restrictions on capital outflows including remittance of profits and interest.

The authorities began to rethink these policies after following them for several decades. The reasons varied over time. For the earliest cases in the 1970s (Argentina, Chile, Uruguay), new ideological currents arose with the return of newly minted Ph.D.s from the United States. A second wave followed in the 1980s (Bolivia, Costa Rica, Mexico), when countries were heavily influenced by the debt crisis, the accompanying role of the international financial institutions, and new conservative leadership in the industrial countries. The 1990s were the key decade, however, as the pioneering countries moved further along the path toward the market and most of the rest of the region joined them, encouraged in part by the positive examples of neighbors, especially Chile, and the disappearance of the socialist bloc in Europe. Nonetheless, ideological and international factors also continued to play a role in governmental decisionmaking.

The reform package was made up of a number of separate but related policies. Price controls were reduced or eliminated, import restrictions were lifted, state-owned firms were privatized, tax rates were lowered and shifted from income to consumption, and labor regulations were made more flexible. Another important component of the reforms centered on the financial system. In this sphere, two changes are often conflated that are really separate policies. One is the deregulation of domestic financial activities, for example, freeing interest rates on loans and deposits, lowering reserve requirements, ending directed credit, and making it easier for new firms to enter the market. The other is the liberalization of international financial transactions, including the elimination of controls on capital flows, the end of regulation on offshore borrowing by financial and nonfinancial firms, and the suppression of multiple exchange rates.

Financial liberalization has been arguably the most controversial of all the structural reforms. While government decisions to lower tariffs, sell state-owned enterprises, or increase labor market flexibility have certainly encountered opposition, it has typically been concentrated in certain groups that face losses as a result of the changes. Financial liberalization, by contrast, has a far broader impact across all sectors of the economy. In addition, the financial sector is generally regarded as the most fragile part of the economy, subject to dramatic swings stemming from changes in economic or political variables or even shifts in market psychology. Nonetheless, domestic financial liberalization is second only to trade liberalization in terms of its implementation record, and it has advanced more (relative to its starting point) than any other reform in the Latin American

Figure 1-1. *Economic Reforms in Latin America, 1990–2000*[a]

Index (0 – 100)

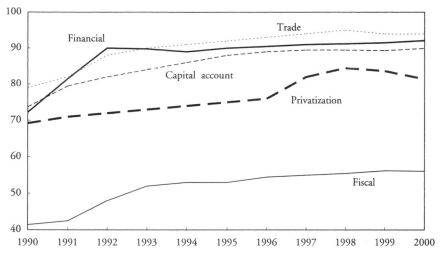

Sources: ECLAC (2001, p. 47), based on Morley, Machado, and Pettinato (1999).

a. Indexes range from 0 (complete government control) to 100 (no government intervention). They are normalized according to the following formula: $I_{it} = (\text{Max} - IR_{it})/(\text{Max} - \text{Min})$, where I_{it} = index value for country i, year t; Ir_{it} = raw value of reform measure, country i, year t; MAX = maximum value of reform measure for all countries, all years; MIN = minimum value of reform measure for all countries, all years.

region; see figure 1-1. Moreover, although opposition to the reforms has generally increased since the late 1990s, when growth rates began to fall after the Asian crisis, the reversion of domestic financial liberalization has been limited.

Latin America's Financial Sector Today: Stylized Facts

Financial liberalization greatly changed the characteristics of the financial sector in Latin America. In particular, the liberalization process created new rules by which the system operates. The new rules, in turn, led to a number of additional changes, such as ownership in the sector and the nature of the government's role. Other dimensions, however, displayed far less variation. Indeed, many characteristics—especially the shallowness of the financial system as a whole and the failure to develop a capital market segment—remained surprisingly similar to the prereform period; proponents had argued that financial liberalization would produce more dramatic and extensive advances. Combining the differences and similarities, we can portray the financial sector today in terms of six stylized facts.

First, Latin America's financial systems remain bank based, meaning that bank credit is more important than other forms of finance such as the flotation of bonds or stock market offerings. Nonetheless, bank credit as a share of GDP is very low in comparison with industrial economies or other developing countries, and it has grown slowly since the early 1990s. On average across the region, bank credit represented only 41 percent of GDP in 2003; the figure was 96 percent in East Asia and 94 percent in the Group of Seven (G-7) countries. Another characteristic that sets Latin America apart is the low share of total bank credit that goes to private borrowers rather than the public sector (22 percent versus 82 percent in East Asia). Short maturities also characterize bank credit, especially from private sector banks, so that firms must continually roll over credit or find other ways to finance investment.[3]

Second, trends in bank behavior have been highly volatile in recent years, and crises have become more frequent in the wake of financial liberalization. Moreover, a link has developed between banking and currency crises, leading to the emergence of so-called twin crises. World Bank data show that Latin American countries had the highest average number of financial crises in the last three decades, at 1.25 per country. Former Soviet bloc countries and sub-Saharan Africa followed with 0.89 and 0.83, respectively. East Asia had only 0.38 crises per country, which approaches the 0.21 level of the Organization for Economic Cooperation and Development (OECD). Latin American countries were also the most likely to have recurrent crises: 35 percent of the countries in the region suffered two or more crises, compared with 8 percent in East Asia and none in the OECD.[4]

Third, bank ownership has changed in two main ways. Many public sector banks have been privatized, with some being sold to local individuals or firms and some to foreigners. In the process, the share of foreign ownership in the banking sector has increased; even banks that were initially privatized through sale to local owners have often been bought by foreigners at a later stage. Recent BIS data, which compare ownership patterns for 1990 and 2002, indicate that the share of assets in government-owned banks in the six largest Latin American countries fell from 46 to 22 percent. Domestic private ownership also fell during this period (from 47 to 32 percent), leaving foreign owners as the major group that gained market share (from 7 to 47 percent). East Asia also saw a rise in foreign ownership, but government ownership rose simultaneously in response to the Asian crisis of 1997–98. Reprivatization is ongoing in East Asia, however, with an important share of assets being purchased by foreigners, so these trends are likely to change in the near future.[5]

3. Data for Latin America and East Asia are from table 5-2; for the G-7 economies they are calculated from IMF, *International Financial Statistics Yearbook*. For countries included in Latin America and East Asia, see section on methodology below. See also García-Herrero and others (2002); Liso and others (2002); IDB (2004) on the general characteristics of Latin American banks.

4. Data are from IDB (2004, p. 30). See also Kaminsky and Reinhart (1998) for a comparison of crises in Latin America and East Asia. Kaminsky and Reinhart (1999) introduce the concept of twin crises.

5. See table 3-2. For earlier comparative analysis, see Litan, Masson, and Pomerleano (2001); foreign bank strategies in Latin America are analyzed in ECLAC (2003, part III).

Fourth, capital markets, the other major source of formal sector finance, remain incipient in most countries of the region. Bonds outstanding represented only 37 percent of GDP in 2003, while stock market capitalization was 34 percent. Comparable figures for East Asia were 60 percent and 80 percent, and for the G-7 they were 141 percent and 100 percent, respectively. On the positive side, Latin American markets grew substantially in the 1990s, albeit with two caveats. First, with respect to bond markets, the large majority of funds in Latin America are going to the public sector; private sector finance represents only 8 percent of GDP (37 percent in East Asia). Second, on the stock market side, capitalization figures greatly overestimate their importance in Latin American economies. New issues (primary markets) have virtually dried up, representing only around 2 percent of GDP in recent years. In addition, the number of listed firms fell between 1990 and 2003. In both markets, liquidity is low as most stocks and many bonds are not traded; this fact discourages entry into the markets since investors cannot exit if they wish.[6]

Fifth, because of the characteristics just described, the financial sector— including both banks and capital markets—has made less of a contribution to economic growth in Latin America than is possible and desirable. A good deal of evidence purports to show that finance is an important determinant of growth in all countries, although analysts disagree on the channels.[7] Our focus in this book is on finance for investment. Investment as a share of GDP is very low in Latin America compared to the high-growth economies of East Asia; the average figures for the period 1990–2003 were 20 percent and 35 percent, respectively.[8] While many factors play a role in explaining low investment rates, evidence from several sources suggests that finance is a particular constraint in the Latin American case, which is logical given the shallow financial markets in the region.[9] Another important factor in the finance-investment relationship is the maturity structure of finance and the lack of a long-term segment in most countries of Latin America today. Indeed, the higher investment ratios in the early postwar period may have been partially due to the availability of long-term government finance. In indirect terms, finance for consumption and mortgages is in its infancy, so demand from these sources is failing to stimulate further investment.

6. Data on bonds outstanding and stock market capitalization for Latin America and East Asia are from tables 5-3 and 5-4. G-7 figures are from Standard and Poor's (2005) and the BIS website (www.bis.org/statistics/qcsv/anx16a.csv). New issues are from Mathiesen and others (2004). Litan, Pomerleano, and Sundararajan (2003) provide information on capital markets in developing countries; World Bank (2004c) analyzes Latin American capital markets.

7. The most up-to-date review of the literature on finance and growth is Levine (2004); see also World Bank (2001, part II). On how the channels of influence may differ depending on the level of development of a particular economy, see Rioja and Valev (2004a, 2004b).

8. Data are from World Bank, *World Development Indicators* (online).

9. See, for example, IDB (2001, chapter 2); Kantis, Ishido, and Komori (2001); Batra, Kaufmann, and Stone (2003). On Latin America in particular, see Pollack and García (2004).

Sixth, access to finance remains severely limited throughout most of the Latin American region, an issue that is closely related to finance and growth. The deficiency in finance for consumers and prospective homeowners is segmented by income group, with lower income earners being especially penalized. Likewise, small and medium-sized enterprises have significant difficulties in obtaining finance. Both bond and stock markets are clearly limited to the largest firms in any given country, so bank finance is the sole alternative to self-finance for smaller firms.[10] The only comparable data on access to finance across Latin American countries are from the World Bank's World Business Environment Survey, which shows that SMEs generally face substantially greater problems than large firms in obtaining access to finance. The difficulties, however, vary by country. For example, only 25–30 percent of small firms in Brazil, Chile, Colombia, and Venezuela report that finance is a major obstacle, while over 50 percent do so in Argentina, Mexico, and Peru. Individual country data, discussed in chapters 6 through 8 of this book, explain some of the reasons for the intraregional differences. Interregional variation is also important: East Asian firms are much less likely than Latin American firms to cite finance as a major obstacle to their operations, since they have access to much deeper financial markets.[11]

Substantive and Methodological Contributions

The book aims to explain these characteristics of the financial sector in Latin American countries. It is the first book-length study of the financial sector as a whole in the region, including banks as well as capital markets. We argue that both components of Latin America's financial system are weak in comparison with East Asia, which we use as a benchmark. In our search for explanations, we make both substantive and methodological contributions to the debates on finance for development that are taking place in the academy as well as the policy world.

In substantive terms, we differ from the new, but increasingly dominant, trend in the literature to place the blame for Latin America's weak financial markets on public banks, overregulation, and a refusal to acknowledge that small size makes full-scale integration with international financial markets the best policy option.[12] While we agree that most public banks have been poorly managed, that heavy-handed and inept regulation and supervision can undermine markets, and that small size is a hindrance, we argue that the solutions need not be total privatization, substitution of private monitoring for public supervision,

10. This is also true of access to the international financial markets, in that only a handful of very large, well-known firms can raise money there.
11. World Bank website (info.worldbank.org/governance/wbes).
12. Chapters 2 through 5 provide extensive literature reviews that document the new views and contrast them with traditional approaches.

and complete integration with international capital markets. More pragmatic solutions need to be considered that take into account the particular circumstances—political as well as economic—in individual countries.

With regard to public banks, a substantial amount of privatization has already taken place, as development and commercial banks have been closed, sold, or merged with private domestic or foreign institutions. Nonetheless, a significant number remain, and the question is what to do with them. One answer is to move toward full privatization as quickly as possible, and in some cases this may be the only answer. For example, the Governor of Bolivia's central bank has argued that it was impossible for Bolivia's public banks to be improved sufficiently, such that the best solution was to eliminate them—which was done.[13] At the same time, there are circumstances in which democratic political decisions have been made to the effect that privatization is not acceptable. Costa Rica is an example here. What can be done under these circumstances?

Our evidence, as explained in chapter 3, suggests that strong institutions may be able to overcome many of the typical problems with public banks. Cleaning their balance sheets, putting competent professionals in charge, and requiring them to compete without special advantages is an alternative to privatization where citizens have decided that they want the public sector to maintain control of certain spheres of the economy. Discussions of exactly this type took place in Costa Rica in the mid-1990s.[14] Similar decisions seem to have been made to maintain Brazil's National Bank for Economic and Social Development (BNDES) and Banco do Brasil and Chile's BancoEstado as public institutions, and similar steps have been taken to require them to operate in an efficient manner. The literature warns of rent seeking, corruption, and a possible contradiction between the economic and social functions of public banks. Our argument is not that public banks should return to the position of power they held in most Latin American countries in the early postwar years. Rather, if citizens so desire, and a strong institutional context can be created, public banks can do a reasonable job in terms of efficiency and in carrying out certain social functions.[15] We also find that weak institutions can undermine otherwise efficient banking institutions.

On regulation and supervision, an important public role clearly needs to be maintained. As discussed in chapter 4, we find (weak) evidence that corroborates the studies by private monitoring advocates with respect to a negative relationship between government-based supervision and bank performance. Likewise, we find a positive relationship between performance and private monitoring indicators. At the same time, we also find evidence of the procyclical tendencies that are

13. Morales (2005).
14. Personal interview with a former Costa Rican official.
15. The Bolivian example is useful in this sense. In an extremely poor country, with weak institutions and few skilled personnel, a solution à la Costa Rica, Chile, and Brazil may indeed be impossible.

the justification for prudential regulation and supervision. The disagreement is not about the empirical relationships, but the conclusion that private monitoring can adequately deal with the problems of stability that plague financial institutions as a result of collective action problems. We see private monitoring and public regulation and supervision as complements, not substitutes, and we join in the call for greater transparency, more public information, director liability, and outside audits to become part of a government-based system of prudential regulation and supervision. Our evidence suggests, however, that it would be a serious mistake to rely exclusively on private initiative.

Finally, on the issue of international integration, we again find space for a middle ground that others do not seem to see. For very small economies, such as those in Central America or the Caribbean, vibrant domestic capital markets are probably not feasible, just as economies of scale make it impossible to support certain nonfinancial sectors. Nevertheless, participation in international financial markets is not the only alternative. While a few large borrowers can access such resources, participation in the international markets is an illusion for the vast majority of firms—even large firms in a local context. We propose that attention be paid to a regional option in those cases, especially where other regional integration agreements already exist. Regional financial markets are not easy to construct, but East Asian governments have been moving in this direction, and Latin America's regional development banks provide an important resource for supporting the necessary infrastructure. Flexibility is needed with respect to possible solutions to the size problem.

In summary, we are not opposed to the new calls for a greater private role (in bank ownership and in regulation and supervision) and greater openness (with respect to participation in international financial markets). We propose, however, that more emphasis be placed on the context in which domestic financial markets operate. By strengthening the macroeconomic and institutional context in individual countries, as well as establishing rules for cautious financial integration at the international and the regional levels, more space is created to take account of local conditions and preferences. This, in turn, increases the chances of making proposals that are relevant to policymakers. Another aspect of the focus on context is the role of governments in creating, completing, and strengthening markets in which the private sector can operate. It is too often forgotten in the new literature that private initiative depends on the context.[16] We develop these ideas more fully in the remainder of the book.

Beyond discussions of the structure of financial markets and their governance, we also want to propose that more attention be paid to two problems

16. We refer to what some call *market-enhancing policies*, often seen as an intermediate position between laissez-faire capitalism and a government-centered version. See Aoki, Kim, and Okuno-Fujiwara (1997); in particular, the chapter by Hellmann, Murdock, and Stiglitz (1997) discusses the link between finance and market-enhancing policies.

that are prevalent throughout the region in terms of existing financial systems. One is the need for a long-term segment, which will support investment and help to raise Latin America's very low rates of capital formation and thus support faster economic growth. We point to a number of experiences that may offer models of how to proceed and make some recommendations on possible steps, but our main aim is to put the issue on the agenda. A second problem that also requires more attention than it has received is how to expand access to financial markets for micro, small, and medium-sized firms. In most countries, the government and a small group of very large firms have no financial constraints in that they can move at will among international markets, domestic capital markets, local banks, and nonbank finance. Their smaller counterparts have much greater difficulties, and under current circumstances they have too few options in the formal financial system. Again, a number of experiences may be adaptable across countries, and we hope to stimulate more discussion of this issue since it has important social and economic ramifications.

Most of the literature that we have discussed in the previous paragraphs is based on large-sample regression studies combining cases from both industrial and developing countries. These studies offer important insights and ways to test hypotheses, but we are troubled by the inclusion of countries with widely divergent levels of development without partitioning the sample to see if relationships are due to this factor. A number of recent studies show that the financial behavior of the two groups of countries differs substantially. In addition, large-sample studies always require the use of highly simplified measures of very complex realities that cannot take adequate account of qualitative distinctions. We argue that these are serious problems, which require an effort at compensation if we are to draw the proper lessons for policymaking.

Our way of dealing with these methodological problems—and an important contribution of the book—is to work at several levels of analysis and to use several methodologies. Our principal approach is small-sample comparative analysis of a dozen countries from Latin America and East Asia, but we also look at three country case studies in a comparative perspective. Another approach is to engage in theoretically informed case studies of single countries; a number are cited in the chapters that follow. Economic historians are in the best position to exploit within-country time series data, which can produce results that complement those from cross-country studies of large or small samples.

Our main comparative referent is East Asia, which we argue is the developing region with the greatest similarities to Latin America and the one that has the most lessons to offer Latin America. Table 1-1 contrasts some of the most important macroeconomic and financial indicators of the two regions. Latin America clearly lags behind on all of them, although the region has much more experience with managing crises, a point that proved to be of interest to East Asia after the Asian financial crisis of 1997–98.

Table 1-1. *Latin America and East Asia: Economic Indicators, 1965–2003*

Indicator	Latin America	East Asia
GDP growth rates		
1965–80	6.0	7.3
1981–90	1.6	7.8
1991–2000	3.3	7.7
2001–03	0.4	6.8
Export growth rate[a]		
1965–80	−1.0	8.5
1981–90	3.0	9.8
1991–2000	8.7	12.1
2001–03	2.0	12.7
Savings rate[b]		
1965	22.0	22.0
1990	22.0	35.0
2000	20.0	35.0
2003	21.0	41.0
Financial depth[c]		
1990	63.0	141.0
1995	86.0	185.0
2000	104.0	203.0
2003	112.0	236.0
Inflation[d]		
1965–80	31.4	9.3
1981–90	192.1	6.0
1991–2000	84.1	7.7
2001–03	6.0	3.1

Sources: World Bank (1992) for GDP growth, export growth, savings, and inflation, 1965–90; World Bank, *World Development Indicators* (online) for GDP growth, export growth, and savings, 1990–2003; IMF, *International Financial Statistics Yearbook* for inflation, 1990–2003; table 5-1 for financial depth.

a. Merchandise exports only for 1965–90; goods and services for 1990–2003.
b. Gross domestic savings as share of GDP.
c. Bank credit plus bonds outstanding plus stock market capitalization as share of GDP.
d. Consumer price index.

Within the two regions, we disaggregate to a number of cases that share an important set of characteristics; this is the middle-income group that is frequently referred to as *emerging market economies*. Given data problems, the particular set of countries varies somewhat from chapter to chapter, but we try to keep a core group intact. In Latin America, we focus on Argentina, Brazil, Chile, Colombia, Mexico, Peru, and Venezuela. In Asia, the cases are Indonesia, Korea, Malaysia, the Philippines, Singapore, Taiwan, and Thailand. Table 1-2 shows the population and per capita GDP for these countries. In Latin America, population ranges from 16 million to 177 million, and per capita GDP from $4,900 to $11,500. For East Asia, the range is 4 million to 215 million and $3,400 to $24,500, respectively. On average, East Asia's population slightly

Table 1-2. *Latin America and East Asia: Population and Per Capita GDP, 2003*

Region and country	Population (millions)	GDP per capita[a]
Latin America[b]	61.4	7,951
Argentina	38.4	11,586
Brazil	176.6	7,767
Chile	15.8	10,206
Colombia	44.4	6,784
Mexico	102.3	9,136
Peru	27.1	5,267
Venezuela	25.5	4,909
East Asia[b]	65.4	12,964
Indonesia	214.5	3,364
Korea	47.9	17,908
Malaysia	24.8	9,696
Philippines	81.5	4,321
Singapore	4.2	24,481
Taiwan	22.6	23,400
Thailand	62.0	7,580

Sources: World Bank, *World Development Indicators* (online); Republic of China (2004) for Taiwan.
a. Dollars (purchasing power parity).
b. Unweighted average.

exceeds that of Latin America, while the per capita GDP differential is much larger.

In the chapters on changes in the financial system, we make use of quantitative data sets that have been gathered by others, putting them into comparable form to the extent possible to be able to describe and explain the differences between and within regions. In the chapters on the impact of the changes, we switch to country case studies of Chile, Mexico, and Brazil. These three not only have the most sophisticated financial systems in Latin America, but they also show three rather different approaches to finance—based on different ownership patterns—in the new market-oriented era. By combining quantitative and qualitative methods, we provide both a broad comparative overview and a nuanced analysis of the interaction of individual characteristics and global trends.

The dependent variables differ in the two parts of the book. In the initial chapters, we are trying to explain the characteristics and changes in Latin America's financial sector and how it differs from that of the more successful East Asian region. In the later chapters, we want to understand the financial sector's contributions to economic success in Latin America itself, where success is defined as a combination of stability, economic growth, and equity. These are broad and ambitious goals, but they are necessary to discover the extent to which the financial sector is pulling its weight in the economic development process and what steps can be taken to improve its performance.

Overview of the Book

The rest of the book is divided into two substantive parts, followed by a policy-oriented conclusion. Part I consists of four chapters that analyze changes in the financial sector over the past fifteen years. Chapter 2 starts with the financial liberalization process. It looks at how much liberalization has taken place in Latin America in comparison with other regions, the relationship between financial liberalization and crisis, and the characteristics of the rescue operations if a crisis occurs. The main findings are that Latin America has liberalized its domestic financial sector extensively, but in an unusually volatile way. Domestic liberalization was accompanied by international liberalization, while macroeconomic stability and prudential regulation lagged behind. Institutions also tended to be weak, which was a disadvantage: good policies require good institutions, and these take time to develop. The combination helped to promote twin banking and currency crises, which were extremely expensive to resolve—in terms of both opportunity costs for government revenues and other costs such as lost GDP, high real interest rates, and falling asset prices. These negative consequences lasted for many years after the crises themselves had subsided. Looking at these facts, we conclude that a gradual approach to liberalization should be pursued to give the authorities time to develop an adequate policy and institutional environment in which to cope with the new challenges.

Chapter 3 begins an examination of three other trends that were associated with financial liberalization and crisis. The focus of this chapter is on changes in ownership of the banking sector. We confirm the generally accepted trend toward less public and more foreign ownership, but we find that substantial heterogeneity still exists. Looking at banking systems within countries, rather than individual banks across countries, we find that East Asia behaves as the new literature predicts: foreign-dominated banking systems perform best, public systems worst, and private domestic systems in the middle. The situation in Latin America is more complex: foreign-dominated banking systems behaved less well than predicted, but public systems performed better. To explain these anomalies, we turn to the role of institutions. Incorporating institutional variables reinforces the results from East Asia and enables us to account for the unexpected findings in Latin America. We conclude that with strong institutions, public banks can perform reasonably well, while weak institutions can undermine the operations of even world-class foreign banks.

Chapter 4 examines another aspect of the government's role in the financial sector. Regulation and supervision were loosened as part of the financial liberalization process, and banks frequently took advantage of the laxity to behave in ways that led to crises. In the postcrisis period, new, more sophisticated systems of prudential regulation and supervision were introduced. It has recently been argued, however, that the new rules are stifling financial development and that private monitoring is a preferable approach. Our findings suggest that private monitoring can be a useful supplement to government-based regulation, but the problems of procyclicality that characterize the financial sector require that governments provide stability as a public good. We also emphasize the interrelationship of macroeconomics and banking regulation and examine the increased role played by international actors in setting rules on regulation and supervision. In this context, an important agenda item for the coming years is the impact of the new BIS agreement on the financial systems of developing countries.

Chapter 5 turns from banks to the capital markets, the other key element of the financial system. While neither banks nor capital markets have been shown to be superior to the other as a source of finance, evidence is growing about the advantages of having both. Latin American bond and stock markets, however, are weak in comparison to their East Asian counterparts, with the possible exceptions of Chile and Brazil. Our findings suggest several reasons for the discrepancy: better macroeconomic performance in East Asia, stronger institutions in East Asia, and the availability of U.S. capital markets as an alternative to domestic markets for large firms in Latin America. Nonetheless, Latin American governments have recently begun to promote domestic capital markets with some success. One method is to create institutional investors, especially through the privatization of pension funds. Others include mandating greater transparency and accountability in the financial sector as a whole and strengthening corporate governance in nonfinancial enterprises. A worrisome issue is new evidence on possible negative interactions between domestic and international financial systems.

Part II of the book shifts from regional analysis of changes in the financial system to case studies of how the changes manifested themselves in individual countries and their impact in terms of growth, investment, and access to finance. Chapter 6 begins with the Chilean case. In the mid-1970s, Chile became the first country in Latin America to embark on a sustained program of financial liberalization. After a serious crisis in the early 1980s, the country was a pioneer in revamping its regulatory and supervisory systems. Since 1990, the Chilean financial sector has been the most successful in the region in terms of depth, efficiency, and stability. These characteristics, in turn, have contributed to a virtuous circle with the highest rates of investment and growth in Latin America. The financial sector model is a combination of domestic and foreign banks; in addition, a single, well-managed public sector bank pursues both social and economic goals. Capital market depth exceeds that of any neighboring country. Reasons for the good performance include the bank clean-up in the 1980s, a stable macroeconomic and institutional environment, and a gradual international reopening after the crisis. Capital market deepening has depended heavily on demand by institutional investors. Despite good performance, challenges remain: increasing long-term finance and liquidity and expanding access for small and medium-sized firms are among the principal ones.

Chapter 7 focuses on Mexico. Mexico's financial reforms began a decade after those in Chile and were followed by a major crisis in 1994–95. As a result, the Mexican government also reformed its banking laws and institutions. It not only reprivatized the banks taken over during the crisis, but eventually sold almost all domestic banks to foreigners; nearly 85 percent of bank assets are now controlled by foreign institutions. While this ownership structure offers potential opportunities, they have yet to be realized. Capital markets are weak, although the government has been promoting them in the last few years. The main problem with Mexico's banks, both foreign and domestic, is that they are not lending to the private sector, especially to private firms. Credit as a share of GDP is extraordinarily low, even in comparison with other countries in the region. This drought in the credit markets has not been a problem for the largest corporations, which can obtain funds internationally, but it has created serious difficulties for the large majority of firms. Despite an upswing since 2003, the negative implications for investment and growth are clear. Reviving bank credit is clearly Mexico's biggest challenge; closely related is the need to improve the country's institutions and expand access to finance for households and small firms.

Chapter 8 turns to Brazil, whose financial sector presents some interesting contrasts to those of Chile and Mexico. First, Brazil also liberalized its financial sector, but to a lesser extent than the other two countries. It still retains several very large and powerful public banks. The other major players are private domestic banks. Foreign competition, while increasing, is less important than in Chile or Mexico. Second, rather than waiting for a financial crisis to erupt, the Brazilian government cleaned up the banking system and revamped its laws and institutions after some serious problems emerged following a successful macroeconomic stabilization program in the mid-1990s. Third, Brazil has a long history of promoting capital markets, and it has some of the largest, most sophisticated markets among developing countries. Nonetheless, problems also remain in Brazil. Credit is scarce because banks prefer to hold government bonds rather than lend, and interest rates and spreads are extraordinarily high as a result of continuing macroeconomic problems. Not surprisingly, investment has been low and growth has been volatile. In addition, access to finance is limited, despite new programs in this area by the public banks.

Part III concludes with a summary of findings and a set of policy recommendations. The recommendations address the most important challenges facing the Latin American region if banks and capital markets are to be strengthened so that they can play a greater role in supporting economic development. The overall message is that emphasis should be placed on changing the environment in which the markets operate, with particular focus on macroeconomic stability, institutional development, and links with the international economy. In addition, market-enhancing policies must be developed to resolve the two major problems we have identified: the lack of long-term finance for investment and the scarcity of finance for small and medium-sized firms. Both need to be resolved if the Latin American region is to overcome the low growth rates of recent years and the long-term heritage of inequality.

PART I

Changes in Latin America's Financial System since 1990: Comparisons with East Asia

2

Financial Liberalization, Crisis, and the Aftermath

Financial liberalization in the past two decades has profoundly transformed financial systems in developing economies around the world. Broadly speaking, these changes have occurred in three stages, although differences are found across countries and perhaps across regions. First, liberalization changed the rules under which financial sectors operate. Whereas previously governments had a strong influence on the volume, price, and destination of loans, private sector institutions now make such decisions on their own. This shift has had important implications for investment and growth, as well as for who has access to finance. Second, in many cases financial liberalization was followed by financial crisis. These crises required rescue programs absorbing large amounts of fiscal revenues and resulted in steep losses of output and social dislocations. Third, the resolution of the crises further changed the characteristics of financial systems. They brought governments back into the picture, although in a different capacity than in the past, and they brought about significant changes in the ownership of financial institutions.

Given the magnitude of these transformations, any study of the financial sector in the current period must begin with a clear understanding of the liberalization process, both the new opportunities it creates and the new challenges it poses. This chapter thus provides essential background for the rest of the book. We define liberalization as domestic financial deregulation and demonstrate that the major Latin American countries have made deep changes—deeper than those in East Asia, which is our main benchmark. We then test several hypotheses about when liberalization will be followed by crisis. Our results indicate that the policies accompanying liberalization—namely, macroeconomic management, capital account opening, and regulation and supervision—are the main determinants of whether a crisis will occur. Institutions are also important because they influence governments' ability to carry out sound policies, but institutions take a long time to nurture. Finally, we provide evidence of the devastating impact of financial crises, including the long-lasting nature of their damage to affected economies. Given the importance of institutions and policies for avoiding crises, we conclude that gradual liberalization has the best chance of a positive outcome.

The chapter is organized in five sections. The first presents our framework and hypotheses for studying liberalization. The second examines statistics on financial liberalization in developing countries, with particular emphasis on Latin America and East Asia. Section three turns to the relationship between liberalization and crisis; it looks at both the theoretical literature and empirical evidence to understand how liberalization and crisis are linked. Section four analyzes short-term rescue mechanisms, their fiscal and other costs, and their degree of success. (Longer-term aspects of the rescue programs are considered in later chapters.) The final section concludes.

Financial Liberalization: Literature and Hypotheses

In the early postwar period in most developing countries, domestic financial systems were dominated by the banking industry. Banks were tightly controlled by economic authorities, either because of concern about financial stability or because banks were an important instrument of development strategy. Rent seeking was also a frequent motivation. Controls were of various types. First, interest rates on both deposits and loans were set by the government. The real rates were often negative, at least ex post, as inflation exceeded nominal rates. Second, reserve requirements were very high, so the commercial banks had little freedom to expand their portfolios. Third, governments issued administrative directives for the allocation of a substantial share of commercial bank credit. Fourth, governments either prohibited banks from engaging in international lending and borrowing or limited the volume and uses of such funds. Finally, government-owned banks were responsible for a large amount of the lending that took place, often intermediating between external sources of credit and local borrowers. Together, these characteristics were referred to as financial repression.

Proponents of reform saw financial repression as leading to low savings rates, since depositors received low or negative interest on their funds; low monetization of the economies; limited access to credit, especially for small and medium-sized firms; and credit directed to borrowers on the basis of political connections, rather than the profitability of their projects. Financial liberalization would remove these burdens, they argued, enabling countries to mobilize increased volumes of resources, deploy them more efficiently, and thus accelerate investment, productivity, and growth.[1]

Opponents of liberalization were much more cautious. Even those who agreed with the criticisms of financial repression worried that the proposed solution could be worse than the problems it was meant to resolve. One concern was that the mechanisms already in place to mobilize resources—however flawed they might be—would be replaced by speculative forces that would result in crisis, chaos, and economic decline. These problems would be magnified if domestic liberalization were accompanied by external financial liberalization, such that large, volatile capital flows could overwhelm weak local banks. Another concern was that long-term finance would disappear in a liberalized system, and access to finance would be limited to a small group of large firms and wealthy households.[2]

We argue in this chapter that both positions embody some elements of truth. The outcomes depend heavily on the way liberalization policies are implemented, the other policies that accompany them, and the institutional framework in which the changes take place.[3] The outcomes also depend on the international context for liberalization, but that is beyond the control of the developing countries themselves.

We begin by defining what we mean by *financial liberalization*. The term is used in different ways in the literature, which helps explain some of the confusion and disagreement. For our purposes, financial liberalization refers to the partial or complete elimination of government-imposed restrictions on domestic financial behavior, so that economic agents can make their own decisions with regard to the volume, price, timing, and purpose of financial transactions. Two elements of this definition are of particular note. First, the definition does not imply that complete liberalization is involved; rather, the emphasis is on the direction of change. Put another way, we do not conceive of the process as a dichotomous choice of repression or liberalization, but as a range of possible points on a spectrum. Second, we do not include international financial liberalization as part of the definition per se. The two usually go together in practice,

1. The early arguments along these lines were made by McKinnon (1973) and Shaw (1973). The classic review of the literature is Fry (1995). More recent reviews include Caprio, Honohan, and Stiglitz (2001); Demirgüç-Kunt and Detragiache (2005).

2. Fry (1995) reviews half a dozen types of critiques of the McKinnon-Shaw thesis. Major examples include neostructuralists, such as Taylor (1983), and market failure approaches, such as Stiglitz (1994). For an updated version of Stiglitz's argument, see Caprio, Honohan, and Stiglitz (2001, chap. 2). On Latin America in particular, see Ffrench-Davis (2005).

3. An interesting complementary approach is found in Lee (2003), who argues that the literature on financial liberalization went through three phases: deregulation per se; the need for macroeconomic stability and dealing with imperfect financial markets; and the identification of institutional preconditions.

Table 2-1. *Relationship between Financial Liberalization and Outcomes*

Dimensions	Positive outcomes	Negative outcomes
Implementation	Gradual and extensive	Rapid and complete
Other economic policies		
Macroeconomic	Prices and real economy stable	Instability in one or both
International	Partial liberalization	Complete liberalization
Regulatory	Tight regulation/supervision	Loose regulation/supervision
Institutions	Strong	Weak

as components of a more generalized move toward greater reliance on the market. We find it useful, however, to consider international liberalization as one of the policies that might accompany domestic financial liberalization.

Based on this definition, we present a framework for analyzing the liberalization process, which includes the variables mentioned: implementation, accompanying policies, and institutional context. Table 2-1 summarizes a simple model of financial liberalization, according to these dimensions. The broadest question is whether the liberalization process is successful, where success (as defined in the introductory chapter) includes financial stability, increased rates of growth, and broader access to finance by lower-income households and small enterprises. Whereas the book as a whole addresses all three goals, in this chapter we concentrate on the first, asking under what conditions liberalization will have a positive outcome (stability) versus a negative one (crisis).

With regard to implementation, the key distinction involves speed and extent. Policies accompanying liberalization center on three components: macroeconomic policy (the approach to price stability, deficits, exchange rates, and real economic stability), international financial policy (the extent and sequencing of capital account opening), and regulation and supervision (adherence to international standards). The strengthening—or creation—of institutions includes the legal framework and protection of contracts, as well as government organs (such as central banks, regulatory and supervisory agencies, and the judicial system). The international political-economic context in which domestic financial liberalization takes place also influences the outcome, but developing countries cannot control this factor, so we do not include it in our scheme.

Our hypotheses, as spelled out in table 2-1, are that success in financial liberalization is optimized by (1) a gradual process of liberalization that eventually leaves decisions to private sector actors (if public sector banks continue, they should be run on a transparent and efficient basis with clear objectives); (2) a policy combination of macroeconomic stability with a competitive exchange rate, partial opening of the capital account following domestic liberalization, and prudential regulation preceding liberalization; and (3) an institutional framework with a strong legal system and competent operating agencies. In the discussion that follows, we test these hypotheses qualitatively by examining experiences in individual countries.

The follow-up to financial liberalization and crisis, if one occurs, is a rescue package and institutional change. These processes have generally been less controversial than financial liberalization itself. Most experts have been quite pragmatic about the prescription of rescue policies, and most governments have used some combination of market-based and government-managed programs. Nonetheless, the debate continues on the extent to which governments should rescue ailing institutions. Moral hazard is a particular concern, but the use of public moneys to bail out private actors has also been a political issue in some cases.[4]

Despite differences of opinion on these several issues, a commonly accepted set of stylized facts can be identified with respect to the empirical process of financial liberalization, crisis, and rescue in recent years. Financial liberalization occurred in most developing countries. It was frequently undertaken without an adequate regulatory environment in place. Newly liberated banks increased loans very rapidly without proper credit analysis or provisions for losses; moral hazard and adverse selection were frequent problems. In the extreme, banks took advantage of loose regulation by engaging in fraudulent activities. Unless authorities acted expeditiously and effectively, crisis resulted, possibly facilitated by a volatile economy and policies that stimulated large capital inflows. To prevent a systemic meltdown, governments intervened to rescue the banks—even if such intervention ran counter to their ideological predilections. Short-run policies included takeover of insolvent institutions, recapitalization, purchase of nonperforming loans, and support for debtors. Longer-term policies involved divestiture of intervened banks, which often resulted in increased foreign ownership, and an improved system of regulation and supervision. Whether this sequence led to a strong performance by the recovering financial system depended on the details of policy design and implementation.

Financial Liberalization: Empirical Trends

Financial liberalization has been a broad-based process in recent decades, involving developed as well as developing countries. Several data sets are available that enable us to compare Latin America with other regions, as well as to compare countries within Latin America. Using a cross-regional sample makes it possible to assess whether Latin America's financial liberalization had unique characteristics or whether the worldwide process has been basically the same everywhere.

---

4. For examples of a pragmatic, mixed approach versus one that argues for a particular alternative, see Calomiris, Klingebiel, and Laeven (2004) and Honohan and Klingebiel (2003), respectively.

The most useful for our purposes is a World Bank data set that includes OECD countries, Latin America, and East Asia during the period 1973–2002.[5] The overall index is composed of three subindexes: domestic financial liberalization (our definition), international liberalization, and stock market liberalization. Each subindex, in turn, is made up of several indicators. Domestic financial liberalization includes eliminating regulations on deposit and lending interest rates, allocation of credit, and foreign currency deposits. International liberalization is measured by the end of regulations on offshore borrowing by financial and nonfinancial institutions, multiple exchange rate markets, and controls on capital outflows. Stock market liberalization is gauged by the abolition of regulations on foreign acquisition of shares in the domestic stock exchange, repatriation of capital, and repatriation of interest and dividends. All of the indexes vary between 1.0 and 3.0, with larger numbers indicating greater liberalization.[6]

The Liberalization Index in International Comparison

Figure 2-1 plots the monthly variation of the overall index for the three groups of countries. It shows that the OECD countries already had substantially more liberalized financial markets than the other two regions at the beginning of the period, and—with the exception of a brief period in the mid-1970s—they advanced steadily until the early 1990s.[7] At that time, they reached the most liberalized position possible on the index and stayed there throughout the following years. The East Asian countries followed a similar path, but they began at a much lower point and had yet to reach full liberalization in 2002. The region attained its highest point (2.7 on the index) in the mid-1990s and continued at that level except for a slight drop around the time of the Asian financial crisis. That reversal was remarkably small, considering the tremendously negative impact of the crisis in the Asian countries.

In some ways, Latin America lies between the OECD and Asia. It began in an intermediate position in 1973 and ended between the other two in 2002. In the intervening years, however, Latin America demonstrated distinctive characteristics. First, the initial increase in the 1970s was very rapid; indeed, the Latin American index actually exceeded that of the OECD countries for a brief period

5. Only fourteen OECD countries are included: Canada, Denmark, Finland, France, Germany, Ireland, Italy, Japan, Norway, Portugal, Spain, Sweden, the United Kingdom, and the United States. OECD members Mexico and Korea are included with their respective regions. The seven Latin American countries are Argentina, Brazil, Chile, Colombia, Mexico, Peru, and Venezuela. The East Asian cases are Hong Kong, Indonesia, Korea, Malaysia, the Philippines, Taiwan, and Thailand. We have excluded Hong Kong, since its entrepôt status gives it atypical characteristics.

6. The index is described in Kaminsky and Schmukler (2003). The numerical data are found at the following website: siteresources.worldbank.org/DEC/Resources/financial_liberalization_index.xls.

7. The small decline in the OECD index was due to the influence of Denmark, Italy, and especially Portugal, all of which had activist governments in the mid-1970s.

Figure 2-1. *Financial Liberalization Index, by Region, 1973–2002*[a]

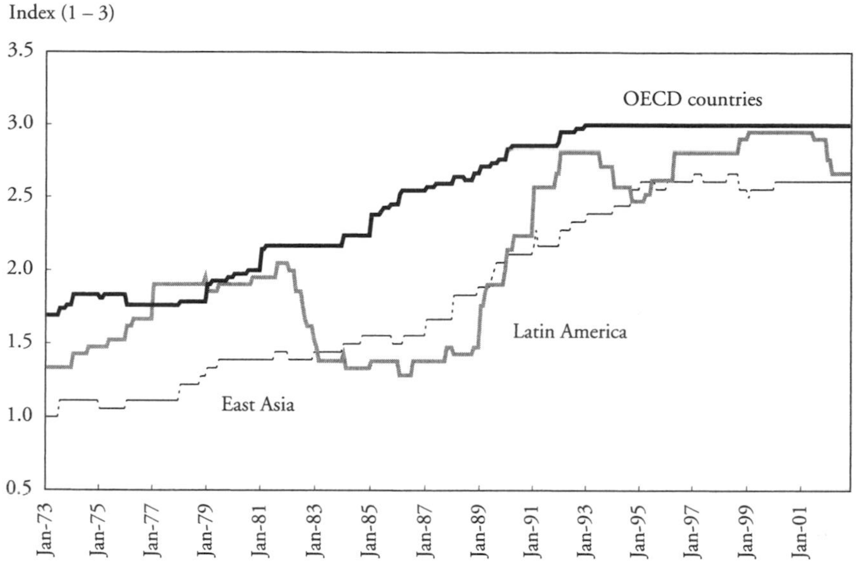

Index (1 – 3)

Source: World Bank website (siteresources.worldbank.org/DEC/Resources/financial_liberaliza-tion_index.xls).

a. See text for definition of index. OECD countries include Denmark, Finland, Ireland, Norway, Portugal, Spain, and Sweden. Latin America includes Argentina, Brazil, Chile, Mexico, Peru, and Venezuela. East Asia includes Indonesia, Korea, Malaysia, the Philippines, Taiwan, and Thailand.

in the mid-1970s. This rise was followed by a sharp and extended reversal during the debt crisis of the 1980s, in contrast to the much milder reaction in the Asian region in the 1990s. Only in 1988 did the liberalization process begin anew, and for the next several years the speed surpassed any period in any other region. From 1994 to 2002, there was again a good deal of stop-go movement. In other words, Latin America as a region pursued a much more volatile liberalization path than East Asia or the OECD.[8]

Since our definition of financial liberalization concentrates on domestic processes, we examine that component of the index separately for the same three regions (see figure 2-2). The pattern for the OECD and East Asian countries mirrors trends already seen in figure 2-1, while domestic liberalization in Latin America shows even greater volatility than was found in the overall index. In the 1970s, domestic financial markets in Latin America were significantly more open than in the OECD region. That gap ended with the debt crisis, however, when Latin American governments reversed their policy stance. By the 1990s, Latin America had joined the OECD countries at the highest level of liberaliza-

8. This finding is consistent with other characterizations of Latin America as an extremely volatile region on many indicators (see, for example, IDB, 1995).

Figure 2-2. *Domestic Financial Liberalization Index, by Region, 1973–2002*ᵃ

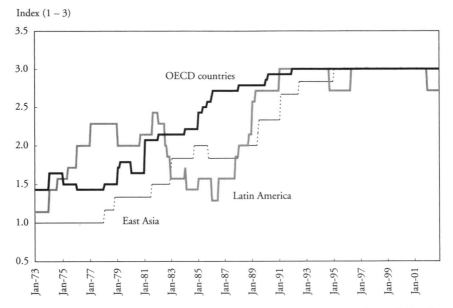

Source: World Bank website (siteresources.worldbank.org/DEC/Resources/financial_liberaliza-tion_ index.xls).
a. See figure 2-1 for lists of countries included; see text for definition of index.

tion, with the exception of limited reversals in the period around the Mexican crisis in 1995 and later in Argentina in 2001–02. East Asia remained slightly less open than Latin America and the OECD until 1995, as it did on the broader index.

The Liberalization Index in Latin America and East Asia

Figure 2-3 disaggregates the components of the index for Latin America. The overall index and the domestic financial component are the same trends presented above; data for liberalization of the capital account of the balance of payments and the stock market are added. As the figure shows, the domestic financial sector was the leading edge of liberalization, almost always exceeding the overall index. The capital account displayed the greatest volatility: it began as the most liberalized part of the index, fell to complete closure in the late 1980s, became completely liberalized in the later 1990s, and then fell off again. Stock markets were liberalized more slowly and smoothly.

In general, the seven Latin American countries for which data are available followed the volatile path displayed by the region as a whole. The main exception was Colombia, as shown in table 2-2, which presents individual country data for the overall index. Aside from a few months in 1986, Colombia followed

Figure 2-3. *Latin America: Components of Financial Liberalization Index,*
1973–2002[a]

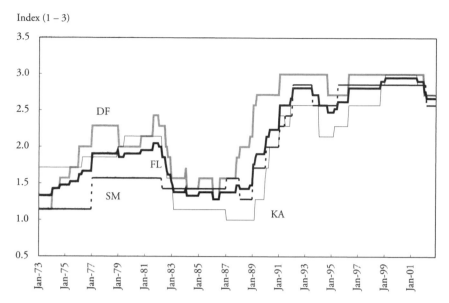

Index (1 – 3)

Source: World Bank website (siteresources.worldbank.org/DEC/Resources/financial_liberaliza-
tion_ index.xls).

a. FL is the full financial liberalization index; DF is the domestic financial liberalization index;
SM is the stock market liberalization index; KA is the capital account liberalization index. See text
for definitions.

a gradual strategy of financial opening throughout the 1973–2002 period, and
it was the only one of the seven that did not have full financial opening by
2002. Chile also followed a less volatile path than its neighbors. After reaching
an index level of 2.0 in 1980, on the eve of its major financial crisis, the index
dropped back to 1.0 for a single year, and then gradually reopened to reach 3.0
in the late 1990s.

The domestic component of the financial liberalization index paralleled that
of the overall index. Again, Colombia was the most stable reformer, reaching
full liberalization in 1981 and remaining at that level with only a brief, very partial reversal in 1986. Chile reached full liberalization earlier, in 1976, but had a
more drawn-out retrenchment in the 1980s. The remaining five countries had
much more volatile histories with domestic liberalization.[9] The other information in the World Bank index that is especially useful for our purposes concerns
trends in international financial liberalization (capital account opening) and its
relationship to domestic financial liberalization. In Brazil, Chile, and Colombia,

9. Calculated from the disaggregated data for the index; see note 6 (in this chapter) for access
information.

Table 2-2. *Latin America: Financial Liberalization Index, 1973–2002*[a]

Year	Argentina	Brazil	Chile	Colombia	Mexico	Peru	Venezuela
1973	1.0	1.3	1.0	1.0	1.7	1.7	1.7
1974	1.0	1.3	1.3	1.1	2.0	1.7	1.7
1975	1.0	1.3	1.6	1.3	2.0	1.7	1.7
1976	1.3	2.0	1.7	1.3	2.0	1.7	1.7
1977	2.3	2.0	1.7	1.3	2.0	1.7	2.3
1978	2.4	2.0	1.7	1.3	2.0	1.7	2.3
1979	2.7	1.3	1.9	1.3	2.0	1.7	2.3
1980	2.7	1.3	2.0	1.4	2.0	1.7	2.3
1981	2.7	1.3	2.0	1.7	2.0	1.7	2.6
1982	1.6	1.3	1.9	1.7	1.6	1.3	3.0
1983	1.0	1.3	1.0	1.7	1.0	1.3	2.4
1984	1.0	1.3	1.3	1.7	1.0	1.3	1.7
1985	1.0	1.3	1.7	1.7	1.0	1.3	1.7
1986	1.0	1.3	1.7	1.3	1.0	1.3	1.7
1987	1.2	1.3	2.0	1.7	1.0	1.0	1.7
1988	1.7	1.7	2.0	1.7	1.1	1.0	1.0
1989	2.4	2.0	2.0	1.7	1.9	1.0	2.2
1990	3.0	2.3	2.5	1.7	2.0	1.0	3.0
1991	3.0	2.5	2.5	2.3	2.4	2.3	3.0
1992	3.0	2.7	2.7	2.3	3.0	3.0	3.0
1993	3.0	2.7	2.7	2.3	3.0	3.0	2.7
1994	3.0	2.3	2.7	2.3	3.0	3.0	1.4
1995	3.0	2.6	2.7	2.3	3.0	3.0	1.4
1996	3.0	2.7	2.7	2.3	3.0	3.0	2.7
1997	3.0	2.7	2.7	2.3	3.0	3.0	3.0
1998	3.0	2.7	2.8	2.4	3.0	3.0	3.0
1999	3.0	3.0	3.0	2.7	3.0	3.0	3.0
2000	3.0	3.0	3.0	2.7	3.0	3.0	3.0
2001	2.7	3.0	3.0	2.7	3.0	3.0	3.0
2002	1.1	3.0	3.0	2.7	3.0	3.0	3.0

Source: World Bank website (siteresources.worldbank.org/DEC/Resources/financial_liberalization_index.xls).

a. For definition of index, see text.

capital account opening lagged domestic financial trends during most of the 1973–2002 period. For these three countries, full capital account opening occurred only in the late 1990s. In Argentina and Peru, trends in domestic and international policy were quite similar, while international policy was more open than domestic policy in Mexico and Venezuela. The majority of the countries thus deviated from our expectation that the two processes would move at more or less the same pace. In the case of Mexico and Venezuela, the closer economic relationships with the United States and the influence of the oil markets are probably major explanatory factors. For Brazil, Chile, and Colombia, the

Table 2-3. *East Asia: Financial Liberalization Index, 1973–2002*[a]

Year	Indonesia	Korea	Malaysia	Philippines	Taiwan	Thailand
1973	1.0	1.0	1.3	1.0	1.0	1.0
1974	1.0	1.0	1.7	1.0	1.0	1.0
1975	1.0	1.0	1.3	1.0	1.0	1.0
1976	1.0	1.0	1.3	1.3	1.0	1.0
1977	1.0	1.0	1.3	1.3	1.0	1.0
1978	1.7	1.0	1.4	1.3	1.0	1.0
1979	1.7	1.0	1.9	1.3	1.0	1.3
1980	1.7	1.0	2.0	1.3	1.0	1.3
1981	1.7	1.0	2.0	1.5	1.0	1.3
1982	1.7	1.0	2.0	1.7	1.0	1.0
1983	2.0	1.0	2.0	1.7	1.0	1.0
1984	2.0	1.0	2.3	1.7	1.1	1.0
1985	2.0	1.0	2.3	1.7	1.3	1.0
1986	2.0	1.0	2.0	1.9	1.3	1.0
1987	2.0	1.0	2.0	2.0	2.0	1.0
1988	2.4	1.3	2.0	2.0	2.0	1.3
1989	2.8	1.3	2.0	2.0	2.2	2.0
1990	3.0	1.3	2.0	2.0	2.3	2.0
1991	2.4	1.7	2.6	2.0	2.3	2.0
1992	2.3	1.7	2.7	2.0	2.3	2.9
1993	2.3	2.0	2.7	2.0	2.3	3.0
1994	2.3	2.0	2.6	2.7	2.3	3.0
1995	2.3	2.3	3.0	2.7	2.3	2.9
1996	2.3	2.7	3.0	2.7	2.3	2.7
1997	2.3	2.7	3.0	2.7	2.7	2.4
1998	2.3	2.7	2.1	2.7	2.9	3.0
1999	2.3	2.3	2.0	2.7	3.0	3.0
2000	2.3	2.3	2.3	2.7	3.0	3.0
2001	2.3	2.3	2.3	2.7	3.0	3.0
2002	2.3	2.3	2.3	2.7	3.0	3.0

Source: World Bank website (siteresources.worldbank.org/DEC/Resources/financial_liberalization_index.xls).

a. For definition of index, see text.

pattern reflects the attempt to maintain control over macroeconomic and financial policy through restricted international opening.[10]

Individual East Asian countries also demonstrated differences among themselves and with Latin America, as shown in table 2-3. Overall, the East Asian countries were less inclined toward financial liberalization than their Latin American counterparts. By 2002, only two countries—Taiwan and Thailand—were completely open according to the World Bank index for overall financial liberalization, and even they arrived at this position only in the late 1990s. In

10. While this policy preference in Chile is well known in recent times, it is interesting to find it in the early years of the military government as well.

Figure 2-4. *East Asia: Components of Financial Liberalization Index, 1973–2002*[a]

Index (1 – 3)

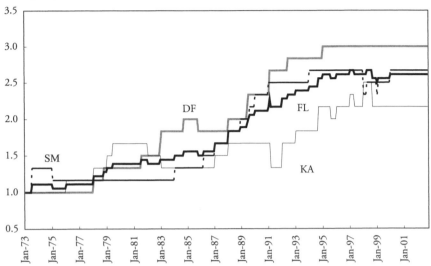

Source: World Bank website (siteresources.worldbank.org/DEC/Resources/financial_liberaliza-tion_index.xls).

a. FL is the full financial liberalization index; DF is the domestic financial liberalization index; SM is the stock market liberalization index; KA is the capital account liberalization index. See text for definitions.

terms of the liberalization process, the Philippines and Taiwan implemented a gradual, smooth opening; so did Korea, except for a reversal following the 1997–98 crisis. Malaysia and Thailand were especially prone to reversals, which occurred at various points, including the crisis, as governments tried to manage the liberalization process. Indonesia opened more rapidly than its neighbors, but then quickly reversed course even before the crisis struck.

Unlike in Latin America, domestic financial liberalization was a laggard in East Asia until the mid-1980s (see figure 2-4). By the late 1980s, four countries were still completely closed as far as domestic indicators were concerned; all liberalization had taken place in the capital account or the stock market. By the mid-1990s, however, all had index scores of 3.0 for domestic liberalization, and these scores did not change during the crisis. It was the capital account that was partially or completely closed in the latter period.[11] The data suggest a more cautious attitude toward financial liberalization than was found in Latin America.

To summarize, Latin America was similar to East Asia and the OECD in that financial liberalization was a policy choice prevalent in all three groups of countries in 1973–2002. Nonetheless, Latin America was distinctive in that the

11. Calculated from disaggregated data for the index; see note 6 (in this chapter) for access information.

region demonstrated substantially greater volatility in the liberalization process that did its counterparts elsewhere. This volatility spanned the entire period covered by the World Bank index, but it was especially pronounced during the debt crisis of the 1980s, when all countries reversed their liberalization policies. No similar policy change was found in Asia in the 1990s; only a very brief and mild reversal occurred in a few countries (Korea, Malaysia, and Thailand). Latin America was also more positively disposed toward liberalization than its Asian counterparts. Comparisons among Latin American countries suggest some interesting differences. Colombia and Chile showed less volatility than the others; together with Brazil, they were also reluctant to open the capital account completely until the last few years of the sample period. Argentina, Mexico, Peru, and Venezuela experienced sharper and more frequent policy reversals than the other three, and international liberalization accompanied or even led domestic liberalization. The next section examines whether these differences are related to the presence or absence of crises in the region.

Financial Liberalization and Crisis

The Asian financial crisis and the earlier Mexican experience spawned a large literature on new causes of crisis. Moreover, although Camdessus referred to Mexico as the first crisis of the twenty-first century, the case displays close similarities to the Chilean crisis of 1981–83.[12] The analysis of new causes began with the argument that the recent crises were not examples of the old macroeconomic syndrome seen throughout the postwar period, whereby a large fiscal deficit and loose monetary policy led to a devaluation that had negative impacts on the economy and thus on bank loan portfolios.[13] Nor were they the result of microeconomic problems in particular banks, leading to panics that spread to the banking system as a whole and sometimes undermined the currency as a result of rescue policies. Rather, new relationships had begun to appear.

New Explanations for Crises

While most economists agreed that something new was happening, they differed on the key elements of the new paradigm. Two separate approaches emerged initially: one concentrated on domestic characteristics, while the other focused on international factors and contagion. Over time, some degree of consensus developed to the effect that both domestic and international processes were involved, perhaps in a necessary-sufficient relationship.

12. Camdessus (1995). See Edwards (1996) on the comparison between Chile and Mexico.

13. It is common to speak of two generations of such models. The first focused on government attempts to defend the currency, followed by a speculative attack after reserves fell to some critical level (for example, Krugman, 1979). The second was more complex: a speculative attack could result from either a predicted deterioration of economic fundamentals or a self-fulfilling prophecy (for example, Obstfeld, 1986).

The domestically oriented approach argued that structural and policy distortions in the countries concerned were the main causes of the crises—even if market overreaction and herding made them more severe than would otherwise have been the case. The early version of this approach, put forth by the International Monetary Fund (IMF) with respect to the Asian crisis, focused on four alleged problems.[14] First was overinvestment relative to domestic savings, which—given the lack of fiscal deficits—was the counterpart of large current account deficits and increasing (short-term) foreign capital inflows.[15] Second were deficiencies in macroeconomic management, mainly pegging exchange rates to the dollar but also ignoring some underlying demand pressures. Third were financial sector weaknesses, including inadequate regulation and supervision, poor corporate governance, lack of transparency, and imprudent lending. Fourth was the international environment, but the focus was on trade and declining competitiveness rather than financial flows and contagion.

One of the most influential academic analyses following the domestic approach was that of Corsetti, Pesenti, and Roubini, who centered their argument on three manifestations of moral hazard.[16] At the corporate level, firms made unwise investments with the supposition that they would be bailed out if they got into serious difficulties. At the financial level, banks borrowed excessively abroad and lent excessively at home, enabling unprofitable investment to continue. Although the financial sector was characterized by weak regulation and supervision, low capital adequacy, nonmarket criteria for project selection, and outright corruption, the close bank-corporation-government nexus again set up the expectation that no bank would be allowed to fail. The international dimension of moral hazard involved foreign banks lending in ways that resembled their local counterparts, assuming that they would be rescued by local governments or the IMF if the need arose. These internal weaknesses made the countries vulnerable to a reversal of capital inflows.

The other approach to explaining the crises agreed that these domestic weaknesses were present, but pointed out that they had existed for a long time, yet the crisis countries had nonetheless been highly successful. Understanding the reasons for the crises was argued to require a focus on new relationships with the international financial markets. In particular, the liberalization of the capital account of the balance of payments in developing countries had enabled banks

14. IMF (1997). Successive issues of the *World Economic Outlook*, after this first reaction in the early months of the crisis, reflected the increasing convergence of opinions across the initial domestic-international divide.

15. In the 1997 analysis, the IMF pointed out that in Mexico the issue was overconsumption, not overinvestment (IMF, 1997, pp. 10–11). The same could also be said for the other Latin American countries, where savings and investment have always been far lower than in East Asia.

16. Corsetti, Pesenti, and Roubini (1998a, 1998b). The popularized version of the moral hazard argument centers on the concept of crony capitalism. See, for example, Kang (2001) on Asia and Haber (2002) on Latin America.

and corporations to borrow large amounts of capital from abroad, but these same flows could easily be reversed if a political, economic, or even psychological shock occurred. These outflows, or "sudden stops," were the main sources of the crises.[17] This argument was frequently accompanied by a sharp criticism of the international financial institutions—especially the International Monetary Fund—both for promoting capital account opening and for the conditionality on their rescue packages, which were said to have exacerbated the crises.[18]

Radelet and Sachs provide a technical version of this argument, centering their analysis on "the intrinsic instability of international lending," or what they call self-fulfilling crises.[19] Lenders initially were eager to pour large amounts of money into countries that were seen as good risks because of rapid growth and other positive features. A shock of whatever kind could generate sudden demands for repayment, however, which turned into a panic as each creditor tried to get out first. In such cases, individual creditors acted rationally, but the collective outcome led to costly crises that were not necessary. Central to the argument is the distinction between illiquidity and insolvency. A liquidity crisis occurs when a solvent, but illiquid, borrower is unable to obtain fresh funds from the international markets because of collective action problems. Such a situation creates multiple equilibria. One equilibrium is where loans are rolled over by most or all lenders, the solvent borrower continues to carry out its business activities, and the lenders receive their payments as scheduled. A quite different equilibrium involves a panic among lenders, where no one is willing to roll over loans; this is often termed herd behavior. The situation is unstable because it is possible to shift from one equilibrium to the other almost instantaneously, on the basis of changing market psychology.[20]

One of the problems with both approaches—in addition to the tendency to focus on one explanation or the other, rather than the relationship between them—is the blurring of banking and currency crises. The literature on so-called twin crises addresses this distinction. Kaminsky and Reinhart, together with others who have built on their pathbreaking work, stress the need to separate the two types of crisis since they are related, but different.[21] In historical terms, Kaminsky and Reinhart find many currency crises but few banking crises before financial liberalization ended the tightly controlled financial systems in developing countries. In the 1980s and 1990s, by contrast, both were frequent. The general pattern was for banking crises to precede currency crises, being set off by financial liberalization, credit booms, and excess liquidity. A banking crisis

17. See Calvo (1998) for an elaboration of the term *sudden stops*.
18. See, for example, Stiglitz (2002, chap. 4). A critical, but more measured, approach to the role of international financial institutions can be found in Dooley and Frankel (2002, chaps. 10 and 11).
19. Radelet and Sachs (1998).
20. See Masson (1999) for a discussion of multiple equilibria.
21. Kaminsky and Reinhart (1999).

undermined the currency, leading to devaluations that, in turn, exacerbated the banking problems. The peak of a banking crisis generally followed a currency crisis.

Other analyses of twin crises emphasize the relationship with financial liberalization even more. Glick and Hutchinson, using a much larger sample than Kaminsky and Reinhart, come to the conclusion that twin crises are limited to financially liberalized, emerging market economies; only in that group were robust results obtained.[22] Demirgüç-Kunt and Detragiache also find that financial liberalization increases the likelihood of bank crises, even after they control for various macroeconomic factors. At the same time, their results indicate that strong institutions (such as respect for rule of law, a low level of corruption, and good contract enforcement) are a mitigating factor. They consider this a reason for a gradual approach to financial liberalization, since institutions cannot be built rapidly.[23] Mehrez and Kaufmann arrive at complementary conclusions, stressing that lack of transparency increases the probability of a crisis following financial liberalization.[24]

Financial Crises in Latin America and East Asia

Latin American countries have suffered many financial crises in the postwar period. The vast majority were either currency crises detonated by excess domestic demand or banking crises set off by problems in individual institutions that spread to the system as a whole. After the start of the economic reform process, which prominently featured both domestic financial liberalization and opening of the capital account, the region witnessed three dramatic twin crises of the "new" type. One reaches back to the early 1980s, and it is no coincidence that it took place in Chile, which was the first country to undertake sustained economic reforms beginning in the 1970s. The second was Mexico in 1994–95, accompanied by spillover effects in Argentina. The third example again took place in Argentina, beginning in 2001.[25]

In East Asia, currency and banking crises were much less frequent and milder when they occurred. Indeed, the deep crises of 1997–98 were almost uniformly described as unexpected, and the governments were unprepared to respond adequately—in contrast with their Latin American counterparts, which had much more experience, even if they had been dealing with different types of crisis in the past. We discuss the Latin American cases in detail in later chapters; here, we summarize the main points to see how these cases fit the theoretical propositions in the literature. We also want to see how the Latin American crises were similar

---

22. Glick and Hutchinson (2001).
23. Demirgüç-Kunt and Detragiache (1998a).
24. Mehrez and Kaufmann (2000).
25. Many other banking crises have occurred in Latin America in recent years, but they have typically been due to problems in individual banks that spread to other institutions.

Table 2-4. *Latin America and East Asia: Characteristics Preceding Financial Crises*
Index and percent

Region and country	Crisis date[a]	Liberalization index[b]		Fiscal deficit[c]	Current account[c]	Short-term debt[d]	Credit[e]
		Domestic	International				
Latin America[f]		3.0	2.6	−1.4	−4.0	149.2	10.5
Argentina	2001	3.0	3.0	−2.4	−3.2	112.6	−7.2
Brazil	1999[g]	3.0	2.0	−7.7	−4.3	70.2	4.9
Chile	1981	3.0	2.0	5.4	−7.1	82.0	36.8
Colombia	1998	3.0	2.0	−3.7	−4.9	58.7	8.2
Mexico	1994	3.0	3.0	0.0	−7.0	610.5	26.9
Peru	1994–99[g]	3.0	3.0	0.7	−5.9	76.5	23.0
Venezuela	1994	3.0	3.0	−2.3	4.3	34.2	−19.0
East Asia[f]		3.0	2.0	−0.5	−2.5	167.9	17.0
Indonesia	1997	3.0	1.0	−0.7	−2.3	198.1	15.1
Korea	1997	3.0	2.0	−1.5	−1.6	262.8	13.8
Malaysia	1997	3.0	3.0	2.4	−5.9	71.9	21.0
Philippines	1997[g]	3.0	2.0	0.1	−5.3	162.3	30.8
Taiwan	1997[g]	3.0	2.0	−1.6	2.4	n.a.	7.7
Thailand	1997	3.0	2.0	−1.9	−2.0	144.5	13.5

Sources: World Bank website (siteresources.worldbank.org/DEC/Resources/financial_liberalization_
index.xls) for liberalization index; IMF, *International Financial Statistics Yearbook* (2004, lines 80, 78ald
and 22d) for fiscal deficit, current account, credit; World Bank (2004a) for short-term debt; ADB (2004)
for Taiwan data.

n.a. Not available

a. Year when crisis started.

b. One year prior to crisis; Mexico data for 1994 and Asian countries for 1997 (because crisis occurred
near end of year).

c. Fiscal deficit and current account as share of GDP; one year prior to crisis.

d. Short-term debt as share of reserves; one year prior to crisis.

e. Change in credit to private sector; three years prior to crisis.

f. Unweighted average of countries shown in table.

g. Date when crisis might have been expected.

to, and different from, those in East Asia. Table 2-4 provides data to help in the
comparison. It includes a number of variables that have been associated with
financial crises.

We begin with Chile as the earliest of the twin crises in our sample. The
Chilean crisis derived in large part from an extreme version of financial liberalization, reflecting the antigovernment ideology of the military regime that took
power in 1973. State-owned banks were quickly sold off to (subsidized) private
buyers, extensive controls on the financial sector were abolished, and the capital
account was partially opened. At the same time, macroeconomic policy used the
exchange rate as a nominal anchor to cut inflation, and capital inflows offset
large current account deficits in the face of fiscal surpluses. Banks took advantage of the unregulated conditions to pump up loans, including many to related

borrowers, and ignored potential losses. A severe banking crisis erupted in 1981. The following year, the situation was complicated by a balance-of-payments crisis, leading to a devaluation of the fixed exchange rate that worsened the banking crisis. The latter was marked by the insolvency of the majority of the private national banks and finance houses, which were taken over or liquidated by the Superintendent of Banking. By mid-1982, the crisis had become a systemic one, extending to many of the largest corporations, which also ended up in government hands.[26]

The Mexican crisis thirteen years later was extraordinarily similar. Indeed, experts asked how Mexico could have failed to heed the lessons from a relatively recent case in its own region.[27] Mexico also moved from an environment of state-owned banks and strong financial repression to a private-sector-dominated, loosely regulated financial system in the space of a few years from the late 1980s to the early 1990s. The credit boom was very similar, as were the insider lending and the failure to make adequate provisions for possible losses. Although Mexico did not have a fixed exchange rate, the currency was informally linked to the dollar in the context of a tripartite agreement designed to lower inflation. Again like Chile, there was no significant budget deficit, but the large volume of capital inflows served to finance large current account deficits, driven by an overvalued peso. A first dissimilarity was a superficial one—the currency crisis broke first, in December 1994, and the devaluation brought down the banks. Nonetheless, many of the banks had been insolvent earlier, although their condition was hidden by lax government accounting standards.[28] More importantly, Mexico's international relationships were far more favorable than Chile's had been a decade earlier: Mexico joined the OECD and the NAFTA agreement went into effect just months before the crisis struck. The external dimensions of the Mexican crisis were thus mitigated by a large loan from the U.S. Treasury and the IMF, while Chile had had to deal with its problems on its own.[29]

The third twin crisis in the Latin American region occurred in Argentina. Ironically, Argentina in the mid-1990s appeared to be a good example of a crisis that was overcome by prompt and effective government action. Caught in the tidal wave of the Mexican collapse, and constrained because its currency board system prevented the central bank from functioning as a lender of last resort, the country suffered a run on its banks, which lost 12 percent of their deposits in four months. The run was stopped by a large loan from the IMF and World Bank, together with a local "patriotic bond" purchased by the banks and large corporations. The authorities beefed up the system of regulation and supervision and negotiated a contingent credit line with foreign banks, which consti-

---

26. See chapter 6 for references.
27. See, for example, Edwards (1996).
28. See the discussion of different definitions of nonperforming loans in Haber (2005).
29. For references on Mexico, see chapter 7.

tuted a proxy lender of last resort. Growth resumed, and the banks more than regained the deposits they had lost. In terms of capital adequacy ratios, Argentine banks were among the most solid in the world, although other indicators were less positive.

The picture turned bleak again toward the end of the decade, however, owing to a combination of international shocks and internal political and economic factors. A large and growing current account deficit resulted from the overvalued exchange rate, and a severe recession after 1998 undermined fiscal revenues and the banks' portfolios. The currency board prevented the central bank from providing liquidity (although other mechanisms compensated to some extent). Notwithstanding a brief respite following the election of a new president and another IMF package, conditions deteriorated sharply in 2001. A "voluntary" debt restructuring was carried out to help relieve fiscal pressures, but by the end of the year the government froze all bank deposits to avoid devaluing the currency. In part because of opposition to this move, months of political chaos resulted. Early 2002 saw a large devaluation and the end of the currency board, together with a default on the country's foreign debt obligations. The unique factor in the Argentine case, in contrast to Chile or Mexico, was that the government targeted the banks to pay much of the cost of the crisis. To protect debtors, bank assets and liabilities were converted to local currency at different exchange rates, leaving the banks insolvent. The government's default on its own obligations, a large part of which were held by the banks, deepened the latter's problems.[30]

Although Latin America and East Asia appeared to share similar characteristics of financial repression in the past, significant differences separated the two regions. In particular, East Asia's banking systems were an integral part of a development strategy that produced the highest growth rates in the world over the thirty-five-year period from 1960 to 1995.[31] For most of that time, however, East Asia's banks had very little autonomy to make loan decisions; rather, governmental authorities provided funds and directed their use to promote particular industries and firms. This meant that regulation and supervision were weak if they existed, central banks were under the control of finance ministries, and banks lacked skills at credit evaluation. The differences that existed across countries were less important than the similarities from the perspective of an East Asia-Latin America comparison.[32]

---

30. On Argentina, see Kiguel (2001); de la Torre, Levy-Yeyati, and Schmukler (2003); Fanelli (2003); Daseking and others (2004); Díaz Bonilla and others (2004).

31. For a summary, see World Bank (1993). Alternative interpretations are found in Amsden (1994); Fishlow and others (1994); Stiglitz and Yusuf (2001).

32. The most important differences were between the Northeast Asian countries (Korea and Taiwan, as well as Japan) and those in Southeast Asia (Indonesia, Malaysia, the Philippines, and Thailand). The former were much more closed and state-dominated, while the latter were more open and more dependent on the private sector, including foreign capital.

By the mid- to late 1980s, however, banking systems in East Asia were already beginning to change. This was partly due to structural shifts in their own economies, but it also reflected the fact that the East Asian countries had become major players in world markets and the industrial countries complained that their banks provided unfair advantages. A review of table 2-3 shows that all six economies—Indonesia, Malaysia, the Philippines, and Thailand in Southeast Asia and Korea and Taiwan in Northeast Asia—became more open in this period, regardless of the level of openness that prevailed previously. The former group started the liberalization process much earlier than the latter, but all six pushed forward in the five years between 1983 and 1987. The particular pattern of liberalization varied, however, as we discuss below.

Of the six, four became engulfed in dramatic financial crises a decade later.[33] To the external world, the events appeared to begin suddenly in July 1997, when Thailand was forced to devalue the baht. In reality, the problems began much earlier, and financial liberalization again set the stage as it had in Latin America. After suffering financial instability in the early 1980s, Thailand recovered and grew at an average rate of 9 percent between 1987 and 1996. The country implemented many structural reforms in this decade, including a comprehensive domestic financial liberalization and the opening of the capital account. The proper institutional safeguards were not in place before the changes took place, however. This combination led to a credit boom, which was stimulated by capital inflows that averaged over 9 percent of GDP during the period and which translated into very high investment in the productive sectors and a hike in asset prices. By the mid-1990s, the negative consequences of the boom—plus adverse international conditions—were beginning to appear: exports slowed, the current account deficit rose, stock market prices fell, several corporations ran into difficulties, and the portfolios of banks and finance companies deteriorated. The government tried various stopgap measures, but it could not use a high interest rate policy because of the weakness of the financial sector. The authorities ultimately floated the baht, which quickly depreciated, exacerbating the untenable position of the banks.[34]

One country's problems turned into a regionwide crisis when contagion spread from Thailand to three of its neighbors during the second half of 1997, but internal weaknesses had already built up in other Asian economies. The other Southeast Asian countries that were severely damaged by the crisis— Indonesia and Malaysia—shared some characteristics with Thailand, although Malaysia pursued a more heterodox policy stance both before and after the crisis. Indonesia carried out its domestic financial liberalization in two stages, in

33. Useful overviews of the East Asian crises are found in Lindgren, García, and Saal (1999); Lee (2003).

34. On Thailand's financial crisis, see Vajragupta and Vichyanond (1999); Alba, Hernández, and Klingebiel (2001); Nidhiprabha (2003); and Warr (2004).

1983 and 1988, as the result of declines in the price of oil, a key export. An important consequence was a rapid rise in the number of banks and the volume of credit, as well as the displacement of the state banks from their previously dominant position. Indonesian authorities tried to improve regulations in step with the liberalization, but these were not enforced. In addition, substantial related lending took place, and banks were subjected to political pressures from groups near the Suharto government. At the macroeconomic level, government policies both allowed private sector agents to borrow abroad and encouraged them to do so through high domestic interest rates and obstacles to particular types of domestic finance. Capital inflows—frequently short-term flows—led to an overvalued exchange rate and an enlarged current account deficit. Contagion from Thailand came both through pressure on the currency and the refusal of foreign banks to roll over loans.[35] The main differences in the Malaysian case were a more gradual financial liberalization process and the continuation of more controls even in the late 1990s. The level of technical expertise at the central bank and the regulatory agencies was also higher than elsewhere in Southeast Asia. Together, these factors meant that Malaysia's level of vulnerability was lower in comparison with its neighbors.[36]

The country whose crisis constituted the biggest surprise to outsiders and insiders alike was Korea, which had become a major economic powerhouse, especially in terms of its export capacity. Partly as a result of its economic position, Korea was under pressure to liberalize its financial system, and it began to do so in the late 1980s. The plan was to carry out the liberalization gradually to avoid the kind of vulnerabilities that others had encountered. In the early 1990s, however, Korea began negotiations to join the OECD, which led to an acceleration of both internal and external reforms. As is now generally acknowledged, the sequencing of the liberalization process was poorly planned, and a very large short-term debt was built up through borrowing by both financial and nonfinancial firms. These processes provided the conditions for contagion to spread from Southeast Asia to what appeared to be one of the strongest economies in the world.[37]

Analysis of Financial Liberalization and Crises

This brief survey, together with the literature based on broader samples of countries and using quantitative methods, demonstrates the close link between financial liberalization and twin crises. Moreover, a look back at table 2-4 confirms that the twin crises in our study were of the new type. That is, they took place

35. Indonesia's crisis is discussed in Ghosh and Pangestu (1999); Nasution (1999, 2002); Pangestu and Habir (2002).
36. On Malaysia, see Jomo (2001); Dornbusch (2002); Kaplan and Rodrik (2002); Chin and Jomo (2003). For a comparison of the experiences of Indonesia and Malaysia, see Nasution (1998).
37. On Korea, see Hahm (1999); Cho (2002); Coe and Kim (2002); Ahn and Cha (2004).

when fiscal and monetary indicators were in relative balance, although a number of other problems were certainly present, especially current account deficits.[38] We finish this section by returning to the hypotheses presented earlier to determine whether the variables cited there can help specify the nature of the relationship between financial liberalization and crises. We also bring in cases where crises did not occur or where they were of a different type than the new twin crises to help clarify our argument.

Of the thirteen Latin American and East Asian countries included in the World Bank indexes, seven suffered financial problems that belong to the category of new twin crises.[39] In each case, financial liberalization appears to have set off a process that led to a crisis. Three sets of variables were proposed in table 2-1 to disaggregate the concept of financial liberalization and to help explain the juxtaposition of liberalization and crisis. They were the speed, extent, and sequencing of domestic financial deregulation, the policies that accompanied the latter, and the institutions to support the new system.

Reviewing the evidence, the first set of variables seems less important than the others. All thirteen cases, including both crisis and noncrisis countries, had completely opened their domestic financial systems in the period immediately preceding the crises. Moreover, whether they opened gradually or abruptly does not appear to be a crucial factor in distinguishing among cases. Some that opened very rapidly suffered crises (for example, Argentina and Chile), while others did not (such as Peru). In terms of sequencing, the relationship between external and internal opening—together with the presence or absence of adequate regulation and supervision—was more important than the sequencing of dimensions of internal opening.

The central differences across cases were determined by the policies that accompanied domestic financial liberalization. The key macroeconomic variable turned out to be the exchange rate. If the rate was fixed, whether formally or informally, it tended toward overvaluation and thus current account deficits, especially in the presence of an open capital account. Policy toward the capital account, in turn, was also crucial, most importantly with respect to the rules on short-term inflows; foreign direct investment and official loans were much less disruptive. The most explosive combination was an abrupt opening to short-term flows when domestic liberalization was taking place simultaneously or had occurred in the recent past. Under these conditions, there was a pent-up

---

38. In this sense, we agree with Kaminsky and Reinhart (1999), who insist that not everything was done well in these countries, such that more was at issue than an undeserved speculative attack. Some disagreement has arisen with respect to current account deficits, in particular. For example, in the period preceding the Mexican crisis, the finance minister argued that the deficit existed because investors wanted to put money into Mexico and it was thus a positive sign rather than a danger. Needless to say, others disagreed strongly.

39. The World Bank indexes actually cover fourteen countries, but as mentioned earlier, we excluded Hong Kong because of its particular characteristics as an entrepôt.

demand for external finance, while domestic financial institutions had little or
no experience in the international markets. Finally, adequate regulation and
supervision were rarely in place before domestic financial liberalization, leading
to the familiar phenomenon of a lending boom without concern for losses. The
typical pattern was for the strengthening of regulation and supervision to be
part of postcrisis cleanup rather than precrisis preventive strategy.

The third set of variables was relevant because good policies could not be
designed and implemented without adequate institutions in place. At the broadest level, adherence to the rule of law and the existence of a judicial system that
protects private property provide an appropriate environment of expectations, as
well as the mechanisms to enforce the law so that banks follow prudent lending
practices. More concrete examples of important institutions on the public sector
side include central banks that are free of intense political pressure on monetary
policy and regulatory and supervisory agencies that can set and enforce rules.
On the private side, commercial banks must have both the skills and the incentives to carry out thorough credit analysis of potential borrowers and to make
lending decisions on the basis of project potential rather than insider connections. Credit bureaus and rating agencies provide useful back-up support to the
banks in the lending process.[40]

What about the countries that did not suffer twin crises? Can they shed any
light on the relationship between financial liberalization and crises? Six of the
thirteen cases—Brazil, Colombia, Peru, and Venezuela in Latin America, plus
the Philippines and Taiwan in East Asia—did not encounter twin crises of the
new type, although most had serious problems with their banks. These cases can
be divided into three categories: potential twin crisis situations, where governments acted preventively; less developed economies that did not attract much
short-term capital; and economies that had other kinds of banking problems.

The prime exemplars of the first category are Brazil in Latin America and the
Philippines in East Asia. When the Mexican crisis occurred, Brazil's banks were
already weak because of the hyperinflation the country had suffered and the
adjustment they had to make after the successful 1994 stabilization program.
The disappearance of inflationary gains as a source of profit led Brazil's private
banks to expand credit, especially to consumers. In the presence of a high interest rate policy and rising unemployment, the credit boom led to a rise in nonperforming loans. Public banks faced special difficulties as a result of their limited capacity to restructure their portfolios and their high operational costs. The
key point is that the Brazilian authorities did not wait for a full-blown crisis to
erupt, but took the initiative to reduce the number of banks, restructure those
that were in difficulty but could be saved, recapitalize the system in general,
allow foreign banks to enter the market, expand the powers of bank regulators,

40. See similar results in Demirgüç-Kunt and Detragiache (1998a).

and increase requirements for capital adequacy and transparency. Proof of the effectiveness of the measures was the lack of a serious banking crisis in the face of the January 1999 devaluation.[41] In the case of the Philippines, the government also took preventive action under the Aquino and Ramos governments. Balance sheets were cleaned after the abuses of the Marcos period, and prudential regulations were strengthened in terms of capitalization requirements, auditing requirements, loan loss provisions, and limits on related lending.[42]

The Philippines also fits into the second category of countries that might well have developed twin crises, but did not because they did not receive much short-term capital inflow. Both the Philippines and Peru had liberalized their domestic financial systems and opened their capital accounts (in the case of Peru, the financial reforms were some of the most radical in the world). Nonetheless, these two countries suffered few problems in relative terms, in part because they were perceived as less attractive investment sites than their more successful neighbors in Asia and Latin America, respectively. For example, much more of their foreign debt was owed to official creditors than was the case with their regional counterparts. Peru also had a large quantity of reserves to back up its debt (and one of the few floating exchange rates in emerging markets in the 1990s).[43]

The third category—countries with other types of crises—also comprises cases in both East Asia and Latin America. Taiwan escaped the 1997 crisis that ravaged the rest of East Asia, in large part because of its huge foreign exchange reserves and perhaps its slower liberalization, but it nonetheless had serious banking problems. The difference with respect to its neighbors is that these problems had no external detonator. They resulted from the bursting of asset bubbles in real estate and the stock market, together with problems in the old public banking sector, which led to low profitability and a high share of nonperforming loans.[44] On the Latin American side, Colombia and Venezuela had crises that were reminiscent of older-style financial problems. Both had large fiscal deficits and crises that spread from particular banks (Banco Latino in Venezuela) or particular segments of the financial sector (cooperatives and savings and loan institutions in Colombia).[45]

In summary, these examples of countries that did not suffer the new type of twin crisis show that government policy can make a difference in crisis prevention. One lesson centers on improving regulation and supervision before a twin crisis breaks (as in the cases of Brazil and the Philippines). Another concerns

41. For references, see chapter 8.
42. On the financial problems in the Philippines, see Hutchcroft (1999); Montes (1999); Gochoco-Bautista (2003).
43. Given Peru's lack of a crisis, literature is scarce; see IMF (1998b, 2004d).
44. On Taiwan, see Yang and Shea (1999); Chow and Gill (2000); Montgomery (2002, 2003).
45. On Venezuela, see García-Herrero (1997); de Krivoy (2000). On Colombia, see Uribe and Vargas (2002).

debt management and the need to avoid large short-term foreign debts (for example, Taiwan, with little debt of any kind, and Peru and the Philippines, with emphasis on long-term debt from official lenders). Ironically, a number of the countries that escaped crisis did so because they were perceived to be less attractive than their neighbors, whether for economic or political reasons. Successful countries must be particularly aware of the pitfalls that their very success can generate.[46]

Rescue Programs: Costs and Outcomes

Rescue programs typically consist of both short- and long-term elements. The latter, which involve structural change as well as new institutions and policy directions, are the subject of the next three chapters. Here we concentrate on the immediate response, including the characteristics and costs of the rescue programs. We also examine the outcomes five years after the crises in our sample (or the latest available observations) to see to whether the rescue operations were successful. Success is defined by a country's performance on three economic variables: the GDP growth rate, the investment-to-GDP ratio, and the credit-to-GDP ratio.

Several taxonomies of short-term rescue measures are discussed in the literature. We focus on the provision of liquidity, recapitalization, the removal of nonperforming loans from bank balance sheets, and the temporary takeover or the closing of insolvent institutions. In ascending order of interventionism, these are the most common measures among the cases we are examining. Their purpose is to deal with the immediate hemorrhaging of the financial institutions through restoration of confidence in the banking system. It is also to keep credit flowing by improving bank balance sheets. Whether these short-term goals are achieved depends on the severity of the crisis and the context in which it takes place (for example, the overall level of confidence in the government, support from international actors, the behavior of other economic variables, and the ability of existing institutions to function in tumultuous times). Measures are also generally taken to help debtors. While these are intimately connected to support for creditors, they are beyond the scope of our analysis.[47]

The need for liquidity can involve either domestic or foreign currency. The former is simply an extrapolation of the normal function of a central bank as lender of last resort. The microeconomic difficulty in a crisis situation is deciding whether a particular bank is solvent but illiquid, and thus a candidate for

---

46. See Ffrench-Davis (2001) for a discussion of the special problems of successful countries.

47. Measures to help debtors can either help or hurt creditors. In Argentina, for example, a more favorable exchange rate was applied to bank liabilities than to assets, leaving the banks insolvent. On measures to help debtors, including corporate restructuring and its relation to bank restructuring, see Collyns and Kincaid (2003, chap. 5); Hoelscher and Quintyn (2003, chap. 7).

support, or whether it is insolvent, in which case other measures are called for. The macroeconomic problem is the trade-off between providing sufficient liquidity to satisfy the banks' needs versus providing so much that it increases inflation and undermines the value of the currency—and helps provoke a twin crisis, as discussed earlier. The situation is more complex if the need for liquidity concerns foreign exchange, since it requires the use of the (always limited) stock of international reserves. The ability to call on international assistance is crucial under these circumstances. If the central bank cannot provide liquidity in the case of local currency or if international help is not available (or is not considered desirable) in the case of foreign currency, then nonmarket solutions are likely to be used, such as a deposit freeze or capital controls. This was what happened in Argentina and Malaysia, respectively, in comparison with the other crises we have examined.

Recapitalization goes beyond the temporary need for greater liquidity to deal with the solvency of an institution. Today, a minimum capital-asset ratio of 8 percent for internationally active banks is mandated by the Bank for International Settlements; some country regulators demand an even higher ratio. If a bank falls below the required level, the least interventionist solution is for the government to require recapitalization. Recapitalization can come through market operations, whereby current shareholders provide additional capital or banks issue new shares. Alternatively, if this is impossible, the government can provide temporary assistance. Often a combination is used. In Mexico, for example, for each two pesos the government put in, the banks had to contribute one peso.

Further support can be provided through the removal of nonperforming loans from bank balance sheets. A broad array of techniques has been tried, some more successful than others. In principle, individual banks or groups of banks can set up such an arrangement; Thailand took this route in the early months of its crisis. A more common approach involves a government-controlled asset management company, such as those set up in Indonesia, Korea, Malaysia, and eventually in Thailand. Mexico's deposit insurance agency performed a similar function, as did Chile's central bank. Argentina's solution remains to be determined. The incentives embodied in the particular arrangements are very important in whether they lead the banks to resume lending. Many experts believe such incentives were not provided in the Mexican case, where credit as a share of GDP fell until recently, whereas they were in Chile, where credit began to expand earlier in the process. In Asia, Korea has been more like Chile, whereas Thailand and Indonesia have been more similar to Mexico.

Finally, in the most extreme situations, a government agency can take control of banks or even close them. Depending on the treatment of depositors, the latter can be very expensive. Also, if it is done poorly, closing banks may make crises worse (as happened in Indonesia). If banks are hopelessly insolvent, however, keeping them open may be the worst decision. With potentially viable

Table 2-5. *Latin America and East Asia: Cost of Financial Crises*
Percent

Region and country	Crisis year[a]	Fiscal cost[b]	GDP loss[c]	Interest rate[d]	Asset prices[e]	Inflation[f]
Latin America[g]		26.4	−10.2	38.4	−54.0	41.6
Argentina	2002	n.a.	−11.0	44.6	−54.7	40.3
Chile	1982	33.5	−13.4	46.0	n.a.	31.2
Mexico	1995	19.3	−6.2	24.7	−53.3	53.3
East Asia[g]		28.6	−9.5	11.9	−70.4	47.2
Indonesia	1998	52.3	−13.1	3.3	−78.5	79.4
Korea	1998	23.1	−6.7	21.6	−45.9	7.2
Malaysia	1998	4.0[h]	−7.4	5.3	−79.9	5.0
Thailand	1998	34.8	−10.8	17.2	−77.4	10.7

Sources: Hoelscher and Quintyn (2003, p. 41) for fiscal cost; Collyns and Kinkaid (2003, pp. 27, 30) for GDP loss; Claessens, Klingebiel, and Laeven (2003, p. 150) for interest rates, except Argentina and Chile, which were calculated from IMF, *International Financial Statistics Yearbook* (2001, 2004); Claessens, Klingebiel, and Laeven (2003, p. 3) for asset prices, except Argentina, which was calculated from Standard and Poor's (2005); Collyns and Kinkaid (2003, pp. 29, 31) for inflation, except Argentina, which was calculated from IMF, *International Financial Statistics Yearbook* (2004).

n.a. Not available.

a. Peak year of crisis.

b. Net fiscal cost as share of GDP.

c. Decline in GDP in first year of crisis.

d. Peak real money market rate during crisis year.

e. Largest monthly drop in real stock market index during crisis year relative to January of previous year.

f. Cumulative consumer price index for 12 months beginning 1 month prior to crisis.

g. Unweighted average of countries shown in table.

h. Honohan and Klingebiel (2003) an alternative source on fiscal cost, whose data are generally similar to the source used here—have a very different figure for Malaysia (16.4 percent).

banks, temporary government intervention provides an opportunity to restructure and recapitalize them before reprivatizing them at a later stage. The goal is usually to keep the banks functioning (the "open bank" solution) as part of the goal of maintaining credit, but a management change is almost sure to occur. In our cases, all governments closed or merged banks, such that the number of financial institutions fell substantially in comparison with the precrisis period. In addition, all governments took over some or most banks and later began to reprivatize them.

These various types of support—together with assistance for both household and corporate debtors—are likely to be extremely costly to the countries involved. The most commonly cited costs are fiscal outlays. As shown in table 2-5, these range from 4 percent of GDP to 52 percent in the cases we are examining. The median was 28 percent, with Latin America and East Asia showing very similar levels. Although not included in the table, the countries without twin crises had substantially lower costs. Several studies try to determine why fiscal costs vary across cases.[48] Here we are mainly interested in underlining the magnitude of lost opportunities—since the government funds that go into bank rescues cannot be used for other activities, whether public sector investment projects or social services—and asking how Latin America fared in comparison with East Asia.

The costs are not limited to absorption of government revenues. Others include lost GDP, increased government debt, lack of credit, weakened firms, and perhaps high inflation.[49] Moreover, rescues frequently involve an income transfer to the wealthiest groups in society, which can be debilitating to a government in political terms, and poverty is likely to be negatively affected, which also has political as well as social and economic costs.[50] Table 2-5 provides indicators of some of these other costs. GDP losses in the worst year of the crises averaged nearly 10 percent, while interest rates and inflation rose substantially and asset prices plummeted. The main differences between Latin America and East Asia on these other measures were much higher real interest rates in the former and a steeper fall in asset prices in the latter.

A final point to keep in mind is that crises are not usually resolved quickly. On the contrary, the effects of a serious crisis will last for years.[51] Although measuring the lingering impact of a crisis is very difficult, table 2-6 provides some tentative estimates by looking at the variables mentioned earlier—that is, GDP growth, investment, and credit to the private sector—in the five years after a crisis. GDP, corrected to eliminate the recovery portion of postcrisis growth, was substantially lower in the five years after the crisis than in the comparable period before. The regional data for both Latin America and East Asia show that corrected growth rates fell more than two-thirds, on average. The only exception was Mexico, whose large devaluation enabled it to increase its exports to an average of 14 percent per year between 1995 and 2000; this meant that the decline in growth was smaller than in other countries.[52]

In the case of the investment ratio, the East Asian countries suffered declines between the five years just before the crisis and the five-year postcrisis period. The impact was smaller in Latin America, perhaps because investment ratios were already at such low levels in the latter. With respect to credit to the private

48. Honohan and Klingebiel (2003), for example, argue that accommodating policies lead to higher fiscal costs, while Claessens, Klingebiel, and Laeven (2004) stress the role of institutions in determining the cost of crises.

49. Recent evidence of the independent negative effects of banking crises on GDP (as opposed to the effects of a general economic downturn) is provided by Dell'Ariccia, Detragiache, and Rajan (2005), who compare sectors that are more and less dependent on external finance. Their finding that the former are especially hard hit is taken to mean that crises per se are causing loss of GDP.

50. On poverty and crises, see Cline (2002); Baldacci, de Mello, Inchauste (2004).

51. Other analyses of crisis duration find faster recovery, especially with respect to GDP growth. One of the reasons is that the studies do not correct for recovery, thus conflating recovery and growth. See, for example, Demirgüç-Kunt, Detragiache, and Gupta (2000).

52. Calculated from the ECLAC website (www.eclac.cl/estadisticas).

Table 2-6. *Latin America and East Asia: Performance Five Years before and after Twin Crises*
Percent

Region and country	Crisis year[a]	GDP precrisis[b]	GDP postcrisis[c]	Investment precrisis[d]	Investment postcrisis[e]	Credit precrisis[f]	Credit postcrisis[g]
Latin America[h]		4.8	1.5	20.3	20.7	38.7	27.7
Argentina[i]	2002	2.6	−2.0	16.0	15.0	24.0	11.0
Chile	1982	7.9	2.9	23.0	23.0	53.0	54.0
Mexico	1995	3.9	3.5	22.0	24.0	39.0	18.0
East Asia[h]		7.8	2.5	38.4	23.1	114.5	93.3
Indonesia	1998	7.6	0.6	31.6	16.0	61.0	24.0
Korea	1998	7.1	4.2	38.2	29.4	73.0	104.0
Malaysia	1998	8.7	2.8	42.0	21.8	158.0	142.0
Thailand	1998	7.9	2.2	41.7	25.2	166.0	103.0

Source: World Bank, *World Development Indicators* (online).
a. Peak year of crisis.
b. Average growth rate five years before crisis.
c. Average growth rate five years after crisis (subtracting crisis decline to correct for recovery).
d. Average ratio of investment to GDP five years before crisis.
e. Average ratio of investment to GDP five years after crisis.
f. Average ratio of credit to private sector to GDP five years before crisis.
g. Average ratio of credit to private sector to GDP five years after crisis.
h. Unweighted average of countries shown in table.
i. Only one year after crisis (2003).

sector, the ratio generally tended to remain much lower five years after the crisis than in the prior peak. There were, however, two exceptions. Chile and Korea, the two countries that arguably did the best job of responding to their respective financial crises, saw credit as a share of GDP increase, although the postcrisis figures for Chile are artificially high because of accounting procedures connected with the crisis resolution.[53]

Conclusions

Financial liberalization has transformed the financial sector in developed and developing countries alike in recent decades. These changes have been especially significant in Latin America and East Asia because of the extent to which governmental authorities intervened in financial decisionmaking in the preliberalization period. In both regions, the financial system had been a key tool for governments in their attempts to industrialize their economies and to determine who should have access to credit. Financial liberalization changed this approach in profound ways that are still being understood.

53. The same was true for Mexico, but the drop in credit in Mexico was so large that even the accounting inflation did not lead to positive figures.

A first change concerned the actors who make decisions about bank credit. On the most superficial level, this involved a transfer of authority from government bureaucrats to private sector bankers. In reality, the shift was more complex. The government has not totally withdrawn, although its new role varies from country to country. In most cases, some public sector financial institutions remain, although they are usually run according to rules similar to those of the private sector. Moreover, the government continues to regulate the financial sector, as in the rest of the world, but its tools are different now. In particular, governments use prudential techniques rather than top-down directives. Government supervision of banks may also be complemented by private monitoring (through disclosure, external ratings, external audits, and so on).

A related change concerned the basis for making decisions. Again, a superficial characterization is that profit maximization at the individual institutional level has replaced the use of finance as an element of national development strategy. There is truth to this view, but other goals were always present, and they continue to be relevant today. For example, market share remains a concern of many banks, even when this interferes with profit maximization. Likewise, providing help for friends, family, and other insiders can rival the interests of a bank qua institution. Family-owned banks are particularly prone to such motivations, although this ownership form is becoming less common.

Finally, these changes have had important implications for the economy. Credit for consumption is increasing at the expense of investment; this shift stems partly from the decreasing role of public sector banks, but less directed credit is also required from private banks. Specific allocations of credit for agriculture, industry, and small firms are declining in favor of credit to the service sector and to larger firms. Interest rates are determined by the market, and real rates tend to be higher than in the past; maturities may also be shorter. All of these factors mean that governments must rethink the tools they have available for managing their respective economies.

In addition to these important changes in the rules of the game, financial liberalization has also frequently been associated with financial crises. As we have shown, financial crises are very expensive. Fiscal costs have been as high as 50 percent of GDP in the case of twin (banking and currency) crises, with clear opportunity costs in terms of the funds used for rescue operations. Losses of GDP, interest rate hikes, declines in asset prices, and other problems magnify the costs far beyond the usual focus on fiscal outlays. Another point is that these costs are not all paid in a single year: our data show that lower GDP growth, investment, and credit still prevailed half a decade after the crises. The evidence also indicates that crises are especially costly to the poor, which is a serious issue in developing countries.

The message is not that financial liberalization should be avoided. Many aspects of financial liberalization are now widely accepted in both Latin America and East Asia. Rather, greater care is needed with respect to the policies that accompany domestic financial liberalization, such as macroeconomic policy, opening of the capital account, and regulation and supervision. The institutions that enable these policies to be implemented adequately need time to be created and strengthened, which argues for a gradual approach to financial liberalization—and probably any other major structural changes.

In the next several chapters, we discuss the longer-term results of financial crises and overall trends in the financial sector of developing countries. These include changes in ownership, especially the increase in foreign ownership of banks; an improvement in the quality of regulation and supervision of the banking sector; and the diversification away from almost exclusive reliance on banking toward expanding capital markets. All three of these trends offer advantages—although foreign ownership is more controversial than the other two—but they could come about without the huge costs of a financial crisis. This should be the goal of developing countries, both the public and private sectors.

3

Changes in Ownership:
Public, Private, and Foreign Banks

B ank ownership in emerging market economies has been transformed by
financial liberalization. Two main policy changes have driven the process:
the market share of public sector banks has been reduced, and the share of foreign banks has been allowed to increase. As a secondary consequence, private
domestically owned banks have generally lost market share. This outcome—
which is still evolving and varies across regions and countries—came about in
two stages. As part of the liberalization process itself, state-owned banks were
sold to the private sector, both domestic and foreign. If a crisis occurred, however, governments often saw themselves forced to renationalize many banks, followed by another round of privatizations. The second trend, toward more foreign ownership, came about in both stages. Foreign banks sometimes took part
in the original privatizations, but more frequently they waited till the second
round. Foreigners also bought out local private owners through mergers and
acquisitions.

Why is ownership important? Do different ownership structures lead to different economic, social, or political outcomes? Who benefits and who loses from
public versus private domestic versus foreign ownership of banks? Like financial
liberalization itself, these are highly controversial, ideologically charged questions, and the thrust of opinion has changed substantially in recent years. In the
early postwar period, public banks were considered to be a positive force for
development, and foreign banks were seen as pilfering resources from developing countries. The reverse is now the dominant view.

Our contribution to these debates is based on a comparative analysis of bank ownership in Latin America and East Asia. While we confirm the generally accepted trend toward less public and more foreign ownership, we find that substantial heterogeneity still exists. Looking at banking systems within countries, rather than individual banks across countries, we find that East Asia behaves as the new literature predicts: foreign-dominated banking systems perform best, public systems worst, and private domestic systems in the middle. The situation in Latin America is more complex: foreign-dominated banking systems behave less well than predicted, but public systems perform better. To explain these anomalies, we turn to the literature on institutions. Incorporating institutional variables reinforces the results from East Asia and enables us to account for the unexpected findings in Latin America. We conclude that with strong institutions, public banks can perform reasonably well, while weak institutions can undermine the operations of even world-class foreign banks.

The chapter is organized in five sections. The first reviews the literature on ownership, institutional environment, and performance and presents two hypotheses to be evaluated. The second examines data on trends in ownership over the past fifteen years, paying special attention to Latin America and East Asia. The third section analyzes evidence on the performance of different ownership patterns with respect to efficiency and stability, while the fourth studies the impact of institutions on performance. The final section concludes.

Bank Ownership, Performance, and Institutions: Literature and Hypotheses

The overall goal of this section is to suggest hypotheses about the impact of ownership patterns on the performance of banking systems, but we must start with the component parts as they are discussed in the literature: public sector banks and foreign banks. Very little has been written about either private domestic banks or the advantages of different mixes of ownership. We contribute in this direction and also discuss the impact of the institutional environment in which the different types of banking systems operate.

Public Sector Banks

Opinion about public sector banks has changed significantly in the last two decades, moving in conjunction with views about the public sector role in the economy of developing countries more generally. During much of the postwar period, state-owned banks were considered an important component of development strategies, in particular strategies geared toward industrialization. This was the case in both Latin America and East Asia.[1]

1. There has been some misinterpretation of the historical rationale for state-owned banks. Following La Porta, López-de-Silanes, and Shleifer (2002), various authors cite some of the leading

Economists of the influential structuralist school in Latin America saw state-owned development banks as necessary to provide finance for investment by both public and private enterprises in the growing industrial sector, since private sector banks were unwilling to offer long-term loans.[2] Based on this view, banks such as Nacional Financiera (Nafin) in Mexico and the National Development Corporation (Corfo) in Chile were established as early as the 1930s to intermediate between sources of international finance and local firms. Brazil's National Bank for Economic and Social Development (BNDES) followed in the 1950s.[3] In the developing countries of East Asia, state control of banks came about through the influence of the Japanese economic model, in which public control was a key element. The clearest intellectual advocacy in the western literature of a state role in that region came fairly recently in attempts to explain East Asia's extraordinarily high growth rates. Authors such as Amsden and Wade extol the virtues of state ownership or control of banks, and even the World Bank's *East Asian Miracle* has some positive things to say about government control of finance, although limiting its partial endorsement to Japan, Korea, and Taiwan.[4]

The World Bank study identifies three targets for state-controlled credit: specific industries or firms that are considered crucial for investment and growth and that produce externalities for the rest of the economy; certain types of firms that are believed to need support, such as exporters or small and medium-sized enterprises (SMEs); and social objectives, such as the expansion of health care and housing or the extension of financial services to rural areas. Like the Latin American structuralists, Amsden and Wade concentrate on the first set of objectives, providing various examples in Korea and Taiwan, respectively, where directed credit stimulated investment. Amsden also highlights Korea's ability to discipline firms that did not perform adequately so as to avoid the heavy losses that have characterized most state-owned financial institutions; the World Bank echoes her analysis with respect to this point.

Beyond promoting growth, other justifications for state ownership of banks include support for governments' stability and equity goals. Private banks are frequently considered to be procyclical, increasing credit in good times and withdrawing it when the economy sours. In the extreme, this behavior can lead to financial crises. Public banks, in turn, are argued to be both able and willing

development economists of the postwar period—Lewis, Myrdal, and Gerschenkron—as advocates of public sector banks in developing countries. In reality, these early economists were discussing the need for a strong state role in general. Moreover, all were talking about socialist economies: Lewis (1950) was writing about a central planning model; Myrdal (1968) was referring to South Asian countries, which he characterized as socialist; and Gerschenkron (1962) was analyzing Russia, both before and after the Bolshevik Revolution. They gave little emphasis to banks, except for Gerschenkron's discussion of private banks in Western Europe.

2. See discussion in Cárdenas, Ocampo, and Thorp (2000); Bulmer-Thomas (2003).

3. See Brothers and Solís (1966), Larraín and Selowsky (1991) on Nafin and Corfo, respectively. The history of BNDES, which was BNDE until the 1980s, is discussed in BNDES (2002).

4. Amsden (1989); Wade (1990); World Bank (1993).

to lend in a countercyclical pattern, thus providing a public good in the financial sector.[5] It is further argued that state banks are required to serve less-privileged groups and individuals. Several categories of potential clients are involved. The main focus of this book is on small firms, but others include vulnerable sectors (such as agriculture and housing) and households in poor neighborhoods or distant locations. Since private sector financial institutions tend to find such clients unprofitable, public banks are again providing a public good.[6]

In the recent wave of literature on finance and growth, by contrast, state-owned financial institutions have come under heavy attack. The principal theoretical argument against them is the alleged political motive behind lending, as opposed to the developmental or social motives that dominated the earlier analyses. This argument is closely related to the rent-seeking critiques of the state role in the economy more generally, claiming that "governments acquire control of . . . banks in order to provide employment, subsidies, and other benefits to supporters, who return the favor in the form of votes, political contributions, and bribes."[7] Given such motives, credit is likely to fund inefficient projects, which—even if they are actually carried out—will have low rates of return at the microeconomic level and undermine productivity and growth at the macroeconomic level.

A growing empirical literature analyzes the impact of state-owned banks. Based mainly on large-sample, cross-country regression studies rather than individual country experiences, this new literature finds high state ownership of banks to be correlated with low growth rates, low efficiency, low profits, high volumes of nonperforming loans, and corruption. La Porta, López-de-Silanes, and Shleifer took the lead in these studies. They argue that their findings support the political rather than the developmental view in that efficiency, growth, and productivity have negative (and sometimes statistically significant) coefficients in the regressions they ran, while controlling for other relevant variables.[8]

Levy-Yeyati, Micco, and Panizza come to somewhat more nuanced conclusions after reviewing a variety of studies on the effects of state-owned banks. For example, they find that the La Porta results are sensitive to sample and period: when they reran the data with another sample, the data lost their statistical significance. Moreover, they cite other empirical studies that find more positive results, such as Micco and Panizza, who report that public sector lending is less

5. This includes regional or international public sector banks. See ECLAC (2002); Titelman (2003).

6. Banks such as Nafin and Corfo have now become second-tier banks, working with first-tier private banks; SMEs are their primary clients. BNDES operates through both first- and second-tier arrangements and also targets SMEs.

7. La Porta, López-de-Silanes, and Shleifer (2002, p. 266).

8. La Porta, López-de-Silanes, and Shleifer (2002). Similar conclusions are reported in Barth, Caprio, and Levine (2001a); World Bank (2001); Galindo and Micco (2003); Caprio and others (2004).

procyclical than that of private banks.[9] Their conclusion: "While we find no evidence that the presence of state-owned banks promotes economic growth or financial development, we also find that the evidence that state-owned banks lead to lower growth and financial development is not as strong as previously thought."[10]

The Levy-Yeyati, Micco, and Panizza paper also introduces an issue that is important for our analysis. In addition to developmental, social, and political views about government ownership of banks, they add the concept of an agency view. This approach stresses the difficulty for public banks to carry out intended (developmental) goals, given the political pressures to which they are subjected. Others broach the same point, when they write of the tendency for reforms of public banks to fail in their objectives of providing better management.[11] We return to the question of "good" versus "bad" public sector banks in our discussion of the institutional environment in which they operate.

Foreign-Owned Banks

Foreign banks had an earlier origin than did public banks in Latin American economies, dating back to the nineteenth and early twentieth centuries, when they provided the main source of finance for capital accumulation in the export sectors. International bond issues were also important, despite frequent defaults.[12] In the postwar years, however, foreign banks were often nationalized or marginalized as governments assumed a greater role in economic affairs. A more complex relationship existed in East Asia, where colonial control lasted longer than in Latin America.[13]

Not surprisingly, the reemergence of foreign banks, mainly as a result of the liberalization process in the 1990s, introduced many new issues and sharp differences of opinion about the advantages and disadvantages of their presence in developing countries. Three main arguments were presented in favor of increased foreign presence. First, it was argued that foreign banks would bring new technology, embodied in both hardware and management techniques, which would raise productivity in their own institutions and spread to local ones as well. The sector as a whole would thus become more efficient. Second, foreign banks would have access to international sources of capital, from both their own home institutions and the international capital markets, and so could contribute to the deepening of local financial sectors. Third, because of their

9. Micco and Panizza (2004).

10. Levy-Yayeti, Micco, and Panizza (2004, abstract).

11. See, for example, Hanson (2004). A variant of the same argument is found in de la Torre (2002), who identifies a syndrome whereby public banks try to improve efficiency and profitability to the point where they lose much of their social rationale for existence. They thus move back toward social goals, only to encounter economic problems again.

12. Stallings (1987); Bulmer-Thomas (2003).

13. On Japanese control of finance in Korea, for example, see Eckert (1991) and Woo (1991).

access to external sources of finance, foreign banks would be a positive force for stability in the face of financial turbulence. Another contribution to stability would come from their home central banks and regulatory agencies, which would both monitor their banks' behavior and help local regulators to increase their skills.[14]

While not opposing foreign banks across the board, other experts and policy-makers are more cautious. Two main concerns are behind their reluctance to open doors too widely to foreign entry; they mirror the reasons discussed earlier for supporting public sector banks. In terms of macroeconomic and financial stability, many worry that foreign banks are too large for local agencies to super-vise. They are concerned that foreign banks will serve as conduits for large capital inflows, which can destabilize macroeconomic behavior. These experts and policymakers are also apprehensive that vulnerable groups in local societies—low-income households, distant regions, declining sectors, and small firms—will be left without credit and other financial services.[15]

A substantial amount of research has been carried out to measure the impact of foreign banks on developing economies. These studies claim to find a positive relationship with efficiency and stability in local financial markets; the impact on access is less clear. In general, the impact of foreign banks seems to be less positive in developed than in developing economies. Since most of the evidence comes from the former, Clarke and others suggest that this may lead to an underestimation of the benefits to the latter.[16]

Several studies show that foreign banks are more efficient than their domestic counterparts in developing countries, but not in advanced economies. Indica-tors used to measure efficiency include profitability, overhead costs, and prob-lem loans; higher values on each are interpreted as indicators of less competition and lower efficiency.[17] Claessens, Demirgüç-Kunt, and Huizinga go on to look at changes that occur when foreign banks enter a domestic market. They find that increased foreign bank presence has a statistically significant effect in lower-ing profits and overhead costs; negative but insignificant relationships result for net interest margins and loan loss provisions. The positive impact on efficiency is found to occur with the initial entry of foreign banks, before they acquire a large market share.[18] Lensink and Hermes extend this analysis by disaggregating the data for high- and low-income countries. They find that the relationship

14. There is a good deal of consensus on these arguments; see, for example, Mathieson and Roldós (2001).

15. One of the most influential critiques is Stiglitz (1994). A useful and balanced study of the impact of foreign direct investment in the financial sector was recently carried out by the Bank for International Settlements; see BIS (2004).

16. Clarke and others (2003).

17. Demirgüç-Kunt and Huizinga (1999); Claessens, Demirgüç-Kunt, and Huizinga (2001); Mathieson and Roldós (2001).

18. Claessens, Demirgüç-Kunt, and Huizinga (2001).

varies between the two. Specifically, in low-income countries, the costs of domestic banks increase with the entry of foreign banks since they have to make new investments in order to compete. In high-income countries, costs either go down or stay the same.[19]

Another issue concerns the relationship between foreign banks and stability. Several analysts find, after controlling for other variables likely to produce banking crises, that greater foreign presence is a stabilizing factor. They use foreign ownership as one of the variables in a regression analysis designed to explain worldwide banking crises; the relationship proves to be a negative one.[20] Other studies concentrate on Latin America—which is not surprising, given the region's proclivity toward crises. Crystal, Dages, and Goldberg report that foreign banks have higher provisioning or higher reserve coverage than local banks and are generally more aggressive in addressing loan quality deterioration.[21] Others find that foreign bank lending has not declined significantly during crisis periods in Latin America, if it comes through local subsidiaries rather than cross-border sources. Related findings are that foreign subsidiaries moderate the tendency toward international capital flight during crises by providing a local venue where nervous depositors can put their money.[22]

Finally, with regard to access, evidence on the behavior of foreign banks is scarce. In one of the most widely cited studies, Clarke and others analyze lending patterns in four Latin American countries in the late 1990s. They conclude that foreign banks generally lend a smaller share of their funds to SMEs than do domestic banks, but this result is accounted for by the behavior of small foreign banks. Larger institutions in two of the four countries actually lend more to SMEs than do local banks.[23] Another study by some of the same authors uses survey data to ask about finance for SMEs. It finds that foreign banks are more likely to finance large firms than small ones, but that the latter nonetheless get more credit than they would otherwise have had.[24] Other researchers suggest that if foreign banks concentrate on large firms, this may encourage other banks to seek out smaller clients.[25] Of course, this positive impact is not likely to occur if many local banks are driven out of business.

Hypothesis on Ownership and Performance

By the early 2000s, the arguments for and against public and foreign banks had become quite familiar. Much less has been said about the relative merits of private domestic banks.[26] These institutions are implicitly seen as falling between

19. Lensink and Hermes (2004).
20. Demirgüç-Kunt and Detragiache (1998b).
21. Crystal, Dages, and Goldberg (2001).
22. Dages, Goldberg, and Kinney (2000); Peak and Rosengren (2000); García-Herrero and Martínez Peria (2005).
23. Clarke and others (2002).
24. Clarke, Cull, and Martínez Peria (2001).
25. Bonin and Abel (2000); Jenkins (2000).
26. Mian (2005) compares the three.

the other two types of banks. As private institutions, they are governed by profit considerations, so they are less likely than public banks to lend for political reasons and suffer the negative consequences. At the same time, they are less likely to be up-to-date with respect to banking technology or to have access to the deep pockets of their foreign competitors. Nonetheless, they are more familiar with local conditions and so perhaps are more willing to support local firms, especially SMEs, which are crucial to economic and social development processes.

Another topic that has not been discussed is whether certain ownership combinations might be particularly advantageous. We know that economies dominated by any one of the three ownership types face problems. An economy completely reliant on private domestic banks will be cut off from external sources of capital and innovation, undermining the growth potential of the financial sector itself and the economy more generally. At another extreme, domination by foreign banks may be good for the largest firms, but the gap relative to SMEs is likely to widen. In addition, foreign domination may arouse political protest against perceived infringement of sovereignty, which in turn can have negative effects on the business environment.[27] Finally, economies in which public sector banks have a very large market share will have the same disadvantages as economies in which local banks dominate, but inefficiency is likely to be greater. Given that competition can help to bring out the positive features of banks and suppress the negative ones, a mixed financial framework might offer advantages over "pure" ownership structures.

Based on the recent literature and the above extensions, our first hypothesis is that foreign-dominated banking systems will perform best, while public-dominated systems will deliver the worst performance. Systems dominated by private domestic banks will fall in between. We would also expect combined systems to do well, but we have insufficient evidence to place them in a rank ordering.

Institutional Environment

When we move from cross-country analysis, where the units are individual banks, to within-country analysis, where the units are banking systems, it is possible—and desirable—to take into account the environment in which banks operate. The environment consists of a great many factors, ranging from geographical location to political system to cultural background. We are particularly interested in the institutional environment and how it affects banking system performance. Institutions are defined as formal and informal rules that shape the behavior of individuals and organizations by reducing uncertainty.[28]

27. On the issue of bank ownership and sovereignty, see Makler and Ness (2002).
28. This definition comes from the work of North (1990) and those following his lead; a common alternative is to define institutions as organizations. On the implications of using one or the other definition in the Latin American context, see Graham and Naím (1998).

A growing number of authors argue that institutions are among the most important determinants of economic growth, and several even claim to have found evidence that institutions trump all other factors. Much of the contemporary literature on institutions and growth dates back to North's work on U.S. economic history.[29] The current focus, however, is mostly on the developing world.[30] Econometric analysis of the relationship is now abundant. Acemoglu, Johnson, and Robinson are leaders in this enterprise, and they are also among the strongest advocates for the primacy of institutions as a causal factor. In their review of the literature on institutions and growth, they state the following: "Although cultural and geographical factors may also matter for economic performance, differences in economic institutions are the major source of cross-country differences in economic growth and prosperity."[31]

An important aspect of the debate on institutions and growth is the issue of potential reverse causality. That is, do better institutions cause higher growth and higher income, or does higher income bring about better institutions, or both? The strongest proponents of institutions as the independent variable are World Bank economists, who have created a large data set to measure institutions.[32] Using new empirical techniques, Kaufmann and Kraay reconfirm a strong positive link from institutions (or governance, in their terminology) to growth. More controversially, they find a weak, or even negative, relationship in the opposite direction.[33] Others continue to believe in a two-way causal process or argue that institutions are the dependent variable.[34]

As we move from economic growth in general to the role of the financial sector in particular, the focus is on the positive influence of high-quality institutions on both the depth of the banking sector and the development of capital markets. The two, in turn, are said to promote growth. La Porta, Lopéz-de-Silanes, and Shleifer again play an influential role, not only making the intellectual argument that the legal system (especially the protection of property rights) is crucial in determining financial development, but also devising a methodology and data set to test the hypothesis. Their key insight is that current financial

29. North (1961).

30. Engerman and Sokoloff (1997, 2002) helped to make the transition with their comparative analysis of growth in the United States and other New World countries. Acemoglu, Johnson, and Robinson (2001, 2002) extend this line of research to other parts of the developing world.

31. Acemoglu, Johnson, and Robinson (2004, pp. 2–3). Others who agree with this conclusion include Rodrik, Subramanian, and Trebbi (2002); Easterly and Levine (2003). A more policy-focused interest in institutions and growth arose from the disappointment with the economic reforms process of the 1980s and 1990s. One response was to point to the need for a so-called second generation of reforms that would be centered on better institutions, thus leading to stronger growth. See, for example, Burki and Perry (1998); Kuczynski and Williamson (2003).

32. See Kaufmann, Kraay, and Mastuzzi (2004). We provide more information on this data set later in the chapter.

33. Kaufmann and Kraay (2002).

34. On the two-way causal process, see, for example, Lora (2002); Pritchett (2002). On institutions as the dependent variable, see Glaeser and others (2004).

rules, and thus outcomes, vary according to legal origin. Specifically, countries following the English common law tradition protect property rights most diligently and thus have deep financial systems, while those following French civil law are at the opposite end of the spectrum. German and Scandinavian traditions lie in between.[35]

Levine and various colleagues further develop the idea of the legal proxy for linking institutions and finance. They show that the most relevant aspect of legal origin is difference in adaptability, arguing that the French tradition is more rigid than the British or German. Systems that can adapt to changing conditions promote financial development more effectively than those that cannot.[36] In a study of the Mexican case, Haber goes beyond the legal origins approach to look at the relationship between institutions, finance, and development more broadly. He argues that three types of institutions will lead bankers to increase the availability of credit: those that protect them from having their property expropriated, those that allow them to enforce debt contracts, and those that encourage them to behave prudently. More controversially, he adds that all three derive from a fundamental set of institutions that limits the authority and discretion of government.[37] Whatever the channels, the evidence increasingly demonstrates that institutions—in part through their impact on finance—are instrumental in promoting economic growth.[38]

Hypothesis on Ownership, Institutions, and Performance

Institutions have not received much attention in the literature on ownership and bank performance as a result of the methodology used to study the topic. Drawing on the works just discussed, we want to introduce institutions into the debate on ownership. Specifically, our second hypothesis argues that the institutional context within a country can either reinforce or offset the expected advantages or disadvantages deriving from a particular ownership type. Strong institutions are particularly important in countries with state-dominated systems, as they can potentially counteract the problems typical of public banks. The same holds for mixed systems, in which public banks are part of the ownership combination. For private or foreign-dominated systems, strong institutions can reinforce their positive characteristics, whereas weak institutions can undermine them. Which institutions are most relevant? Regulation and supervision are clearly important, and we address them in the next chapter. Here we take a

---

35. La Porta, López-de-Silanes, and Shleifer (1997, 1998).

36. Levine (1998, 1999); Beck, Demirgüç-Kunt, and Levine (2003).

37. Haber (2004).

38. On institutions and finance in several Latin American countries, see the book produced from an Inter-American Development Bank project, especially the chapters by Cristini, Moya, and Powell (2001); Fuentes and Maquieira (2001); Monje-Naranjo, Cascante, and Hall (2001); Pinheiro and Cabral (2001).

broader approach, looking at rule of law and general characteristics of the government, in addition to regulation.

Trends in Bank Ownership

Over and above the differing views about the advantages and disadvantages of public versus private ownership of banks, a clear consensus has developed about recent trends. Throughout the developing world, less public and more foreign ownership of banks has emerged over the last fifteen years. Important differences remain, however, across regions and individual countries as a result of historical context and policy decisions.

Regional Trends in Bank Ownership

Comparable data are hard to come by with respect to ownership. One reason is that definitions make a great deal of difference. Some studies report the share of assets, loans, or deposits accounted for by ownership type; others base their categories on ownership of a certain share of assets (50 percent is the typical cutoff point) before control is reported. The former approach tends to show a higher ownership for foreign banks, although not necessarily for public banks, since the latter share is likely to be quite high if it exists. In addition, some studies of public sector bank ownership are limited to commercial banks, while others include development banks; if development banks exist, they will obviously increase the public share. Finally, the treatment of foreign bank branches versus subsidiaries often varies, again giving rise to differences across works purporting to study the same phenomena.[39]

Table 3-1 shows the best estimates available for long-run changes in bank ownership, based on a data set compiled by La Porta, López-de-Silanes, and Shleifer.[40] It provides information on ownership status of the ten largest banks in ninety-two countries in 1970, 1985, and 1995 based on the share of assets held. The sample includes industrial, developing, and transition economies. While these data do not separate private domestic from foreign ownership, they are useful for two reasons.[41] First, they offer a twenty-five-year perspective that begins before financial liberalization and ends after a substantial part of it had taken place. Second, the data enable us to compare across regions, including the industrial countries as well as subgroups of developing and transition economies.

Beginning with the broadest categories, we see a shift from public to private banking in both industrial and developing countries, although the percentage

39. The biggest problem with these definitional differences is that the authors frequently fail to specify which definitions they are using.
40. La Porta, López-de-Silanes, and Shleifer (2000, 2002).
41. We calculated private ownership as a residual from the La Porta, López-de-Silanes, and Shleifer data, which are limited to the share of public ownership.

Table 3-1. *Ownership Structure of Banking Systems around the World, 1970–95*
Unweighted average (percent)

Region	1970		1985		1995	
	Government	*Private*	*Government*	*Private*	*Government*	*Private*
Developed	37.0	63.0	31.6	68.4	21.8	78.2
Developing	65.6	34.4	62.6	37.4	48.8	51.2
East Asia Pacific	49.1	50.9	45.7	54.3	41.1	58.9
Eastern Europe	90.2	9.8	96.0	4.0	49.9	50.1
Latin America	65.8	34.2	54.8	45.2	40.1	59.9
Middle East	55.4	44.6	55.1	44.9	54.2	45.8
South Asia	94.7	5.3	97.9	2.1	87.5	12.5
Sub-Saharan Africa	40.8	59.2	48.5	51.5	33.6	66.4

Sources: Calculated from La Porta, López-de-Silanes, and Shleifer (2000, 2002).

change is much larger in the latter. The share of private sector ownership rose by 24 percent in industrial countries between 1970 and 1995, but it increased by 49 percent in the developing world. In both cases, the majority of the change came about in the ten years between 1985 and 1995. Among developing regions, the most dramatic shift took place in the former socialist bloc, which began with almost all its banks in state hands. The share fell to little more than half during the period under study. The other big change occurred in Latin America, where nearly two-thirds of banks were public in 1970, declining to two-fifths by 1995.[42] Other regions, including East Asia, saw much smaller changes, although that region is especially heterogeneous.

Table 3-2 provides a more detailed look at three developing regions during a more recent period. It is based on data from the Bank for International Settlements (BIS) for all three ownership categories—public, private, and foreign—for the years 1990 and 2002. The trends are consistent with those found in table 3-1. In Latin America and in Eastern Europe, government ownership fell, foreign ownership increased, and private domestic ownership contracted somewhat. The situation was more complex in East Asia. While foreign ownership increased in most cases, it fell in the two places where foreign ownership was the highest in the region. Government ownership also rose, especially in those countries where financial crises occurred in the late 1990s. This seemingly contradictory result came about because governments felt obliged to intervene when bank survival was threatened or when bank crises seemed likely to spill over into the rest of the economy. They are now in the process of divesting these assets, but the process has not yet been completed.

42. In percentage terms, the second biggest change was in South Asia, but this was from a very low base, and the 1995 total for private sector ownership was only 12.5 percent.

Table 3-2. *Ownership Structure of Banking Systems in Emerging Markets,*
1990 and 2002
Percent

Region and country	1990			2002		
	Government	Private	Foreign	Government	Private	Foreign
Asia						
China	100	0	0	98[a]		2
Hong Kong	0	11	89	28[a]		72
Indonesia	96[a]		4	51	37	13
India	91	4	5	80	12	8
Korea	21	75	4	30	62	8
Malaysia	n.a.	n.a.	n.a.	72[a]		18
Philippines	7	84	9	12	70	18
Singapore	0	11	89	0	24	76
Thailand	13	82	5	31	51	18
Latin America						
Argentina	36	54	10	33	19	48
Brazil	64	30	6	46	19	27
Chile	19	62	19	13	46	42
Mexico	97	1	2	0	18	82
Peru	55	41	4	11	43	46
Venezuela	6	93	1	27	39	34
Eastern Europe						
Bulgaria	100[a]		0	13	20	67
Czech Republic	78	12	10	4	14	82
Estonia	n.a.	n.a.	n.a.	0	1	99
Hungary	81	9	10	27	11	62
Poland	80	17	3	17	10	63
Russia	94[a]		6	68	23	9
Slovakia	100[a]		0	5	9	85

Source: BIS (2004, p. 9).
n.a. Not available.
a. Disaggregated data are not available.

Bank Ownership in Latin America

The two data sets already discussed provide an idea of general trends in bank
ownership in Latin America. The substantial drop in government control and
the rise in foreign ownership are in line with the analysis of the previous chapter,
which documented rapid—if volatile—financial liberalization in the region.
Table 3-3 focuses on individual country behavior, including that of some
smaller countries. It is based on a recent World Bank data set, which has information for 2001.[43]

43. The definition of ownership is based on answers to a two-part question: what fraction of
the banking system's assets is in banks that were (a) 50 percent or more government
owned and (b) 50 percent or more foreign owned at the end of 2001? See World Bank website

Table 3-3. *Latin America: Ownership Structure of Banking Systems, 2001*
Percent

Category and country	Ownership type		
	State	*Private*	*Foreign*
Mainly foreign			
Mexico	0	17	83
Panama	12	29	59
Mainly private			
Colombia	18	60	22
Ecuador	14	79	7
El Salvador	4	84	12
Guatemala	3	88	9
Honduras	0	81	19
Peru	0	57	43
Venezuela	7	50	43
Mainly public			
Costa Rica	62	15	23
Mixed			
Argentina	32	36	32
Brazil	32	38	30
Chile	13	40	47

Source: World Bank, *World Development Indicators* (online).

The table reveals that ownership patterns are far from homogeneous. We can identify four subgroups. A first group consists of countries where foreign capital dominates the banking system. Only two Latin American countries clearly fall into this category: Mexico, where foreign banks account for nearly 85 percent of banking assets, and Panama, a regional financial center with nearly 60 percent foreign ownership. A second group is made up of countries where private domestic institutions account for the majority of the banking system. The countries that most clearly fit this pattern are among the smallest. In Ecuador, El Salvador, Guatemala, and Honduras, private domestic banks represent around 80 percent of assets. In Colombia, Peru, and Venezuela, private banks account for between 50 and 60 percent of the total. A third group is centered on state-owned banks. While this situation was quite typical of Latin America in the early postwar years, by 2000 only Costa Rica had maintained this kind of system, with a majority of its banking sector (62 percent) in public hands. Finally, a last group is characterized by mixed ownership, where no single type represents more than half of total assets and where all ownership types are represented. This group includes Argentina, Brazil, and Chile.

(econ.worldbank.org/external/default/main?theSitePK=478060&contentMDK=20345037&menu PK=546154&pagePK=64168182&piPK=64168060), questions 3.8.1 and 3.8.2.

Table 3-4. *East Asia: Ownership Structure of Banking System, 2001*
Percent

Category and country	Ownership type		
	State	Private	Foreign
Mainly foreign			
Hong Kong	0	11	89
Singapore	0	11	89
Mainly private			
Malaysia	0	81	19
Philippines	11	74	15
Thailand	31	62	7
Mainly public			
China	98	0	2
Indonesia	51	37	13
Vietnam	75	10	15
Mixed			
Korea	40	30	30

Sources: World Bank, *World Development Indicators* (online); Fitch Ratings (2003) and IMF (2003d) for Vietnam.

Bank Ownership in East Asia

East Asia also displays a good deal of heterogeneity in bank ownership. Table 3-4, which is based on the same World Bank data set as the previous table, reveals several clusters that are superficially similar to those found in Latin America. When we look more closely, however, the characteristics of the clusters and their distribution vary in important ways.

We first note that two East Asian countries—Hong Kong and Singapore— are heavily reliant on foreign banking (nearly 90 percent of total assets). These two city states, which are regional financial centers, also have very large foreign production sectors that match their banking facilities. In this sense, they are similar to Panama, but very different from Mexico. A second group of countries has mainly private banks. In the Southeast Asian nations of Malaysia, the Philippines, and Thailand, over 60 percent of the banking system is in private domestic hands; many of these banks have traditionally been family-owned franchises. Third, a large majority of the banking sector in China and Vietnam is still state owned, reflecting their socialist economic history. We also place Indonesia in this group. Although public ownership is only slightly over 50 percent, the characteristics of its banking sector are similar to the state-dominated group. The fourth group, consisting of mixed ownership, is small in the East Asian region. South Korea is currently the only clear example, but several East Asian countries are moving toward mixed systems as banks taken over during the crisis are reprivatized, often being sold to foreign owners.

Ownership and Performance

Having examined the literature on bank ownership, as well as ownership characteristics and trends in the two regions, we now return to the two hypotheses presented earlier. The first leads us to ask how different types of banking systems, defined by ownership characteristics, compare in performance. We also want to examine whether the Latin American and East Asian regions display significant differences with respect to this question and, if so, why. It is very difficult to test this hypothesis, for a variety of reasons. First is the problem of definitions and cutoff points. Exactly what share of total bank assets must pertain to a particular ownership type to be classed as domination? Second, we have very few examples of each of the respective ownership types. Third, getting adequate and comparable data is problematic. This exercise should therefore be regarded as exploring some initial evidence that, if it proves useful, should be reconsidered later with a larger sample.

Tables 3-5 and 3-6 show a number of indicators for banks in East Asia and Latin America, with the banks grouped into the categories that were identified in the previous section. The indicators include a broad characteristic of the economies (per capita income); four indicators of bank efficiency (private sector credit/GDP, overhead costs/net income, nonperforming loans/credit, and profitability[44]); and three indicators of stability (the capital ratio, provisions/nonperforming loans, and Moody's bank ratings). The Moody's rating is an assessment of the financial strength of each bank in a given country, weighted by assets.[45] Unfortunately, lack of data makes it impossible to provide a systematic treatment of access to finance.

Given the exploratory nature of this exercise, we start by asking two questions with respect to the tables. First, do the variables characterizing the four ownership types cluster around certain values? Second, are these values consistent with the predictions of the literature we have examined? Positive answers to both questions, but especially the first, would provide some initial validation of the categories we have defined.

---

44. Profitability is included here since it is typically used in this type of analysis. Profitability has been interpreted in two opposing ways, however. On the one hand, low profitability is sometimes taken as an indicator of poor performance and low efficiency, especially among public sector banks (for example, Levy-Yeyati, Micco, and Panizza, 2004). On the other hand, low profitability is also seen as the result of competition and greater efficiency (for example, Demirgüç-Kunt, Levine, and Min, 1998). Because of this ambiguity, we interpret profitability based on the other characteristics of each individual case.

45. The Moody's rating measures the probability that a bank will need outside help, not whether it will receive it. Factors taken into account include individual bank fundamentals and the operating environment (such as the prospective performance of the economy, the structure and relative fragility of the financial system, and the quality of banking regulation and supervision). See the definition for Bank Financial Strength Rating on Moody's website (www.moodys.com).

We look at East Asia first, since the relationship between ownership and performance is clearest there, and we then contrast Latin America with the Asian cases. As table 3-5 indicates, the best performance on most indicators is found in high-income Hong Kong and Singapore, with their foreign-dominated banking systems. Indeed, the banks in these two financial centers are among the strongest in the world. Both countries' financial sectors are deep and stable, the banks are extremely efficient, nonperforming loans are low, capital ratios and provisions are high, and they receive very high marks from the rating agencies. While profitability is on the low side, in this case we interpret low profits as an indicator of competition rather than systemic weakness. The foreign-owned banking systems in these city-states are consistent with the productive systems, where foreign investment is also very prominent. Partially as a consequence, high foreign ownership has not aroused local hostility as it has in some Latin American cases.

The countries with mainly private banking systems—Malaysia, Thailand, and the Philippines—are from middle-income Southeast Asia. The Southeast Asian nations have traditionally been open economies that relied heavily on trade, and from the mid-1980s they received large amounts of foreign investment, especially from their Northeast Asian neighbors. Nonetheless, their largely family-owned banks were protected from foreign ownership. The rapid growth in these economies over the last several decades was abruptly halted in 1997 by a financial crisis from which they are only now recovering. Thus, despite their financial depth, they have high nonperforming loans, low provisions, and low stability scores from the rating agencies. The Philippines, while fitting in this category in most ways, displays differences that have led it to be referred to in Asia as a quasi–Latin American country. Because it was relatively poor and less attractive to foreign capital than its neighbors in the 1990s, it was not initially affected as much as they were when foreign capital withdrew during the crisis. Later, however, the crisis spilled over into the Philippine economy, raising its nonperforming loans and lowering its efficiency.

The public-dominated banking systems in East Asia are archetypical examples of the negative characteristics discussed in the literature. They are found in the poorest countries in the region—although these countries have been growing rapidly. With the important exception of China, they have lower credit ratios than others in the region. They also have very high nonperforming loans and low stability ratings. Both China and Vietnam are in transition toward capitalist economies, despite their attempts to maintain authoritarian political systems. Many of their current problems derive from their socialist pasts, when state-owned banks financed money-losing state enterprises, thus leading to huge volumes of nonperforming loans.[46] Indonesia is a different case in that it is not a

46. While nonperforming loan measures are hard to define in most countries, they are especially so in these two cases. In China, for example, some experts believe that nonperforming loans were at least double the official figure shown in table 3-5; see, for example, Lardy (2001).

Table 3-5. *East Asia: Performance by Ownership Type of Banking Systems, 2003*

Category and country	Per capita income[b]	Credit ratio[c]	Efficiency[d]	Nonperforming loans[e]	Return on assets[f]	Return on equity[g]	Capital ratio[h]	Provisions[i]	Moody's rating[j]
Mainly foreign[a]	26,730	132	45.3	3.6	0.9	11.8	16.7	107.8	68.5
Hong Kong	26,189	151	47.2	3.9	0.8	13.5	15.4	n.a.	62.3
Singapore	27,270	112	43.3	3.2	0.9	10.1	17.9	107.8	74.7
Mainly private[a]	3,129	69	68.8	14.3	1.1	12.0	14.7	54.4	23.2
Malaysia	4,965	97	n.a.	13.9	1.4	17.1	13.7	38.9	33.3
Philippines	1,239	31	68.8	16.1	1.1	8.5	16.3	51.5	20.4
Thailand	3,182	79	n.a.	12.8	0.7	10.5	14.0	72.8	15.8
Mainly public[a]	851	84	n.a.	18.2	0.9	22.1	16.8	143.2	6.5
China	1,024	148	n.a.	22.0	0.1	n.a.	11.2	n.a	10.0
Indonesia	1,090	20	n.a.	17.9	1.6	22.1	22.3	143.2	3.0
Vietnam	438	n.a.	n.a.	15.0	n.a.	n.a.	n.a	n.a	n.a.
Mixed	15,291	95	43.3	2.6	0.5	12.3	10.5	109.4	18.3
Korea	15,291	95	43.3	2.6	0.5[k]	12.3[k]	10.5	109.4	18.3

Sources: World Bank, *World Development Indicators* (online) for per capita income and credit; IMF (country reports) for efficiency, Vietnam data; IMF, *Global Financial Stability Report* (September 2004 and April 2005) for nonperforming loans, return on assets, return on equity, capital ratio, provisions, Moody's Ratings.

n.a. Not available.

a. Unweighted averages of countries shown in table.
b. Per capita GDP in 1995 dollars.
c. Credit to private sector as share of GDP.
d. Operating expenses as share of gross operational margin.
e. Nonperforming loans as share of total loans, excluding loans sold to asset management firms.
f. Profits as a share of assets.
g. Profits as a share of equity.
h. Bank regulatory capital as share of risk-weighted assets.
i. Provisions as share of nonperforming loans.
j. Financial strength index (0 = lowest, 100 = highest).
k. Average of 2002–04.

transition economy, but most of its postwar history was played out under a corrupt authoritarian ruler who used the banking system to finance personal and political objectives. This experience left the banks with a large overhang of nonperforming loans.

Korea, the lone current example of a mixed banking system in East Asia, was the most aggressive in bringing the financial crisis under control. The decline of nonperforming loans to less than 3 percent is the best indicator of its success, together with its high score on efficiency. One of the ways that Korea battled the effects of the crisis was to open its banking sector to foreign ownership when it began to reprivatize the banks taken over during the crisis. Initially, the foreign owners were equity firms, but more recently some major international banks have entered the market. At the same time, Korea maintains several well-run development banks despite the government's avowed intention to reprivatize all of the commercial banks. This combination led to the current mixed system, which others in the region are beginning to imitate. Its low Moody's rating, when compared to the favorable performance indicators, is due to the overly rapid switch from corporate to consumer lending as another result of the crisis. As a consequence, significant problems in the credit card industry slowed economic growth starting in 2003 and caused new difficulties for the banking sector.[47]

Overall, then, the banking systems in the East Asian countries not only share characteristics within each group, but the groups behave as the literature predicts for specific types of banks. The foreign-dominated systems are the strongest, the public sector systems are the weakest, and the private domestic systems lie in between. The new mixed banking system in Korea also appears to be working well, approaching the success of the foreign-ownership countries on several indicators.

Latin America presents some interesting exceptions to this clear pattern (see table 3-6). We begin the discussion as before with the countries characterized by foreign domination of their banking systems—namely, Mexico and Panama. Both are middle-income countries within the Latin American region, but their economies and banking systems differ in major ways. Panama's strong performance is similar to that of other financial centers, featuring a high credit-to-GDP ratio together with high efficiency and profitability. Mexico's performance has been much weaker. Since the 1994–95 crisis, when foreign banks purchased the large majority of bank assets, Mexico has not experienced many of the advantages that foreign institutions are expected to bring. The new foreign owners have recapitalized the banks, lowered nonperforming loans, and increased profits. On the other side of the ledger, however, they have made money mainly through increasing fees and commissions and holding risk-free government bonds rather than financing new activities that need capital. Mexico is a particularly inauspicious case for such heavy foreign ownership. Unlike Panama and the

47. On these current problems in the Korean banking system, see IMF (2003c, 2005b).

Table 3-6. *Latin America: Performance by Ownership Type of Banking Systems, 2003*

Category and country	Per capita income[b]	Credit ratio[c]	Efficiency[d]	Nonperforming loans[e]	Return on assets[f]	Return on equity[g]	Capital ratio[h]	Provisions[i]	Moody's rating[j]
Mainly foreign[a]	3,607	52	55.8	3.2	1.9	20.0	14.2	167.1	39.6
Mexico	3,717	16	74.2	3.2	1.7	14.2	14.2	167.1	39.6
Panama	3,496	87	37.4	n.a.	2.0	25.7	n.a.	n.a.	n.a.
Mainly private[a]	1,896	24	77.5	5.4	1.1	16.1	12.7	101.4	16.0
Ecuador	1,812	20	88.5	7.9	1.9	12.7	12.2	127.3	8.3
El Salvador	1,790	41	73.1	2.8	1.0	9.8	n.a.	n.a.	n.a.
Guatemala	1,544	18	78.4	7.1	0.4	6.8	n.a.	n.a.	n.a.
Honduras	713	38	81.9	3.8	1.1	12.0	13.0	36.8	n.a.
Colombia	2,321	20	79.7	6.8	2.4	17.0	12.4	98.3	24.2
Peru	2,438	22	81.1	5.8	1.1	10.8	13.3	141.1	23.3
Venezuela	2,655	10	60.1	7.7	6.2	44.0	n.a.	103.7	8.3
Mainly public	4,093	31	69.2	1.7	2.1	19.5	16.5	145.9	n.a.
Costa Rica	4,093	31	69.2	1.7	2.1	19.5	16.5	145.9	n.a.
Mixed[a]	5,733	34	65.6	12.2	0.1	4.2	15.7	125.9	26.9
Argentina	7,071	11	n.a.	30.5	-2.5	-20.6	14.0	81.2	0.0
Brazil	4,577	29	65.7	4.4	1.6	16.4	18.9	165.6	24.3
Chile	5,552	62	65.4	1.6	1.3	16.7	14.1	130.9	56.5

Sources: World Bank, *World Development Indicators* (online) for capita income and credit; *Latin Finance* (August 2004) for efficiency, nonperforming loans, return on assets, return on equity for El Salvador, Guatemala, Honduras, Panama; IMF, *Global Financial Stability Report* (September 2004) for nonperforming loans, return on assets, return on equity, capital ratio, provisions, Moody's Ratings.

n.a. Not available.

a. Unweighted averages of countries shown in table.
b. Per capita GDP in 1995 dollars.
c. Credit to private sector as share of GDP.
d. Operating expenses as share of gross operational margin.
e. Nonperforming loans as share of total loans, excluding loans sold to asset management firms.
f. Profits as a share of assets.
g. Profits as a share of equity.
h. Bank regulatory capital as share of risk-weighted assets.
i. Provisions as share of nonperforming loans.
j. Financial strength index (0 = lowest, 100 = highest).

two East Asian financial centers, its domestic productive sector is nationally based, so production and finance are mismatched.[48] While the poor performance in recent years might arguably represent a necessary transition toward a stronger banking system in the future, this outcome remains very much to be seen.

In Latin America, unlike East Asia, the countries dominated by private domestic banks are the poorest in the region. These are Central American and Andean countries that have not developed to the same extent as their neighbors. In recent years, political conflicts have exacerbated the economic problems, particularly in the Andean region. Earlier political conflicts in Central America have subsided, although they have not been overcome entirely. Not surprisingly, their low level of development and political instability has limited their attractiveness for foreign investors, including banks. Only 13 percent of total assets are held by foreign banks in El Salvador, Guatemala, and Honduras, while the figure is less than 30 percent for Andean countries. Their financial institutions thus remain locally owned, but the domestic banks have been unable to support their economies adequately. They are characterized by the lowest credit-to-GDP ratios, the lowest efficiency ratings, the highest nonperforming loans, the lowest profitability, and the lowest stability ratings in Latin America. While the Central American and Andean subgroups display important differences, both are located at the low end of the performance range.

One of the surprises we uncovered is the relatively good performance by Costa Rica, despite the fact that public banks account for almost two-thirds of total assets. The literature, as well as the East Asian cases, led us to expect a much weaker showing. In comparison with its Latin American counterparts, Costa Rica has a fairly high per capita income, and it has traditionally been seen as a wealthy and stable exception in the Central American region. Of the thirteen Latin American countries in table 3-6, Costa Rica ranks second on nonperforming loans and the capital ratio, third on profitability, and fifth on efficiency and credit as a share of GDP.[49] Costa Rican citizens have made it clear that they do not want to privatize major state-owned assets, including the banking system. At the same time, Costa Rican governments have recognized that if they are to maintain economic control, they must provide a stable and efficient system. They have been relatively effective, according to the indicators cited, although Costa Rica has not escaped the typical Latin American problem of lack

48. One of the results of the mismatch is political opposition to foreign ownership. In Mexico, such opposition has manifested itself primarily in attacks on the banks' owners for allegedly fraudulent activities of their predecessors in making bad loans that were eventually paid for by the taxpayers. The fact that the banks had been purchased by foreigners undoubtedly increased the opposition, which probably would have occurred in any case.

49. These data pertain only to onshore banking operations. Costa Rican private banks also have offshore operations, which are only partially supervised by national authorities. The offshore operations began in the days when private banks were heavily restricted in terms of what activities they could pursue; the possibility of phasing them out is currently under discussion.

of financial depth in the banking system. Nonetheless, the country provides evidence that it is possible to maintain a sound banking system in the face of democratic opposition to privatization.

Finally, the three countries in the mixed-ownership group are the wealthiest in the Latin American sample (though still far below the high-income Asian cases). Unlike the three previous groups, this group shows wide variation in performance. Each country has a significant public sector banking presence, but the results vary dramatically. Argentina, with a still unresolved financial crisis, has two of Latin America's worst-performing state banks. The other two countries in this group—Chile and Brazil—have some of the strongest banks in the region, including their public sector institutions. Overall, the two have relatively deep financial sectors, strong efficiency scores, low nonperforming loans, and high evaluations on stability. Chile is substantially stronger than Brazil on the last two items, while Brazil has a higher capital ratio and provisions. With respect to profitability, the two are in the middle ranks because of strong competition in the two markets. The good performance of the public sector banks (as well as the banking systems as a whole) is noteworthy. Both governments have taken decisive steps to clean up their banking systems, improve corporate governance, and strengthen regulation with positive results.

Ownership, Institutions, and Performance

Our second hypothesis, concerning the impact of the institutional context on bank performance, is also difficult to study. The problems of measuring bank performance, as discussed previously, are now compounded by the problem of measuring the impact of institutions. We want a broad concept of institutions that goes beyond bank regulation and supervision, which is the subject of the next chapter. A World Bank project on governance provides a useful methodology and a data set that disaggregates governance into six components. Four are relevant institutional factors that can be expected to affect bank behavior: government effectiveness (that is, quality of bureaucracy, credibility of government's commitment to policies, quality of public service provision), regulatory quality (appropriate balance between market orientation and government control), rule of law (effectiveness and predictability of judiciary, enforceability of contracts), and control of corruption (extent to which society is free of the need to pay bribes at the microeconomic level and the avoidance of elite capture of the state at the macroeconomic level). The project combines twenty-five data sets created by eighteen organizations to quantify the components of governance in the 199 countries that are included in the database.[50]

---

50. Kaufmann, Kraay, and Mastruzzi (2004) explain the methodology of the project, and associated data files provide data for each country and each variable for 1996, 1998, 2000, and 2002.

Table 3-7. *Latin America and East Asia: Institutional Quality Index, 2002*[a]

Region and country	Rating	Ranking	Region and country	Rating	Ranking
Latin America	−0.21	n.a.	East Asia	0.36	n.a.
Chile	1.39	3	Singapore	2.05	1
Costa Rica	0.67	5	Hong Kong	1.44	2
Mexico	0.06	8	Korea	0.73	4
Panama	0.03	9	Malaysia	0.62	6
Brazil	−0.08	10	Thailand	0.19	7
Peru	−0.30	13	China	−0.22	11
El Salvador	−0.37	14	Philippines	−0.25	12
Colombia	−0.41	15	Vietnam	−0.51	16
Guatemala	−0.56	17	Indonesia	−0.80	20.5
Honduras	−0.67	18			
Argentina	−0.71	19			
Ecuador	−0.80	20.5			
Venezuela	−0.92	22			

Source: Calculated from World Bank website (www.worldbank.org/wbi/governance/govdata).
n.a. Not available.

a. Institutional characteristics are defined by World Bank as government effectiveness, rule of law, regulatory quality, and control of corruption; see text for explanation.

Using 2002 data on government effectiveness, regulatory quality, rule of law, and control of corruption as measures of institutional quality, we assign a rating and ranking to thirteen Latin American and nine East Asian countries, as shown in table 3-7. A number of points are of interest for our analysis. First, institutional quality in Latin America, according to this measure, is well below that of East Asia. The unweighted average ratings are −0.21 for Latin America versus 0.36 for East Asia. Likewise, only four of thirteen countries in Latin America receive positive ratings compared with five of nine in East Asia. On the individual components, Latin America is strongest on regulatory quality and weakest on rule of law, while East Asia scores best on government effectiveness and worst on corruption control.

Second, a comparison of tables 3-5 and 3-7 reveals that the institutional scores for the East Asian countries are highly correlated with income levels, which in turn are highly correlated with the type of banking system and performance. These relationships are not as close in Latin America. Insofar as a strong correlation exists, it causes a problem since we are interested in the relationship between institutions and performance, and income may determine both. As mentioned earlier, there is an ongoing debate about the relationship

Criticisms of these data have been raised, some of which are addressed by the authors themselves. Those who agree with the spirit of the exercise criticize the use of data on perceptions, rather than the underlying factors themselves; the possible bias of these perceptions; and the sometimes rapid changes in institutions that are expected, by definition, to change only slowly. Others (such as Przeworski, 2004a, 2004b) have more profound objections to the very idea of measuring the impact of institutions, given the methodological problems of dealing with counterfactuals.

between institutions and income. The World Bank group argues that the causal relationship runs from institutions to income and not in the other direction.[51] Our concern is different, though related: do institutions affect bank performance beyond any effect that per capita income level may have? We suspect that all of the relationships run in both directions, but—at the least—institutions are a mechanism through which income affects bank performance.

Third, the institutional characteristics in East Asia seem to reinforce ownership in terms of explaining performance (see tables 3-5 and 3-7). That is, the strongest institutions are found in foreign-based banking systems, which have the best performance in the region. The next strongest are in the private-dominated systems, which perform second best, and the weakest institutions are in the poorly performing public-bank systems. But what are the mechanisms involved? Exactly how do institutions affect performance? Based on the institutional measures from the World Bank study, we can outline three channels of influence. First, respect for rule of law gives private institutions, including banks, the confidence to make long-term investments, since they have some reasonable certainty that their money will be safe. Second, high regulatory quality (by the World Bank definition) means that rules will be established in a way that is consistent with market mechanisms, which is also conducive to entrepreneurial initiative. Finally, an effective and honest government bureaucracy provides some assurance that laws and rules will be implemented fairly. All of these mechanisms mean that banks are more likely to make the commitments that will lead to better performance.[52]

Fourth, institutions help to explain some of the unexpected results in the relationship between ownership and performance in Latin America (see tables 3-6 and 3-7). As we have seen, Mexican banks perform less well than predicted for a foreign-dominated banking system. They have low efficiency scores and a low volume of credit as a share of GDP. Indeed, the credit ratio fell throughout most of the past decade. The reasons are discussed in some detail in chapter 7; here we simply point out that the low quality of Mexican institutions can be expected to inhibit performance. The two institutional components on which Mexico has negative scores are rule of law and corruption. These problems lessen the willingness of the new foreign bank owners to take the risk of making loans, since they are unsure if they will be able to recover their money. Arguing along the same lines, Haber and Musacchio make a more specific case that lack of contractual security shapes bank performance in Mexico.[53]

51. See Kaufmann and Kraay (2002), as well as the critiques accompanying their article (Lora, 2002; Pritchett, 2002).

52. Returning to the issue of relying on perceptions about institutions in the World Bank indicators, it is precisely perceptions that are important in determining whether investors will risk their money.

53. Haber and Musacchio (2005). The use of a single country study over time is an alternative way to study the impact of institutions on bank behavior.

The opposite situation seems to have occurred in Costa Rica. Whereas the literature tells us that public sector banks are generally characterized by poor performance, Costa Rica has a relatively good record within the Latin American region, featuring high efficiency, low nonperforming loans, good profitability, and strong stability. An important part of the explanation for this unexpected result is the environment in which Costa Rica's banks operate. On the one hand, the country is known for its political and economic stability. On the other, its strong institutions (namely, good regulation, low corruption, and adherence to the rule of law) have enabled the Costa Rican government to follow its citizens' desire to maintain public sector services that function effectively.[54] In the mid-1990s, the U.S. Agency for International Development (USAID) financed a program specifically designed to strengthen financial institutions in Costa Rica. Private banks have been promoted to increase competition for public banks; one of the largest public banks was closed for not following government regulations; and the central bank has been extremely conservative in its management style. This is not to imply that the Costa Rican financial sector has no problems. Although the government is taking steps to improve the situation, the public banks still enjoy some advantages compared to their private sector counterparts, and the offshore banking sector is only partially supervised. Compared with its neighbors, however, Costa Rica's banks rank highly.[55]

Finally, the three Latin American countries with mixed banking systems— Chile, Brazil, and Argentina—have very different performance records. Chile has by far the strongest financial system in the region; Brazil has a medium record in the Latin American context; and Argentina has a very weak banking system that has been unable to escape from the crisis that has ravaged the country since the late 1990s. The institutional characteristics of the three would predict exactly these outcomes.

Chile's institutions are the strongest in the Latin American region and are exceeded only by Hong Kong and Singapore in our sample. Chile is known for its adherence to the rule of law, the competence of its central bank and finance ministry, and its stable macroeconomic performance since it emerged from a financial crisis in the mid-1980s. These characteristics have helped the sole state-owned commercial bank receive high marks from rating agencies and international financial institutions. Brazil falls in the middle of our sample of Latin American and Asian countries (ranking tenth out of twenty-two on our institutions index). Its only positive score is on regulatory quality, but it also has

54. Several cases of high-level corruption have recently been uncovered in Costa Rica, but in both relative and absolute terms, the country remains an exception to the pattern of corruption in neighboring countries.

55. Personal interview with a former Costa Rican government official. See also two publications by the long-time central bank governor (Lizano, 2003, 2005). For a critical, but supportive, analysis of Costa Rica's banking system, see IMF (2003b, 2004c).

Figure 3-1. *Latin America and East Asia: Institutional Quality Index versus Credit to Private Sector*[a]

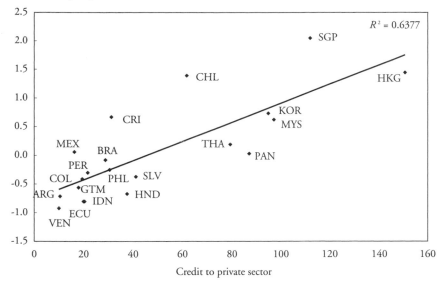

Institutional quality index

Source: World Bank, *World Development Indicators* (online) for credit; table 3-7 for institutional quality index.

a. Institutional quality index (for 2002) consists of government effectiveness, rule of law, regulatory quality, and control of corruption. Credit to the private sector (for 2003) is share of GDP.

very capable economists and bankers in its economics ministries. The country privatized most of its public sector banks in recent years, and its two largest remaining government-owned banks are generally acknowledged to be run on a highly professional basis. Argentina's institutions, by contrast, compete with Indonesia and Venezuela at the bottom of the scale. The economic performance of the country has been especially volatile, and corruption has long been considered a serious problem. Other indicators, however, have declined significantly in recent years due to political and economic instability, including a major debt default and freezing of bank deposits. In this environment, Argentina's two main public sector banks have had particularly poor records in terms of nonperforming loans, efficiency, and profits.

In short, countries with strong institutions can have well-functioning public sector banks, while those with weak institutions not only will have clear difficulties with public banks, but also will not be able to take advantage of private banks.[56] Figures 3-1 to 3-3 map the relationships between institutions and three of the performance measures shown in the tables. They include credit as a share

56. Latin America provides many examples of the latter in addition to Mexico. The countries dominated by private domestic banks have both the weakest performance indicators and the weakest institutions.

Figure 3-2. *Latin America and East Asia: Institutional Quality Index versus Nonperforming Loans*[a]

Institutional quality index

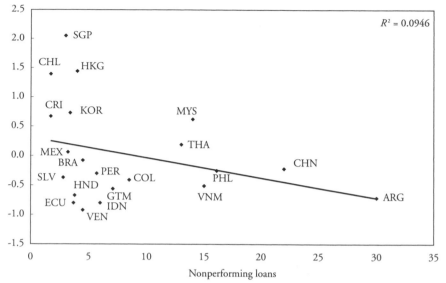

Nonperforming loans

Sources: IMF, *Global Financial Stability Report* (September 2004) and *Latin Finance* (August 2004) for nonperforming loans; table 3-7 for institutional quality index.

a. Institutional quality index (for 2002) consists of government effectiveness, rule of law, regulatory quality, and control of corruption. Nonperforming loans are for 2003.

of GDP, nonperforming loans as a share of total loans, and Moody's ratings as an indicator of stability. All confirm the expected relationships: better institutions are associated with more credit, fewer nonperforming loans, and higher Moody's scores. The closest fit is between institutions and the Moody's ratings (R^2 = 0.83), followed by credit to the private sector (R^2 = 0.64).[57] The lowest correlation (R^2 = 0.09) is found between institutions and nonperforming loans, a variable that is notoriously difficult to measure and subject to varying definitions across countries.

Since the three figures show East Asian as well as Latin American countries, they highlight some of the differences across the two regions. The Asian countries generally outperform their Latin American counterparts. More are located in the upper quadrants, indicating positive scores on institutions; only China, Indonesia, the Philippines, and Vietnam are located on the lower part of the graph. For Latin America, only Chile and Costa Rica are clearly in the upper quadrants; Mexico, Panama, and Brazil are near the middle; while the others fall

57. China has been eliminated from this graph since credit to state-owned firms (the majority of total credit) is combined with credit to the private sector, thus producing a misleading statistic.

Figure 3-3. *Latin America and East Asia. Institutional Quality Index versus Moody's Ratings*[a]

Institutional quality index

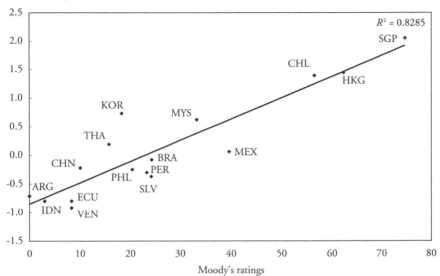

Moody's ratings

Source: IMF, *Global Financial Stability Report* (September 2004) for Moody's Ratings; table 3-7 for institutional quality index.

a. Institutional quality index (for 2002) consists of government effectiveness, rule of law, regulatory quality, and control of corruption. Moody's ratings are for 2003.

to the bottom. The East Asian countries also tend to be above the trend line, indicating performance even better than their institutional scores would predict, while the Latin American countries are generally below. The Latin American countries with private sector banks are all in the lower left-hand quadrant of the graphs, indicating the combination of the poorest quality institutions and the worst performance.

Conclusions

The data presented in this chapter confirm the worldwide trend in bank ownership toward less emphasis on public participation and a greater role for foreign owners. This process has occurred in both Latin America and East Asia. Despite these common trends in the two regions, we find that ownership remains quite heterogeneous from country to country. Unlike most of the literature, we focused on the ownership characteristics of the banking systems within countries rather than on particular types of banks across countries. Based on the characteristics of the banking systems, we identified four groups of countries in each region: a first group in which foreign ownership dominates, a second in which local private ownership is the most common form, a third in which public banks still control the majority of bank assets, and a fourth in which mixed ownership prevails.

When we tried to match performance data to the ownership characteristics of the banking systems, we found that the two regions behaved in somewhat different ways. The pattern in East Asia fits what our first hypothesis would predict. That is, foreign-dominated systems perform best, followed by local private ownership. The countries with predominantly public banks fared the worst. Performance by the single mixed ownership system fell between the foreign and private domestic systems. In Latin America, by contrast, the situation is less clear-cut. The best performing banking system (Chile) has mixed ownership, followed first by the only public-sector-dominated banking system in the region (Costa Rica) and then by the two foreign-dominated banking systems (Mexico and Panama). The worst performers tend to be those countries where private domestic banks dominate. The mixed group varies greatly, including the best performer, a middle-level one, and one of the worst performers.

To explain these findings, we turned to the second hypothesis: the relationship between performance and institutional characteristics of the respective countries. In East Asia, institutions reinforced the previous findings. The best institutions were found in the countries with the best-performing banking systems and vice versa. In Latin America, institutions contributed to explaining the anomalies found. Costa Rica has strong institutions, which helps explain why its state-dominated banking system works much better than the literature would lead us to believe. The same is true for the mixed cases. Chile has the strongest institutions in the region, which has enabled its single public bank to perform well. Brazil has a larger public presence, which makes the management task more difficult, and its institutions are also weaker than those in Chile. The result is a mid-level performance. Argentina had enormous institutional deficiencies by 2002, which compounded the performance problems deriving from the financial crisis in that country. Finally, institutions also help explain why the foreign-dominated banks in Mexico have not performed as well as expected. In East Asia, the two foreign-controlled banking systems were the top performers in those two countries, but Mexico's institutions are far weaker than those of its East Asian counterparts and not even very strong in the Latin American context.

In summary, adding the institutional dimension helps explain the relationship between bank ownership and performance. For example, the analysis suggests that public banks can perform well according to commonly used indicators—but only if the country's institutional framework is strong. Other examples, such as Argentina, China, Indonesia, and Vietnam, show the difficulties in managing public banks in the face of weak institutions. At the same time, foreign banks can perform extremely well, as seen in East Asia, but there is no guarantee—especially in the context of relatively weak institutions, as found in Mexico. The message, then, is that the real world is more complex than some of the literature would lead us to believe. We need to look at individual cases to understand the ways in which ownership characteristics affect performance and how banking systems interact with their institutional environments.

4

Toward Stability:
Regulation, Supervision,
and the Macroeconomic Context

The financial crises of 1994–95 and 1997–98 sounded wake-up calls to Latin America and East Asia, respectively, indicating that regulation and supervision needed to be strengthened. But what exactly does strengthening regulation and supervision mean? Until recently, the phrase would have been universally interpreted as tightening government regulations on capital adequacy, classification of problem loans, and provisions for expected losses at individual banks. It would also have been associated with giving supervisors more power and autonomy to enforce the regulations. In the last few years, however, a new view has been put forth that posits the superiority of private monitoring of banking systems over the traditional public approach. According to this new view, regulators and supervisors should concentrate on getting banks to disclose as much information as possible so customers can evaluate their quality and decide which ones to patronize. These market mechanisms, it is argued, force banks to behave prudently and to provide resources to society as needed. A third approach also relies on governmental supervision, but it differs from both of the others in that it focuses on the macroeconomic level. It is primarily concerned with the ways in which procyclical practices can undermine the financial stability of the system as a whole.

Our first aim in this chapter is to present the ongoing debates among these three perspectives and to ask if they are mutually exclusive or complementary. The discussion is a more specific instance of the one begun in the last chapter, where we considered a broad range of institutions, from government effective ness to support for rule of law to control of corruption. Now we focus on a particular type of institution that is central to any study of the financial sector. Strengthening government-based regulation and supervision has been a typical response to crises that have occurred in developing countries following financial liberalization, but private monitoring has also increased in many cases. We explore the choices that individual governments have made in this respect.

We also extend the discussion to take into account two other elements that are essential to understanding the impact of regulation and supervision on the stability of banking systems. The first is the macroeconomic context. On the positive side, low inflation, stable growth rates, and policies to cope with international capital flows and external debt can provide support for banking systems. On the negative side, macroeconomic shocks, such as high interest rates, asset bubbles, devaluations, and capital flow reversals, can cause problems for even the strongest systems, especially those in developing countries. The second element encompasses international rules and best practices, such as those established by the Bank for International Settlements (BIS) and the International Monetary Fund (IMF). Such rules also have both positive and negative implications for banking. Given these interactions, regulation and supervision—however defined—can no longer be considered in isolation.

Our own analysis indicates that private monitoring is positively related to bank performance, while government-based regulation and supervision have a very weak negative relationship. We also find abundant evidence that procyclicality is a major problem; in particular, it was an important cause of twin (banking and currency) crises in emerging market economies in the 1980s and 1990s. We conclude that complementarities exist among the three approaches to regulation and supervision, and they should be emphasized in policymaking. Private monitoring—especially increased transparency and public disclosure of bank information—should certainly be incorporated into bank regulations. Given the interconnections among banks and the fact that rational behavior for individual institutions can undermine the stability of the overall system, however, we disagree with the idea that private monitoring could substitute for government-based regulation and supervision. We also argue that regulation and supervision should look for ways to dampen procyclical tendencies in bank behavior. Insofar as the new BIS accord encourages procyclical behavior, as some experts claim, this is a serious problem that will need to be dealt with as implementation proceeds.

As in the other chapters, we explore these topics in the context of a comparison between emerging market economies in Latin America and East Asia. The first section looks at the literature just mentioned and outlines several hypotheses to be evaluated. The second section presents data on the current state of regulation and supervision in Latin America and East Asia, including changes that have come about as a result of recent crises. The third section evaluates the hypotheses, using both quantitative data on regulation and supervision across countries and case study materials on specific national experiences in the two regions. The last section concludes.

Regulation and Supervision: Literature and Hypotheses

Regulation and supervision have become controversial topics in much the same way that bank ownership has aroused new debates. Indeed, some of the same analysts are involved in both sets of discussions, and some of the arguments about private versus public control are brought to bear. For our part, we suggest that macroeconomic and international contexts play an important role in determining the impact of regulation and supervision, just as we argued in the previous chapter that ownership needs to be seen within a broader institutional context. Macroeconomic stability—or the lack thereof—is a crucial element that affects both individual banking institutions and banking systems as a whole. At the same time, while decisions on regulation and supervision used to be considered the exclusive purview of nation-states, it is now generally accepted that international organizations will standardize approaches across countries through proposing and trying to enforce rules and best practices.

Approaches to Regulation and Supervision

Three approaches to regulation and supervision are currently on the international agenda. The first, which we call the traditional approach, dominates practice in individual countries.[1] The other two represent intellectual critiques made by analysts with close ties to important international organizations, and they thus form part of the policy discussion. The traditional approach is a microprudential one that focuses on individual banks and their performance indicators, particularly those that relate to stability.[2] Comparisons are with a peer group of other institutions. The main aim is to make sure that individual banks are sound, under the assumption that if all individual institutions meet requirements, then the system as a whole will be safe. This approach relies on government regulation of bank behavior and government supervisors to enforce the regulations. It is regarded as appropriate by most governments and rating agen-

1. Although we call this approach traditional, it has only been used in developing countries for a relatively brief time. Until financial liberalization took place, regulation largely consisted of orders from the finance ministry or central bank with respect to interest rates, credit allocation, and so on. The concepts of prudential regulation and supervision are new to most Latin American and East Asian countries, although they are well established in the industrial world. A discussion of them can be found in any textbook on money and banking; see, for example, Mishkin (2001, chap. 11).

2. For the definition of a microprudential approach, in contrast to a macroprudential one, see Borio (2003, especially pp. 2–4).

cies. The international financial institutions also accept substantial parts of this approach, although they go beyond it.

One set of criticisms of traditional government-based regulation and supervision is also based on a microprudential model in that the unit of analysis is the sum of the individual banks in a given country, and no account is taken of the relationships among them or the impact of macroeconomic shocks to the system as a whole. The methodology involves cross-country regressions using variables from a large number of developed and developing countries. Such analysis has become feasible through a World Bank–sponsored database that provides detailed information on the characteristics of regulation and supervision in over 150 countries, based on surveys of bank supervisors in 1999 and 2003. Barth, Caprio, and Levine—the creators of the database—use it to analyze the impact of different kinds of regulation and supervision on outcomes including bank development (credit to the private sector as a share of GDP), stability (lack of a systemic crisis in recent years), efficiency (administrative costs as a share of assets), and integrity (control of corruption).[3]

The results of their analysis are controversial. Contrary to the accepted wisdom of most governments and the main international financial institutions, they find that greater supervisory power and regulations restricting banks' activities are negatively correlated with bank development and efficiency and positively related to financial fragility and corruption. In a symmetrical fashion, they find a positive relationship between bank development and private sector monitoring, defined by an index that includes the use of outside auditors, evaluations by rating agencies, accounting disclosure and director liability, and the avoidance of explicit insurance schemes. Results with respect to capital regulations are ambiguous, but the authors interpret them as nonpositive. While they generally decline to make specific policy recommendations on the basis of their findings, the authors nonetheless criticize two of the three pillars of the new Basel Accord being forged by the BIS. These include the use of capital regulations and the reliance on official supervisory mechanisms as a means of enforcement. They praise the third pillar—namely, the use of market discipline—but refer to it as the underdeveloped element of the agreement.

The analysis becomes even more controversial when Barth, Caprio, and Levine place their findings in a general political-economic context, arguing against government interventions in a variety of forms. These include bank ownership, which links their findings to those discussed in the previous chapter. They base their position on the premise that politicians will use bank supervisors

3. An early paper, based on the 1999 survey, is Barth, Caprio, and Levine (2001a); a book based on both data sets is Barth, Caprio, and Levine (2005). For a sample of others working in this same line, see Shleifer and Vishny (1998) on the general topic of the government role in finance; Blum (1999) on capital requirements; Claessens and Klingebiel (2001) on the scope of bank activities; Demirgüç-Kunt and Detragiache (2002) on deposit insurance.

to promote pet projects, banks will be able to capture regulators, and political and legal institutions will not be able to contain these forces. The proper role for government, they argue, is to create institutions that require disclosure and hold bank officials responsible, rather than giving additional power to supervisors and increasing the restrictions on bank behavior.

A very different critique moves from a micro- to a macroprudential model and focuses on the procyclicality of the financial system.[4] The problem includes, but goes beyond, the concern with asymmetric information. It has to do with at least two processes. First, increasing confidence among individual investors tends to generate a self-fulfilling rise in asset prices. As investors become more optimistic, they try to expand their asset holdings at a pace that is far more rapid than the expansion in supply. Booms in asset prices then tend to corroborate past expectations, leading to further optimism. Individual risk assessment thus changes with the state of collective enthusiasm. Second, banks also behave in a procyclical way, even though the mechanisms involved are slightly different. Waves of optimism in the banking sector lead to an expansion of lending, which affects the level of aggregate demand and thus the income and cash flow of consumers and the productive sector. In times of expansion, real and financial asset prices increase, as does the value of collateral. Through these self-fulfilling processes, banks tend to increase their leverage and thus their vulnerability to changes in the variables that affect their risks: economic activity and level of employment (credit risk), borrowing interest rates (liquidity risk), and asset prices (market risk). The contention is that individual actors cannot or will not take into account the impact of their actions on the rest of the system, creating a collective action problem that requires the government to step in to provide a public good in the form of financial stability.[5]

Saying that government action is necessary for addressing procyclicality problems does not mean that regulation and supervision are functioning appropriately at the present. Indeed, proponents of this approach identify significant deficiencies in current versions of regulation and supervision. Perhaps the most serious involves misinterpretation of the timing of risk. While risks are generated during a boom as a result of the processes mentioned above, they are commonly viewed as increasing as an economy slows and reaching their peak during a recession. The fact that they materialize only when growth slows does not mean that greater risk is present, but bankers, supervisors, and rating agencies act as if risks were greater. This leads to increased provisions and a reduction in loan volume as risk aversion rises. With less access to credit, borrowers cannot

---

4. BIS representatives are especially prominent in putting forward these arguments. See, for example, BIS (2000); Crockett (2000, 2001); Borio, Furfine, and Lowe (2001); Turner (2002); Borio (2003). A call for modeling these processes is found in Goodhart (2004). On the Latin American region in particular, see Hausmann and Gavin (1996); Ocampo (2003).

5. On international financial stability as a public good, see Underhill (2001).

keep up on their payments, and it becomes harder for economies to emerge from a recession.

Economists and regulators who adhere to this view of the financial sector have suggested a number of policy proposals. They argue that lengthening the time horizon over which risk is measured and managed is a necessary precondition for any improvement. One proposal is for greater discretion in the use of supervisory instruments. For example, greater provisions could be required in a boom period if it was thought that risk was being assessed improperly. Likewise, an increase in capital requirements could be sought if capital inflows were considered very risky. A related prescription is to use a rule to bring about the same kind of countercyclical effect without having to rely on supervisory discretion.[6] Another proposal uses monetary policy to address imbalances in the financial system. This idea has been under discussion recently in the context of whether central banks should target asset price increases as well as inflation in goods and services. A less far-reaching proposal is to have monetary authorities give more prominence to the problems of risk to try to shift views on the issue to include the need to avoid procyclicality.[7]

Regulation, Supervision, and Macroeconomics

Not surprisingly, the two microprudential approaches do not see the macroeconomic environment as particularly relevant to their concerns. It is rarely mentioned in discussions involving what we call the traditional approach. Likewise, the economists who argue for a private-sector-based regulatory and supervisory system limit themselves to using inflation or growth as control variables in some of their equations. The intimate relationship between the financial sector and macroeconomics is axiomatic for the procyclicality approach, but the tendency is to emphasize the link in which finance is the independent variable.[8] We want to underscore the fact that the impact of macroeconomics on finance—and on the regulatory and supervisory process—is equally important.

A major concern of the BIS economists and others studying procyclicality, in addition to the possibility that it can generate financial crises, is the effect it can have on the real economy. The macroprudential approach thus embodies the linkage from finance to macroeconomic variables insofar as its goal is to avoid large output losses. Indeed, the devastating nature of crises in emerging market economies in the 1990s appears to be a major factor in the spurt of literature on these topics, as we have already discussed in chapter 2. We presented data on the

6. Countercyclical supervision has been used by the Bank of Spain. For a discussion, see Fernández de Lis, Martínez, and Saurina (2001); Ocampo (2003).

7. Economists following this approach have also criticized the new Basel Accord; in their case, however, it is because the accord may increase procyclicality, as discussed later.

8. See, for example, Borio, Furfine, and Lowe (2001). We do not mean to imply that macroeconomic causes of crises have not been considered; we merely want to underline their importance and discuss some of the mechanisms.

scale of output loss over and above the fiscal costs of crises. The negative impact on asset prices and interest rates is also important in considering the mechanisms behind output losses.

The opposite relationship, from macroeconomics to finance, becomes relevant for explaining the source of financial stress. For example, a sudden increase in interest rates can cause a rise in delinquencies if loans have been made at floating rates; alternatively, the banks will be directly squeezed if their cost of funds rises in the face of fixed-rate assets. An abrupt fall in asset prices will threaten banks to the extent that they are holding large stocks of securities or real estate. A devaluation can cause financial chaos if currency mismatches are prevalent in bank portfolios. And a reversal of capital inflows is likely to trigger a decline in growth rates, which will lead to an increase in nonperforming loans. The fact that these shocks are at the macroeconomic level means that they will affect all banks, although the impact will vary somewhat depending on the characteristics of individual institutions—in particular, their levels of capital, liquidity, and the soundness of their assets. If the shocks are strong enough, they can undermine regulatory and supervisory systems as well as causing problems for banks. The recent Argentine experience, which we examine later, is an example of the potential for damage. The macroeconomic context must thus be taken into account in order to understand the origins, development, and impact of financial instability.[9]

International Pressures on Banking Regulation

In part because of the systemic factors discussed in the previous sections, banking regulation is no longer left exclusively to national authorities. While many of the changes in regulation and supervision in emerging economies came in response to events in individual countries or in regions more broadly (for example, the impact of the Mexican crisis of 1994–95 or the East Asian crisis of 1997–98 in their respective geographical areas), developments at the international level have also played a role. The BIS and the Basel Committee on Banking Supervision have been most influential in putting these issues onto the agenda and homogenizing standards for developed and developing countries alike. Following the Asian crisis, they were joined by the Financial Stability Forum (FSF), which brings together finance ministers, regulators, and central bank authorities to coordinate actions among the industrial countries with respect to financial issues. This process also affects developing countries, despite their lack of a voice to express their concerns.[10]

9. For discussion of regulation and supervision in the context of macroeconomics, see Hausmann and Gavin (1996); Lindgren, García, and Saal (1996); IMF (1998a); World Bank (1999); Ocampo (2003); Studart (2003).

10. The BIS expanded its membership in the mid-1990s to fifty-five, including most of the emerging market economies. Membership in the Basel Committee and the FSF, however, is limited to the major industrial countries (plus Hong Kong and Singapore in the case of the FSF), so it is difficult for the developing countries to present their viewpoints on issues of concern to them.

International standards themselves are currently in a state of flux, and recently agreed changes pose new challenges to developing country institutions. The Basel Capital Adequacy Accord (Basel I), introduced in 1988, was a milestone in banking regulation. The 8 percent minimum capital requirement for internationally active banks, which was adopted by over a hundred countries, clearly improved financial stability. Nonetheless, critics claimed that the approach was too rigid and simplistic and that it did not correspond to actual levels of risk. Developing countries were especially troubled about the rules providing incentives for short-term over long-term lending.

Basel II was meant to correct the problems identified by introducing more complex alternatives for determining risk, including the use of models developed by individual banks. Some experts studying the potential impact on developing countries fear that the new approach will have a negative impact on those economies through two channels. First, the new risk categories may overestimate the risk of lending to developing countries and thus lead to a significant decline in the volume of loans or a large increase in their cost. Second, the new mechanisms for adjusting capital requirements may formalize procyclical tendencies already inherent in regulation and supervision and thus increase the frequency of crises that have an especially negative impact on the developing world.[11] Other problems from the developing country viewpoint include the anticipated difficulties in evaluating and monitoring the new bank-based models and the fear that the criteria of industrial country banks and regulators will be imposed upon them.[12]

In addition to negotiating international agreements, the BIS—in collaboration with the IMF and the World Bank—tries to influence more specific aspects of the financial sector in developing (and other) economies. The most important instrument with respect to banking is the Core Principles for Effective Banking Supervision. These specify the recommended powers of supervisors, their duties, and their access to information.[13] Since the BIS itself lacks the capacity to evaluate the implementation of the standards, it must rely on others. Key partners are the IMF and the World Bank, which in 1999 began to conduct joint Financial Sector Assessment Programs (FSAPs) among their member countries. The FSAPs are geared toward assessing risks and vulnerabilities in the financial sector, with a focus on possible macroeconomic shocks. A major technique is stress testing, whereby shocks are simulated to determine their impact on individual banks and national financial systems as a whole.

---

11. For critiques along these lines and policy proposals, see Reisen (2000); Griffith-Jones (2003); Griffith-Jones and Persaud (2005). Powell (2005) makes a different, but related, critique that focuses on the problems of the private sector and SMEs in particular. Gottschalk and Sodré (2005) also express concern about the implications for SME lending, based on a study of Brazil.

12. Personal interviews with banking and supervisory authorities in several Latin American countries.

13. The Core Principles can be found on the BIS website (www.bis.org).

While the assessments are allegedly voluntary, governments face a good deal of pressure to participate. Some 120 had done so by mid-2005, but regional participation varied substantially: three-quarters of North, Central, and South American countries had taken part (excluding the United States), but only about one-third of East Asian countries had enlisted.[14] This difference is reflected in regulatory and supervisory practices in the two regions. Despite increased efforts to move away from a one-size-fits-all approach, the FSAPs and the Basel Accords are mechanisms through which individual countries have lost autonomy in setting policy on regulation and supervision.[15]

Hypotheses on Regulation and Supervision

Several hypotheses suggest themselves as a result of this brief review of the literature on regulation and supervision. A first relates to the debate about the relative merits of public versus private supervision. Using the new empirical evidence that is now available, we test the hypothesis that private monitoring has a more positive impact on bank performance in Latin America and East Asia than does traditional regulation and supervision. A second hypothesis focuses on the other debate, which concerns macro- as opposed to microprudential models and their relationship to systemic stability. We look for evidence of the procyclicality that is central to the macroprudential approach and how it might relate to trends in regulation and supervision in the two regions. In addition, we ask whether any data show that macroeconomic shocks have played an important role in undermining regulatory and supervisory systems in Latin America or East Asia. Third, the increased international influence on techniques of regulation and supervision implies that they should become more similar over time. We assess the available evidence to see whether this hypothesis is supported.

Regulation and Supervision: The State of the Art

Drawing on a database sponsored by the World Bank, we sketch out the current situation with respect to regulation and supervision of the banking sector in many Latin American and East Asian countries in 1999 and 2003.[16] It enables us to compare across the two regions in terms of regulation and two types of supervision: the traditional government-based approach and private sector monitoring. We concentrate on the data for 1999, but provide some indications of important changes as of 2003. The changes may be useful in tracing the impact of crises on regulation and supervision.

---

14. IMF and World Bank (2005, pp. 8–11).

15. The most recent review of the program is described in IMF (2005a) and IMF and World Bank (2005). Most of the country evaluations are posted on the IMF website (www.imf.org), although governments have to agree to make them public.

16. See Barth, Caprio, and Levine (2001b) for a description of the database, which we mentioned earlier in the chapter.

Table 4-1. *Latin America and East Asia: Bank Regulation, 1999*

Region and country	Minimum capital-asset ratio (%)	Actual risk-adjusted capital ratio (%)	Capital stringency index (0–6)[a]	Bank entry index (0–3)[a]	Overall bank activities index (0–4)[a]	Overall regulation index (ORI)[b]
Latin America						
Argentina	11.5	16.4	6.0	2.0	1.8	37.7
Brazil	11.0	15.8	3.0	3.0	2.5	35.3
Chile	8.0	12.3	3.0	2.0	2.8	28.1
Mexico	8.0	13.0	5.0	2.0	3.0	31.0
Peru	9.1	12.7	5.0	1.0	2.0	29.8
Venezuela	10.0	14.0	2.0	1.0	2.5	29.5
Average	9.6	14.0	4.0	1.8	2.4	31.9
East Asia						
Indonesia	8.0	12.5	2.0	3.0	3.5	29.0
Korea	8.0	9.3	5.0	1.0	2.3	25.5
Malaysia	8.0	12.8	1.0	2.0	2.5	26.3
Philippines	10.0	18.0	2.0	1.0	1.8	32.7
Singapore	12.0	20.0	5.0	2.0	2.0	41.0
Taiwan	8.0	10.4	3.0	1.0	3.0	25.4
Thailand	8.5	12.2	3.0	2.0	2.3	27.9
Average	8.9	13.6	3.0	1.7	2.5	29.7

Source: World Bank website (econ.worldbank.org/external/default/main?theSitePK=478060&contentMDK=20345037&menuPK= 546154&pagePK=64168182&piPK=64168060).

a. Possible range of index in parentheses.

b. Sum of individual components.

Table 4-1 begins with a set of indicators on banking regulation in six Latin American and seven East Asian countries. The best known indicator is the minimum capital-asset ratio, currently set at 8 percent by the BIS through the Basel I agreement. Most governments seem to regard the 8 percent minimum as inadequate. Less than half of the thirteen set their own minimums at the official 8 percent level, while the remainder have higher ratios; Argentina, Brazil, and Singapore top the list with required ratios between 11 and 12 percent. The actual risk-adjusted ratios are even higher. With two exceptions, all countries maintain ratios above 12 percent, and several are more than double the 8 percent minimum. These ratios are in line with recommendations from Latin American regional organizations that developing countries should set ratios above the international norm, given the greater volatility of their economies in comparison with industrial countries and the extremely high cost of banking crises.[17]

Several other indexes are also presented in table 4-1. The capital stringency index includes adherence to the BIS guidelines, as well as various measures of the degree to which leverage is limited.[18] The bank entry index measures the dif-

17. See, for example, Hausmann and Gavin (1996); ECLAC (2002).

18. For precise definitions, see Barth, Caprio, and Levine (2001b).

ficulty in setting up new banks in a given country; specifically, it reflects the types of assets that count toward the capital-asset ratio. The bank activities index concerns whether banks can engage in various nonbanking activities (such as securities, insurance, and real estate).

The data presented in table 4-1 clearly show that regulation has many dimensions, with countries being stricter on some than on others. Nonetheless, tendencies toward cross-country patterns do emerge. To measure these tendencies, we present a summary index (the overall regulation index), which is the sum of the five components. The last column in the table presents the result of these calculations. The indexes indicate that Latin America has a slightly more stringent regulatory system than East Asia. Latin American scores are higher than those of East Asia on every item except banking activities. Among individual countries, however, Singapore has the strictest regulation, followed by Argentina and Brazil. At the low end is Chile, together with three East Asian countries: Korea, Malaysia, and Taiwan. With the exception of Singapore, then, the strongest economies have lower levels of regulation, while more problematic economies have higher levels.

Table 4-2 uses the same data source to examine trends in government-based bank supervision. While more attention is typically devoted to the topic of regulation, the best regulations have little relevance if they are not enforced. The main index with respect to supervision is the supervisory power index. It is the summation of sixteen measures of supervisory power to deal with abnormal situations encountered—the greater the power, the higher the index. Brazil has the highest ranking on the supervisory power index, followed by Indonesia and Singapore. The lowest scores are in Korea, Mexico, and Taiwan. Other indexes include a prompt correction index that measures whether supervisors have to intervene when a bank's indicators of problems reach a certain level. The power to declare banks insolvent and the power to restructure banks are subcomponents of the supervisory power index. Finally, the forbearance index indicates the extent to which supervisors have power to decide on their own whether to enforce rules; higher decision leeway is said to give supervisors greater power.

As with regulation we calculate an overall supervisory index as the sum of the component parts (see the last column of table 4-2). Latin America again has a slightly higher overall score than East Asia. Brazil has the highest score of the thirteen countries, followed by Indonesia. Others with strict supervisory capacity are Peru, the Philippines, and Venezuela, while Malaysia, Taiwan, and Thailand are at the lowest end. Substantial differences exist between the rankings on regulation and supervision. Only Brazil is found in the top group of countries on both indexes. Again, a tendency exists for the strongest economies to be more lenient, but Argentina and Mexico are certainly exceptions to this rule.

A different approach to supervision is embodied in the private monitoring index, which is shown in table 4-3. The idea behind private monitoring is that

Table 4-2. *Latin America and East Asia: Bank Supervision, 1999*

Region and country	Supervisory power index (0–16)[a]	Prompt corrective action index (0–6)[a]	Restructuring power index (0–3)[a]	Declaring insolvent power index (0–2)[a]	Forbearance discretion index (0–4)[a]	Overall supervision index (OSI)[b]
Latin America						
Argentina	12.0	0.0	3.0	2.0	3.0	20.0
Brazil	15.0	6.0	3.0	2.0	1.0	27.0
Chile	11.0	3.0	3.0	2.0	0.0	19.0
Mexico	10.0	3.0	3.0	2.0	1.0	19.0
Peru	14.0	4.0	3.0	2.0	1.0	24.0
Venezuela	14.0	5.0	3.0	2.0	0.0	24.0
Average	12.7	3.5	3.0	2.0	1.0	22.2
East Asia						
Indonesia	14.0	6.0	2.0	2.0	1.0	25.0
Korea	10.0	4.0	3.0	2.0	1.0	20.0
Malaysia	11.0	2.0	3.0	2.0	0.0	18.0
Philippines	12.0	6.0	3.0	2.0	1.0	24.0
Singapore	14.0	0.0	3.0	1.0	2.0	20.0
Taiwan	9.0	3.0	3.0	1.0	1.0	17.0
Thailand	11.0	0.0	3.0	2.0	2.0	18.0
Average	11.6	3.0	2.9	1.7	1.1	20.3

Source: World Bank website (econ.worldbank.org/external/default/main?theSitePK=478060&contentMDK=20345037&menuPK= 546154&pagePK=64168182&piPK=64168060).
a. Possible range of index in parentheses.
b. Sum of individual components.

rather than giving power to government supervisors to enforce regulations, governments should use their power to compel banks and other financial institutions to reveal information to the public about their balance sheets and their policies. Corporations and even individual citizens will then supposedly be able to monitor bank behavior and choose to deal with the ones that follow the soundest policies. A variety of methods are thought to enhance public knowledge. Components include whether an external audit is required, the share of the ten largest banks that are rated by international rating agencies, the degree of accounting disclosure, director liability, and the absence of an explicit deposit insurance scheme.

Our overall private monitoring index does not display much variance. Scores, which could range from zero to eight, actually vary between 4.4 and 7.0. The main reason is that on many of the variables, either all (or nearly all) countries comply or none of them do. In the former category are the requirement for a certified audit, director liability, and the use of subordinated debt. Likewise, all reject the advice to eschew deposit insurance, ignoring the opinion of some experts who see it as leading to moral hazard and diverting attention from the

Table 4-3. *Latin America and East Asia: Private Monitoring, 1999*

Region and country	Certified audit (0–1)[a]	Credit agency rating (0–1)[a]	Director liability (0–1)[a]	Disclosure (0–3)[a]	Deposit insurance (0–1)[a]	Subordinated debt (0–1)[a]	Private monitoring index (PMI)[b]
Latin America							
Argentina	1.0	1.0	1.0	2.0	0.0	1.0	6.0
Brazil	1.0	1.0	1.0	2.0	0.0	1.0	6.0
Chile	1.0	0.5	1.0	2.0	0.0	1.0	5.5
Mexico	1.0	1.0	1.0	1.0	0.0	1.0	5.0
Peru	1.0	0.5	1.0	2.0	0.0	1.0	5.5
Venezuela	1.0	0.4	1.0	1.0	0.0	1.0	4.4
Average	1.0	0.7	1.0	1.7	0.0	1.0	5.4
East Asia							
Indonesia	1.0	1.0	1.0	2.0	0.0	1.0	6.0
Korea	1.0	1.0	1.0	3.0	0.0	1.0	7.0
Malaysia	1.0	1.0	1.0	2.0	n.a.	1.0	6.0
Philippines	1.0	0.6	1.0	3.0	n.a.	0.0	5.6
Singapore	1.0	1.0	1.0	3.0	n.a.	1.0	7.0
Taiwan	0.0	1.0	1.0	2.0	n.a.	1.0	5.0
Thailand	1.0	0.9	1.0	1.0	0.0	1.0	4.9
Average	0.9	0.9	1.0	2.3	0.0	0.9	5.9

Source: World Bank website (econ.worldbank.org/external/default/main?theSitePK=478060& contentMDK=20345037 &menuPK=546154&pagePK=64168182&piPK=64168060).
a. Possible range of index in parentheses.
b. Sum of individual components.

quality of banks. On the overall index, Korea and Singapore reach seven points out of a possible eight on private monitoring; a number of countries in both regions have scores of six (Argentina, Brazil, Indonesia, and Malaysia). The lowest scores are in Mexico, Taiwan, Thailand, and Venezuela. The relationship between private monitoring and government-based regulation and supervision is clearly complex. Some countries (namely, Brazil and Indonesia) are high on both, but new countries also appear with high scores on private monitoring (including Korea and Malaysia). The correlation coefficient between the private monitoring index and the overall supervisory index is 0.37.

The regional averages are also of interest. For the first time, East Asia has a higher score than Latin America. Looking back over the three tables, Latin American countries have more pervasive regulation and stronger government-based supervision, on average, while East Asian countries score higher on private monitoring. None of the differences are very large, however. We discuss reasons for these differences in the following section.

The Barth, Caprio, and Levine surveys enable us to compare the 1999 data with data for 2003. While only four years separate the two surveys, some inter-

Table 4-4. *Latin America and East Asia: Country Changes in Regulation and Supervision, 1999–2003*[a]

Region and country	Changes in overall regulation index (ORI)	Changes in overall supervision index (OSI)	Changes in private monitoring index (PMI)
Latin America			
Argentina	<<	<<	=
Brazil	>>	=	=
Chile	>	>	>
Mexico	>>	>	>
Peru	=	<	=
Venezuela	>>	<	>
Average	>	<	=
East Asia			
Korea	=	>>	=
Malaysia	=	=	>
Philippines	<<	>	>>
Singapore	<	=	=
Taiwan	>	>>	>>
Thailand	>	<	>
Average	=	>	>

Source: World Bank website (econ.worldbank.org/external/default/main?theSitePK=478060&contentMDK=20345037 &menuPK=546154&pagePK=64168182&piPK=64168060).

a. =: change between 0.3 and –0.3; >: change between 0.3 and 2.0; >>: change beyond 2.0; <: change between –0.3 and –2.0; <<: change beyond –2.0.

esting changes occurred, mainly at the individual country level. Table 4-4 shows the most important ones. The regional averages for the three indexes do not show any clear-cut trends. In Latin America, regulation was stepped up slightly, while supervision stringency fell by a similar amount. The opposite pattern was found in East Asia: regulatory provisions remained constant, but government-based supervision was strengthened. With respect to private sector monitoring, East Asia increased its efforts, while Latin America remained constant. The most important changes between 1999 and 2003 were found at the individual country level, especially those involving response to crises, as we discuss in the next section.

Regulation, Supervision, and Financial Performance

The survey data described above provide the basis for evaluating two of our three hypotheses. One involves the relative benefits to be obtained from official supervision as opposed to private monitoring. We can also use the data to investigate the impact, if any, of international pressures on developing country governments to follow best practices in regulation and supervision. Best practices may well include aspects of both types of supervision. With respect to the hypothesis on the relationship between macroeconomics, procyclicality, and regulation and supervision, we have to turn to a different kind of data and look at individual country experiences over time.

A Challenge to Traditional Views

Our first hypothesis tests, for a particular subset of countries, the claims regarding the superiority of private monitoring over official supervision of banks. Barth, Caprio, and Levine find positive results when using a large sample that combines developed and developing countries. Examination of their scatter plots, however, suggests that their results may be driven by different behavior between these two groups of countries, since the former tend to cluster in one corner of the graphs.[19] We try to replicate their results using a more homogeneous subsample of middle-income countries from Latin America and East Asia. Our methodology is much simpler, centering on bivariate analyses through scatter plots and trend lines. We concentrate on the dependent variable that they call bank development, proxied by bank credit to the private sector as a share of GDP. We also follow their lead in combining the 1999 survey with credit data for 2003 to provide the longest possible period between the operation of the regulatory and supervisory processes and the impact on credit. In addition, however, we present information from the 2003 survey and contrast the results obtained with those from the 1999 data.

Figure 4-1 plots the relationship between credit ratios and the overall regulation index for the two regions. The correlation is negative—more regulation is associated with lower credit ratios—but it is exceedingly weak ($R^2 = 0.05$). Singapore is an outlier in the graph; removing it strengthens the relationship greatly ($R^2 = 0.50$). With or without Singapore, however, the two variables clearly have a negative link that is repeated in several other forms in the following pages.

To explore the negative link, imagine four quadrants in figure 4-1 based on the average values of the two variables.[20] The lower right-hand quadrant consists of the strongest East Asian economies; in other graphs, Singapore joins them. These countries have the highest credit-to-GDP ratios, as well as relatively low levels of regulation. Chile hovers in the middle—the country with the highest credit ratio in Latin America, but far below the main Asian countries—and is just inside that same quadrant. In the upper left-hand quadrant are half of the Latin American countries, with the remainder just below the dividing line. This group has low credit ratios, but high scores on regulation. This group also includes the Philippines (frequently referred to as a quasi–Latin American coun-

19. As described in chapter 3, evidence on several variables indicates very different relationships for banks from industrial and developing countries.

20. The average ratio for credit to the private sector to GDP is 60 percent; the average for the ORI is 30.7.

Figure 4-1. *Latin America and East Asia: Credit to the Private Sector versus Regulation*[a]

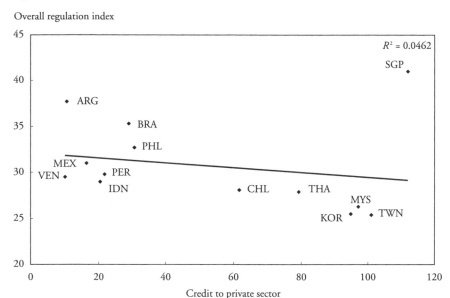

Overall regulation index

Credit to private sector

Sources: Table 4-1 for overall regulation index; IMF, *International Financial Statistics Yearbook* (2004, line 22d) for credit to private sector.

a. Overall regulation index (for 1999) is defined in table 4-1. Credit to the private sector (for 2003) is share of GDP.

try) and Indonesia (the weakest of the East Asian group and still profoundly affected by the 1997–98 crisis).

Regional differences are thus driving the relationship to a substantial extent. In terms of regulation, the East Asian countries tend to place greater emphasis on what is frequently called administrative guidance than on legal obligations, which makes them appear to have lighter regulation than Latin America. This difference is beginning to disappear as a result of international pressures, but some aspects linger. The important exception is Singapore, whose exceptional-ism among its East Asian neighbors can be explained in at least two ways. One is the country's authoritarian tradition, evident at least since independence in 1965. Strong regulations exist with respect to all aspects of life in this city state; until recently, for example, it was illegal to chew gum in the street. In addition, however, Singapore is an important international financial center, and its survival depends on its being perceived as a safe place to do business.

Figure 4-2, which illustrates the link between credit and supervision, displays a pattern very similar to that of credit and regulation, except that Singapore is no longer an outlier. Under these circumstances, a much stronger negative relationship appears ($R^2 = 0.41$). There is some reordering among the two groups of

Figure 4-2. *Latin America and East Asia: Credit to the Private Sector versus Supervision*[a]

Overall supervision index

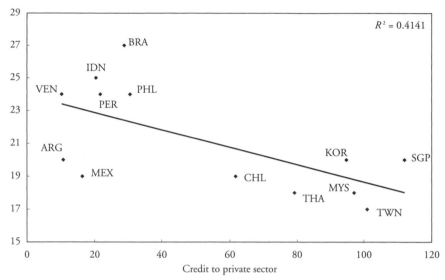

Credit to private sector

Sources: Table 4-2 for overall supervisory index; IMF, *International Financial Statistics Yearbook* (2004, line 22d) for credit to private sector.

a. Overall supervision index (for 1999) is defined in table 4-2. Credit to the private sector (for 2003) is share of GDP.

countries in line with differences between regulatory and supervisory tendencies. On the Latin American side, Brazil's supervision is stronger in relative terms than its regulation, while Argentina and Mexico are the opposite. Among East Asian countries, Korea is similar to Brazil, while Singapore follows the same pattern as Argentina and Mexico. The central message of figure 4-2 is that stricter supervision is associated with lower credit levels, but it may well be a spurious relationship in that both are influenced by more general regional characteristics and historical experiences, as discussed above.

Complementing the analysis of regulation and supervision is figure 4-3, which presents data on the correlation between credit to the private sector and private sector monitoring. Here, for the first time, we find a positive relationship, albeit a weak one ($R^2 = 0.17$). The East Asian subsample is divided, with Korea and Singapore showing high scores on private monitoring and Taiwan and Thailand lower scores. The Latin American group is also dispersed, with Argentina and Brazil at the high end and Venezuela in the lowest position. Chile, as usual, is in the middle with respect to both variables.

Before we explore the overall implications of these data, it is useful to review the results of a similar analysis of the 2003 survey data. Table 4-5 summarizes

Figure 4-3. *Latin America and East Asia: Credit to the Private Sector versus Private Monitoring*[a]

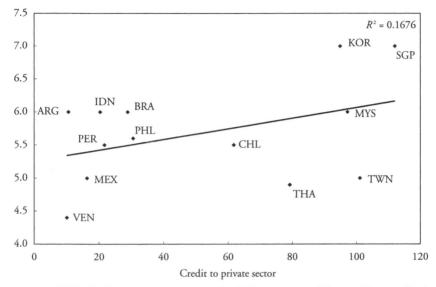

Private monitoring index

Credit to private sector

Sources: Table 4-3 for private monitoring index; IMF, *International Financial Statistics Yearbook* (2004, line 22d) for credit to private sector.

a. Private monitoring index (for 1999) is defined in table 4-3. Credit to the private sector (for 2003) is share of GDP.

and compares the two sets of results. Like the overall regulation index for 1999, that from the 2003 survey also has a negative relationship with financial depth. While it is stronger than what we found previously, it is still weak ($R^2 = 0.12$). The main difference with respect to 1999 is that Singapore is less isolated, and it is balanced by a decline in Taiwan's regulation level. The differences between the two data sets are not significant, however.

The relationship between credit and the overall supervision index, by contrast, completely disappears between 1999 and 2003 ($R^2 = 0.00$ in the latter year). This unexpected result stems from three large changes: both Korea and Taiwan substantially increased the power of their supervisors between 1999 and 2003, while Argentina did the opposite. Korea underwent a profound process of structural change after the 1997–98 financial crisis; its government took a much more aggressive approach to restructuring than any of the other Asian crisis countries. As discussed in chapter 2, a typical component of postcrisis restructuring is tightening regulation and supervision. Taiwan, which escaped the earlier crisis, was in serious problems of its own by 2003, based on bubbles in its real estate and stock markets, among other factors. Tighter supervision resulted from trying to deal with this situation. At the other end of the spectrum,

Table 4-5. *Latin America and East Asia: Regulation, Supervision, and Credit,*
1999 and 2003
R squared

Index	1999	2003
Credit and overall regulation index (ORI)[a]	0.05	0.12
Credit and overall supervision index (OSI)[a]	0.41	0.00
Credit and private monitoring index (PMI)[a]	0.17	0.36

Sources: Calculated from data in tables 3-5, 3-6, 4-1, 4-2, 4-3, and 4-4.
a. Credit to the private sector as a share of GDP; see text and tables 4-1 through 4-4 for definitions of indexes.

Argentina in 2003 was still in the midst of a crisis in which the banking sector was deeply involved. The banks had been targeted by the government to pay a substantial part of the costs of the crisis through the way in which the devaluation was implemented. This process jeopardized the supervisory functions of the central bank. Interestingly, the Argentine policy was countercyclical, while that of Korea and Taiwan was procyclical. The latter would be predicted by the literature on cycles; the Argentine exception is linked to political factors in that country.[21]

In contrast to the ambiguous overall findings on regulation and supervision, private monitoring became more closely associated with private sector credit in the 2003 survey data ($R^2 = 0.36$, versus $R^2 = 0.17$ in 1999). Across the board, countries in both regions either maintained high scores on private monitoring or raised them. Particularly large increases occurred in the Philippines and Taiwan, which increased both government-based supervision and private monitoring. Five other countries—Chile, Malaysia, Mexico, Thailand, and Venezuela—also stepped up private monitoring, though to a lesser extent. At the same time, three of the five increased or maintained their level of government-based supervision.

What begins to become clear, especially in the 2003 data, is that there is no real contradiction between strong supervision of the traditional government-based sort and private monitoring. Indeed, private monitoring—or at least the greater amounts of disclosure, transparency, and information that are used as indicators—is very much part of the new best practices that the international institutions and others are pushing. The attempt to portray them as alternatives, with the recommendation that strong traditional supervision be replaced by private monitoring, is not in tune with reality in developing countries themselves. This is especially the case in light of the concerns that we address later regarding financial crises and instability.

21. After substantial political turmoil in 2001–02, the new Argentine president took a very aggressive stance against international norms, organizations, and markets. This type of political reaction did not occur in other twin crisis countries for reasons that are beyond the scope of this analysis.

International Influence

By the early 1990s, several international and regional organizations were stressing the importance of better financial regulation and supervision. These concerns were greatly magnified by the Mexican crisis of 1994–95 and especially by the Asian crisis of 1997–98. In both cases, the diagnosis of the causes of the crises focused heavily on deficiencies in regulation and supervision. What was meant by this? Documents from the BIS, the IMF, the World Bank, and regional organizations indicate that better regulation and supervision involves both tighter prudential regulation of such items as capital adequacy, asset quality, provisioning, and the use of international accounting standards, as well as greater disclosure. Since disclosure is the essence of the private monitoring paradigm, the two seem to be related in a positive way.

Useful documents for exploring this proposition are the most recent reports on the IMF/World Bank Financial Stability Assessment Program (FSAP).[22] The issues discussed cover the most common recommendations to come out of the FSAP evaluations. These include the need to improve corporate governance of financial institutions (two-thirds of FSAPs), expand legal and judicial frameworks (half), strengthen governance of oversight agencies (half), reinforce supervisory staff (half), improve data and reporting systems (half), and increase competition (one-fifth). This clearly encompasses both traditional supervision and private monitoring.

Another recent IMF document reveals the relationship between IMF/World Bank evaluations and the macroprudential approach advocated by the BIS and others.[23] This document makes it clear that systemic stability is the main focus of the FSAPs. The financial soundness indicators employed in the FSAPs are placed squarely within a macroprudential framework. Of special note is the emphasis on credit booms and their role in increasing systemic vulnerability and the transmission of macroeconomic shocks through the banking system. Stress testing is the instrument of choice for measuring the vulnerability of individual countries' financial systems.

Given the high-profile recommendations of the BIS and associated organizations and the prevalence of the FSAPs, it is interesting to ask about their impact on the financial management of individual countries. Since the current FSAPs are one-shot evaluations, we cannot look at changes over time. If the influence of the international organizations is strong, however, we would expect improvements in the scores on the Barth-Caprio-Levine surveys and increased homogeneity across countries—especially in our middle-income sample. Table 4-6 enables us to check on these points. The table shows that the combined sample

22. See IMF (2005a); IMF and World Bank (2005).
23. IMF (2004b).

Table 4-6. *Latin America and East Asia: Summary Statistics on Regulation and Supervision, 1990–2003*

Index	Latin America Mean	East Asia Mean	Latin America and East Asia Mean	Standard deviation
Regulation 1999	31.9	29.7	30.7	4.97
Regulation 2003	32.9	29.8	31.4	4.77
Supervision 1999	22.2	20.3	21.2	3.13
Supervision 2003	21.0	22.0	21.5	4.42
Private monitoring 1999	5.4	5.9	5.7	0.80
Private monitoring 2003	5.7	6.6	6.2	0.64

Source: World Bank website (econ.worldbank.org/external/default/main?theSitePK=478060& contentMDK=20345037&menuPK=546154&pagePK=64168182&piPK=64168060).

registered an increase in all three categories: regulation, government-based supervision, and private monitoring. Nonetheless, the increases were very small. Within regions, the pattern held for East Asia, while Latin America saw a reversal in terms of government-based supervision because of the large changes in Argentina. We also calculated standard deviations to see if these became smaller between the 1999 and 2003 surveys, which would indicate increased homogeneity. They fell with respect to regulation and private monitoring, but increased for supervision. Again, the changes were all small, but they indicate some tendency toward greater similarity across countries.

Financial Fragility and Procyclicality

The third hypothesis that we evaluate involves the interaction between macroeconomics and the financial system. In particular, we look for evidence in the Latin American and East Asian cases of the procyclicality that is the basis for the macroprudential justification of regulation and supervision. As explained at the beginning of the chapter, the problems result from lending booms that accompany the upswing of business cycles as borrowers and lenders alike respond to high and growing expectations. While it appears that risks are low in the early part of a cycle, in reality vulnerabilities build up as banks find it difficult to distinguish among potential clients, all of whom appear to be good risks. The likely result is adverse selection and perhaps also moral hazard. Only as the cycle wears itself out do the underlying weaknesses become obvious. At that point, lending is curtailed as regulations are tightened and risk aversion sets in, although risks are really no greater than they were before. This exacerbates the economic slowdown.

We find an extreme version of this typical cyclical pattern in the three Latin American and four East Asian countries that suffered twin (banking and currency) crises between the early 1980s and the late 1990s. As shown in chapter 2, the crises followed financial liberalization, which loosened or eliminated the regulatory restrictions that prevailed during the preceding period of financial repression. While the deregulation of financial markets brought many benefits, a major problem was that an alternative framework of prudential regulation and supervision, appropriate for a modern financial system, was not yet in place.

To complicate matters further, capital account opening generally accompanied domestic financial liberalization. Both banks and nonfinancial enterprises sought credit in the international markets, sometimes to supplement local sources or sometimes because high domestic interest rates led them to substitute international for domestic credit. The absence of adequate regulatory restrictions on foreign currency liabilities, together with lack of experience in international markets, led to a very rapid buildup of debt. Much of it was on short terms since this was cheaper than longer-term credit.

A third element, which exacerbated the two previous problems, was macroeconomic policy. For differing reasons in the various cases, exchange rates were closely linked to the dollar. In Latin America, an exchange rate anchor was used to lower inflation. In East Asia, an undervalued exchange rate was used to promote exports. In the former situation, trade deficits built up as lack of competitiveness resulted from an overvalued exchange rate, while in the latter the dilemma was nearly the opposite. Undervalued exchange rates and other government support helped to make East Asian countries exporting powerhouses and eventually saturated markets for their main products. In both regions, current account deficits were an important element of the foreign exchange problems that led to devaluations. Those devaluations, in turn, either triggered or exacerbated banking crises. We examine these experiences in detail to understand the implications for regulation and supervision.

We divide the twin crisis countries into the two regional groups since the details of the overall stories vary across regions. Intraregional variation was also present, but it was less significant because of shared structural characteristics and historical experiences among neighboring countries.[24] To highlight both the commonalities and differences, figure 4-4 presents data on growth rates of domestic credit to the private sector and international liabilities to the banking sector during the six years before and after the twin crises. In other words, we are looking at trends in credit and in an important source of funding for those credits. Every case features a lending boom in the period preceding a crisis. With the exception of Korea, credit fell off sharply after the crisis and remained at low levels for a substantial period, contributing to low growth or even recession in the respective countries. International liabilities also rose, but the relative magnitude of the increases with respect to domestic credit varied across the two regions.

---

24. See Stallings (1995) for a discussion of the sources and impacts of regional differences.

Figure 4-4. *Latin America and East Asia: Credit to Private Sector and International Liabilities*[a]

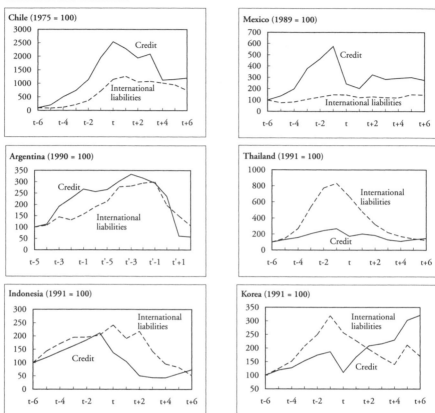

Sources: IMF, *International Financial Statistics Yearbook* (2001, 2004).

a. Six years before crisis (*t* – 6) = 100. For Chile, crisis year is 1981; Mexico, 1995; Argentina, 1995 and 2001; Thailand, 1997; Indonesia, 1997; and Korea, 1997. Credit and international liabilities are in constant (2000) dollars.

The historical experiences of Chile in the early 1980s and Mexico in the early 1990s closely reflect the process outlined above. In both cases, credit booms were facilitated by lax regulatory systems that failed to oversee the banks and by legal systems that failed to prevent fraudulent activities within the banking industry. With the advantage of hindsight, it becomes clear that both moral hazard and adverse selection were in play.

The Chilean crisis represented in figure 4-4 took place much earlier than the others.[25] Financial liberalization in Chile occurred after the military coup in 1973, followed by a crisis in the early 1980s. Credit in Chile in the six precrisis

25. For details and references on Chile, see chapter 6.

years increased an astounding twentyfold.[26] International liabilities rose tenfold, but in relative terms the latter amount seems small, as seen in the first panel in the graph. This lending binge had a very low starting point: credit as a share of GDP in the early 1970s had reached unusually low levels, and the economy had been closed in financial terms. The increase was facilitated by very lax regulation, which was part of the military government's ideology in opposition to state intervention. The banks were quickly privatized and formed the basis for new conglomerates that engaged in very aggressive and risky transactions. A substantial share of the new loans went to related parties and nonperforming loans proliferated, but adequate provisions were not made.

These microeconomic practices took place in a macroeconomic context that greatly increased vulnerability. The exchange rate was used to lower inflation from the three-digit levels it had reached in 1973. In the process, competitiveness fell and the trade deficit ballooned. The current account deficit reached nearly 15 percent of GDP in the months before the crisis. These deficits had to be financed by large-scale capital inflows, some of which were represented by the bank liabilities seen in figure 4-4. Shocks came in the form of bank failures in 1981, followed by a large devaluation in 1982; this set off a crisis that lasted for several years and cost the economy around 40 percent of GDP in fiscal costs alone. The decline in domestic credit exacerbated the recovery problems. One of the results in the postcrisis period was a substantial strengthening of regulation and supervision.

The Mexican experience with uncontrolled lending was surprisingly similar to that of Chile, although it took place a decade later.[27] Credit rose nearly sixfold between 1989 and 1994, but international liabilities to the banking sector did not grow very fast. This was one area in which Mexico maintained strong regulatory requirements. Prudential regulation was generally underdeveloped because the banks were nationalized in 1982 and run by government decree for nearly a decade before they were reprivatized in the early 1990s. Since the new owners paid very high prices, they were willing to engage in risky practices to recoup their costs and begin making profits. Nonperforming loans built up rapidly. Again like Chile, macroeconomic problems exacerbated those at the microeconomic level. A semifixed exchange rate anchored a stabilization program, leading to large trade and current account deficits and matching capital inflows. In the Mexican case, the crisis was triggered by a set of political shocks in the election year of 1994. A devaluation at the end of the year both revealed the extremely weak situation of the banks and led to their bankruptcy.

26. The amplitude of the Chilean cycle was magnified by exchange rate trends. Using constant local currency, the increase was "only" tenfold. Exchange rate trends also affected some of the other cases to a more limited extent, but the basic pattern of booms in domestic credit and international borrowing were found with either measure.

27. See chapter 7 on Mexico.

The Argentine case is more complicated since the country suffered two separate financial crises in the 1990s.[28] Financial liberalization, which began in the early 1990s, lifted most of the controls on domestic and foreign operations of the financial system that had been imposed during the previous period of high inflation and external constraints. Liberalization took place in the context of an exchange-rate-based stabilization program embodied in a currency board. Price stability and the fixed exchange rate regime abruptly reduced both inflation and exchange rate risk. This created a fertile environment for the rapid growth of financial activity, but it also led to maturity and exchange rate mismatches.

Until 1994, the situation appeared quite promising. Deposits and loans grew rapidly, while peso and dollar lending rates fell significantly. These results were a mix of several important features: a monetization process caused rapid growth of deposits in the banking sector; an increase of foreign capital inflows led to the dollarization of both liabilities and assets; and the increased competition among banks and the improvement of overall confidence resulted in a rapid expansion of credit, as is evident in figure 4-4. Given the currency board rules, which made monetary and credit policy dependent on foreign capital inflows, foreign liabilities rose more rapidly relative to domestic credit than in Chile or Mexico.

In 1995, however, the Argentine economy and banking sector were hit hard by the spillover from the Mexican crisis. Under the currency board system, the only instrument that domestic monetary authorities had for facing potential capital outflows was to allow domestic interest rates to rise. This rise, in turn, provoked an increase of arrears and defaults and reduced the confidence of depositors, leading to significant withdrawals. Despite steps by the central bank, the banks lost 12 percent of their deposits in the first four months of 1995.

In the aftermath of this first crisis, a set of measures was introduced to restructure the sector by injecting more capital, promoting mergers and acquisitions, and creating incentives for the expansion of foreign banks. A deposit insurance scheme was also introduced, and a new system of reserve requirements was introduced to reduce leverage. In the second half of the 1990s, private bank provisions in relation to total credit increased substantially, liquidity within the banking sector rose, and the capital adequacy ratio was maintained at levels far beyond those established by the Basel I guidelines. Foreign banks more than doubled their share of the market between 1994 and 1999. In sum, the banking sector became more solid, which explains why its ability to deal with the emerging market crises that characterized the late 1990s was far superior to what was observed after the Mexican crisis. Nonetheless, macroeconomic policies—especially the currency board—eventually undermined these improvements as the banking sector and the economy as a whole fell into crisis after the devaluation

28. On Argentina, see Kiguel (2001); de la Torre, Levy-Yeyati, and Schmukler (2003); Fanelli (2003); Daseking and others (2004); Díaz Bonilla and others (2004).

in January of 2002. Regulatory and supervisory improvements were swept away in the process, as domestic credit and international borrowing fell.[29]

The East Asian crisis countries differed from their Latin American counterparts in a number of important ways. They had a thirty-year history of high growth and low inflation, and they had strong external sectors as a result of their export orientation. One element of this high-growth model was the use of the financial sector as a channel to implement government industrialization policies. While the model was most highly developed in Northeast Asia, Southeast Asia shared a significant number of these characteristics. In the late 1980s and early 1990s, all of these countries began to dismantle their extensive controls, including those pertaining to the financial sector.

The last three panels in figure 4-4 (Indonesia, Korea, and Thailand) show some interesting differences compared with the patterns in Latin America. While each Asian country saw significant growth of credit in the period preceding the 1997 crisis, the increases were not as large as those in Argentina, Mexico, or—especially—Chile. Credit to the private sector more or less doubled in Indonesia and Korea, while it tripled in Thailand. Unlike Latin America, however, international liabilities in all three East Asian cases outpaced the growth rate of domestic credit.[30] This pattern reflects East Asia's history of more closed financial sectors. Once they were given the authorization to move into international capital markets, both banks and nonfinancial corporations did so with a vengeance since they were without many constraints on the part of the respective governments.

Thailand stands out among its neighbors for both the size of its credit increase and the growth of international liabilities; the latter rose eightfold between 1991 and 1997. A significant portion of these liabilities were probably contracted through the offshore banking center, the Bangkok International Banking Facility, but transparency was low so the details are unclear. Financial liberalization, both domestic and international, set the scene for a decade of rapid GDP growth, which averaged 9 percent per year between 1987 and 1996, fed by the credit boom and capital inflows. As the economy grew and asset prices ballooned, bank portfolios deteriorated. Large current account deficits ultimately depleted reserves, and the baht was floated in July 1997, undermining Thailand's banks and setting off the crisis that spread rapidly to its neighbors.[31]

29. For an elaboration of these issues in Argentina, Brazil, Chile, and Mexico, see Stallings and Studart (2003).

30. This does not mean that international liabilities were larger than domestic credit. On the contrary, one reason the former grew so rapidly was a relatively low starting point. Domestic credit as a share of GDP started from a high level. Thus, the amplitude of the various curves is heavily influenced by initial conditions, but all cases display a rapid rise of credit and international liabilities.

31. On Thailand's financial crisis, see Vajragupta and Vichyanond (1999); Alba, Hernández, and Klingebiel (2001); Nidhiprabha (2003); Warr (2004).

Indonesia saw credit double in the six years leading up to the crisis, and international liabilities closely tracked the growth of credit, as illustrated in figure 4-4. Following financial liberalization in the late 1980s, the number of banks and volume of credit began to rise. Many of the loans were to related borrowers; this was an especially serious problem in Indonesia as a result of the crony capitalism under the Suharto regime. The government actually encouraged companies to borrow abroad by its high interest rate policies. Short-term capital inflows accompanied trade and current account deficits, so that Indonesia had the internal characteristics that made it vulnerable to contagion following the devaluation of the baht.[32]

In Korea, like Thailand, international liabilities far outpaced the growth of credit, although the latter nearly doubled. The relatively low increase in credit was partly due to its substitution by off-balance-sheet items that enabled the banks to compete with the growing nonbank sector. Korea's financial liberalization began in the late 1980s, but it accelerated in connection with negotiations to join the OECD in the early 1990s. The newly opened capital account enabled financial and nonfinancial firms to borrow abroad; much of the debt was contracted on short terms. Although it had a much stronger and more diversified economy than its neighbors, it also succumbed to the regional crisis, as its foreign exchange reserves were exhausted and its financial institutions fell into bankruptcy.[33]

Korea stands out from the other countries shown in figure 4-4 in that credit fell only briefly during the crisis and then began to grow again. It exceeded its previous peak by 1999 and continued rising, thus underpinning the recovery that was more rapid than in other cases.[34] Another credit boom occurred, involving credit cards and consumer lending as the banks tried to diversify their portfolios in the absence of investment-led demand for credit. A second mini-crisis took place in Korea in 2003 as a direct result of the consumer credit buildup. The better state of the banking sector, including improved regulation and supervision, helped to keep these problems under control in comparison with 1997–98.

In summary, these six cases provide ample evidence of the procyclicality and resulting financial fragility that continue to worry the international financial institutions. The argument that they were extreme cases and not representative of normal trends is true only up to a point. The same underlying tendencies are also at work in less dramatic circumstances. Recent examples center on the sig-

32. Indonesia's crisis is discussed in Ghosh and Pangestu (1999); Nasution (1999, 2002); Pangestu and Habir (2002).

33. On Korea, see Hahm (1999); Cho (2002); Coe and Kim (2002); Ahn and Cha (2004).

34. Argentina had a similar pattern, but it resulted in a second, much more serious, crisis. Mexico's rapid recovery was a temporary one—based on exports to the United States—without access to credit. The lack of credit has become a serious problem in Mexico, as discussed in chapter 7.

nificant increase in consumer credit in many developing economies. The Korean experience is likely to be the first of many problematic experiences in this regard.

Conclusions

Several different approaches to regulation and supervision are currently competing for the attention of policymakers, especially those in developing countries. One is the traditional, microeconomic approach that focuses on the stability of individual banks in order to protect their depositors. From this perspective, the more regulation and supervision, the better. A challenge to this perspective has recently been mounted by experts who provide evidence that stricter regulation and supervision are negatively correlated with financial depth, efficiency, and even stability. These results come out of large-sample econometric studies that combine data on both developed and developing countries.

We replicated these results for a smaller, more homogeneous sample of countries in Latin America and East Asia. We found a weak negative relationship between regulation and bank development, defined as credit to the private sector as a share of GDP, and a stronger negative correlation between bank supervision and credit ratios. We also found a positive relationship between credit and private monitoring.

Concluding from these results that governments of developing countries should be encouraged to pull back from regulation and supervision and rely on private monitoring would be to ignore another set of problems that is the focus of the third approach to regulation and supervision. This approach is advocated by international financial institutions, which are concerned with the stability of the overall financial systems of individual countries and—given increased international interdependence—of the world financial system as a whole. Macroeconomic shocks face all banks simultaneously, and they are thus beyond the purview of individual institutions. Moreover, individual actors, behaving in a perfectly rational way, can increase risks for the financial system as a whole.

Some of these problems arise from a misinterpretation of the timing of risk and result in inappropriate regulatory response. Risks increase during a boom, but they only become apparent in the slowdown process. At that point, the appearance of greater risk causes regulation to be tightened, risk aversion to increase, and the two together become a drag on economic growth. Macroeconomic policies frequently exacerbate this procyclicality. We provided evidence supporting this perspective through examining data on lending patterns among countries that suffered twin crises in the 1980s and 1990s.

The solution to these apparently contradictory sets of evidence and concerns would seem to be smarter regulation and supervision, not less regulation and supervision. More disclosure and a better informed public should certainly be part of any set of policy recommendations with respect to the financial sector. The private monitoring paradigm is an important contribution to policy for the future, but it needs to be carefully integrated into existing prudential regulations that have proved valuable in the period after financial liberalization put these issues onto the agenda.

At the same time, the arguments for macroprudential regulation and supervision must be taken into account as well. Those advocating this approach are also critical of existing regulation and supervision—although for different reasons than those supporting private monitoring. They believe that existing regulation and supervision are procyclical and thus exacerbate problems of instability. Recommendations on this side include, above all, a longer time horizon for regulators. In addition, regulators need to find ways to limit the increased vulnerabilities during boom periods (to manage the boom, as some put it) and to avoid overtightening during recessions. They also must look for ways to identify and protect the financial system against macroeconomic shocks, whether exogenous or endogenous. While proposals for countercyclical regulation and supervision would be very difficult to carry out in practice, some solutions to the problems of cyclicality must be sought. These issues are especially pressing at the moment because of the possibility that the new Basel Accord itself may increase procyclical behavior and magnify instability.

5

From Banks to Capital Markets:
New Sources of Finance

Emerging market economies—including Latin America and East Asia—have traditionally had bank-based financial systems, with small, poorly developed capital markets. Bond markets have tended to be shallow, heavily dominated by government debt, and with low turnover. Stock markets have likewise featured few issues, and most have not been traded with any frequency. Thus, the banking system has provided the main source of finance for both public and private borrowers. Recent financial liberalization reforms changed the way that banking systems operate by limiting government controls over interest rates and over the volume and recipients of credit. While they also provided some stimulus for capital market development, no dramatic changes have occurred to match those found in banking.

According to one strand of the literature, this situation does not pose any particular problem since bank-based systems provide a perfectly viable source of finance; indeed, the majority of the industrial countries have bank-based systems. The so-called Anglo-Saxon model, based on strong capital markets, is an anomaly even among industrial economies. Another line of thought suggests that it is important to have capital markets in addition to the banking system because capital markets provide a useful alternative to bank finance domestically and lower dependence on volatile foreign capital flows for public and private borrowers alike. They also offer new savings instruments and information on benchmark interest rates.

We agree with the argument that capital markets are a useful complement to banking systems, but the chapter demonstrates that Latin America trails far behind East Asia and the industrial countries in terms of capital market development and financial depth more generally. Lack of diversification toward capital markets is especially problematic for the investment process in Latin America, given the region's low levels of domestic bank credit. Three factors have hindered capital market development: lack of macroeconomic stability, lack of strong institutions, and the existence of international (especially U.S.) financial markets as an alternative to domestic markets. While we would expect structural reforms to stimulate capital markets—as they did in Chile—they were generally carried out in a problematic way such that the full advantages were not obtained. Financial liberalization, followed by financial crises, was a prominent example. We argue that Latin American policymakers should take steps to promote markets by advancing further in the macroeconomic policy area and strengthening institutions, especially corporate governance. Governments may also have to take proactive measures to stimulate the participation of new actors through legal changes and other incentives.

This chapter compares capital market development in Latin America with that in East Asia. The first section reviews the literature about the role of capital markets, their relative importance, and the determinants of their performance. It also presents several hypotheses about the reasons for Latin America's lagging performance. The second section provides data on financial market trends in Latin America and East Asia since 1990. The third section analyzes the differences between the two regions in light of the hypotheses. The final section concludes.

Capital Market Performance: Literature and Hypotheses

In an influential study published more than two decades ago, Zysman popularized the idea that financial systems can be divided into three types: a system based on capital markets (as in the United States and Great Britain), a credit-based system administered by governments (such as France and Japan), and a credit-based system dominated by financial institutions (like Germany). Zysman, a political scientist, is interested in this distinction because of the implications for government policy and relations among political actors. He believes that financial systems influence governments' capacity to intervene in the economy and the types of political conflicts that emerge. Specifically, the book argues that private sector firms dominate economy and society in the U.S.-U.K. type of arrangements, government policies are key factors in economies like Japan and France, and negotiated solutions prevail in German-style structures.[1]

In the economics field, an equally influential book by Allen and Gale looks at the same five countries, although the authors collapse Zysman's two credit-based systems and speak only of banks versus markets. Their principal aim is to criti-

1. Zysman (1983).

cize standard economic theory about the allocation of resources through financial markets. They set out "to develop theories that better capture how resources
are allocated in practice and understand the normative properties of different
systems," but they are also interested in comparing the advantages and disadvantages of market-based versus credit-based (intermediated) systems. Criticizing
this simplistic dichotomy, they argue that each system has advantages and disadvantages. They conclude that different institutions can perform the same functions and that the ideal system relies on both.[2]

A third book of interest for our topic, an edited volume by Demirgüç-Kunt
and Levine, brings two new elements to the discussion of banks and markets.
First, they move away from the industrial countries and focus on the developing
world. In this sense, they look more to Goldsmith as an antecedent than to the
authors just mentioned.[3] Second, they provide empirical data, including a new
database, with which to compare the operation of the two types of systems
across a large number of countries. Echoing Allen and Gale, they do not find
either type to be superior; rather, they argue that the crucial point is how well
either functions. They advise governments to focus on legal, regulatory, and policy reforms that improve the operation of both banks and markets.[4]

Developing countries tend to be located on one extreme of the spectrum
between banks and capital markets, since the requirements for setting up banking systems are much less stringent than for markets. Thus, even moving toward
Allen and Gale's ideal of a combined system would require additional effort to
promote capital markets. By the late 1990s, economists, business people, government officials, and the international financial institutions were all calling for
more movement in this direction. Asian governments have been especially eager
to promote the growth of bond markets in the aftermath of the financial crisis
of the late 1990s, in the belief that the crisis would have been less severe if markets had been more developed.[5]

Particular emphasis has been placed on the so-called missing market for government and corporate bonds. The term derives from the fact that stock markets
are more common than bond markets in developing countries, in part because
the upside of a bond is limited by the interest rate, while an equity claim has an
unlimited upside and so can compensate for high risk.[6] Those urging support

2. Allen and Gale (2000).
3. Goldsmith (1969).
4. Demirgüç-Kunt and Levine (2001).
5. The Asian Development Bank (ADB), the Asian Development Bank Institute (ADBI), and
the UN Economic and Social Commission for Asia and the Pacific (ESCAP) have carried out studies and made recommendations on how to strengthen the bond markets in the Asian region. See,
for example, ESCAP (1998); Kim (2001); Yoshitomi and Shirai (2001). Latin American governments have been less concerned with these issues, although the Inter-American Development Bank
(IDB) recently published a volume on the capital markets (Dowers and Masci, 2003), and the IDB
itself has sponsored programs to stimulate the development of financial markets.
6. See BIS (2002, box 2) for a discussion on "why equity markets may exist where bond markets fail to thrive."

for the missing market offer a variety of explanations for the importance of an active bond market.[7] First, a bond market is the only means of establishing a market-determined interest rate, which will help investors calculate the opportunity costs of alternative investments. Second, in the absence of a bond market, savers will have fewer investment choices and thus a lower volume of savings may be mobilized. Third, firms will face a higher cost of funds without a bond market and may be biased toward short-term investments in trying to match maturities. Fourth, to compensate for the lack of a domestic bond market, firms and governments may borrow abroad and thus take excessive foreign exchange risks. Fifth, in the absence of a deep bond market, the banking sector becomes more significant than it would be otherwise, which makes the economy more vulnerable to crises.

Other experts concentrate on specific institutional needs to justify the call for increased emphasis on bond markets. From the government's perspective, for example, a bond market is useful for financing fiscal deficits without increasing inflation or taking on exchange rate risk and for running monetary policy. Firms and households also need access to bond markets to obtain long-term finance for investment and mortgages.

Finally, an argument that has become increasingly common combines some of the justifications above: namely, domestic capital markets provide an alternative to borrowing abroad and thus avoid the risks and volatility that the latter entails. The head of the International Monetary Fund (IMF) capital market division recently stated, "The efforts to develop local securities markets have been motivated by a number of considerations, especially the desire to provide an alternative source of funding in order to self-insure against reversals in capital flows."[8] He went on to quote Alan Greenspan's well-known comment that smoothly functioning bond markets can act as a "spare tire" to use when other sources of funds dry up.

The new interest in capital markets has sparked an increasing amount of analysis aimed at better understanding how they operate. Although most of the studies concern equities, bond markets are also considered. Topics of interest include the relationship of capital markets to economic growth and investment, the circumstances under which they work best, their links to other forms of finance, and differences or similarities across regions. While strong overlaps exist with the literature we have already discussed on the functioning of banking systems, some new topics are also introduced.

Theoretical models are ambiguous on whether stock markets are positively or negatively linked to economic growth. For example, the literature contains arguments both for and against markets' capacity to monitor firm behavior; this

7. See Herring and Chatusripitak (2000, especially pp. 14–24). Others make similar arguments.
8. Hausler, Mathieson, and Roldós (2003, p. 21).

debate is essentially the reflection of the one about banks versus markets. Given these disagreements, the recent empirical analysis is especially important. One of the most frequently cited articles is that by Levine and Zervos, which examines evidence on a set of developed and developing economies over the period 1976–93.[9] They study several measures of stock market performance as predictors of economic growth: size (market capitalization as a share of GDP), trading value (volume traded as a share of GDP), and the turnover ratio (volume traded as a share of market capitalization). Several measures of growth are also used: GDP, capital stock, and productivity. To assess whether stock markets and banks are substitutes or complements, they include both in their analysis, together with various control variables. Their conclusion is that both stock markets and banks are independent determinants of growth, but the relevant factor in stock markets is liquidity, not size.

If we assume that financial markets are positively linked to investment and growth, what has stimulated their growth and what determines their depth and liquidity? The financial system reforms, which were the main subject of chapter 2, are an important part of the answer to these questions. Financial liberalization both served as a signal to potential participants in the markets that a government was committed to private sector participation in the economy and opened space for market mechanisms to function. Other reforms were also important. Opening the capital account made foreign participation in the markets possible; privatization provided new firms that were eager to obtain funds; and pension reform brought in new actors on the demand side. In addition, the reforms generally led to increased macroeconomic stability, which was very positive for the development of capital markets. Control of inflation was important for both stock and bond markets, while the size of government budget deficits was crucial in determining the characteristics of the latter.[10]

Reforms of the economy as a whole were complemented by changes that were specifically oriented to improving capital market functioning. A study by the World Bank identifies five such areas in Latin America: creation of supervisory agencies, establishment of insider trading laws, and improvement of custody arrangements, trading systems, and clearing and settlement processes. By 2002, between 88 and 100 percent of Latin American countries had implemented such changes.[11] More generally, corporate governance was also strengthened to protect the rights of investors, including minority shareholders.[12]

9. Levine and Zervos (1998). Levine (2004) mentions a number of criticisms of the article, including difficulties with causality, the measurement of liquidity, the possibility of spurious correlation, and the failure to include other parts of the financial markets in the analysis. Demetriades and Andrianova (2004) provide more fundamental criticisms.

10. On the economic reforms in Latin America, see Stallings and Peres (2000).

11. World Bank (2004c, chap. 2, figure 9).

12. On corporate governance, see Shleifer and Vishny (1997); Oman (2001); Oman, Fries, and Buiter (2003). On corporate governance in the financial sector, see Litan, Pomerleano, and Sundararajan (2002).

The literature suggests that in addition to reforms, institutions are important in determining how well the markets operate. As in chapter 3, we use the term *institution* to refer to formal and informal rules that help to eliminate uncertainty. La Porta, López-de-Silanes, and Shleifer propose the use of a country's legal origins as a proxy for the type of institutions that would be found later; they consider legal origins to be particularly important with respect to property rights.[13] The authors argue that the English common law tradition leads to better protection of property rights than German and Scandinavian traditions. French civil law is said to be the least protective of such rights.

This type of approach has also been extended to the analysis of stock markets. In a series of papers, La Porta and colleagues study the relationship between legal origin and various measures of stock market performance, including size of the markets, number of listed firms, initial public offerings (IPOs), and ownership concentration.[14] Their cross-country regressions generally support their hypotheses. They also look at more specific measures of investor protection—including rule of law, antidirector rights, and one-share one-vote rules—and find similar conclusions for some of the measures.

In a recent paper, they confirm that "law matters," but argue strongly that private enforcement is more relevant than public rules.[15] In this sense, they complement the position of Barth, Caprio, and Levine, discussed in chapter 4, who make a similar argument for the banking sector. In particular, La Porta, López-de-Silanes, and Shleifer find that having an independent regulator or the ability to impose criminal sanctions is not important, while extensive disclosure requirements and simple procedures for investor recovery of losses are associated with larger stock markets.

A final set of papers focuses on the relationship between domestic and international capital markets. In their analysis of Latin America's capital markets mentioned above, World Bank economists confirm that macroeconomic stance, institutions, and economic reforms are positively associated with domestic stock market development. They also find, however, that activity in international markets increases as a result of these factors. Indeed, examination of the ratio of international to domestic stock market activity indicates that they have a larger impact on Latin American participation in stock markets abroad. Evidence is compiled from both descriptive statistics and econometric analysis; it includes several measures of stock market performance—capitalization-to-GDP ratios, turnover, and new issues. Similar evidence is found for government bond markets, although data problems preclude analysis of corporate bonds.[16]

13. La Porta and others (1998).
14. La Porta and others (1997, 1998).
15. La Porta, López-de-Silanes, and Shleifer (2003).
16. World Bank (2004c, chap. 3).

Going further, Levine and Schmukler find negative ramifications in terms of the effects of international activity on domestic markets in Latin America. The most important is a decrease in the liquidity of local markets. As more firms issue stock and bonds abroad, liquidity falls dramatically on local capital markets. Small size and concentration further these problems. Some firms have left local markets altogether and moved to international stock markets in the United States or Europe, usually as a result of purchase by multinational corporations.[17]

The issue of size is a significant one for this group of World Bank economists. They stress the relationship between the size of an economy and the development of its capital markets, including bond and stock markets; in both cases, a strong positive relationship is found. The conclusion drawn is that smaller countries should concentrate their efforts on integrating themselves with the international capital markets, rather than trying to create capital markets at home. They also argue that regional markets do not provide a good alternative because costs will be higher than on international exchanges.[18] Contrary to the World Bank approach, Asian governments have been promoting regional markets. They are attempting, for example, to form a regional bond market in addition to the system of swaps that is already in place.[19]

Our interest in this chapter is to examine why Latin America has lagged behind other regions, particularly East Asia, in this area of finance, just as it did in banking. Based on the literature just discussed, we present four hypotheses. First, we suggest that macroeconomic performance is an important determinant of capital market development. Higher growth, lower inflation, and higher savings rates would be expected to increase the size (and perhaps the liquidity) of bond and stock markets. Second, the implementation of reforms— including financial liberalization, privatization, and pension reform—should favor capital market development. At least two channels may be relevant: reforms are a signal to investors, and they provide new actors and instruments that help the markets function better. Third, we argued in chapters 3 and 4 that institutions play an important role in determining bank performance; we believe the same is likely to hold with respect to stock and bond markets. We hypothesize that stronger institutions will be associated with larger markets and perhaps with higher liquidity. Finally, participation in international markets could have a negative impact on domestic capital markets. Local actors may see international markets as a substitute, thus relieving pressure for local market development. Moreover, internationalization may undermine local markets by shrinking liquidity.

---

17. Levine and Schmukler (2004).
18. World Bank (2004c, chap. 3); Claessens, Klingebiel, and Schmukler (2002).
19. Recent analyses of the Asian regional market initiatives include Amyx (2004); Ma and Remolona (2005); Park and Park (2005).

Comparing Financial Market Trends across Regions

Several recent empirical studies help to identify trends in capital markets in emerging economies, especially bond markets.[20] Their message is that domestic capital markets have been expanding, although fairly unevenly across regions and individual countries. This expansion has generally been accompanied by growth of domestic bank credit and increased use of international financial markets. Thus, domestic capital markets do not seem to have displaced other sources of finance, although a better understanding of the relationship among the various markets would be helpful.[21]

We begin with an overview of the financial system in Latin America and East Asia. Table 5-1 compares the structure of the financial markets as a whole, including banks, bonds, and equity, over the period between 1990 and 2003.[22] These data provide the opportunity to contrast both the overall depth of the financial markets in the two regions and the relative weight of the different components. The principal measure used in this table (and most of the others in the chapter) is outstanding amounts of finance as a share of GDP, which shows the importance of the volume of finance relative to the size of an economy. Dollar figures are also shown to compare the absolute size of the markets, both between the two regions and with the international capital markets; the latter will be an element of the discussion below on the viability of local markets.

Several important points emerge from the top panel of the table. First, in 2003, domestic financial markets as a whole in East Asia were twice as deep as those in Latin America (236 percent of GDP as opposed to 112 percent). Each individual component echoed the gap between the two regions, although the difference was especially prominent in the banking sector. Second, the relative strength of East Asia has been present at least since 1990. When measured as a share of GDP, the East Asian advantage shrank somewhat over the period. The growth rate of total domestic finance as a share of GDP in Latin America was 78 percent, compared with 67 percent for East Asia. This divergence, however, was due exclusively to the fact that GDP grew three times as fast in East Asia (7.5 percent annual average increase versus 2.6 percent in Latin America). In absolute terms, finance in East Asia grew more rapidly: 253 percent in nominal dollar terms, compared with 180 percent in Latin America. Third, a similar pattern unfolded in the capital market segment (bonds and stock markets). Latin

20. See, for example, United Nations (1999); BIS (2002); Masuyama (2002); Dowers and Masci (2003); Litan, Pomerleano, and Sundararajan (2003); World Bank (2004c).

21. For two different approaches to the complementarities between banks and securities markets, see Levine and Zervos (1998) and Hawkins (2002).

22. This kind of exercise entails significant data problems, so the numbers should only be taken as approximations, although we believe that the trends are accurate. Different sources produce different figures for the same variables, and the same source can even produce different estimates in different publications! Problems also arise since the data are aggregated in U.S. dollars, which introduces distortions stemming from exchange rate variations.

Table 5-1. Latin America and East Asia: Composition of Domestic Financial Sector, 1990–2003

Measure and region	Bank claims[a]			Bonds outstanding[b]			Stock market[c]			Total		
	1990	1995	2003	1990	1995	2003	1990	1995	2003	1990	1995	2003
Relative size of markets (share of GDP)												
Latin America[d]	34	33	41	17	21	37	12	25	34	63	86	112
East Asia[e]	63	71	96	30	31	60	48	72	80	141	185	236
Share of total finance (percent)[f]												
Latin America	55	42	37	26	27	31	19	32	32	100	100	100
East Asia	46	41	41	19	18	26	35	42	34	100	100	100
Absolute size of market (billions of dollars)												
Latin America	340	500	639	162	319	540	121	383	563	623	1,202	1,742
East Asia	471	981	1,463	190	433	915	355	1,007	1,210	1,016	2,421	3,588

Sources: See references for tables 5-2, 5-3, and 5-4.
a. Total claims by deposit money banks.
b. Total bonds outstanding.
c. Stock market capitalization.
d. Weighted averages; includes Argentina, Brazil, Chile, Colombia, Mexico, Peru, and Venezuela.
e. Weighted averages; includes Indonesia, Korea, Malaysia, the Philippines, Singapore, Taiwan, and Thailand.
f. Calculated on the basis of absolute size of market.

America saw a bigger increase as a share of GDP, but growth was virtually identical in absolute terms. Thus, the combined bond and stock market share of GDP in 2003 in Latin America was still only about half that in East Asia.

The second panel of table 5-1 shows the relative importance of the three financial sector components within each region. The three were fairly evenly distributed in Latin America in 2003, while in East Asia, bank credit was somewhat more important than either of the other components. Some shifts occurred over time. For Latin America, the most obvious trends were the reduced importance of bank credit and the increased role of capital markets. The changes were less marked in East Asia.

The third panel shows the absolute size of the markets. By 2003, total financial market size was $3.6 trillion in East Asia, more than twice the size of Latin American markets at $1.7 trillion. Capital markets (bonds and stocks) in Latin America increased from a little less than $300 billion to $1.1 trillion between 1990 and 2003. East Asian markets grew from $550 billion to $2.1 trillion in the same period. Since the capital markets expanded at about the same rate in the two regions, the large gap was not reduced. These regional figures need to be broken down by country, since the markets are currently organized on a national basis. When we combine bonds outstanding and stock market capitalization, five countries had markets that exceeded $200 billion in 2003: Brazil ($535 billion) and Mexico ($271 billion) in Latin America; and Korea ($776 billion), Taiwan ($536 billion), and Malaysia ($267 billion) in East Asia. This compares with an average of around $5 trillion for the five largest OECD markets in bonds alone.[23]

Table 5-1 focuses on amounts outstanding for each component. Another way to look at the process is to focus on recent trends in financial flows. Flow data for the period 1997–2002 reinforce some of the differences observed in the data on stocks but reverse others. The overall amount raised by the two regions in domestic and international markets was about the same—around $2.3 trillion over five years. In both cases, the vast majority came from domestic markets. Other patterns were quite different. Bank credit was much more significant for East Asia than for Latin America; bonds were much more important for Latin America (especially for the public sector) than for East Asia. The stock market faded in both regions, especially Latin America. In general, the public sector was the main borrower in Latin America, raising $2 trillion, while the private sector received only $260 billion. The situation was reversed in East Asia, as $1.6 trillion went to the private sector and $700 billion to the public sector.[24]

We now examine the three components separately, including the differences among countries within regions. We begin with bank claims, as shown in table

23. Data on bonds are from the BIS website (www.bis.org/statistics/qcsv/anx16a.csv); stock market capitalization is from Standard and Poor's (2005).
24. Calculated from data in Mathieson and others (2004, pp. 6–9).

Table 5-2. *Latin America and East Asia: Domestic Bank Credit, 1990 and 2003*
Percent of GDP

Region and country	Total credit[a]		Credit to private sector[b]	
	1990	2003	1990	2003
Latin America[c]	34	41	23	22
Argentina	26	36	16	11
Brazil	45	46	31	29
Chile	48	64	45	62
Colombia	18	32	16	20
Mexico	22	42	15	16
Peru	19	25	8	22
Venezuela	19	16	17	10
East Asia[c]	63	96	55	82
Indonesia	50	39	46	20
Korea	56	99	53	95
Malaysia	82	118	69	97
Philippines	27	54	19	31
Singapore	96	141	84	112
Taiwan	76	124	60	101
Thailand	74	91	65	79

Sources: IMF, *International Financial Statistics Yearbook* (2001, 2004); Republic of China (2004) for Taiwan.

a. Total claims by deposit money banks (IFS lines 22a–g, 22bx, 22cg).

b. Claims on private sector by deposit money banks (IFS line 22d).

c. Weighted averages of countries shown in table.

5-2.[25] In addition to providing data on the overall trends already described, the table compares credit to the private sector with total credit in each economy. The dominant message is that the private sector got much more credit in East Asia than in Latin America. Private sector credit in Latin America remained less than 25 percent of GDP throughout the period studied, while it increased from 55 to 82 percent in East Asia. The private sector share of total credit was also much higher in East Asia: 87 percent in 1990, falling slightly to 85 percent in 2003. For Latin America, the figures were 68 percent and 54 percent, respectively. In other words, not only did the Latin American private sector receive a smaller share of existing credit, but the gap increased over the period. Moreover, a huge gap remained in terms of GDP share, and this is the most important factor in terms of its impact on growth.

25. The data in these tables are from international sources, which have attempted to standardize them across countries. Thus, substantial differences often exist with respect to national data in individual countries because of different methodologies and the inclusion of different items. The differences are likely to be most significant with respect to bank credit, both in total and to the private sector. They will be evident in comparing the tables in this chapter with those in chapters 6 through 8.

Table 5-3. *Latin America and East Asia: Domestic Bonds Outstanding,*
1990 and 2003
Percent of GDP

Region and country	Total bonds		Bonds for private sector[b]	
	1990	2003	1993	2003
Latin America[a]	17	37	2	8
Argentina	8	17	0.1	10
Brazil	n.a.	61	n.a.	11
Chile	35	57	11	28
Colombia	3	28	0.3	n.a.
Mexico	23	24	1	3
Peru	n.a.	8	n.a.	4
Venezuela	n.a.	n.a.	n.a.	n.a.
East Asia[a]	30	60	21	37
Indonesia	n.a.	32	n.a.	3
Korea	36	74	30	55
Malaysia	74	95	18	56
Philippines	21	30	n.a.	n.a.
Singapore	30	64	16	23
Taiwan	18	56	15	29
Thailand	10	40	7	18

Sources: BIS website (www.bis.org/statistics/qcsv/anx16a.csv) for total bonds, (www.bis.org/statistics/qcsv/anx16b.csvamounts) for private sector bonds; World Bank, *World Development Indicators* (online) for GDP; Republic of China (2004) for Taiwan GDP.
n.a. Not available.
a. Weighted averages of countries shown in table.
b. Includes both corporate and financial sector bonds outstanding.

Table 5-2 also shows data for the seven Latin American and seven East Asian countries for which data are most readily available. With one exception, they are also the largest emerging market economies in each region.[26] A pattern appears here that recurs with all our data: some countries in each region have much deeper financial markets than others. Indeed, the differences within regions are sometimes as important as those across regions. In terms of total bank credit, Chile has had access to much more credit than other Latin American economies. In East Asia, the situation has been more even across countries, although Indonesia and the Philippines lagged behind. The same general pattern holds for private sector credit, which actually fell as a share of GDP between 1990 and 2003 in a number of countries in both regions (namely, Argentina, Brazil, Venezuela, and Indonesia).

26. China is by far the largest emerging economy in the Asian region. It is not included for two main reasons: there are very serious data problems for China, and including China in weighted averages would overwhelm the rest of the East Asian region, making comparisons with Latin America quite difficult.

Table 5-3 shows total domestic bonds outstanding and bonds issued by the private sector. Data problems are more severe for bonds than for bank loans, so several countries are missing from the table for 1990. It is not clear if the data are unavailable or if there were no bond issues; in any case, they would not have been large. For the private sector, data are only available as of 1993 and again for selected countries. East Asia far outpaces Latin America in total bonds outstanding as a share of GDP, but an even greater difference exists for private sector bonds (including both the corporate and financial sectors). While the private sector share increased in both regions, by 2003 the private sector in Latin America still accounted for only 22 percent of total bonds outstanding (representing 8 percent of GDP). In East Asia, the private sector represented 62 percent of total bonds (37 percent of GDP). On the other side of the ledger, then, the public sector accounted for nearly 80 percent of bonds in Latin America, but less than 40 percent in East Asia.[27]

Again, we find substantial differences within as well as across regions. Chile and Brazil dominate the bond markets in Latin America, since Brazilian bond markets are larger than bank claims. Korea and Malaysia are the largest participants in East Asian bond markets. A very large gap nonetheless remains between the leading economies in the two regions: the two East Asian leaders represent 55 percent of GDP in private sector bonds, while the figure is less than 20 percent for their Latin American counterparts.

The stock market is potentially an important source of finance for private firms, but the figures for market capitalization give a greatly inflated view of their role. As noted earlier, issuance of shares on the markets (the so-called primary markets) fell to a very low level in both regions over the last five years of the sample period (to only 2 percent of GDP in Latin America and 8 percent in East Asia).[28] This compares with market capitalization figures of 34 percent and 80 percent of GDP, respectively (see table 5-4). Individual countries display some changes relative to bank loans and bonds. While the two largest stock markets in Latin America (in terms of GDP share) are again found in Chile and Brazil, Malaysia and Singapore top the list in East Asia.

Table 5-4 also shows the turnover ratio, which is an indicator of how active the secondary market is in each country or region. The measure is defined as the total value of shares traded during a given period, divided by the average market capitalization for the period. The ratio is important because investors are more willing to put money into a liquid stock market (with a high turnover ratio) than an illiquid one. More active trading also provides more accurate pricing of individual issues and improves the allocation of resources. The data show that turnover in East Asia vastly exceeds that in Latin America (152 percent versus

---

27. It is interesting to note that the public sector share grew as a result of the financial crisis of 1997–98 in East Asia. In 2001, the public sector share was only 32 percent.

28. Mathieson and others (2004, pp. 6–9).

Table 5-4. *Latin America and East Asia: Domestic Stock Market Indicators,*
1990 and 2003

Region and country	Market capitalization[a]		Turnover ratio[b]		No. of listed firms		Price indexd[c]	
	1990	2003	1990	2003	1990	2003	1990	2003
Latin America[d]	8	34	30	20	1,624	1,238	326	1,288
Argentina	2	30	34	6	179	107	268	1,033
Brazil	4	48	24	32	581	367	41	369
Chile	45	119	6	10	215	240	839	3,227
Colombia	4	18	6	3	80	114	300	783
Mexico	12	20	44	21	199	159	761	2,145
Peru	3	27	n.a.	6	294	197	n.a.	357
Venezuela	17	4	43	4	76	54	552	182
East Asia[d]	48	80	145	152	1,792	4,576	445	401
Indonesia	7	26	76	34	125	333	99	34
Korea	42	54	61	237	669	1,563	483	414
Malaysia	110	162	25	34	282	897	138	140
Philippines	13	29	14	9	153	234	870	828
Singapore	93	159	n.a	71	150	475	n.a.	n.a.
Taiwan	78	129	430	185	199	669	632	637
Thailand	28	83	93	117	214	405	381	346

Sources: World Bank, *World Development Indicators* (online), based on Standard and Poor's (2000, 2005).

n.a. Not available.

a. Market capitalization as share of GDP.

b. Value of shares traded to market capitalization.

c. 1984 = 100 except Peru, where 1992 = 100; and Indonesia, where 1989 = 100.

d. Weighted averages of countries shown in table.

20 percent, respectively, in 2003); indeed, turnover actually fell in Latin America during the past decade. This is a serious problem. Evidence shows that liquidity, rather than market size, is most closely linked to economic growth.

Turnover appears to be related to the absolute size of market capitalization—as opposed to share of GDP, which is our basic measure in this chapter. Of the five stock markets with capitalization over $100 billion, four (Brazil, Mexico, Korea, and Taiwan) had the highest turnover in their respective regions, although Brazil and Mexico were well below their Asian counterparts. Chile is an interesting case in that it has the largest stock market in terms of GDP in Latin America but a very low turnover; the reasons are discussed later.

A look at the number of firms listed on each stock market over the period 1990–2003 reveals that the two regions started out at very similar levels: 1,624 in Latin America and 1,792 in East Asia. By 2003, however, the number of listed firms in Latin America had fallen to 1,238, while it had more than doubled in East Asia to 4,576. Every country in the Asian sample showed buoyant

Table 5-5. *Latin America and East Asia: Holders of Domestic Debt Securities,*
2000
Percent of GDP

Region and country[a]	Central banks	Commercial banks	Institutional investors	Other financial institutions	Nonresidents	Other
Latin America[b]	10	31	33	29	0	6
Brazil	22	30	0	49	0	0
Chile	0	31	62	7	0	0
Colombia	25	20	46	2	0	7
Mexico	0	57	13	29	1	0
Peru	3	16	43	14	0	24
East Asia[b]	5	50	12	17	1	17
Indonesia	0	96	0	4	0	0
Korea	2	63	20	14	2	0
Malaysia	7	0	0	24	1	68
Thailand	11	39	26	24	0	0

Source: BIS (2002, p. 29).

a. No data are available for Argentina, Venezuela, the Philippines, Singapore, and Taiwan.

b. Unweighted averages of countries shown in table.

growth, while only two in Latin America grew at all. This "delisting" phenomenon has serious implications for market liquidity, as discussed below. The trend in number of listed firms complements the data on market capitalization, clarifying the relative role of price and volume increases. These data suggest that price increases were most important in Latin America, while volume increases dominated in Asia. More direct evidence of this fact is provided in the last column of the table. The leading price index of emerging market stocks indicates that East Asian share prices fell slightly between 1990 and 2003, while Latin American prices rose by 300 percent in dollar terms.[29]

A final set of data that is essential for analyzing domestic capital markets concerns the purchasers of bonds and stocks. Table 5-5 sheds some light on this issue, although data are difficult to compile and country-specific categories make them hard to interpret; the data are also limited to debt securities. Nonetheless, some useful points can be extracted from the table. First, commercial banks are the dominant purchasers in East Asia, holding half of all bonds; in Latin America, the banks' share is less than one-third. Second, the single largest category of purchaser in Latin America is institutional investors (that is, private pension funds, insurance companies, and investment funds of various kinds). The third major difference concerns the category "other," which includes indi-

29. Standard and Poor's (2000, 2005). While prices fell in East Asia after the crisis in 1997–98, faster price rises in Latin America were not due exclusively to this factor. In 1996, for example, the year before the crisis, the Asian index was 403, while the Latin American index was 649 (1984 = 100).

Table 5-6. *Latin America and East Asia: Outstanding Amounts of International Finance, 1995 and 2003*
Percent of GDP

Region and country	International bank loans[a]		International bonds		International equity[b]		Total	
	1995	2003	1995	2003	1995	2003	1995	2003
Latin America[c]	15	29	4	19	1	2	20	50
Argentina	16	28	6	68	2	5	24	101
Brazil	11	22	3	17	0	2	14	41
Chile	33	70	1	14	2	3	36	87
Colombia	13	15	2	17	0	0	15	32
Mexico	22	34	9	12	4	2	35	48
Peru	11	22	0	4	0	2	11	28
Venezuela	16	22	5	17	0	0	21	39
East Asia[c]	34	30	4	11	1	4	39	45
Indonesia	24	17	2	4	1	3	27	24
Korea	17	17	5	10	1	3	23	30
Malaysia	24	59	8	23	2	4	34	86
Philippines	13	30	4	31	3	4	20	65
Singapore	255	148	1	24	2	11	258	183
Taiwan	12	22	1	7	1	8	14	37
Thailand	40	27	4	6	1	5	45	38

Sources: BIS website (www.bis.org/statistics/hcsv/hanx9a_int.csv) for bank loans, (www.bis.org/statistics/qcsv/anx15b.csv) for bonds; IMF, *Global Financial Stability Report* (September 2004) and unpublished data for equity.

a. Includes cross-border loans and foreign currency loans from local offices of foreign banks.
b. Equity outstanding is sum of cumulative emissions since 1991.
c. Weighted averages of countries shown in table.

vidual investors and corporations. This group is much more significant in Asia than in Latin America. These different types of buyers are important because they have different portfolio requirements. To take the two extremes, institutional investors tend to buy and hold, while individual investors are much more likely to trade frequently. The investor profile is probably related to the turnover rate reported in table 5-4—assuming that owners of stock and bonds behave in similar ways.

Thus far, we have focused on domestic financial markets, but governments and the private sector have an alternative source at the international level. International banks can provide loans to borrowers in emerging market economies (either through the head offices or through local branches in emerging economies themselves), and actors in emerging markets can also issue bonds or equity internationally. Table 5-6 provides information on international bank loans, bonds, and equity outstanding in 1995 and 2003. Here we find a somewhat different pattern than in the previous tables: international finance in 2003 constituted a larger share of GDP (50 percent) in Latin America than it did in East Asia (45 percent). The data further show that international finance as a share of total finance (domestic and international) was 31 percent in Latin America versus 16 percent in East Asia. Nonetheless, the addition of the international component does not offset the differences in domestic finance between the two regions.

If we disaggregate the figures for bank loans and bond issues from the international markets, we find results that are similar to those for the domestic markets in terms of the public-private allocation. For Latin America, nearly two-thirds of the bonds issued in international markets were by governments in 2003. The range is from 31 percent in Chile to 96 percent in Peru. Only 16 percent was issued by nonfinancial corporations in Latin America, versus 35 percent in East Asia; the remainder in both cases was issued by local financial institutions. Thus, in Latin America, both domestic and international bond markets were largely the province of governments needing to finance deficits. The opposite was the case in East Asia, where private sector firms were the main issuers of debt. With respect to bank loans, the picture is more nuanced. The public sector received only a slightly larger share of total international loans in Latin America in 2003 (22 percent) than in East Asia (19 percent). Among private sector entities, the nonfinancial sector in Latin America was the major borrower: about 60 percent of total loans was obtained by this sector. In East Asia, a fairly even division was found between financial and nonfinancial borrowers.[30]

Analysis of Financial Market Trends

The previous section identified important differences between domestic financial markets in Latin America and East Asia along a number of dimensions. The most important are much deeper and more liquid markets in East Asia than in Latin America and a stronger emphasis in Asia on providing resources to the private sector. Latin America's greater participation in international financial markets offers some counterbalance, but not enough to make up for East Asia's advantage in the domestic sphere. In addition, international capital market participation may be a double-edged sword, offering important benefits in terms of the volume and price of finance while also providing channels for contagion in periods of financial crisis and perhaps undermining the operation of domestic markets. In this section, we examine evidence about the hypotheses presented earlier to explain the differences between the two regions. The hypotheses focus on the macroeconomic environment, structural reforms, the quality of institutions, and the role of international financial markets in the two regions.

---

30. Calculated from the BIS website. For international bonds, see www.bis.org/statistics/qcsv/anx12.csv; for international bank loans, see www.bis.org/statistics/hcsv/panx9a.csv.

Table 5-7. *Latin America and East Asia: Macroeconomic Indicators, 1965–2003*
Percent

Indicator	Latin America[a]	East Asia[a]
GDP growth rates		
1965–80	6.0	7.3
1981–90	1.6	7.8
1991–2000	3.3	7.7
2001–03	0.4	6.8
Inflation[b]		
1965–80	31.4	9.3
1981–90	192.1	6.0
1991–2000	84.1	7.7
2001–03	6.0	3.1
Savings rate[c]		
1965	22	22
1990	22	35
2000	20	35
2003	21	41

Source: World Bank (1992) for 1965–90; World Bank (2004a) for GDP growth and inflation in 1991–2003; World Bank, *World Development Indicators* (online) for savings in 2000–03.
a. Broad definitions of Latin America and East Asia.
b. Consumer price index.
c. Gross domestic savings as share of GDP.

Macroeconomic Environment

One reason that East Asia's domestic financial markets are twice as deep as those in Latin America (and the gap is widening) has to do with differences in macroeconomic performance. Table 5-7 compares the two regions with respect to three macroeconomic variables that are of particular relevance for financial sector development: the domestic savings rate, GDP growth, and inflation.

The savings rate is obviously important since it is a nation's savings that are recycled through the financial system. As the table shows, savings rates in East Asia were nearly double those in Latin America in the last fifteen years of the sample period, despite starting at the same level in the 1960s. East Asian savings rates after 1990 were around 37 percent of GDP, on average, compared with 21 percent in Latin America. A variety of reasons have been suggested to account for the difference, including higher growth rates, lower inflation rates, and the greater need to provide for education and social security in Asia. This list suggests that the three macroeconomic variables are closely interrelated and constitute a package of factors rather than several independent ones.

Inflation rates are relevant because they influence people's willingness to hold local currency and financial instruments priced in that currency. While there is consensus on this general point, disagreement arises on the level of inflation that may discourage people from holding financial assets. Some analysts have suggested a threshold below which inflation is not very important.[31] In any case, Latin America's inflation rates during the 1980s were far higher than any possible threshold, averaging nearly 200 percent as a result of hyperinflation in several countries. The region's record improved substantially in the 1990s (although the average rates shown in table 5-7 are skewed upward because of Brazil); by the early 2000s inflation was in the single digits. A measure of the changed environment is the fact that significant devaluations in Latin America in the late 1990s did not increase inflation, since the demand for money increased. Nonetheless, East Asia's lower, stable inflation history over recent decades would be expected to support greater financial depth.

The role of growth is more complex. As described in earlier chapters, most scholars currently argue that the dominant causal relationship between finance and growth runs from the former to the latter, but they also agree that this is a messy area and that feedback and simultaneity are probably involved.[32] In this sense, deep financial markets may facilitate growth, but high growth rates also stimulate financial markets, forming a virtuous circle. More generally, growth will call forth some kind of finance; the question is whether it is robust and sustainable or fragile and short-lived. Growth rate volatility is also relevant, since high volatility generally reduces investors' willingness to put money into financial markets.

East Asia's growth rates were the highest in the world in the 1960–90 period and remarkably stable. They remained high in the 1990s, until the crisis of 1997–98. Latin American growth, while strong in the early postwar decades, lagged that of East Asia and fell sharply in the 1980s as a result of the debt crisis. It then picked up in the early 1990s, only to fall back after the Mexican financial crisis of 1994–95. The halts in growth in both regions correlate with problems in the financial markets. In Latin America, a serious credit crunch developed in the banking sector in several countries (especially Mexico) after 1995, while in East Asia, stock market capitalization fell substantially after 1997–98, leading to a temporary stagnation in volume of finance outstanding.

To illustrate the relationship between macroeconomic performance and capital market development, figures 5-1, 5-2, and 5-3 correlate savings rates, inflation, and GDP growth with market capitalization in Latin America and East Asia. As expected, the relationships with savings and growth are positive and that with inflation is negative. The strongest is with savings ($R^2 = 0.52$), followed by growth ($R^2 = 0.32$) and inflation ($R^2 = 0.28$).[33]

---

31. See, for example, Boyd, Levine, and Smith (2001).

32. For a discussion, see Demetriades and Andrianova (2004).

33. The correlations between the three macroeconomic variables and bonds outstanding were generally lower than with stock market capitalization; the exception was with GDP growth, where the correlation was higher ($R^2 = 0.39$ versus $R^2 = 0.32$). Correlations between macroeconomic variables and turnover were very weak.

Figure 5-1. *Latin America and East Asia: Market Capitalization versus Gross Domestic Savings*[a]

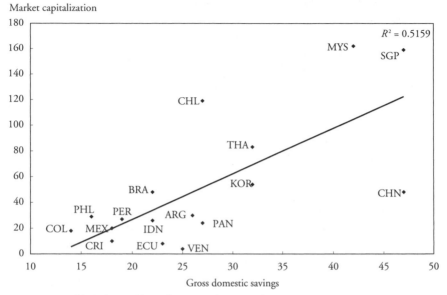

Source: World Bank, *World Development Indicators* (online).
a. Market capitalization (for 2003) and gross domestic savings (for 2003) are both shares of GDP.

Figure 5-2. *Latin America and East Asia: Market Capitalization versus GDP Growth*[a]

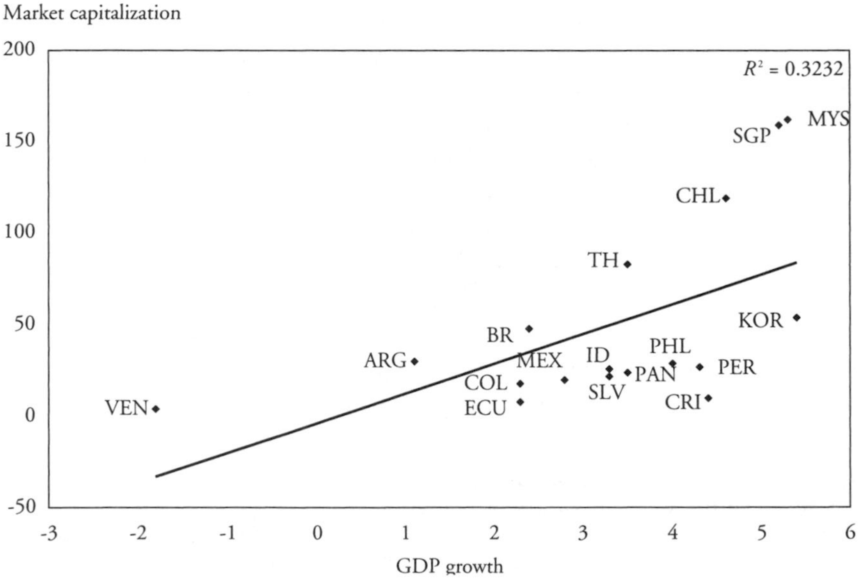

Source: World Bank, *World Development Indicators* (online).
a. Market capitalization (for 2003) is share of GDP; GDP growth is the average of 1994–2003.

Figure 5-3. *Latin America and East Asia: Market Capitalization versus Inflation*[a]

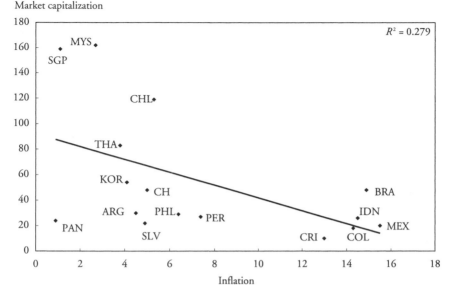

Market capitalization

$R^2 = 0.279$

Inflation

Source: World Bank, *World Development Indicators* (online).
a. Market capitalization (for 2003) is share of GDP; inflation is the average change in the consumer price index for 1994–2003.

Structural Reforms

A second factor in explaining the differential size and performance of capital markets involves the role of structural reforms. The reforms have a double function: as a signal to private investors and as practical instruments that can promote capital market growth. We focus on three reforms: financial liberalization, privatization, and pension reform. Unfortunately, data to support cross-regional comparisons are scarce. Several attempts have been made to measure reforms in Latin America, but we are not aware of any comparable data sets for East Asia.[34] We thus use proxies to make our comparisons, drawing on several tables and figures in earlier chapters.

We start with financial liberalization, which enables the private sector (domestic and foreign) to make decisions on financial issues, rather than having them imposed by the government. Here we do have reform measures for both regions. Chapter 2 presented a financial liberalization index made up of three component parts: domestic liberalization, capital account opening, and stock market deregulation. Those data showed that Latin America's financial sector overall was somewhat more open at the end of 2002 than that of East Asia, if we

34. On Latin America, see Burki and Perry (1997); Morley, Machado, and Pettinato (1999); Lora (2002).

discount Argentina's backsliding (see figure 2-1 in chapter 2). The main difference had to do with the capital account, which remained more closed in East Asia.

A second reform is privatization. Privatization tends to result in large private firms that need new sources of capital, since they no longer have access to government revenue to top up retained earnings. The new firms are likely to become more efficient and profitable than their government-run predecessors, but external funds will still be needed. As a result, they may well be listed on a local stock exchange and take steps to issue bonds. While we do not have data for overall privatizations in East Asia, the data on bank privatizations from chapter 3 provide an indicator of trends in the two regions. Table 3-1 revealed that public ownership of banks decreased much more rapidly in Latin America than in East Asia in 1970–95. However, while a good deal more privatization occurred in Latin America, the share of private-owned banks was about the same in the two regions by 1995. Data from table 3-2, by contrast, indicate that between 1990 and 2002, private banks in Latin America increased their control from 54 to 78 percent of total assets, while in East Asia, on average, government ownership increased as a result of the crisis. Although this rise in government control was generally temporary, the renationalized banks would not have been candidates for flotation on the local stock exchanges, as happened in Latin America.[35]

Finally, we turn to pension reform. Again no comparable data are available, but table 5-5 showed who purchased debt offerings in the two regions at the beginning of the current decade. In Latin America, institutional investors (mainly pension funds) were the single largest group of debt holders, accounting for 33 percent of the total. They were followed by commercial banks, with 31 percent, and other financial institutions, with 29 percent. In East Asia, by contrast, 50 percent of debt was held by commercial banks and only 12 percent by institutional investors. The conversion of pay-as-you-go government pension programs to fully funded private schemes in Latin America began in Chile in 1981. The Chilean system was later adapted in many other countries in the region, especially in the 1990s, including Argentina, Bolivia, Colombia, El Salvador, Mexico, Peru, and Uruguay. Although Brazil has not privatized its pension system, it does have a complementary voluntary system whose assets are invested by fund managers. In East Asia, government pension systems have not been abandoned, yet several countries have large government-controlled provident funds that are actively managed; the largest are in Malaysia and Singapore.

Managed pension funds, whether controlled by the public or private sector, are important players in local debt and (perhaps) stock markets. The question is

35. On privatization in developing countries, see Gupta (2000); Kagami and Tsuji (2000); Bortolotti and Siniscalco (2004); Nellis and Birdsall (2005). On Latin America, see Chong and López-de-Silanes (2005).

whether they can invest in private sector securities or only in government paper. Where the former is the rule, the funds have become an important stimulus on the demand side for long-term private sector securities. Pension funds in Chile, for example, are widely credited as being a major factor in bolstering securities markets, and the same is beginning to occur in Mexico. In most cases, however, they are limited to providing a noninflationary way to finance government deficits. Brazil's complementary funds are mostly in government debt, with a small share in private equity and bonds. Table 5-8 shows total assets as a share of GDP for the Latin American and East Asian managed funds. The largest funds are in Chile, Malaysia, and Singapore. (In dollar terms, however, Brazil's funds are larger than Chile's.) In most cases, government securities predominate. Equity investment is very small, although investment in corporate and especially financial sector securities is more common.[36]

Quality of Institutions

Our third hypothesis about why East Asian capital markets are deeper than those of Latin America concerns the quality of the institutions in the two regions. Chapter 3 explored the influence of institutions in determining banking sector performance. Institutions are even more important with respect to the capital markets, where the issue of confidence is crucial. We correlated the index of institutions shown in table 3-7 with the size of capital markets; the result is shown in figure 5-4. The relationship is strongly positive (R^2 = 0.66). The main outliers are Costa Rica, whose market capitalization is much smaller than would be predicted by the high quality of its institutions, and Malaysia and Hong Kong, which have larger markets than expected. In contrast to market size, virtually no relationship exists between institutions and liquidity (the turnover ratio). Liquidity appears to be more closely linked with the strategy of investors, rather than the characteristics of the markets. In particular, liquidity is likely to be lower in countries where pension funds play an important role, since they tend to buy and hold. This is more typical of Latin America than of East Asia, where banks and individuals are the main investors. We discuss other reasons for low liquidity in Latin America later.

The above indicators are measures of the way societies and economies as a whole function, or the quality of governance. They are extremely important in determining the environment in which business decisions are made, but a more specific set of institutions is equally relevant. These are elements of corporate governance, which is defined as the institutions and practices through which suppliers of finance to corporations ensure that they will get a return on their

---

36. On pension reform in Latin America and East Asia, see Holzmann and Hinz (2005). A more extensive analysis of the Latin American experience and its impact on financial markets is found in Gill, Packard, and Yermo (2004). On Chile, see Uthoff (2001); Corbo and Schmidt-Hebbel (2003). On Brazil, see Studart (2000).

Table 5-8. *Latin America and East Asia: Allocation of Pension Fund Assets, circa 2002*[a]

Region and country	Total[b]	Share of GDP	Asset allocation (percent of total)						
			Government securities	Corporate bonds	Financial institutions[c]	Equities	Investment funds	Foreign securities	Other
Latin America									
Argentina	11.7	11.3	76.7	1.1	2.6	6.5	1.8	8.9	2.4
Bolivia	1.1	15.5	69.1	13.4	14.7	0.0	0.0	1.3	1.5
Brazil[d]	47.7	10.4	54.3	2.2	23.0	27.7	0.0	0.0	11.5
Chile	35.5	55.8	30.0	7.2	34.2	9.9	2.5	16.2	0.1
Colombia	6.3	7.7	49.4	16.6	26.6	2.9	0.0	4.5	0.0
Costa Rica	0.1	0.9	90.1	4.6	5.3	0.0	0.0	0.0	0.0
El Salvador	1.1	7.4	84.7	0.5	14.4	0.5	0.0	0.0	0.0
Mexico	31.5	5.3	83.1	14.8	2.1	0.0	0.0	0.0	0.0
Peru	4.5	8.1	13.0	13.1	33.2	31.2	0.8	7.2	1.6
Uruguay	0.9	9.3	55.5	4.3	39.6	0.0	0.0	0.0	0.5
East Asia									
Indonesia	6.9	4.0	n.a.	n.a.	n.a.	n.a.	n.a.	n.a.	n.a.
Malaysia	54.4	57.3	37.0	19.0	21.6	21.7	0.0	0.0	0.0
Philippines	7.4	9.5	n.a.	n.a.	n.a.	n.a.	n.a.	n.a.	n.a.
Singapore	52.9	60.1	100.0	0.0	0.0	0.0	0.0	0.0	0.0
Thailand[e]	11.8	9.3	40.0	n.a.	28.3	8.0	n.a.	n.a.	n.a.

Sources: Yermo (2004) for Latin America, except Brazil; Asher (2002) for East Asia; Armijo and Ness (2004) and OECD (2005) for Brazil.

n.a. Not available.

a. End 2002 for Latin America; varying dates between 1999 and 2001 for East Asia.

b. In billions of dollars.

c. Bank deposits and money market funds for East Asia.

d. Company pension funds only; share attributed to government securities may include some other items.

e. Only partial allocation available.

Figure 5-4. *Latin America and East Asia: Market Capitalization versus Institutional Quality Index*[a]

Market capitalization

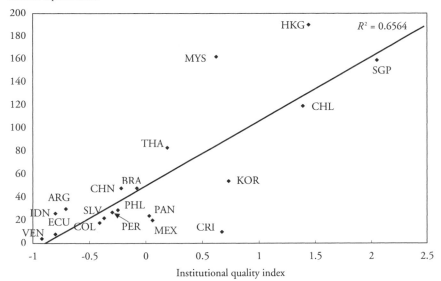

Institutional quality index

Sources: Table 3-7 for institutional quality index; World Bank, *World Development Indicators* (online) for market capitalization.

a. Market capitalization (for 2003) is share of GDP. Institutional quality index (for 2002) consists of an average of four indexes: government effectiveness, regulatory quality, rule of law, and control of corruption.

investment.[37] In a capitalist society, the latter is crucial if risks are to be taken and money is to be invested. Corporate governance has increasingly come to be recognized as a determinant of a country's economic success in the industrial world. Here we assess the extent to which it is influential in the capital markets in our set of emerging economies.

The World Economic Forum (WEF) compiles information on global competitiveness and includes indicators of corporate governance as an important aspect of competitiveness. We selected four of the questions from their annual survey of business executives and converted them into an index. The four questions include availability of information, financial disclosure, insider trading, and regulatory standards.[38] The results of crossing the corporate governance index with market capitalization in Latin American and East Asian countries—

37. Shleifer and Vishny (1997, p. 737). For a broader approach to corporate governance, see Oman (2001); Oman, Fries, and Buiter (2003). On corporate governance in Latin America, see Capaul (2003); for East Asia, see Zhuang and others (2000); for Southeast Asia, see Ho (2005).

38. World Economic Forum (1999). The exact questions are as follows: (1) Is information about business extensive and easily available? (2) Is the level of required financial disclosure extensive and detailed? (3) Is insider trading uncommon in the domestic stock market? (4) Are regulatory standards among the world's most stringent? Each is coded on a scale from one to seven, where

Figure 5-5. *Latin America and East Asia: Market Capitalization versus Corporate Governance Index*[a]

Market capitalization

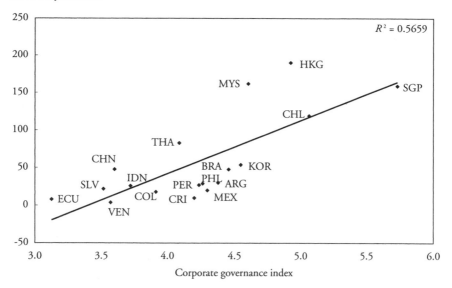

Corporate governance index

Sources: World Economic Forum (1999) for corporate governance index; World Bank, *World Development Indicators* (online) for market capitalization.

a. Market capitalization (for 2003) is share of GDP. Corporate governance index (for 1999) consists of four indexes: availability of information, financial disclosure, insider trading, and regulatory standards.

shown in figure 5-5—produces a similar, but slightly weaker, relationship than we found with the more general indicators of societal governance (R^2 = 0.57). The Asian countries generally fall above the trend line, indicating that their stock markets are larger than would be predicted by the indicators of corporate governance; Hong Kong and Malaysia are examples of this situation. Latin American countries generally have smaller markets than would be predicted. The relationship between the corporate governance indicators and bond issues outstanding is also positive, but much weaker than for stock markets. The same is true for turnover.

La Porta, López-de-Silanes, and Shleifer provide an alternative to the WEF data.[39] They create two sub-indexes within a framework for comparing public and private enforcement in terms of their impact on various indicators of market size and performance. Public enforcement includes attributes of supervisors;

seven is the most positive response. The survey included 3,934 respondents in fifty-eight countries in 1999. It now has a much wider coverage, but unfortunately the most relevant questions for our purposes are no longer included, so we use the 1999 data.

39. La Porta, López-de-Silanes, and Shleifer (2003).

the investigative powers of supervisors; supervisors' ability to give orders to issuers, distributors, and accountants; and supervisors' ability to issue criminal sanctions. Private enforcement includes measures of disclosure requirements and the rules about burden of proof when an investor wants to recover losses. While they find a positive relationship between capital market development and private enforcement (but not public enforcement), the relationship for the countries we study is much weaker than in figure 5-5. Some of the outliers also cast doubt on the reliability of the indicators. For example, the single highest score for private enforcement is found in the Philippines, while Indonesia and Peru rank higher than Chile; Mexico competes with Ecuador and Venezuela for the bottom places in the index. As a consequence, we consider that the relationship between public and private enforcement needs further research.

International Context

A final hypothesis about capital markets in the two regions centers on the international context. Domestic financial markets provide the vast majority of finance in all emerging economies, but international capital has generally played a significant role, too. The channels through which foreign capital entered have varied over time. Foreign direct investment (FDI) was the most important in the 1950s and 1960s, but it was replaced by syndicated Euroloans in the 1970s. The latter led to a severe debt crisis in the 1980s in Latin America and in some Asian countries. In the 1990s, while FDI again became significant (including important investments in banking, pension funds, and other parts of the financial sector itself), portfolio investment also played a large role. The latter entered via investment in local stock markets and, to a lesser extent, bond markets; bank deposits constituted the main channel in smaller countries with poorly developed capital markets. Most of the foreign portfolio investment dried up after the mid-1990s, however, as international investors became more risk averse.

At the same time, governments, banks, and large nonfinancial corporations in emerging market economies sought funds on international markets by floating bonds, issuing American or global depository receipts (ADRs and GDRs), and borrowing from international banks. As shown in table 5-6, international bank loans reached 29 percent and 30 percent of GDP in 2003 for Latin America and East Asia, respectively. International bonds were 19 percent in Latin America and 11 percent in East Asia, while international equity contributed a smaller amount, accounting for 4 percent of GDP in Asia and 2 percent in Latin America. Those with access to international markets could obtain larger amounts of finance at a lower price than was available locally.[40] Of course, access

40. See Zervos (2004) for detailed information on comparative costs of domestic versus international finance. She focuses on the three countries that are studied in depth in this book: Brazil, Chile, and Mexico. She finds that costs vary widely. In general, debt financing is cheaper than equity, and international issuance tends to be cheaper than domestic issuance (except for Mexico).

to international markets is available only to an extremely limited set of very large and well-established private firms, together with governments and government-owned corporations.

Despite the advantages of participating in international markets, access to these markets has been accompanied by volatility, exchange rate risk, and (all too frequently) financial crises. As discussed in chapter 2, a good deal of controversy exists over the relative weight of domestic and international sources of crisis. At a minimum, however, analysts agree that international financial markets have been the source of serious problems, both for macroeconomic management and for the operation of firms at the microeconomic level.

Several such problems have been identified. The most obvious is that foreign capital tends to move in waves. Large inflows enter as enthusiasm builds for emerging market economies, but these flows can move out as rapidly as they arrived when confidence wanes for whatever reason. (The graphs in figure 4-4 provided dramatic evidence of these cycles in Latin America and East Asia.) These surges and droughts are extremely difficult to manage, given their large size relative to most emerging economies. A related problem is the procyclicality associated with private capital flows, which can produce asset price bubbles that—when they burst—wreak greater havoc on these economies than in the industrial countries with their stronger financial systems. A third problem involves exchange rate appreciation, which is fed by capital inflows and undermines the trade balance—thus increasing the need for more capital inflows.[41]

Beyond these frequently discussed problems, a new dilemma has been highlighted by World Bank economists who have studied Latin America's capital markets and the reasons for their lack of dynamism.[42] While they arrive at conclusions that are similar to ours with regard to the positive impact of macroeconomic performance, reforms, and institutions on the development of domestic capital markets, they find that these same factors are also positively related to Latin American participation in international markets. One of the techniques they use to analyze the phenomenon is to construct a variable that is the ratio of foreign activity to domestic activity. After regressing this variable on reform, macroeconomic, and institutional variables, they conclude that while both domestic market development and internationalization are driven by the same fundamentals, the latter relationship is the stronger of the two. That is, improvements in fundamentals accelerate internationalization. They find similar evidence for government bond markets, although data problems precluded analysis of corporate bonds.

A follow-up question concerns the comparison between Latin America and East Asia on this issue. Our data in table 5-6 indicated that international

41. A recent analysis of these problems in emerging markets is found in Ffrench-Davis and Griffith-Jones (2003).
42. World Bank (2004c); Claessens, Klingebiel, and Schmukler (2004).

finance is more important for the former than the latter. Over 30 percent of Latin America's total finance in 2003 was from international sources, versus 16 percent in East Asia. One explanation for the difference is that geographical and cultural proximity to the United States provided the option of international finance for Latin America, especially in the case of Mexico, which might have made the development of domestic markets seem less urgent than in the case of Asia.

The World Bank study also addresses the impact of internationalization on domestic markets in the two regions and finds it to be negative for Latin America. One of the papers finds that the relationship between fundamentals and accelerating internationalization holds only for Latin America.[43] The authors identify two channels. One concerns migration and spillovers. When Latin American firms issue stock and bonds abroad, liquidity falls on local capital markets. Small size and concentration further these problems. In the extreme case—which has occurred with some frequency in Latin America but not in Asia—firms are delisted locally and transferred to international stock markets in the United States or in Europe. The other channel is trade diversion. When firms internationalize, domestic trading in their shares on local markets increases at the expense of local firms. Thus, while reforms encourage the development of domestic capital markets in direct ways, they can also discourage them indirectly.

In summary, after considering four sets of factors that we would expect to determine the relative dynamism of capital markets in Latin America in comparison with East Asia, we found three that seem to favor the latter region and one that is more positive in the former. The macroeconomic environment clearly suggests that capital markets should function better in East Asia than in Latin America. Likewise, the stronger societal institutions in East Asia should also buttress the capital markets. The difference between the two regions is much smaller with respect to corporate governance institutions, but East Asia still has a slight advantage. Latin America's active participation in international financial markets provides some advantages to the region's firms and governments, but the downsides seem to outweigh the advantages. This is especially the case in light of the World Bank's new evidence that participation in international markets can undermine domestic markets.

Only the more extensive reform effort—financial liberalization, privatization, and pension reform—seems to be more positive for capital market development in Latin America, but it has clearly not been sufficient to offset the other three factors that have benefited East Asia more. One reason is that the reforms have not always turned out as their proponents expected. The financial crises following financial liberalization are perhaps the most dramatic examples, but serious

43. Levine and Schmukler (2004).

economic and political problems have also arisen with privatization. At the same time, pension fund reform—which proved a boon for the growth of capital markets in Latin America—has probably put a brake on the liquidity of Latin American capital markets. Evidence from other researchers suggests that liquidity is the main connection between capital markets and economic growth.

Conclusions

This chapter has provided data on a number of dimensions for comparing the financial markets in Latin America and East Asia. They can be summarized in the following six points. First, the overall financial sector—including both banks and capital markets—is twice as deep in East Asia as in Latin America (when measured as a share of GDP). The gap grew in absolute terms but not as a share of GDP, since output expanded so much faster in Asia than in Latin America. Second, bank claims as a share of GDP grew very slowly in Latin America between 1990 and 2003, in the presence of a serious credit crunch in a number of countries. Loans expanded much faster in Asia, meaning that the credit-to-GDP gap increased. Moreover, a much lower share of bank credit has gone to the private sector in Latin America. Third, bonds outstanding in East Asia grew faster in absolute terms, but not as a share of GDP. Nonetheless, the gap remains very large and, again, a much higher share was captured by the private sector in Asia.

Fourth, stock market capitalization grew rapidly in both regions, although new issues fell off substantially. Price increases played a bigger role in the growth of market capitalization in Latin America than in East Asia. In addition, the number of listed firms fell in Latin America, while it more than doubled in East Asia in the 1990–2003 period. East Asia's markets were also more active in terms of trading volume. Fifth, while Latin America lagged behind East Asia in the domestic financial markets, the gap was partially offset by its greater participation in international markets. The share of international finance in total finance was twice as high in Latin America as in East Asia, but participating in international markets has negative as well as positive effects. Sixth, all of the indicators above display great diversity across individual countries in the two regions. In many cases, intraregional differences are about as important as interregional ones.[44]

We presented four hypotheses to explain the greater market depth in East Asia, which were supported by the evidence on the two sets of cases. First, that region's superior macroeconomic performance since the early 1960s (in the form of higher growth rates, lower inflation, and higher savings) created a propitious environment for the development of capital markets. Second, structural reforms

44. See, for example, Stallings (2005) on the growing similarities between the financial sectors in Chile and South Korea.

in both regions not only provided a positive signal to private investors, but also encouraged new actors on both the supply and demand sides. For example, newly privatized firms were listed on local stock markets, while privatized pension funds were eager to purchase long-term assets. Third, strong institutions promoted capital market development since they increased the confidence of potential investors. These institutions were found at two levels: societal-level governance characteristics and corporate governance indicators. In general, East Asia's institutions were stronger. Fourth, Latin America's greater participation in international capital markets has provided some important benefits in terms of access to deeper markets and lower prices, but it involves high risks in terms of volatility, exchange-rate mismatches, and possible contagion in times of financial crisis. Recent evidence suggests that the interrelationship between domestic and international markets may be penalizing the former. In any case, the option of international participation is limited to governments and a small number of firms.

Latin American countries face many challenges in attempting to broaden access to finance as a step toward promoting higher growth and a better standard of living for their populations. This chapter focused on the role of capital markets, which can provide an alternative to domestic bank finance for certain economic actors and perhaps leave more space in the credit market for others. They also offer new instruments for mobilizing savings and serve as a focus for improving corporate governance and other institutions. While they will never be the dominant source of finance, they can be a useful supplement.

PART II

The Impact of the New Financial System on Investment and Access in Latin America

6

Chile:
Mixed Ownership
Provides a New Model

C hile was the first country in Latin America to embark on a major and sustained program of financial liberalization.[1] It began in the mid-1970s, soon after the military overthrew the elected government of Salvador Allende. The liberalization process, however, resulted in a period of unsustainable and poorly managed lending that ended in a serious crisis in the early 1980s. As part of the recovery process, Chile became a pioneer in terms of restructuring its banks and revamping its regulatory and supervisory system. Since 1990, the Chilean financial sector has been the most successful in the region on a variety of indicators. Thus, the Chilean case can provide lessons, in both a positive and negative vein, for its counterparts in the region. It offers a benchmark for our analysis of other countries.

The Chilean banking system grew steadily from the early 1990s, and it currently enjoys the greatest financial depth among Latin American economies—although these levels are still low by international standards. Improvements were also made in bank efficiency, and lending rates and spreads decreased substantially, an indication that the perceived default risk declined as lending expanded. Capital markets grew during the decade, although growth was less sustained: after a period of rapid increase, they suffered shrinkage for a number of years, but have begun to grow again recently. In the process, the markets have

1. We would like to thank Gabriela Clivio, research director at BBVA Corredores de Bolsa in Santiago, for valuable help with data for this chapter.

increased their role in the financing of households and the productive sector, thanks in large part to the active participation of institutional investors. Stability is another characteristic of the Chilean financial system that stands out vis-à-vis the experiences of neighboring economies. The system was not disrupted by the Mexican crisis (only the stock market was affected significantly) or by the subsequent financial shocks faced by the region in the latter part of the 1990s (although lending did slow with respect to its previous pace). Since 2003, a significant recover has been under way.

In this chapter, we discuss some of the determinants of Chile's financial success story, and we evaluate how recent developments in the sector affect its ability to promote growth and broaden the productive sector's access to financing. The first section presents a brief review of the financial liberalization process and the changes in regulation and supervision that took place after the crisis of 1981–83. The second section discusses changes in the structure of the financial system since 1990. The third section analyzes the relationship between finance, investment, and growth, while the fourth looks at access to credit by different segments of the business sector. The last section summarizes the findings and discusses the challenges that face Chile, despite its positive performance in the last fifteen years.[2]

Liberalization, Crisis, and Response

Chile has been a model of financial stability within the Latin American context since 1990, and the financial system has provided important support for the rest of the economy. Such stability has not always existed, however. The 1980s crisis, in particular, was extremely costly—for the government, enterprises, and consumers, as well as for the banks themselves. Only later did the financial system assume its current characteristics. To shed light on this trajectory, we look back at the financial liberalization of the 1970s to identify the problems it created, examine the crisis of 1981–83 and the government's response, and trace the new system of regulation and supervision that was introduced after the crisis. We also go beyond banking to consider institutional changes in the capital markets.

Financial Liberalization and Its Consequences

At the end of the Allende government in 1973, Chile had one of the most repressed financial systems in the region.[3] The central bank, in conjunction with the finance ministry, set interest rates, maintaining them at negative real levels. The result was a very low volume of financial intermediation; bank credit to the private sector fell to only 6 percent of GDP by 1973.[4] Reserve requirements

2. Two recent papers that deal with some of these same issues are Hernández and Parro (2004, 2005).

3. On financial repression in the early 1970s, see Valdés Prieto (1992) and Fontaine (1996); figures in this paragraph come from those sources unless otherwise noted.

4. Calculated from IMF, *International Financial Statistics Yearbook* (2000, line 22d).

were high (80 percent for sight deposits), and banks were obliged to provide credit to specific sectors that the government wanted to encourage. Moreover, the government directly owned or controlled most of the banks. The traditional state-owned commercial bank (the Banco del Estado) was responsible for 45 percent of all loans, and most other commercial banks were nationalized during the Allende period. The five state-owned development banks administered credit equal to that of the entire commercial banking system.[5]

One of the main objectives of the military junta that overthrew Allende was to liberalize and restructure the financial system, as part of a broader process to establish a market-oriented economy open to the rest of the world.[6] The process was set in motion within months of the military coup, and the changes can be grouped into three categories. A first group involved the end to restrictions on financial intermediation. Directed credit requirements were lifted, reserve requirements were lowered (to 10 percent for sight deposits), and restrictions on foreign borrowing were reduced and eventually eliminated altogether. Second, interest rates were liberalized. By the end of 1975, banks were free to set both lending and deposit rates, subject only to a "conventional maximum" on the former. Third, the banking sector was reorganized. The state-owned commercial banks were sold to the private sector—at subsidized prices—which facilitated the formation of conglomerates (*grupos*) centered on the banks. By the end of 1978, among commercial banks, only the Banco del Estado remained in government hands, although three of the development banks continued to operate under new rules. As part of the privatization process, foreign institutions were permitted to do business in Chile, and finance companies (*financieras*), both regulated and unregulated, were authorized. Finally, there was a movement toward universal banks, eliminating the previous segmentation of the market and lowering barriers to entry.

The decline in regulatory oversight led to serious problems, although they remained disguised until the early 1980s. The banks appeared to be in strong condition based on a number of indicators, especially profit margins. One early sign of potential trouble was the explosive growth of loans, which increased at a real compound rate of 32 percent a year between 1975 and 1981, rising from 12 percent of GDP to 49 percent during the six-year period.[7] An increasing share was going to related borrowers (about 20 percent of loans and 250 percent of capital and reserves by 1982). Despite the rapid growth of credit, interest rates

5. They included the National Development Corporation (Corfo), the Agrarian Reform Corporation (Cora), the National Institute for Agricultural Development (Indap), the Housing Corporation (Corvi), and the National Mining Corporation (Enami).

6. See Ffrench-Davis and Stallings (2001) on the general reform process in Chile; Held and Jiménez (2001) focus on the financial sector reform. Data in the text in the rest of this section come from the latter source unless otherwise indicated. For a critique of the financial reform, see Díaz-Alejandro (1985); Ffrench-Davis (2002).

7. Calculated from IMF, *International Financial Statistics Yearbook* (2000, lines 22a-f); the data refer to claims of deposit money banks on the private and public sectors; they were deflated by the consumer price index.

in the domestic market remained well above international rates, with an average real rate of 20 percent during the six years.

Many banks took advantage of the weak regulatory and supervisory environment to engage in practices that ultimately led to insolvency. Bank management was highly risk-prone. In addition to the related credits, nonperforming loans were not recognized, provisioning for losses was deficient, and an increasing share of loans was financed with external credit, leading to currency mismatches especially after the exchange rate was fixed in 1979. These problems were heightened by the presumption of a government guarantee on deposits. After the rescue of an important bank in 1976, a limited deposit insurance scheme (up to approximately $3,000 per account) was introduced, but public perception was of a much broader guarantee.[8]

Macroeconomic policy exacerbated problems internal to the banks. The rapid decline in external tariffs led to a large number of corporate bankruptcies, especially in the industrial sector. The fixed exchange rate increased competition for domestic firms and made exporting more difficult. This was reflected in large trade and current account deficits, which had to be financed by increased foreign borrowing. In general, the volatile growth rate increased the risks for banks, as their customers fell on hard times. These problems were similar to what would be seen later in other countries throughout the region and beyond.

The Financial Crisis and Government Response

A severe financial crisis erupted in 1981, as a result of the various conditions described above. The following year, the situation was complicated by a balance-of-payments crisis related to the fixed exchange rate. The financial crisis preceded the 1982 declaration of a moratorium in Mexico and the cutoff of external credits to Latin America—in other words, the crisis had domestic roots, although it was exacerbated by international events.

The financial crisis was marked by the insolvency of the majority of the private national banks and *financieras*. Of the twenty-six private domestic banks and seventeen *financieras* in operation, the Superintendency of Banks and Financial Institutions (SBIF, by its Spanish acronym) had to take over the operation of fourteen and eight, respectively, between 1981 and 1986. These included the two largest banks in Chile: the Banco de Chile and the Banco de Santiago. Eight of the intervened banks and all eight of the *financieras* were liquidated, while others were merged with solvent institutions.

A recent study details the government's short-term response and calculates the costs incurred.[9] The liquidation of the sixteen financial institutions was based on their having broken laws and regulations, in addition to their insolvency. Costs were shared between bank shareholders and government institu-

8. All monetary figures cited in this chapter are in U.S. dollars.
9. See Sanhueza (1999, 2001). The longer-term response is discussed in the following section.

tions; the latter's costs amounted to 10.6 percent of GDP. The cost of the liquidation was many times the recognized bad debts of the banks and *financieras*, which suggests the scale of hidden losses. In addition, very little was recovered, indicating extremely weak loan portfolios, an inefficient process of liquidation, or both.

By mid-1982, the crisis had become systemic, extending to solvent institutions with serious short-term liquidity problems. In this case, the solution devised was for the central bank to purchase the banks' bad-loan portfolios with the agreement that they would buy back the assets later; they were not allowed to pay dividends until they did so. The majority of the portfolio purchases centered on the two largest banks, but many other institutions were also involved. The process was very protracted, and one of the banks is still repaying its debts to the central bank. Costs to the government were 6.7 percent of GDP (8.9 percent resources transferred minus 2.2 percent recovery). Beyond dealing with bad debts, most of the banks also needed to be recapitalized. A key mechanism was a program known as popular capitalism, which provided various fiscal incentives for the purchase of new shares in small blocks (2.4 percent of GDP).

While these mechanisms went a long way to getting the banks back into operation, provisions also had to be made for the other side of the problem— the debtors.[10] A preferential exchange rate was established for those with debts in foreign currency, whose problems increased with the devaluation of the peso in mid-1982. In the case of small and medium-sized enterprises (SMEs) and mortgage holders, debts were reprogrammed. These programs together cost the government 16.3 percent of GDP, the large majority of which went to finance the preferential dollar.

The overall process involved more than 35 percent of GDP.[11] Moreover, this represents only the fiscal costs, excluding the loss of GDP resulting from the crisis. The Chilean rescue has been cited as successful, however, in that it required shareholders to assume a significant part of the cost, avoided worsening the problems in the course of the rescue process, and ultimately led to the restructuring of the banking sector so that lending resumed.[12] Outstanding bank claims, as measured in constant local currency, reached a peak in 1982, fell until 1986, and then began to grow again.[13] At the same time, the opportunity cost of the vast amounts of public resources expended was very high, especially in a

10. See Eyzaguirre and Larrañaga (1991).

11. Sanhueza (1999, p. 47); calculations are made with 1983 as a base year.

12. See the comparative analysis in Rojas-Suárez and Weisbrod (1996).

13. Given the fact that a similar program in Mexico contributed to the paralysis of lending in that country, it is worth looking in detail at the mechanisms used in Chile. Despite the high costs and enormous complexity of the Chilean operations, the requirement that banks use their profits to buy back their bad-loan portfolios in a fixed period of time—and not pay dividends until they did so—meant that the Chilean banks had the incentive to expand their loan portfolios to increase revenue. In addition, rapid growth after 1985 made it attractive for the banks to extend credit. Both aspects were different in Mexico.

society characterized by high and growing inequality. A lesson from the Chilean experience is the need to design more efficient and more egalitarian policies before a crisis strikes.

The New System of Regulation and Supervision

After the crisis, a new attitude emerged with respect to regulation and supervision of the banking system. The shift was part of a general move toward increased pragmatism in economic policy, in contrast with the extreme view of the 1970s that less government was better under all conditions.

The banking law of 1986, which became a model for the region, reinforced the powers of the SBIF. Expanding on initiatives that began earlier in the decade, it required that portfolios be ranked by risk category and that provisioning be made for higher risk credits. It also increased the transparency of the process. It tightened policies with respect to credits to individual borrowers and to related parties. The latter term was defined more strictly than under the previous banking law, and related loans were limited to 5 percent of capital if no collateral was provided and 25 percent with collateral. In addition, the total amount of related credit could not exceed bank capital and reserves, and related party credit could not be granted on terms more favorable than those for other borrowers. Capital adequacy requirements were left at the previous levels: leverage could not exceed twenty times capital for banks and fifteen times for finance companies. Definitions were tightened, however. Deposit insurance was eliminated for term deposits, so as to make depositors more vigilant, but all sight deposits were covered, as were accounts of small depositors (up to an amount of about $4,000).[14]

The banking law was modified in 1997 to bring it up to date with domestic and international trends that had emerged over the preceding decade. At this time, Chile adhered to the Bank for International Settlements (BIS) capital adequacy ratio of 8 percent, and BIS risk categories were also adopted. Banks were permitted to expand through such activities as administering mutual and pension funds, leasing, factoring, and financial advising in the domestic market. On the international level, they were allowed to set up subsidiaries and engage in other domestically permitted functions. They could also provide guarantes for clients in the international market. Finally, conditions were created for more banks, both national and foreign, to enter the Chilean market after a decade of closure.[15]

Another innovation of the 1990s was what some banking experts call private monitoring (see chapter 4). That is, supervision was not limited to government activities, but was complemented by increased information so that potential customers could differentiate among competing banks. Indicators of private

14. Held and Jiménez (2001).
15. See Budnevich (2000) on the 1997 modifications to the banking law.

monitoring include whether an external audit is required, the percentage of the largest banks that are rated by international rating agencies, and the degree of accounting disclosure and director liability. Chile has been moving in this direction. Moreover, the marks its banks receive from the rating agencies are the highest in the Latin American region and comparable to those of banks in the industrial countries.[16]

The banking supervisory authorities in Chile see self-regulation by the banks themselves as a crucial complement to government regulation and supervision. This is closely related to the new stress on corporate governance, involving more professional management, independent boards of directors, external auditors (domestic or international), and greater transparency than in the past.[17] The SBIF has abandoned its practice of telling the banks exactly how to evaluate credit risk. Nearly all banks now have their own models for risk evaluation—which must be approved by the authorities—in preparation for implementation of the new Basel II regulatory system. Nonetheless, government supervision continues to be quite strict; extensive quarterly information must be made public, and annual supervisory visits to each bank are routine. Most experts believe that this combination of public and private regulation has made Chile a model for other economies in the region.[18]

Beyond the Banking Sector

While the main thrust of the financial sector reforms centered on banking, attention was also devoted to the development of capital markets. Chilean markets traditionally were very underdeveloped, but the military government technocrats wanted to promote them as a complement to the banking system.[19] New instruments—especially those relating to mortgage finance—were introduced in the late 1970s, but it was not till 1980–81 that the basic legislation was approved to create a new Superintendency of Securities and Insurance (SVS, in Spanish) to regulate issuers and traders and to require the quarterly publication of information by publicly listed companies. The technocrats also developed a solution to the problem of Chile's inflation rate, which was far above international levels. It involved a unit of account, known as the *Unidad de Fomento* (UF), which was indexed to the inflation rate and changed value daily. Originally created in the 1960s for use by savings and mortgage institutions, the UF was extended to financial activities in general in the 1970s, so as to simulate a

16. See various reports from Moody's, Standard and Poor's, and Fitch Ratings.

17. On corporate governance in Chile, see Agosin and Pastén (2003).

18. Marshall (2004b) provides a recent statement of policies on bank regulation and supervision. On the IMF's positive evaluation of the Chilean financial system, see IMF (2004a). Despite positive external evaluation, some experts argue that Chile's regulation and supervision are too strict and that the country should move much further in the direction of private monitoring; see Carkovic and Levine (2002).

19. On the state of the capital markets at the beginning of the military government, see Gregoire and Ovando (1974).

crucial prerequisite to capital market development. Finally, a major reform of the pension system took place in 1981, which was intimately connected to capital market development, as explained below.

Prices on the Santiago Stock Exchange plunged by two-thirds during the financial crisis of the early 1980s, and they did not regain their 1980 level till the end of the decade. The problems created were not nearly as serious as those in the banking sector, however. Consequently, the only significant change in capital market legislation in the 1980s was the requirement that investments eligible for pension fund purchase have ratings by two specialized agencies; this gave rise to the country's risk rating industry. In the mid-1990s, changes were made to liberalize pension fund portfolio limits for stock and bond ownership. Only at the end of the 1990s did the finance ministry introduce major modifications to the securities legislation.

The public tender law of 2000 improved corporate governance, especially through protection of minority shareholder rights, and provided greater flexibility for investment funds. At the same time, the regulatory powers of the SVS were increased, and capital requirements were raised for banks with a high concentration of assets. The capital market reform law of 2001 went further by trying to increase access for small and medium-sized firms, including the establishment of a new stock exchange geared to their needs. It also reduced capital gains and other taxes for certain groups of investors and further liberalized restrictions on pension funds. The second capital market reform law was introduced in 2003 to promote venture capital, lower transaction costs, improve corporate governance and transparency, and set up voluntary retirement accounts to complement the obligatory pension system. A scandal that hit the capital markets in 2003 temporarily slowed the legislation, as methods were sought to prevent such occurrences in the future.[20] An important aspect is better coordination among the superintendencies of banking and financial institutions, securities and insurance, and pension fund administrators. Although the government does not currently plan to consolidate supervision, an informal coordinating system has been introduced. The second capital market reform law proposes to establish a formal committee, serviced by a technical secretariat.

Changes in Structure

Like other Latin American economies, Chile had a bank-based financial system in the 1980s, given the dominant position of banks in the intermediation of funds. The banking sector continued to expand in the 1990s, but bonds and especially stock market capitalization also rose significantly (see figure 6-1).

20. This scandal, which was small by international or even regional standards, concerned theft by rogue traders in a private firm (Inverlink) and the government's main development agency (Corfo). In addition, Inverlink had illegally acquired information from the secretary of the central bank president, leading to the latter's resignation.

Figure 6-1. *Chile: Composition of Financial Markets, 1990–2003*

Percent of GDP

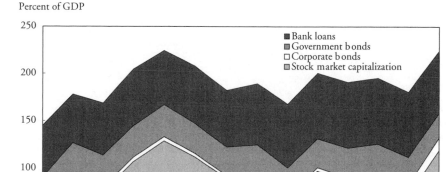

Sources: Tables 6-1 and 6-3.

Indeed, there is now an ongoing debate on whether Chile is moving toward a capital-market-based system.[21] One of the main reasons for the increasing role of capital markets in Chile's financial system was the rapid expansion of the size and role of institutional investors, especially the privatized pension funds. In a very short period, they acquired significant volumes of securities and profited from a buoyant market. At the same time, changes in regulation and a better business environment led to the growth of mutual and foreign investment funds, which created a virtuous circle between the institutional investors and the expansion of the securities markets. International financial markets also welcomed Chilean firms.

The Banking Sector

The banking sector expanded substantially in the two decades between the early 1980s and the early 2000s. In nominal dollar terms, total system assets rose from $20 billion in 1980 to $34 billion in 1990 to $159 billion in 2003. In compound terms, this increase averaged nearly 7 percent annually over the twenty-three-year period from 1980 to 2003. Assets also grew as a share of GDP—from 74 to 188 percent (see table 6-1). Given the crisis of the early 1980s, growth of assets was slower in the 1980s than in the 1990s.[22] Loans and deposits followed similar trends.

21. See Gallego and Loayza (2001).
22. The jump in assets in 1982–85, which declined only gradually, was connected with the bank rescue program.

Table 6-1. *Chile: Assets and Liabilities of the Banking System, 1980–2003*
Percent of GDP

Year	Assets/ liabilities	Loans	Securities	Other assets	Deposits	Other liabilities
1980	74.0	52.1	5.7	16.2	32.8	41.2
1981	77.8	57.8	4.5	15.6	33.7	44.1
1982	129.1	81.9	11.5	35.7	38.7	90.3
1983	147.0	70.2	32.3	44.5	52.1	94.8
1984	202.7	78.9	46.9	76.9	35.4	167.3
1985	218.8	68.2	69.4	81.2	38.1	180.7
1986	191.4	60.2	61.6	69.5	38.7	152.7
1987	163.7	57.3	49.6	56.9	41.2	122.5
1988	132.6	53.8	34.4	44.3	40.1	92.5
1989	123.0	57.8	25.3	39.9	41.6	81.4
1990	124.2	54.5	27.8	41.9	43.0	81.2
1991	99.4	50.9	25.6	22.8	45.4	54.0
1992	96.3	54.6	19.2	22.5	45.6	50.7
1993	103.4	59.7	17.3	26.4	46.8	56.6
1994	118.7	57.3	16.9	44.4	46.1	72.5
1995	120.1	60.5	15.3	44.3	49.1	71.0
1996	118.3	59.5	14.2	44.5	49.2	69.1
1997	133.2	64.3	14.2	54.6	48.2	85.0
1998	133.1	66.8	13.7	52.6	54.5	78.6
1999	160.1	69.2	16.8	74.0	57.9	102.2
2000	178.9	69.2	17.8	91.9	60.6	118.3
2001	192.1	69.5	18.4	104.1	59.6	132.5
2002	181.8	68.4	18.9	94.6	60.2	121.7
2003	188.3	66.0	17.2	105.1	55.4	133.0

Sources: SBIF, *Información Financiera* for 1980–89; SBIF website (www.sbif.cl) for 1990–2003.

While growth was taking place on a fairly steady basis, important changes were occurring among the actors involved. Table 6-2 shows the ownership characteristics of the banking sector in terms of the number of institutions, employees, branches, and share of assets. Foreign banks grew substantially during the period at the cost of private domestic banks, especially in terms of assets. This pattern occurred because foreign banks, other than those setting up branches, entered the market through the purchase of local institutions. Meanwhile, the single public sector institution held its own. As of the end of 2003, private domestic banks represented 46 percent of all institutions, 44 percent of employees, and 32 percent of assets; foreign banks had 50 percent, 37 percent, and 57 percent, respectively, while the public sector bank had 19 percent of all employees and 11 percent of assets.[23]

23. After 2000, the definition of a foreign bank was changed so that only branches of foreign banks are included; subsidiaries are counted as domestic banks. Our analysis in table 6-2 and elsewhere continues to use the previous definition, which is the common one in other countries.

Table 6-2. Chile: Characteristics of the Banking System, 1990–2003

Indicator and year	Private[a]		Public[b]		Foreign[c]		Finance companies		Total	
	Number	%	Number	%	Number	%	Number	%	Number	%
Number of institutions										
1990	14	35	1	3	21	53	4	11	40	100
1995	13	38	1	3	17	50	3	9	34	100
2000	9	31	1	3	18	62	1	4	29	100
2003	12	46	1	4	13	50	0	0	26	100
Number of employees										
1990	20,756	58	8,124	23	4,117	12	2,490	7	35,487	100
1995	23,299	52	8,471	19	5,242	12	7,847	17	44,959	100
2000	15,152	37	7,625	19	16,467	41	1,281	3	40,525	100
2003	16,131	44	7,132	19	13,887	37	0	0	37,150	100
Number of branches										
1990	556	58	182	19	147	16	89	7	974	100
1995	724	59	198	14	179	12	136	15	1,237	100
2000	532	38	294	21	526	37	56	4	1,408	100
2003	611	41	310	21	560	38	0	0	1,481	100
Volume of assets[d]										
1990	6,626	58	1,941	17	2,780	24	143	1	11,491	100
1995	18,937	61	2,404	13	7,667	25	503	2	31,069	100
2000	22,391	31	6,424	9	43,367	60	404	1	72,624	100
2003	30,561	32	10,618	11	54,372	57	0	0	95,550	100

Source: SBIF, *Información Financiera*.
a. Private, domestically owned banks.
b. Government-owned banks.
c. Foreign-owned banks (branches and subsidiaries); 2003 data use the olc definition of foreign banks, based on ownership rather than legal status in Chile.
d. Billions of current pesos.

The share of total assets held by foreign banks increased rapidly after 1993, when they held only 20 percent. By 2000, the Chilean banking sector had one of the highest levels of foreign participation in the region: foreign-controlled banks held 60 percent of total assets and made 45 percent of all loans, although these shares dipped slightly by 2003 as a result of several mergers. As in other Latin American countries, the main foreign presence in Chile comes from Spain (55 percent of foreign-owned assets) and the United States (30 percent). Other countries represented include Canada, Japan, several European countries, and Brazil.[24] Chile was a prime target of foreign bank expansion in the 1990s because of its strong and sustained macroeconomic performance and its political stability.

While the most obvious sign of increased foreign participation in Chile's financial markets is the expansion in the size and power of foreign banks, the holdings of foreign assets by Chilean financial institutions also increased from around $500 million in 1990 to over $2 billion in 2003. Unlike the situation in some neighboring economies, this rise in foreign assets was not overwhelmed by the rise in foreign liabilities. Indeed, the gap narrowed substantially from a 6:1 ratio of liabilities to assets in 1990 to only 2.5:1.0 in 2003.[25] This trend is important for the stability of the banking system, since currency mismatches have become one of the main destabilizing factors associated with banking crises in the region and elsewhere. The healthier trend in Chile is due in large part to the relatively high savings rate in the country, such that the banks can fund most of their activities domestically.

Chile has only one public sector commercial bank, the Banco del Estado de Chile (now called BancoEstado). The share of public ownership of the financial system is thus one of the smallest in the Latin American region (11 percent of total bank assets in 2003). The role of this bank was redefined throughout the 1990s, and it now plays a significant role in supporting SMEs, either directly or through credit insurance mechanisms. It also has an especially large branch network, extending into areas that private banks do not consider sufficiently profitable. As table 6-2 shows, BancoEstado represents only 4 percent of banking institutions and 11 percent of assets, but it nonetheless controls 21 percent of branches. Supporting smaller firms and providing financial services to distant clients are two of the ways that the bank tries to serve a social function befitting a public sector institution, at the same time that it competes with the private sector. Its profitability (approximately equal to the before-tax average for all banks) shows that it is competitive and that its long-term sustainability is based on its own performance, rather than support from the government.[26]

24. Data are from Salomon Smith Barney (2001); see also Calderón and Casilda (2000) on Spanish banks.

25. IMF, *International Financial Statistics Yearbook* (2000, 2004, lines 7.a.d. and 7.b.d).

26. On BancoEstado, see Mena (2005). Beyond the 17 percent corporate tax paid by all firms, public sector firms (including BancoEstado) pay an additional 40 percent of profits, so an after-tax comparison would be misleading.

Chile also continues to maintain three development institutions that provide a limited amount of funding to vulnerable groups of clients, although they are not commercial banks in that they do not take deposits. These include the National Development Corporation (Corfo), which specializes in credit and other services for SMEs; the National Mining Corporation (Enami), which supports small mining firms; and the National Institute for Agricultural Development (Indap). Corfo is a second tier bank that works through the private banking system, while the other two make small amounts of direct loans. In 2003, Corfo disbursed around $60 million in loans plus an additional $13 million through leasing and factoring operations. Indap in 2001, the last year for which data are available, made $15 million in long-term loans and $24 million in short-term credits.[27]

Table 6-2 indicates that Chile's banking sector is relatively small as measured by the number of deposit-taking institutions. Moreover, the number declined from forty in 1990 to twenty-six in 2003. The reduction in the number of financial institutions resulted from the wave of mergers and acquisitions that took place in the last decade, as well as from the exit of several foreign banks with small market shares. Simultaneously, the finance companies were absorbed into the new universal banks when the 1997 banking law permitted the latter to move into nontraditional financial activities such as factoring, custody and transfer of securities, insurance, underwriting, and securitization.

Not surprisingly, the shrinkage in the number of institutions was accompanied by a rise in concentration. The share in loans and investments of the five largest banks fell slightly during the 1980s, from 58 percent in 1981 to 55 percent in 1990. It then rose to 60 percent in 2000, and it jumped to 72 percent in 2003 due to two very large mergers. Spain's Banco Santander combined its flagship bank in Chile with Banco Santiago, a large local bank it already controlled; the resulting institution became the largest bank in the country. At almost the same time, Banco de Chile, long the dominant domestically owned private institution, merged with a mid-sized local bank, Banco Edwards, to become the second largest bank. BancoEstado emerged as the third-ranking institution. By 2003, the ten largest banks represented 91 percent of all loans and investments, while the top three alone accounted for over half.[28]

Capital Markets

Chile's capital markets continue to be shallow compared with industrial countries, but their recent expansion is noteworthy. Unlike other experiences in Latin America, the expansion has been primarily in the form of private securities rather than government debt. This pattern has to do with the supply and demand characteristics of the financial deepening in the 1990s. The fact that investment, including infrastructure and other construction, played a central

27. Calculated from Rivas (2004, appendix).
28. Calculated from the SBIF website (www.sbif.cl).

Table 6-3. *Chile: Stock and Bond Markets, 1981–2003*
Percent of GDP

Year	Stock market[a]	Bonds[b]	Government[c]	Mortgage[d]	Corporate[e]	Total
1981	21.6	9.2	4.9	4.0	0.3	30.8
1982	20.7	15.7	9.3	4.7	1.7	36.4
1983	12.1	25.3	17.3	6.5	1.5	37.4
1984	9.9	31.2	23.2	6.5	1.5	41.1
1985	13.9	60.2	51.8	6.8	1.5	74.1
1986	24.4	57.3	49.5	6.9	0.8	81.7
1987	28.0	51.1	43.6	6.1	1.4	79.1
1988	28.6	42.9	35.1	5.7	2.0	71.5
1989	38.7	38.4	29.5	5.5	3.5	77.1
1990	49.7	46.9	36.2	6.1	4.6	96.6
1991	86.7	46.9	34.7	6.7	5.5	133.6
1992	74.6	46.2	34.3	6.9	5.0	120.8
1993	107.0	46.1	33.0	8.2	4.9	153.1
1994	128.8	48.8	33.6	10.5	4.6	177.6
1995	112.0	46.3	31.5	11.0	3.8	158.3
1996	89.6	46.7	30.0	13.5	3.1	136.3
1997	91.0	47.8	31.6	13.8	2.4	138.8
1998	67.2	46.4	30.8	12.7	2.9	113.6
1999	97.3	47.5	30.3	13.6	3.7	144.8
2000	85.4	49.2	31.1	12.9	5.1	134.6
2001	85.5	53.3	31.0	13.0	9.3	138.8
2002	70.6	53.8	29.9	12.5	11.5	124.4
2003	119.2	51.0	25.7	12.1	13.2	170.2

Sources: IFC (1990, 1995) and Standard and Poor's (2005) for market capitalization; *Informe Financiero del Sector Público* for government bonds; SVS, *Revista Valores* for corporate and mortgage bonds.

a. Market capitalization.
b. Sum of government, mortgage, and corporate bonds outstanding.
c. Central Bank bonds outstanding.
d. Mortgage bonds outstanding.
e. Public and private corporate bonds outstanding.

role in the booming economy explains the increasing demand for long-term financing. At the same time, the 1990s were a period of rapid growth of institutional investors, who were eager to acquire long-term assets.

The value of the four main types of securities traded in Chile increased twelvefold in nominal dollar terms between 1981 and 2003; at the same time, they rose from 31 to 170 percent of GDP (see table 6-3). While all categories expanded in absolute terms, the composition of the capital markets changed substantially. In 1981, stock market capitalization accounted for 70 percent of the market total and bonds for only 30 percent. A decade later, their respective shares were nearly even, only to return toward their initial distribution by 2003. Within the bond category, government bonds were around half of total bonds in 1981, the height of anti-government ideology. They rose to over three-quarters in the early 1990s and then declined over the next decade. A significant point for the capital markets is that, unlike bank lending, they reached a peak both in absolute terms and as a share of GDP in the mid-1990s and then started to shrink, especially after the Asian crisis began in 1997. Only in 2003 did the trend reverse itself; by 2004 they had finally exceeded their earlier peak. A good deal of attention has been devoted recently to trying to explain the shrinkage and other problems in the markets; we return to this question below.

Beyond trends in the total value of securities, several other market characteristics need to be highlighted. The change in the value of securities over time is the result of two factors: new issues and price changes. The former represent the primary markets, while the latter emerge out of the secondary markets. In addition, we are interested in the liquidity of the markets and the number and type of participants.

For the stock market (Bolsa de Comercio de Santiago), changes in market capitalization have mainly resulted from changes in prices on the secondary market, on both the up and down sides (see table 6-4). New issues have been very small relative to the overall market size, which is similar to stock market trends in most countries. Moreover, the number of listed firms actually shrank from its peak in the late 1990s, falling from 295 in 1997 to 240 in 2003. Participants are a small group of very large firms for the Chilean context; the average assets of listed firms were over $600 million in 2004.[29] Liquidity in the stock market, as measured by the turnover ratio (transactions in a particular period divided by market capitalization), has been very low by international standards and falling in recent years; this is also a source of concern.

The bond markets differ from the stock market in several ways. As noted previously, the outstanding stock of government bonds (mainly central bank notes) is much larger than corporate issues. Nonetheless, the ratio has been declining because the central bank has floated far fewer issues recently as a result of a change in monetary policy, while corporate issuance has surged following the drop in interest rates. Table 6-5 illustrates this shift very clearly. The number of issuers has increased, but participants in the bond markets are an even more elite group than firms listed on the stock exchange. In 2003, for example, only thirty-nine new corporate issues were listed with an average flotation of around $75 million. Liquidity in the bond markets is much higher than in the stock market, but this is mainly due to high turnover in central bank paper. Trading in corporate bonds has exceeded that of stocks, but it is nevertheless low by international standards.[30]

The purchasers of stocks and bonds in Chile, unlike most other emerging market countries, are mainly institutional investors, including pension funds,

29. Calculated from the Bolsa de Comercio website (www.bolsantiago.cl).
30. Cifuentes, Desormeaux, and González (2002).

Table 6-4. *Chile: Characteristics of the Stock Market, 1980–2003*

Year	Number of listed firms	Market capitalization[a]	New issues[a]	Volume traded[a]	Turnover ratio[b]	Price index IGPA[c]	Change in index[d]
1980	265	9,400	198	548	5.8	100	n.a.
1981	242	7,050	192	375	5.3	76	−25
1982	212	4,395	170	114	2.6	68	−59
1983	214	2,599	159	59	2.3	57	−42
1984	208	2,106	127	40	1.9	63	−10
1985	228	2,012	150	50	2.5	110	−32
1986	231	4,062	290	298	7.3	262	126
1987	209	5,341	935	498	9.3	344	15
1988	205	6,849	550	650	9.5	460	30
1989	213	9,587	274	826	8.6	758	45
1990	215	13,645	253	785	5.8	1,167	40
1991	221	27,984	183	1,907	6.8	2,484	102
1992	245	29,644	480	2,061	7.0	2,734	8
1993	263	44,622	819	2,765	6.2	3,916	31
1994	279	68,195	926	5,263	7.7	5,425	45
1995	284	73,860	892	11,072	15.6	5,740	5
1996	283	65,940	1,372	8,460	12.8	4,903	−19
1997	295	71,832	1,922	7,426	10.3	4,794	−6
1998	287	51,809	872	4,417	8.5	3,595	−33
1999	285	68,193	1,461	6,874	10.1	5,168	32
2000	258	60,514	1,408	6,083	10.1	4,869	14
2001	249	56,734	411	4,220	7.4	5,398	4
2002	254	48,110	89	3,120	6.5	5,020	16
2003	240	85,534	212	6,544	7.7	7,337	62

Sources: IFC (1990, 1995); Standard and Poor's (2005).
n.a. Not available.
a. Millions of dollars.
b. Volume traded as share of market capitalization (%).
c. Indice General de Precios de Acciones, IGPA (1980=100).
d. Change in dollar terms (%).

insurance companies, mutual funds, and investment funds. The mere existence of institutional investors—many of which are long-term investors by nature, owing to the long-term structure of their contingent liabilities—creates demand for securities. Thus, the simultaneous growth of all institutional investors had profound effects on the demand for securities, their price, and the development of this market, but the pension funds (AFPs, by their Spanish acronym) have been the most important.[31]

---

31. On the impact of Chilean pension funds on the financial markets, see Uthoff (2001); Walker and Lefort (2002); Corbo and Schmidt-Hebbel (2003). Insurance company assets have risen together with the pension funds, since AFP administrators must purchase policies for their clients, but mutual funds are smaller in relative terms than in many other emerging market countries.

Table 6-5. *Chile: Characteristics of Bond Market, 1980–2003*

Year	Number of issuers	Amount outstanding[a]	Number of new listed issues	Corporate[b]	Government	Amount of placement[a]	Corporate[a,b]	Government[a]
1980	7	n.a.	4	4	0	0	0	0
1981	7	1,698	13	13	0	0	0	0
1982	12	2,677	9	9	0	0	0	0
1983	13	3,717	2	2	0	44	44	0
1984	15	4,751	5	5	0	66	66	0
1985	16	8,787	3	3	0	4	4	0
1986	8	8,915	3	3	0	32	32	0
1987	14	9,312	13	13	0	122	122	0
1988	20	8,961	12	12	0	267	267	0
1989	23	9,091	10	10	0	329	329	0
1990	27	12,372	16	15	1	294	294	0
1991	37	13,929	19	17	2	499	365	134
1992	39	16,460	12	12	0	154	152	2
1993	40	16,856	5	4	1	295	279	16
1994	46	19,451	14	13	1	447	406	41
1995	46	23,021	5	5	0	69	69	0
1996	47	22,696	5	4	1	175	135	41
1997	42	25,597	7	6	1	104	83	21
1998	41	24,622	7	6	1	809	798	11
1999	44	24,836	13	12	1	703	693	10
2000	44	27,336	21	20	1	2,312	2,292	20
2001	64	26,779	40	36	4	3,033	2,962	71
2002	70	27,890	40	35	5	3,065	2,160	905
2003	81	28,169	41	39	2	2,957	2,733	224

Sources: SVS, *Revista Valores* for number of issuers, new issues, and placements; table 6-3 for amount outstanding.

n.a. Not available.

a. In millions of dollars.

b. Public and private companies.

The pension fund reform in 1981 led to a significant transfer of resources to the newly created AFPs, and the fund administrators began to seek investments. Initially, they concentrated their growing resources in central bank paper, mortgages, and bank deposits; later they were authorized to invest more heavily in stocks and bonds of Chilean corporations and, still later, to expand into foreign investments. By the end of 2003, pension fund assets exceeded $49 billion (58 percent of GDP). The share of AFP holdings of securities in relation to the total stock of securities increased from around 2 percent in 1981 to 43 percent in 2003. The largest shares were in government, mortgage, and corporate bonds; their role in the equity market was much less pronounced.[32] Table 6-6 shows the evolving allocation of AFP investments by type of asset.

32. Superintendency of Pension Fund Administrators website (www.safp.cl).

Table 6-6. *Chile: Size and Allocation of Pension Fund Portfolios, 1981–2003*

Year	Billions of dollars	Share of GDP	Investment allocation (percent)				
			Government[a]	Financial[b]	Corporate[c]	Foreign[d]	Total
1981	0.3	0.9	28.1	71.3	0.6	0.0	100
1982	0.7	3.6	26.0	73.4	0.6	0.0	100
1983	1.3	6.4	44.5	53.4	2.2	0.0	100
1984	1.8	8.6	42.1	55.7	1.8	0.0	100
1985	1.5	10.7	42.4	56.0	1.1	0.0	100
1986	2.1	12.7	46.6	48.7	4.6	0.0	100
1987	2.7	14.2	41.4	49.4	8.8	0.0	100
1988	3.6	15.1	35.4	50.1	14.5	0.0	100
1989	4.5	18.2	41.6	39.2	19.2	0.0	100
1990	6.7	24.4	44.1	33.4	22.4	0.0	100
1991	10.0	31.2	38.3	26.7	34.9	0.0	100
1992	12.4	31.2	40.9	25.2	33.8	0.0	100
1993	15.9	38.1	39.3	20.7	39.4	0.6	100
1994	22.3	42.1	39.7	20.1	39.3	0.9	100
1995	25.4	40.0	39.4	23.1	37.2	0.2	100
1996	27.5	37.4	42.1	24.6	32.8	0.5	100
1997	30.8	39.0	39.6	30.1	29.0	1.3	100
1998	31.1	40.3	41.0	32.1	21.2	5.7	100
1999	34.5	49.2	34.6	33.7	18.3	13.4	100
2000	35.9	50.9	35.7	35.6	17.6	10.9	100
2001	35.4	55.0	35.0	33.1	18.5	13.4	100
2002	35.8	55.8	30.0	35.0	18.4	16.4	100
2003	49.2	58.2	24.7	27.3	24.0	23.8	100

Source: Superintendency of Pension Fund Administrators website (www.safp.cl).
a. Government and Central Bank notes and bonds.
b. Time deposits, mortgage securities, bonds and shares of banks.
c. Bonds and shares of corporations, investment fund quotas, commercial paper.
d. Investments in mutual funds, bonds, shares, derivatives in foreign markets.

With regard to foreign participation in the financial sector, most of the attention has been directed to the banking industry, given its dominant role, but foreign participation has also been important in the capital markets. One indicator is the share of foreign ownership in the Chilean pension funds: 65 percent of total assets under management in 2001 corresponded to foreign participation (largely Spanish), and over half of the investments represented control of the respective institutions.[33]

While developments in the capital markets were significant in and of themselves, they also played an important role in sustaining the growth of loans and the maturities of assets held by banks. One reason lies in the fact that, after 1991, banks were allowed to intermediate mortgage-backed securities, obtaining fees from such operations. Banks thus became important market makers, placing most of their mortgage-backed securities with institutional investors. This is

33. Salomon Smith Barney (2001).

Table 6-7. *Chile: International Finance, 1991–2003*
Percent of GDP

Year	Banks[a]	Bonds	ADR[b]	Total
1991	34.3	0.9	0.0	35.2
1992	34.2	0.7	0.3	35.2
1993	32.9	1.8	0.9	35.6
1994	37.2	1.4	2.4	41.0
1995	32.9	1.1	2.2	36.2
1996	39.0	2.9	2.5	44.4
1997	45.1	4.1	3.1	52.3
1998	55.2	4.6	3.2	63.0
1999	60.0	6.6	3.2	69.8
2000	66.0	6.6	3.1	75.7
2001	66.1	10.0	3.6	79.7
2002	63.9	13.1	3.5	80.5
2003	67.0	14.3	3.3	84.6

Sources: BIS website (www.bis.org/statistics/hcsv/hanx9a_for.csv) for bank loans, (www.bis.org/statistics/qcsv/anx12a.csv) for bonds; IMF, *Global Financial Stability Report* (September 2004) and unpublished data for ADRs.

a. Bank loans include cross-border and foreign currency loans from local offices of foreign banks.

b. ADRs are the sum of cumulative equity emissions since 1991.

another example of the virtuous circle relating the growth of banks, institutional investors, and capital markets as a consequence of specific policies undertaken by Chilean authorities in the period.

International Finance

Chile's domestic financial system is the largest in the Latin American region, but economic actors nevertheless tap the international markets for additional resources. Of course, only the largest borrowers can do so; in Chile's case, unlike that of Mexico or Brazil, such borrowers are mainly from the private sector. Only about one-third of the total international financial activity corresponds to the government, and some of that share consists of sovereign bonds issued by the government to help establish a yield curve and thus open the way for private firms to enter the markets.

Table 6-7 shows trends in international finance between 1991 and 2003. It also disaggregates the total into three component parts—syndicated bank loans, foreign and international bonds, and American depository receipts (ADRs). Together they amounted to 85 percent of GDP in 2003. By far the largest component was bank loans, representing about 80 percent of the total. While bonds constituted a much smaller share (17 percent), they have been growing much faster than bank loans. ADRs were not very significant, and no new issues have been floated since the late 1990s. Nonetheless Chile does have a presence in international equity markets. Sixteen Chilean firms are listed on the New York Stock Exchange, and seventeen have issued ADRs; not surprisingly, the overlap between the two is very strong.[34] The largest sectoral representation in ADRs is beverages and tobacco (16 percent) and utilities (13 percent). Other sectors that are prominent include merchandising and retail, chemicals, and the multisector holding companies. An additional source of foreign capital is investment in the local stock market. In 2004, about 23 percent of the shares in the top forty companies were in foreign hands ($17 billion out of $75 billion market capitalization).[35]

Finance, Investment, and Growth

Chile's banks and capital markets have performed impressively since 1990, and they were very supportive of the growth process witnessed over the last fifteen years. Having described the main characteristics of the financial system, we now want to identify the factors that were especially positive in the virtuous circle between finance and growth in Chile during this period. In particular, we focus on finance of investment, which in turn is a key determinant of the expansion of output. Table 6-8 provides an overview of sources of finance for the corporate sector according to amounts outstanding. In 2003, while stock market capitalization dominated, other domestic sources accounted for 27 percent of the total and international sources for 16 percent. Some very tentative data are also available for new finance, as opposed to amounts outstanding. While those data are consistent with table 6-8 in terms of the greater significance of domestic versus international finance, they indicate that new equity issues are far less important than the market capitalization figures would lead us to believe.[36]

Bank Credit

The banking sector was marked by rapid growth, increased efficiency, and a high degree of stability. In nominal dollar terms, total claims in the system tripled from $15 billion in 1991 to around $44 billion in 2003. Moreover, lending as a share of GDP rose from 51 to 66 percent (as was shown in table 6-1). Almost all of this credit went to the private sector, since the government had ceased to require finance as a result of budget surpluses. Business firms were the principal recipients, accounting for about 53 percent of the growing volume of credit. Other important users of credit were mortgage holders (19 percent), consumers (9 percent), and those engaged in international trade (9 percent); the remaining 10 percent was shared by smaller users.[37]

34. Information on the NYSE comes from their website (www.nyse.com); ADR information is from the Universal Issuance Guide on the Citibank website (wwss.citissb.com/adr/www/brokers/mn_uni.htm).

35. Data are from the Bolsa de Comercio de Santiago website (www.bolsantiago.cl).

36. IMF (2003a, p. 86). The IMF data are only available through 2002, so they do not capture the upswing of new issues of corporate bonds and stocks beginning in 2003.

37. Calculated from the SBIF website (www.sbif.cl); data are for 2003.

Table 6-8. *Chile: Finance for the Corporate Sector, 1993–2003*
Percent of GDP

| | Domestic finance | | | International finance | | | |
Year	Bank loans[a]	Corporate bonds[b]	Stock market capitalization	Loans[c]	Bonds[d]	Equity[e]	Total
1993	42.2	4.9	107.0	9.0	0.9	0.9	164.9
1994	40.7	4.6	128.8	11.2	0.8	2.4	188.6
1995	43.6	3.8	112.0	11.0	0.6	2.2	173.2
1996	39.6	3.1	89.6	14.3	2.9	2.5	152.1
1997	41.6	2.4	91.0	20.8	3.5	3.1	162.4
1998	43.9	2.9	67.2	23.9	4.0	3.2	145.1
1999	44.2	3.7	97.3	23.8	5.3	3.2	177.5
2000	43.7	5.1	85.4	21.2	5.2	3.1	163.8
2001	48.9	9.3	85.5	25.0	7.4	3.6	179.7
2002	44.7	11.5	70.6	24.9	9.3	3.5	164.5
2003	41.3	13.2	119.2	22.5	7.9	3.3	207.4

Sources: SBIF, *Información Financiera* for bank loans; Table 6-3 for corporate bonds outstanding, stock market capitalization; BIS website (www.bis.org/statistics/hcsv/hanx9a_priv.csv) for international bank loans, (www.bis.org/statistics/qcsv/anx12c.csv) for international bonds; table 6-7 for international equity.
a. Claims by banks on business customers.
b. Outstanding bonds issued by corporations.
c. Claims by international banks on private sector.
d. Outstanding bonds issued by corporations in international markets.
e. ADRs.

Figure 6-2 shows that the annual growth rates of bank credit, investment, and GDP were closely linked during the 1990s. Despite its greater volatility, investment was synchronized with GDP growth throughout the period. At the same time, changes in the volume of credit were strongly correlated with both variables pertaining to economic activity. Peaks and troughs coincided exactly until the last few years, with no lag, making it hard to decipher the causal mechanisms at work.

Figure 6-3 uses monthly data, which provide some additional insights. This figure—which plots the six-month moving average of the growth rate of commercial bank lending to the private sector and the monthly indicator of economic activity (IMACEC)—shows two interesting characteristics of the credit cycle in Chile. First, the growth rate of bank credit was generally higher than that of economic activity. Second, the growth of lending followed the growth of economic activity with a short lag. That is, the supply of credit was quite responsive to demand during the high growth years. In the period of lower economic growth after 1999, however, the relationship shifted, and finance appears to have become less supportive of the growth process. The same divorce between credit and the real economy after 1999 appeared in figure 6-2; this raises a question as to whether the credit-growth relationship changes significantly in periods of low growth or recession. We return to this point later when we examine

Figure 6-2. *Chile: Growth Rates of GDP, Investment, and Credit, 1991–2003*

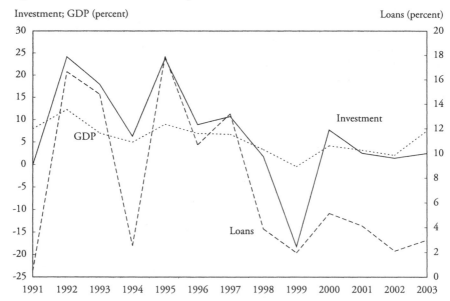

Sources: ECLAC website (www.eclac.cl) for GDP and investment; SBIF website (www.sbif.cl) for loans.

Figure 6-3. *Chile: Monthly Growth Rates of Credit and Output, 1990–2003*[a]

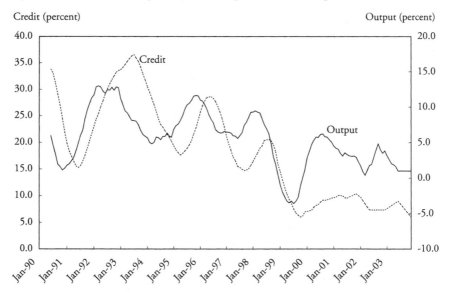

Sources: SBIF website (www.sbif.cl) for credit; Central Bank website (www.bcentral.cl/eng/infoeconomic/seriesofindicators/series01.htm) for IMACEC.

a. Credit is total credit; IMACEC is monthly indicator of economic activity. Both are six-month moving averages.

the quite different patterns in the domestic capital markets and in international finance.

Both macroeconomic and microeconomic factors played a role in the virtuous circle between credit and growth in the 1990s. Institutions have also been important. The stable macroeconomic context is one of the main characteristics distinguishing Chile from its neighbors in the past fifteen years. Several elements have been positively linked with financial development. First, stable, high growth rates (which slacked off toward the end of the 1990s) called forth finance and were supported by it, as we just illustrated in figures 6-2 and 6-3. Second, the lack of fiscal deficits made it easier to control inflation and avoided crowding out the private sector. Third, capital account management meant that less volatility was imported from abroad than would otherwise have been the case. This third policy has been quite controversial, but the benefits appear to have outweighed the costs, given the serious damage that volatility has caused in Chile's own past and in other regional economies.[38]

A manifestation of the links between macroeconomics and finance is evident in the relationship between unemployment levels and nonperforming loans. Figure 6-4 shows that nonperforming loans as a share of total bank credit were already low in the early 1990s, attributable to the strict regulation and supervision and the steady economic recovery in the second half of the 1980s.[39] From 1990 onwards, there was a strong correlation between nonperforming loans and the unemployment rate. As would be expected, the decline in nonperforming loans was reflected in a reduction of the provisions made by banks, owing to the lower risk implicit in lending. While the relationship with unemployment trends is a direct one with respect to consumer lending, it is indirect for many business firms through their ability to sell in domestic markets; for exporters it is not important. All three variables increased with the decline in growth, but they remain at low levels in comparative terms.

The second part of the virtuous circle is related to microeconomic factors, especially the overall cost of financing provided by banks. Table 6-9 shows a significant reduction in nominal lending rates and spreads from 1990 to 2003. At the same time, real loan rates have fluctuated without an overall trend. The falling interest rates and spreads were due to significant cost-reducing improvements and greater efficiency in the 1990s as overall expenses were reduced throughout, and competition forced banks to translate this decline of costs into

38. The two sides of the argument can be found in Agosín and Ffrench Davis (2001); De Gregorio, Edwards, and Valdés (2000).

39. The Chilean definition of nonperforming loans is more lenient than international standards: only the portion of a loan whose payment is overdue is included in the nonperforming loan category, rather than the whole loan. The IMF (2002a, p. 72) estimates that under international standards, Chilean nonperforming loans would be roughly double the current ratio—which is still comparatively low.

Figure 6-4. *Chile: Unemployment, Nonperforming Loans, and Provisions, 1990–2003*[a]

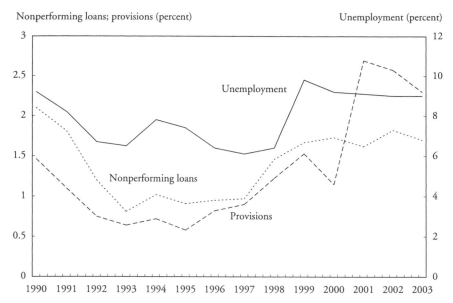

Sources: ECLAC website (www.eclac.cl) for unemployment rate; SBIF website (www.sbif.cl) for nonperforming loans and provisions.

a. Provisions are share of GDP; nonperforming loans are share of total loans; unemployment is urban unemployment.

lower lending rates and operating margins. The lower cost increased the demand for loans, which fed back into higher investment and growth rates.

Institutions have also played an important role in helping the banking sector improve its performance in recent years. Fuentes and Maquieira, for example, argue that institutional development explains the low level of nonperforming loans in Chile. In addition to regulation and supervision, they cite the legal framework, including the judicial system and bankruptcy code, and the increased use of credit bureaus.[40] Hernández and Parro also argue that institutions have made an important contribution to the dynamism of Chile's financial sector more generally. They pay particular attention to the governance factors that we discussed in chapters 3 and 5, including effective government performance, adherence to rule of law, control of corruption, and strong regulation.[41]

Another way to study the relationship between credit and output growth is to move to the sectoral level. The supply of credit to businesses, consumers, and home owners all rose rapidly in 1990–2003. While business loans grew at a strong 8.3 percent a year, the growth of loans for consumption and mortgages

40. Fuentes and Maquieira (2001).
41. Hernández and Parro (2005).

Table 6-9. *Chile: Performance Indicators for the Banking System, 1990–2003*
Percent

Year	Loans ratio[a]	Nominal loan rate[b]	Real loan rate[c]	Spread[d]	Efficiency ratio[e]	Return on equity[f]	Return on assets[g]	Non-performing loans[h]
1990	54.5	48.2	11.8	8.5	49.5	19.9	1.7	2.1
1991	50.9	28.3	16.4	6.3	61.3	15.3	1.3	1.8
1992	54.6	23.8	8.0	5.7	68.6	17.0	1.3	1.2
1993	59.7	24.0	10.5	6.0	63.2	20.6	1.5	0.8
1994	57.3	20.3	10.5	5.3	68.0	19.1	1.5	1.0
1995	60.5	18.1	9.2	4.4	68.0	13.9	1.3	0.9
1996	59.5	17.3	10.1	3.9	66.5	16.6	1.2	1.0
1997	64.3	15.6	9.1	3.6	66.4	13.7	1.0	1.0
1998	66.8	18.4	13.2	4.5	61.4	11.5	0.9	1.4
1999	69.2	11.9	8.6	3.7	60.2	9.4	0.7	1.7
2000	69.2	13.9	10.1	5.1	60.8	12.7	1.0	1.7
2001	69.5	11.3	7.7	5.3	56.2	17.7	1.3	1.6
2002	68.4	7.5	5.0	3.8	55.2	14.4	1.1	1.8
2003	66.0	5.6	2.8	3.3	53.6	16.7	1.3	1.6

Sources: Table 6-1 for loans as share of GDP; Central Bank CD (2000) and website (www.bcentral.cl) for loan rates and spread; SBIF website (www.sbif.cl) for efficiency ratio, return on equity, return on assets, and nonperforming loans.

a. Total loans as share of GDP.
b. Rate for 30–89 day nonadjustable loans.
c. Nominal loan rate deflated by consumer price index.
d. Nominal loan rate minus 30–89 day nonadjustable deposit rate.
e. Operating expenses as a share of gross operational margin.
f. Profits as a share of equity.
g. Profits as a share of assets.
h. Nonperforming loans as a share of total loans.

was even more impressive at 13.4 percent and 11.9 percent, respectively.[42] Disaggregating the figures for business loans indicates that while the pace of growth differed significantly across sectors, credit as a share of production value rose in most cases (see table 6-10). This is a good indicator that bank credit has been playing an increasing role in the financing of productive activities.

The importance of bank credit, however, varied substantially across sectors. The sectors in table 6-10 can be divided into three groups. First are the fastest growing (transport and communications, mining, and electricity and gas). Since they are mainly foreign owned, they do not rely on local bank credit and have the lowest ratios of credit to output. The second group (commerce, finance, and agriculture) had the second highest growth rates and received the most credit per unit of output. The third group (industry, construction, and general services) grew most slowly. They received less credit than the second group, but

42. Data are from the SBIF website (www.sbif.cl).

Table 6-10. *Chile: Credit as a Share of GDP by Sector, 1990–2003*
Percent

Sector	Average 1990–94[a]	Average 1995–99[a]	Average 2000–03[a]	Average 1990–2003[a]	Sectoral growth rate 1990–2003
Agriculture	56.1	55.9	67.9	59.0	4.8
Mining	9.8	8.8	9.1	9.2	6.7
Industry	34.7	33.8	34.0	34.2	4.0
Electricity and gas	9.0	19.9	26.6	17.5	7.3
Construction	53.5	48.4	45.6	49.6	4.5
Commerce	79.7	77.9	88.1	81.1	6.3
Communications/transport	19.2	23.1	22.3	21.4	8.1
Finance	55.3	58.7	57.0	57.0	5.4
Services	27.5	44.9	49.5	39.5	3.3
Total	42.4	45.4	46.9	44.6	5.2

Sources: SBIF website (www.sbif.cl) for credit; ECLAC website (www.eclac.cl) for GDP.
a. Credit to a sector, divided by GDP in that sector.

more than the first. In short, bank credit is related to sectoral growth rates for sectors that are not dominated by large, foreign-owned firms.

Capital Markets and International Finance

Trends in the capital markets were both similar to and different from those just described for banks. Significant growth occurred in the value of outstanding securities: in nominal dollar terms, stock market capitalization and bonds outstanding combined rose more than fourfold between 1990 ($29 billion) and 2003 ($123 billion). This growth was not monotonic, however, especially for the stock market. As noted earlier, market capitalization rose from 1990 to 1995–97, then fell off sharply, and has only recently begun to recover. (Market capitalization was shown in table 6-3 as a share of GDP and in table 6-4 in absolute values.)

The decline of the markets was a major concern for Chilean authorities. Two main explanations were put forward. One was based on a Keynesian type of analysis and focused on the demand for finance. It argued that macroeconomic events, especially the international financial crises of the late 1990s and the resulting slowdown of economic growth in Chile, were the main reason that the markets were less active. Thus, even if the government were to introduce policies to strengthen the stock and bond markets, a return to previous levels of activity would depend on increased demand for finance.

The alternative, supply-side approach pointed out that the slowdown began before the international crisis struck and searched for explanations in the markets themselves, together with policies alleged to be erroneous. Examples were said to include overregulation of domestic markets, taxation of secondary ADRs, capital controls that limited the entry of foreign investors, overly strict rules on pension fund investment, and high transaction costs to enter the domestic markets. According to this approach, the government could take important steps that would improve and revive the markets, and the additional finance would help stimulate growth.[43]

The link between securities markets and investment is less straightforward than that between bank credit and investment. Chile's stock market—like those of other developing economies—is dominated by a small number of large corporations. An even smaller number of firms have floated bonds on the domestic market. Most of these firms also have access to international financial markets, and all can tap local bank finance when they need it. In other words, this small group of large firms—which accounts for the vast majority of all investment—moves among sources of finance, depending on market conditions.

Caballero's analysis of this phenomenon gives a good idea of the mechanisms at work in the financial markets.[44] He argues that Chile remains vulnerable to external shocks, especially those deriving from terms of trade, despite having its macroeconomic house in order. These shocks require finance to keep the real economy from being affected, but international sources generally pull back under such circumstances. Large Chilean firms then shift to domestic capital markets and especially to banks, but the latter do not want to increase credit. Flight to quality results, which essentially crowds smaller firms out of the market. We return to the implications for equality in the next section, but here the point is the negative impact on output and employment.

A study by Gallego and Loayza complements Caballero's work by focusing on investment decisions by large firms in Chile.[45] The authors report that the largest firms (those in which the AFPs can invest) are not financially constrained, although this conclusion holds only for the highest quality group. They also find that large firms' revenue growth is positively related to the depth of the banking sector, but negatively related to stock market capitalization. This surprising result changes, however, when they look at the real value of market capitalization, that is, when they strip out the rise in value from price increases. These results reinforce those of Caballero in that the best-positioned firms can always get access to finance, but their smaller counterparts have significantly greater problems.

Other sources remind us that very large firms have many interests, and the financial resources they seek (and obtain) may be used for many purposes, of

---

43. See Cifuentes, Desormeaux, and González (2002) for an analysis by three central bank officials. They present a mixture of the above arguments, although leaning toward the supply-side approach.

44. Caballero (2002).

45. Gallego and Loayza (2001).

which investment in Chile is only one. For example, Calderón and Griffith-Jones find that ADRs issued by large Chilean firms in the mid-1990s were used almost exclusively for investment abroad.[46] Likewise, the large volume of bonds issued in the domestic market in 2002–03 were not used for investment, but to take advantage of low interest rates to refinance older, high-cost debt.[47]

Given these myriad complicating factors, it is not clear ex ante what kind of relationship might exist between investment and finance through the capital markets. Figure 6-5 provides empirical data on growth of investment and the dollar value of new stock and bond issues. Since the two are alternative forms of raising capital for essentially the same group of firms, it seems reasonable to combine them. The variables display little relationship in the first part of the 1990s. Activity in the markets was quite limited, and no particular correlation with investment trends is apparent. A close relationship emerged with domestic capital markets after 1999, however, as the Chilean economy lost its momentum following the Asian crisis. This is exactly the opposite of the trend with investment and bank loans, as shown in figure 6-2. In that case, bank loans and investment were tightly linked until 1999, and then the relationship disappeared. A possible explanation is that only the largest companies were investing in the low growth years, and they were getting their external resources primarily from the capital markets. A very similar pattern occurs with international finance, in that the link with investment also became much closer as of the late 1990s (see figure 6-6).

Sectoral data for market capitalization reinforce the hypothesis of a link between finance and growth. The five sectors in which growth exceeded the overall GDP rate in the period 1990–2002 were transportation and communications (an annual compound rate of increase of 6.9 percent), electricity and gas (6.3 percent), mining (5.9 percent), commerce (5.8 percent), and banking (4.9 percent). Four of these sectors were the most active on the local stock market, with the highest capitalization and turnover. Only mining—which is dominated by foreign enterprises and the huge state firm, CODELCO—was not heavily represented.[48] Mining firms obtain the large amounts of investment finance they need almost exclusively on the international markets, while firms from the other four sectors use both markets, as Caballero indicated.

While the private sector has had more competition from the public sector in the capital than in the credit markets, crowding out of the former by the latter has not been a problem in Chile. Government bonds—mainly attributable to the central bank policy of sterilizing capital flows—doubled in absolute amounts during the 1990s, but they fell significantly in relative terms (from

46. Calderón and Griffith-Jones (1995).

47. Christian Vinacos and Montserrat Salvat, "Bajas tasas impulsaron mercado de valores," *El Mercurio*, January 3, 2004.

48. Calculated from data on the Bolsa de Comercio de Santiago website (www.bolsantiago.cl), with GDP growth from the ECLAC website (www.eclac.cl).

Figure 6-5. *Chile: Growth Rate of Investment and New Issues of Equity and Corporate Bonds, 1991–2003*

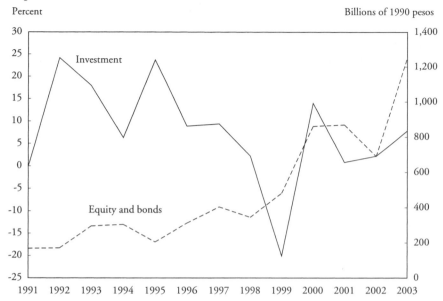

Sources: ECLAC website (www.eclac.cl) for investment; SBIF website (www.sbif.cl) for new issues of stocks and bonds.

Figure 6-6. *Chile: Growth Rates of Investment and International Finance, 1991–2003*

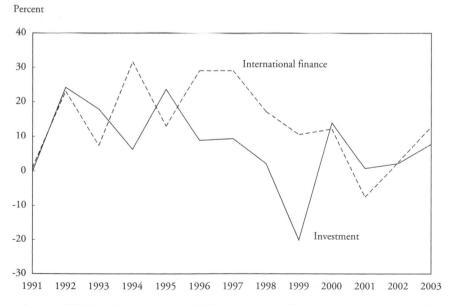

Sources: ECLAC website (www.eclac.cl) for investment; BIS website (www.bis.org), Standard and Poor's (2005), IMF (unpublished) for international finance.

77 percent of the total in 1990 to 50 percent in 2003; see table 6-3). The same was true in the international markets, as we have discussed. In domestic and foreign markets alike, then, the government's austere macroeconomic stance left plenty of space for the private sector to finance itself and thus contributed to the successful economic growth process. This situation stands in stark contrast to many other countries in the region, where governments still absorb a majority of bank loans and especially of bond issues.

Access to Finance for Small Firms

Chile's financial system has made an important contribution to overall growth rates since 1990, but to get a more complete understanding of the impact on growth, employment, and equity, we need to explore the question of who has had access to finance. There are various ways to approach the question of access; here we concentrate on access for the business sector, examining different size categories among firms (large, medium, small, and micro). Most of the emphasis is on formal sector credit from the banking sector, but we also touch briefly on the capital markets.[49]

As noted earlier, the expansion of the credit supply was far superior to that of GDP. The total volume of credit in constant pesos more than tripled between 1990 and 2003. Data on the number of borrowers and average volume of loans present a picture of how the credit market in Chile changed after 1990. The number of bank debtors rose from 1.6 million in 1990 to 4.5 million in 1997, before falling to 3.4 million in 2001 as growth rates fell and defaults drove debtors from the market. A substantial recovery then took place. This trend contrasts with the total amount of credit, which continued to rise in terms of constant pesos, meaning that the average size of loans increased. The overall picture for the period is quite positive. As seen in figure 6-7, the number of borrowers with access to the formal credit market more than doubled between the early 1990s and the early 2000s.[50]

A recent study by Román, based on data from the SBIF, enables us to probe beneath these aggregate figures to analyze trends in access to finance by size of firms in the 1990s.[51] The study defines firm size in the standard Chilean way, according to volume of sales: micro firms are classified as those with sales under $60,000, small firms from $60,000 to $625,000, medium-sized firms from

---

49. Pollack and García (2004) contribute a useful study on access to finance for SMEs. While most of the paper deals with Latin America in general, a chapter on Chile includes data from an unpublished study by García.

50. Many additional sources of consumer lending have become available. Credit from department stores is particularly important. According to the SBIF, the number of nonbank credit cards is around 8 million, more than three times the number of credit cards issued by banks.

51. Román (2003).

Figure 6-7. *Chile: Number of Debtors and Volume of Debt, 1990–2003*

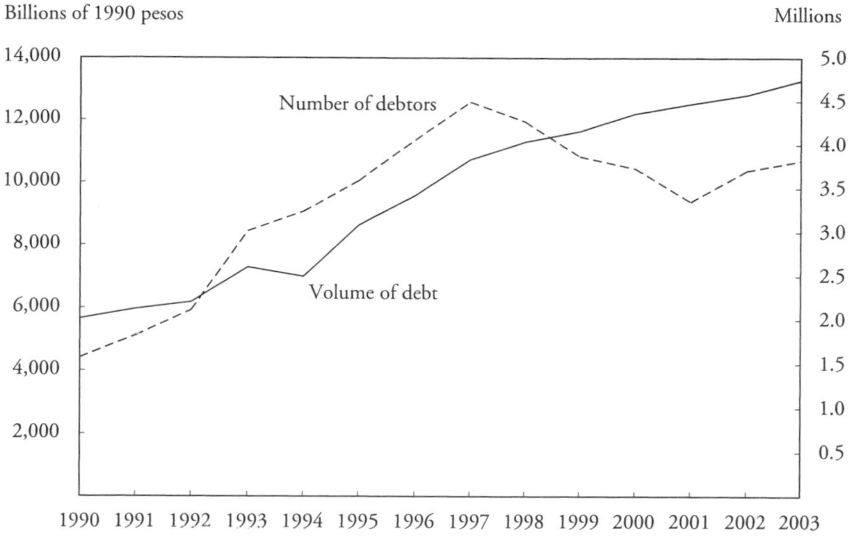

Billions of 1990 pesos   Millions

Source: SBIF website (www.sbif.cl).

$625,000 to $2.5 million, and large firms as those with sales over $2.5 million.[52] In 2000, 83 percent of all firms qualified as micro, 15 percent as small, 2 percent as medium sized, and less than 1 percent as large. In turn, micro firms accounted for 4 percent of sales, small firms for 10 percent, medium-sized firms for 9 percent, and large firms for 77 percent.

Large firms, as would be expected, were much more likely than their smaller counterparts to have access to bank credit. As table 6-11 shows, large firms, despite representing less than 1 percent of all firms, received over 60 percent of the banking credit going to the business sector. Nonetheless, the results of the study are unexpected in at least two ways. First, the table shows that micro, small, and medium-sized firms received a larger share of total credit than their sales share would predict. Large firms, by contrast, received less than their expected share. At the two extremes, micro firms (4 percent of sales) received 10 percent of credit in 2000, while large firms (77 percent of sales) accounted for 64 percent of credit.

A second unexpected finding concerns trends during the period studied (1994–2000). Table 6-12 shows that 78 percent of large firms had access to credit in 2000, but this represented a decline from the 84 percent that had had access in 1994. Likewise, the share of small and medium-sized firms with access

52. These categories are based on the UF accounting unit, which is used to index financial transactions to inflation in Chile. The value of the UF varies from day to day; the size ranges reported above assume a UF equal to $25, which is an average for recent years.

Table 6-11. *Chile: Allocation of Bank Debt by Size of Firm, 1994–2000*
Percent

Year	Micro[a]	Small[b]	Medium[c]	Large[d]	Total[e]
1994	9.1	15.6	13.7	61.7	100.0
1995	9.0	15.0	12.7	63.3	100.0
1996	10.0	16.6	13.7	59.7	100.0
1997	9.9	15.6	12.8	61.8	100.0
1998	9.6	15.2	13.0	62.2	100.0
1999	10.1	15.0	12.4	62.4	100.0
2000	9.9	15.0	11.5	63.6	100.0

Source: Calculated from Román (2003, table 20).
a. Firms with sales less than U.S.$60,000.
b. Firms with sales from U.S.$60,000 to U.S.$625,000.
c. Firms with sales from U.S.$625,000 to U.S.$2.5 million.
d. Firms with sales over U.S.$2.5 million.
e. Excludes "tramo 0," which represents firms with debt but no sales; the share of tramo 0 was 14–15 percent in 1994–96 and 7–9 percent in 1997–2000.

fell slightly. By contrast, the share of micro firms with access to bank credit rose from 32 percent in 1994 to 39 percent in 2000. On both indicators, micro firms do very well when compared with small and medium-sized firms. As we suggest below, this may be due to certain government programs that target micro firms in an especially effective way.

Before moving to programs for micro and small firms, however, we return to the situation of large firms. While the above suggests that these firms have done less well than might have been expected in obtaining bank credit, this is more than offset by other sources of finance. We combined the Román study with data from the IMF and calculated that the 1 percent of large firms receive nearly 85 percent of total finance going to firms (64 percent of domestic bank credit plus all resources from international banks and domestic and international capital markets).[53] Moreover, Caballero's analysis shows that large firms displace smaller firms from the credit markets when economic problems arise.[54] It is in this sense that the large firms are not credit constrained, while their smaller counterparts not only have trouble accessing finance in normal times, but can be squeezed out of the markets altogether in more difficult periods. Undoubtedly a larger-than-usual number of smaller firms goes bankrupt when such a credit crunch occurs.

53. IMF (2003a, p. 86). There is an important inconsistency here regarding the definition of large firms. In terms of bank credit, Román considers the 6,000 largest firms, while fewer than 350 are listed on the Chilean stock exchange. The latter make up the really privileged group in terms of access to finance. The SBIF recently defined a new category, mega firms, encompassing the top 1,000.
54. Caballero (2002).

Table 6-12. *Chile: Allocation of Bank Debt by Size of Firm, 1994–2000*
Percent

	1994			2000		
Size	No. of firms	No. with credit	Percent access	No. of firms	No. with credit	Percent access
Micro[a]	435,852	139,621	32.0	533,479	210,354	39.4
Small[b]	80,099	50,815	63.4	93,842	58,041	61.8
Medium[c]	11,217	8,422	75.1	13,159	9,492	72.1
Large[d]	4,950	4,165	84.1	6,065	4,750	78.3
Total	532,118	203,023	38.2	646,549	282,637	43.7

Source: Calculated from Román (2003, table 16).
a. Firms with sales less than U.S.$60,000.
b. Firms with sales from U.S.$60,000 to U.S.$625,000.
c. Firms with sales from U.S.$625,000 to U.S.$2.5 million.
d. Firms with sales over U.S.$2.5 million.

The high degree of inequality in Chile was recognized as a serious problem by the center-left political coalition that came to power in Chile with the restoration of democracy in 1990. In addition to direct measures to combat inequality and poverty, the new government established several types of programs to provide small and micro firms with greater access to credit and financial services. Central to these efforts were two government financial institutions—the National Development Corporation (Corfo) and BancoEstado.

In the 1980s, Corfo made loans directly to firms. This process proved very costly to the government, generating over $500 million in losses, and the window was closed in 1990.[55] Since then, Corfo has acted as a second-tier bank, providing resources to commercial banks, which on-lend them to firms and households. Some of these funds come from Corfo's government-provided budget, while others come from donor governments in industrial countries. A number of programs with different characteristics are geared to smaller firms' needs for investment funds and working capital. The three largest together provided around $60 million in 2003, a figure that had been declining in previous years. Another important Corfo initiative was providing funds to the banks to restructure the debts of micro, small, and medium-sized firms, which had gotten into financial problems as growth slowed in the late 1990s.[56]

These programs have been useful, but they suffer from at least two kinds of problems. First, they have been relatively small. The $60 million mentioned above represents only a little over 3 percent of the commercial bank credit that goes to SMEs.[57] The restructuring initiative was larger, with original projections

55. Foxley (1998).
56. A description of the programs can be found in Foxley (1998); Dini and Stumpo (2002); Rivas (2004).
57. The 3 percent figure is calculated by multiplying the total credit flows (from IMF, 2003a, p. 86) by percentage of debt held by micro, small, and medium-sized firms (from Román, 2003, table 20).

of $1 billion. However, while Corfo provided $300 million and BancoEstado contributed $200 million, the private sector share of $500 million never materialized. A second problem concerns the definition of SMEs in the Corfo programs. The agency violates its own guidelines in many programs by substantially broadening the universe of firms that can participate. For example, the largest Corfo program for SMEs—a multisectoral fund for investment financing—can be accessed by firms with annual sales up to $30 million (and large firms are defined as having sales over $2.5 million). Corfo will not comment on this inconsistency, but experts hypothesize that the agency is trying to avoid the stigma of new losses by providing funds only to highly creditworthy enterprises.[58]

BancoEstado is a first-tier commercial bank—although with some unique characteristics vis-à-vis its private sector counterparts. Specifically, it tries to combine a profitable portfolio with services to disadvantaged parts of the population. BancoEstado has taken a leading role in serving small and micro firms, both in its role as a lending institution and in coordinating activities by private sector banks. It has innovative programs for small and micro firms, serving over 100,000 clients between the two. Especially with micro firms, the emphasis is on providing a holistic solution to problems of small entrepreneurs, including technical assistance, training, and networking in addition to credit. Use of the Internet and telephone for communication with clients helps to keep overhead costs low.[59]

Equally important is BancoEstado's role in providing support to encourage private sector banks to serve small firms. Since a major reason that such firms lack access is that they do not have collateral or guarantees, the bank administers a program called Fogape (Guarantee Fund for Small Entrepreneurs), which auctions government funds to commercial banks to be used for guaranteeing credit to small firms. Such firms cannot have sales of more than $625,000 and must fulfill the normal standards of eligibility. The program started in 1980; it was revamped in 1997, after which its operations accelerated rapidly. Thus, there were 200 operations with three banks in 1998 and more than 30,000 operations with seventeen banks in 2003; in the latter year, the program provided about $250 million.[60] These amounts are larger than those provided by Corfo, and they go to firms that really match the targeted group of small firms. At the other end of the spectrum, however, BancoEstado also makes loans to very large firms. Indeed, BancoEstado has a very different profile of clients than its private sector competitors, focusing on the smallest and largest segments. Table 6-13 illustrates this point with data on size of loans for BancoEstado, Banco de Chile (the

---

58. Dini and Stumpo (2002).
59. BancoEstado website (www.bancoestado.cl); see also Mena (2005).
60. Fogape website (www.fogape.cl).

Table 6-13. *Chile: Loan Portfolios of Public, Private, and Foreign Banks, 2003*
Billions of pesos and percent

Bank	*Micro*[a] Amount	%	*Small*[b] Amount	%	*Medium*[c] Amount	%	*Large*[d] Amount	%	*Total* Amount	%
BancoEstado[e]	1,615	31.2	1,080	20.8	326	6.3	2,159	41.7	5,180	100
Banco Chile[f]	431	7.1	2,120	34.8	1,427	23.4	2,115	34.7	6,094	100
Santander[g]	717	8.9	3,034	37.6	1,503	18.6	2,815	34.9	8,069	100
Total	2,763	14.3	6,234	32.2	3,256	16.8	7,089	36.6	19,343	100

Source: SBIF, *Información Financiera* (December 2003).
a. Less than U.S.$10,000; original source in UF, calculated as UF = U.S.$25.
b. From U.S.$10,000 to U.S.$250,000.
c. From U.S.$250,000 to U.S.$5,000,000.
d. More than U.S.$5,000,000.
e. Public bank.
f. Largest private domestically owned bank.
g. Largest foreign bank.

largest private domestic bank), and Banco Santander (the largest foreign bank).[61]

In Chile, where the hallmark of the economy is private sector leadership, the main source of finance for small and medium-sized firms is private banks. Virtually all the private banks are now competing for SME clients in order to shore up their businesses and maintain profit margins under highly competitive conditions. There are two main reasons. The margins on SME loans are higher than those for larger clients, and large firms are increasingly using the domestic capital markets and international finance.[62] A variety of new mechanisms are being used to service smaller clients in addition to the traditional types of bank loans. Prominent examples include leasing, factoring, and securitizing. Another type of tool—credit scoring—has come into use for all kinds of banking transactions with small firms and individuals to enable banks to make low-cost decisions about the creditworthiness of potential borrowers.

Medium-sized firms generally have no problem obtaining bank loans, although there were temporary credit shortages in the low-growth period after 1998.[63] Small firms have greater difficulties, in part because of lack of collateral; here the Fogape program is very useful. An additional problem is that credit to SMEs, like credit in general in Chile, is typically in the form of very short-term loans (less than ninety days). Under normal circumstances, these loans are rolled over, but the practice provides the context for a credit crunch to develop in hard times.

61. We are using size of loan here as a proxy for size of firm (that is, large loans are referred to as loans to large firms).
62. Personal interviews with bankers and entrepreneurs in Chile.
63. Personal interviews.

Interestingly, micro firms are better positioned than small firms with respect to loan maturities. Indeed, Román's argument as to why the former fared better than the latter in the late 1990s is based largely on this distinction. A program of particular interest is the IFIS (Financial Institutions) program, administered by the Chilean government's Solidarity and Social Investment Fund (Fosis). Operating in a way analogous to Fogape, Fosis auctions funds to commercial banks, in this case as a subsidy for the high transaction costs associated with loans to micro enterprises. The guarantees are good for only three loans to any one client, since after that time the banks should have the relevant information and the firms should become normal clients. Two private commercial banks initially took the lead in the IFIS program: Banco de Desarrollo, a bank connected to the Catholic Church, and Banco Santander, the large Spanish bank through its subsidiary Banefe. Both used IFIS to develop their own programs of lending to micro firms, and they were then replaced by BancoEstado as the leading partner. In its first ten years of existence, the IFIS program managed to incorporate 123,000 micro firms, giving them access to some kind of banking services.[64] Moreover, the fact that the guarantees require banks to make loans that are of longer duration than are typically provided to SMEs (and at fixed interest rates) makes micro enterprises the beneficiaries of a more stable source of finance.

Overall, the current Chilean government has taken the issue of access to credit seriously, and a number of programs have been developed to try to expand access to smaller firms. Some of them have been more successful than others. BancoEstado is arguably the most important agent in the attempt to broaden access, but Corfo and other agencies also play an important role. In addition, the private sector has become more involved in providing credit for smaller firms, based on the banks' own business motives. In the last few years, for example, several niche banks devoted specifically to small firms have been authorized to begin operations. Indeed, the government argues that the problem for SMEs currently is not lack of credit, but the terms on which it is offered (such as higher interest rates than for larger firms, shorter maturities, greater demands for collateral, and lack of trained personnel to handle their particular needs).[65] Government agencies have a number of proposals on the table, since credit problems for small and especially micro firms—whether quantitative or qualitative—do remain serious, and all agree that much more needs to be done to deal with them.

Conclusions

The Chilean financial system—both the banking system and the capital markets—expanded significantly and performed well in the past fifteen years. In this final section, we highlight the main reasons that the Chilean system has

---

64. In 2002, the number of formal sector micro firms was around 533,000 (Román, 2003, p. 9).
65. Marshall (2004a).

outperformed its counterparts in the region. We also point to some challenges that are still on the horizon.

First, the stability and good performance of the banking sector since 1990 were a direct consequence of the thorough cleanup of the banking industry after the financial crisis of 1981–83 and the improved system of regulation and supervision. At the beginning of the 1990s, Chile already had a solid and modern system of prudential regulation and supervision. Few changes were made during the decade, mostly to comply with the specific rules set by BIS standards for capital adequacy, risk assessment, and disclosure. More self-regulation and better corporate governance were also introduced. Moreover, banks were allowed to expand into a wider range of activities, and foreign banking institutions increased their presence in the Chilean market.

Second, a virtuous circle was created between capital markets and institutional investors. The pension reform of 1981 led to significant transfers of resources to the newly created private pension funds, whose contingent liabilities are, by definition, long-term. Insurance company assets grew in tandem, as obligatory policies were issued for pension-fund beneficiaries, and changes in regulation and a better business environment also permitted a rapid growth of mutual funds and foreign investment funds. Finally, the Chilean government created incentives for the development of specific markets, particularly of mortgage-based securities, and provided the necessary legal framework for the markets to function.

Third, the good performance of the banking and capital markets was aided by the context in which market operations took place. Macroeconomic policy contributed to a stable and growing economy, which had a strong positive interaction with the financial sector, and the capital account of the balance of payments was managed so as to limit volatility from international markets. The favorable macroeconomic environment (which resulted in economies of scale and a decline in default rates), the reduction of public debt and deficits, and the interrelated improvement of microeconomic variables led to the reduction of interest rates, spreads, and thus the cost of credit. It also meant that the public sector was not crowding the private sector out of financial markets. Institutions made an important contribution, too. Since the restoration of democracy in 1990, Chile has been known for respect for the rule of law and an independent judiciary, and corruption is much lower than in most developing countries. Institutions specifically related to the financial sector have also been strengthened through several pieces of legislation.

Fourth, in this environment of growth and stability, the international opening of the credit and capital markets in the 1990s had a complementary role. Not only has foreign ownership increased in both the banking and nonbanking financial sectors, but Chilean firms have become important participants in the markets for syndicated loans, international and foreign bonds, and, to a lesser extent, ADRs and other forms of international equity. The holdings of foreign assets by Chilean financial institutions have also risen substantially. Notably, financial opening and integration took place in the context of low increase in exchange-risk exposure—an important factor in mitigating the impact of external shocks that typically lead to currency mismatches and constitute a source of financial crisis.

Despite these obvious successes, Chile faces several challenges in the coming years. First, the financial stability for which the country is justifiably recognized must be maintained. This may sound simple, but new problems will inevitably arise as the country's financial sector becomes more integrated into international markets, especially since the international financial system itself is continually changing. Moreover, Chile's floating exchange rate has increased volatility, as have more relaxed policies on capital flows and the decision to wean the economy away from indexation. In organizational terms, the Basel II accord will pose new challenges for banking regulators and supervisors. New instruments, including various types of derivatives, require more sophistication on the part of users and regulators alike, and the challenge is heightened by the presence of a number of large foreign banks in the Chilean market. At the same time, this presence may be an advantage if partnerships can be formed with foreign regulators. Overall, the main task is to ensure that macro- and microeconomic policies continue to work together—as they have in the past—to promote a stable financial environment.

Second, if the financial sector is to provide adequate support for investment and growth, increasing long-term finance must be a priority. Chile has moved away from the model of relying on public sector development banks, so private sector alternatives must be nurtured, including public-private partnerships. While it may be possible to create incentives to encourage the banks to lengthen maturities, equal attention should be focused on strengthening the capital markets. One issue is lowering transaction costs so that medium-sized firms can access the markets, but liquidity must also be raised to attract investors. The pension funds have been a great boon for the markets, but they have lowered liquidity, requiring new initiatives to compensate. Some analysts have suggested improving the market infrastructure, standardizing contracts, and increasing the availability of derivatives. Finally, an agenda for investment finance would not be complete without addressing the need for venture capital. Finance for start-ups is essential if Chile is to move toward high-technology sectors. This will probably require the public and private sectors to work together in new ways.

Third, the issue of access to finance is a vital component of the goal of increased equality in Chilean society. As it currently stands, the financial sector is compounding problems of inequality of wealth and income, rather than helping to resolve them, insofar as the share of finance accruing to large firms is even higher than their share of output. Some creative and efficient policies (such as Fogape and IFIS) have been devised by government agencies, and the private institutions have also begun to see opportunities through expanding into lower-income markets. But much remains to be done. The banking system lost over one million customers during the economic downturn of the early 2000s. While most have been won back, a sizable number of Chileans still lack access to financial services. More important from our perspective, additional efforts are needed to expand finance for small and micro firms. Large and medium-sized firms can generally obtain access to finance of various sorts that fit their needs, but their smaller counterparts face serious obstacles—including some of the very regulations that have helped maintain stability in the financial sector. A good starting point would be a thorough inventory of existing programs and policies to see which are working well, how they can be improved, and how they can be expanded to serve the obvious unmet needs.

A final, more general point concerns the way the Chilean government and financial sector perceive the challenges that face them. A comfortable tendency is to measure their performance with respect to other Latin American economies. Chile comes out extremely well in this comparison on most counts. A view toward the future and the need for improving competitiveness, however, suggests that Chile should raise its sights beyond the neighborhood. Some of the high-performing East Asian countries could provide a useful benchmark and possibly provide some ideas about new directions, as the earlier chapters of the book have discussed.

7

Mexico:
Foreign Banks Assume Control

M exico initiated its financial reforms more than a decade after Chile.[1] In the late 1980s, the Mexican government began to eliminate the controls that had characterized the financial sector during much of the postwar period; the reforms accelerated in the early 1990s. Liberalization and a resulting lending boom occurred in the absence of new prudential regulations, however, and they were combined with macroeconomic policies that ultimately led to a foreign exchange crisis and devaluation at the end of 1994. The decline in the currency's value undermined an already weak banking sector, and the government was forced to intervene to prevent a wholesale meltdown. The intervention was carried out in conjunction with a large loan from the U.S. Treasury and the International Monetary Fund (IMF) to support the foreign exchange reserves. Although the immediate crisis was brought under control, the damage was significant, and deep problems remain today.

The period after 1990 can be divided into three parts. From 1990 to 1994, the newly privatized banks expanded credit rapidly, mainly directing it toward the private sector. After the crisis of 1994–95, credit to the private sector fell steadily, but in two different contexts. During the second half of the 1990s, the banks were trying to rebuild their capital, restructure their operations, and meet new regulatory requirements. Thus little lending took place, despite robust eco-

1. We would like to thank Celso Garrido, Professor of Economics at Mexico's Universidad Autónoma Metropolitana Azcapotzalco, for the document he prepared as an input to this chapter. It has been expanded in his own book; see Garrido (2005).

nomic growth. In the first half of the 2000s, two changes occurred simultaneously: growth slowed, and foreign banks made a massive entry into the Mexican market. Only by mid-decade did loans begin to recover, but mainly for consumption rather than production; lending as a whole remains far below precrisis levels. Capital markets followed similar patterns.

The Mexican economy has serious problems in comparison with the other countries we are studying. In particular, it has very low levels of bank credit to the corporate sector, and the capital markets make only a minimal contribution to funds for investment. Overall, domestic finance for firms in Mexico is 28 percent of GDP (measured by amounts outstanding in 2003), whereas the comparable figures for Brazil and Chile are 82 percent and 174 percent, respectively. Finance in East Asia is even more abundant. This does not mean that no Mexican firms have access to finance. On the contrary, a very small group of very large firms has excellent access. The problem concerns the great majority of firms, which are limited to retained earnings and fragile nonbank funding. Until Mexico has a deeper domestic financial system and provides broader access, long-term growth that encompasses the domestic economy as well as exports will be hard to generate.

This chapter assesses the problems in Mexico's financial system and how to convert it into a more dynamic force in the Mexican economy and society. The first section looks at financial liberalization, the crisis, and the aftermath. The second turns to structural changes in the financial sector—banks, capital markets, and the links to international finance, which are especially important for Mexico given its close ties to the United States. The third section analyzes the relationship among finance, investment, and growth in the Mexican case; this is closely linked to the question of who has access to finance (section four). The final section concludes by analyzing the challenges that confront Mexico with respect to improving the performance of finance for production and its role in the economy more generally.

Liberalization, Crisis, and Response

The Mexican financial system has experienced unusual turbulence in the last two decades: nationalization, reprivatization, and deregulation all occurred within a relatively short period of time. Not surprisingly, the process has not been a smooth one. While significant efforts have been made recently to buttress the system and increase the availability of credit, they have not yet achieved success. This history provides the crucial background for understanding the current financial problems Mexico faces. We begin with the steps leading to the bank nationalization, followed by the liberalization process and the disequilibria it created. We then turn to the crisis and the government response, both the short-term rescue and the longer-term institutional changes. We finish by extending the analysis beyond the banks to include the capital markets and how they, too, have changed as a result of financial liberalization and the crisis.

Financial Liberalization and Its Consequences

By the early 1980s, Mexico was considered to be one of the most successful developing countries and was frequently compared with the newly industrialized economies (NIEs) of Brazil, Korea, and Taiwan. As in other NIEs, the state-owned development banks were crucial instruments in Mexico's postwar industrialization drive. The national development bank (Nacional Financiera, or Nafin), in particular, played a key role in intermediating between international finance and domestic firms, both public and private. State banks serving specific groups of clients were also prominent actors, including a foreign trade bank, an infrastructure bank, and several agricultural banks. Together, they controlled a substantial, but varying, share of Mexican bank loans over the years; at some points, their share exceeded 50 percent of total domestic credit. Beyond its direct ownership of the development banks, the Mexican government exercised tight control over private commercial banks through high reserve requirements, interest rate regulation, and directed credit.[2]

The Mexican economy also relied on international capital (both private banks and multilateral institutions), which was especially important in financing state-owned firms in petroleum, energy, and transportation, as well as industry. The resulting buildup of foreign debt in the 1970s, together with the drop in oil prices in the early 1980s, created the conditions whereby Mexico nearly defaulted on its obligations and initiated the so-called lost decade of the debt crisis in Latin America. In Mexico's case, the external financial crisis was linked to the domestic financial sector when the outgoing government of José López Portillo nationalized the private banks in 1982 in an attempt to bring the crisis under control; state ownership was written into the constitution. This act constituted a last attempt at state control of the Mexican economy. A move toward greater reliance on the market began under the successor administration of Miguel de la Madrid (1982–88).[3]

One of the most important sets of market-oriented reforms was centered on the financial sector. Since privatizing the banks would have required a constitutional change, the de la Madrid government worked around the margins by selling nonbank financial institutions, such as brokerage houses and insurance companies. It also diverted government borrowing from banks to the capital markets by increasing the issuance of short-term treasury bills. The big changes, however, came under the administration of Carlos Salinas de Gortari (1988–94). Interest

2. For a discussion of the financial sector in the early postwar period, see Goldsmith (1966); Del Angel-Mobarak (2005). On the relationship between finance and investment in the early period, see FitzGerald (1978).

3. On the bank nationalization, its causes, and its ramifications, see Del Angel-Mobarak, Bazdresch, and Suárez (2005).

rates were liberalized on both assets and liabilities, directed lending quotas were eliminated, and reserve requirements were lowered and then abolished. The constitution was amended to permit the reprivatization of the banks, which took place in only fourteen months between mid-1991 and mid-1992. Buyers had to be Mexican nationals; most had little or no banking experience; and they paid very high prices for their new properties. The last two factors would later be recognized as highly problematic for banking performance.[4]

The banking system's response to liberalization was as expected. Lending grew rapidly (around 30 percent per year in real terms from 1989 to 1994), and the share of loans to the private sector rose from 10 to 40 percent of GDP.[5] Most analysts agree, however, that the first years of privatization were characterized by "reckless—sometimes fraudulent—lending as a result of poor supervision and underdeveloped regulations. Poor credit-analysis procedures and few internal controls characterized the sector during this time. Banks put themselves in a precarious position as their lending outpaced their deposits, and they funded the shortfall through interbank borrowing—mainly from foreign banks."[6] As a consequence, nonperforming loans increased from around 2 percent of total loans in 1990 to 9 percent in 1994, but these official figures should be taken as a lower bound given the government's weak accounting procedures at the time.[7]

In addition to these microeconomic problems, macroeconomic policies also contributed to the buildup of a financial crisis. The use of an exchange rate anchor to control inflation led to overvaluation of the peso, large trade and current account deficits, and strong capital inflows. Initially, most of the inflows were foreign direct investment, thanks to the signing of the North American Free Trade Agreement (NAFTA) with the United States and Canada. Political shocks during the election year of 1994, however, triggered a sharp drop in long-term capital flows and thus dwindling reserves. To limit the decline, the government issued short-term debt that was payable in pesos but indexed to the dollar (*tesobonos*). While the policy was temporarily successful, the hemorrhaging resumed, and by the end of the year, as the new Zedillo administration prepared to take office, it was clear that drastic steps would have to be taken. The peso was floated in December, resulting in a large devaluation.

4. For useful summaries of the buildup to the crisis, see Gruben and McComb (1997); Haber (2005).

5. Marcos Yacamán (2001).

6. EIU (2001, p. 7). Gruben and McComb (1997) contrast two theories about the nature of the problems in Mexico's banking sector: insufficiently competitive or hypercompetitive. The sector appears to have switched from the first to the second in a short time in 1993–94. See also Gruben and McComb (2003).

7. Data are from McQuerry (1999), but see Haber (2005) on different ways to calculate nonperforming loans.

The Financial Crisis and the Government Response

The devaluation of the Mexican peso set off a crisis that severely damaged the country's banking system, as well as its economy more generally. Because Mexican regulations limited banks' foreign exchange exposure, the direct problems created by the devaluation were less significant than in most other countries.[8] Several indirect consequences were more serious. These included a sharp drop in economic activity, a substantial hike in interest rates in an attempt to control inflation, and an increase in the demand for dollars. The resulting inability of debtors to service their obligations increased the already high level of nonperforming loans, which put the banks themselves in danger.

Mexico's response to the twin crises it faced was piecemeal. The authorities feared that open recognition of the full extent of the banking crisis would worsen the external crisis, so they did not deal with the banking crisis comprehensively.[9] In the short run, help came from the new NAFTA partners. Despite opposition from the U.S. Congress, the Clinton administration and the IMF orchestrated what was then the largest financial rescue package in history—some $50 billion.[10] Much of the package went to redeem the *tesobonos*, which made some observers question the motives of the rescue operation, but it enabled the government to restore its foreign exchange reserves and to regain control of its policy instruments. The stringent economic policies worked out between the Mexican government and the IMF permitted the taming of inflation and the resumption of economic growth, mainly through increased exports to the United States as a result of the newly competitive exchange rate. The recovery was very uneven, however, partially because of continuing problems in the financial sector.

A number of measures were introduced to aid the banks in the short run. First, an international liquidity facility was established to enable the banks to meet their foreign exchange obligations. Second, a recapitalization program (Procapte) was set up to help banks meet the 8 percent capital-asset ratio set by the Bank for International Settlements. Banks could raise their capital ratio by creating convertible subordinated bonds, selling them to the deposit insurance agency (Fobaproa), and using the proceeds to augment their capital. If the banks became insolvent, the bonds would be converted to equity under government ownership.[11] Third, banks were allowed to exchange nonperforming loans for ten-year zero-coupon government bonds. (This plan was commonly referred to

8. Some loopholes did exist, however, to get around the regulations; see O'Dougherty and Schwartz (2001).

9. This argument is convincingly made by Krueger and Tornell (1999). In addition, as others have pointed out, a lack of timely information made it hard to grasp the full extent of the crisis; see McQuerry (1999).

10. All monetary figures cited in this chapter are in U.S. dollars.

11. This program was not used much because the market considered participation to be a sign of weakness. See Mackey (1999).

as Fobaproa, since that agency was in charge of taking over the nonperforming loans.) The quid pro quo was that bank shareholders had to inject one peso of new capital for every two pesos of nonperforming loans shifted off their balance sheets. They also had to make provisions for 25 percent of the debt transferred and to hold, not trade, the bonds. Fourth, debtor relief programs were offered to various categories of borrowers—such as credit card and mortgage holders, the agriculture sector, and SMEs—to stretch out loan payments, reprice them in UDIs, and subsidize interest payments.[12] Subsequently, a program of discounts on loan principal was added to end the process (and was thus referred to in Spanish as *punto final*).

The cost of these programs rose each year since the banks' problems were not fully resolved and new nonperforming loans quickly replaced those moved to Fobaproa. In addition, the government bent its own rules by broadening the categories of loans that could be sold to Fobaproa. In 1995 the cost was estimated at 5.5 percent of GDP; by 1996 it had risen to 8.4 percent; and by 1998 it had reached 16.2 percent. More recent estimates run around 20 percent of GDP.[13]

A complementary aspect of the rescue program involved both temporary and permanent changes in bank ownership. The temporary changes centered on the government's takeover of twelve banks, because of either capitalization problems or fraud. The twelve institutions—all quite small—accounted for about 12 percent of the total assets of the banking industry. In general, other banks bought the branch networks of the intervened banks, leaving the assets and liabilities for Fobaproa to dispose of.[14] The more permanent ownership changes involved the expansion of foreign banks. While the opening of the market to foreign banks was part of the NAFTA agreement, it was initially meant to be very gradual and was to be capped at 25 percent foreign ownership. The need for recapitalization, in the absence of local partners with deep pockets, led to an acceleration of the opening process. Foreigners now own the vast majority of Mexico's banking industry. The government hoped that the new foreign owners would not only bring additional capital, but would also introduce new technology—hard and soft—that would make the economy more competitive and help avoid future crises.

The New System of Regulation and Supervision

As the sale of Mexican banks was taking place, other changes were also occurring in the financial sector. President Ernesto Zedillo presented a package of

12. The UDI is a unit of account, indexed to the inflation rate. It was modeled after the Chilean UF.

13. See Krueger and Tornell (1999, table 12) for 1995–98; OECD (2002, p.7) for the recent figure.

14. See Graf (1999) for a list of the individual banks and the way each participated in the various programs for bank rescue. La Porta, López-de-Silanes, and Zamarripa (2002) provide a slightly different list.

banking reforms to the congress in March 1998. The package consisted of two elements. The first was a set of proposals to strengthen the regulation and supervision of the banking sector. In institutional terms, the package proposed to grant autonomy to the bank regulatory agency, the Banking and Securities Commission (CNBV, by its Spanish acronym), and to move it from the finance ministry to the Bank of Mexico. It further sought to dissolve Fobaproa and replace it with two new institutions to carry out its two functions: reselling the assets it had acquired and serving as the nation's deposit insurance agency. The operational changes included the following: (i) a new deposit insurance system, which would end the de facto unlimited deposit insurance that existed previously and increase the oversight of the deposit insurance agency; (ii) stricter accounting standards, which would increase the transparency of credit operations for both supervisors and the public, impose stricter standards for handling past-due loans, and substantially increase loan-loss provisions; (iii) measures to improve lending practices and new laws on credit transactions, aimed at speeding the process of asset foreclosure and broadening the range of property to be used as collateral; and (iv) stricter rules on quality of capital. To reduce possible future exchange rate mismatching, the Bank of Mexico lowered the existing ceilings on foreign currency liabilities and imposed compulsory liquidity coefficients in foreign currency.[15]

The second aspect of the Zedillo package was much more controversial. The president proposed to add the liabilities held by Fobaproa to Mexico's national debt. This move would effectively legalize the status quo, but it required the approval of the congress to change the general law on public debt. Opponents claimed that many of the loans turned over to Fobaproa represented poor business judgments and that some were fraudulent. They argued that it was inappropriate to force taxpayers to assume the cost—especially when they had already paid for the crisis with unemployment and lost income.[16]

Because of the controversy generated by this second proposal, it took many months to gain approval for the reform package as a whole. A compromise was reached at the end of 1998 after nine months of debate. No definitive solution was agreed on the debt nationalization; rather, the annual costs were to be included in each year's budget. Audits were to be carried out on the loans that were assumed by Fobaproa, and the loans were to be returned to the banks if it were determined that they had been improperly handled.[17] The bonds issued by

15. See Marcos Yacamán (2001) for details; also EIU (2001).

16. McQuerry (1999) argues that the situation was especially charged because it came at a time of political transition in Mexico. For the first time in decades, opposition parties in Congress were able to challenge the long-ruling Institutional Revolutionary Party (PRI) effectively.

17. An audit report was commissioned from a Canadian expert, Michael Mackey; see Mackey (1999). In mid-2004, an agreement was finally reached. The banks' current owners agreed to take back $826 million in bad loans and allow a limited audit of another $600 million. See Elizabeth Malkin, "Deal in Mexico Makes Four Banks Absorb Losses from Loans," *New York Times*, July 16, 2004.

Fobaproa were to be replaced by new ones that the banks would hold, remunerated at competitive interest rates, which many experts believe is one of the major causes of the financial sector's problems today. We discuss this issue at length below. Fobaproa was disbanded, as proposed, and replaced by a new deposit insurance agency (Ipab, by its Spanish acronym), but autonomy was not granted to CNBV, the regulatory agency, which continued to operate as a dependency of the finance ministry.

While these changes clearly improved the regulatory and supervisory capacity of the Mexican authorities, many problems remained. At the macroeconomic level, rule of law and contract enforcement were not widely accepted. At the microeconomic level, poor corporate governance continued to characterize both banks and nonfinancial corporations. Moreover, Mexico's regulators face a particular set of problems that have yet to be adequately addressed, either in the literature on banking or in practice. Five of the six largest banks and over 80 percent of bank assets are in the hands of giant foreign institutions. How does this affect the ability of local regulators and supervisors to act? Does it require close cooperation with the regulators in the banks' home countries? If so, how should this be carried out? If Mexican regulators are to take sole responsibility, how can they deal with institutions that are larger and more powerful than they are? These questions will require more consideration in the future.[18]

Beyond the Banking Sector

The financial liberalization process and the resulting crisis were mainly centered on the banking sector, but there were also implications for the capital markets. While the stock market goes back to the late nineteenth century, the modern version of the bond market dates to the introduction of short-term treasury bills (*cetes*) in 1978. The stock market took off with the financial reforms, and by 1993 it had reached the largest capitalization that it has ever attained (50 percent of GDP). The number of listed firms rose: an average of eighteen new public offerings were made each year between 1991 and 1994. The bond market, by contrast, languished, since many institutional requirements were still lacking. The crisis hit the capital markets hard, but the government soon began a multifaceted program to promote them.[19]

A key step was the pension reform law, which was passed in 1995 and began operation in 1997. Largely based on the Chilean reform, the law provided for fully funded pension accounts (*siefores*) to be managed by fund administrators (*afores*). The change greatly expanded the potential base of institutional investors. While the initial rules governing the *afores* required them to invest in government securities, a relaxation of these restrictions later allowed them to

18. Our interviews conducted at the Bank of Mexico indicate that the authorities are aware of this problem and are considering how to deal with it, but it is not a high priority.

19. For information on the capital markets before the crisis, see Martínez and Werner (2002).

move into corporate debt. Nonetheless, government paper still accounts for the vast majority of their assets. Legal initiatives also expanded the scope for the operation of mutual funds and stimulated the formation of rating agencies to evaluate potential issuers in the capital markets. The most recent changes, which took effect in January 2005, allowed Afores to invest up to 15 percent of their assets in Mexican and international equities.[20]

A second important step was the improvement of the legal framework within which the markets operate. As part of a large package of institutional reforms approved in April 2001, corporate governance was strengthened through the establishment of independent board members, auditing committees, protection of minority shareholders, and greater transparency in the corporate sector more generally. The government reforms were complemented by a private sector initiative to draw up a voluntary code of corporate best practices, which emphasizes improvements in corporations' administrative procedures and information transparency.[21] In 2005, the government proposed a new capital market law designed to tighten corporate governance further by increasing publicity for sanctions by regulators, extending the reach of insider trading rules, and changing the role of corporate boards. It would also expand the power of the Banking and Securities Commission and make it easier for medium-sized firms to list on the market. The reform, however, was delayed by opposition in the congress, although it is expected to be approved in 2006.[22]

Market regulation and supervision is headed by the ministry of finance, aided by three agencies of particular relevance for the securities markets—the Banking and Securities Commission, the Insurance Commission, and the Pension Funds Commission. The Mexican Stock Exchange is a self-regulating corporation, operating under a charter from the finance ministry and owned by local brokerage houses. While these agencies generally have a good reputation, they need more resources and autonomy, as well as greater coordination, if the markets are to develop more fully in the coming years.[23]

Changes in Structure

The most salient characteristic of Mexico's domestic financial sector in recent years has been its small size in relation to the magnitude of the country's economy. Debates as to whether the system is bank or market based stem not from the fact that the markets are large and strong, but from the fact that bank credit as a share of GDP is so small.[24] The stock and bond markets are weak in part

20. See Reynoso (2004) on the possible consequences of the new law.

21. The document can be found on the website of the Mexican Stock Exchange (www.bmv.com.mx).

22. See John Authers, "Lobbying Delays Mexico Securities Bill," *Financial Times*, June 20, 2005.

23. See, for example, IMF (2001); OECD (2002); Bank of Mexico (2003).

24. See discussion in Copelman (2000).

Figure 7-1. *Mexico: Composition of Financial Markets, 1990–2003*

Percent of GDP

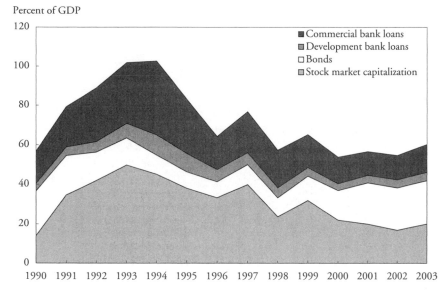

Sources: Tables 7-1 and 7-3.

because of the lack of institutional investors and an adequate legal framework. At the same time, Mexico is closely integrated into the U.S. financial markets, both for government agencies and large firms, making domestic markets somewhat redundant for these key borrowers. Figure 7-1 shows the relative shares of bank credit, bonds outstanding, and stock market capitalization and how these have varied since 1990.

The Banking Sector

The structure of the Mexican banking system changed in three crucial ways in the last quarter century: assets and loans increased and then shrank dramatically in both the 1980s and 1990s; control was passed from the state to private domestic owners and then to foreign banking institutions; and concentration among banks increased substantially although it was already very high. The three trends are intimately interrelated.

Table 7-1 shows the evolution of commercial and development bank loans and deposits in the 1980–2003 period. At the beginning of the 1980s, the commercial banks were private, domestically owned institutions; their loans were expanding, although from a low base. This trend reversed with the bank nationalization in late 1982: loans fell from 21 percent of GDP in 1982 to 15 percent in 1988. The trend reversed again as financial liberalization began, and loans reached a new peak (39 percent) in 1994 before the financial crisis. Since that time, the loan ratio has remained more or less constant, but at a rather low level in comparative terms. Moreover, even the current 34 percent figure is inflated

Table 7-1. *Mexico: Assets, Loans, and Deposits of the Banking System, 1980–2003*
Percent of GDP

Year	Commercial banks			Development banks			All banks		
	Total loans	Loans to private sector[a]	Deposits[b]	Total loans	Loans to private sector[a]	Deposits[b]	Total loans	Loans to private sector[a]	Deposits[b]
1980	17.6	16.2	23.8	13.4	4.1	2.9	31.0	20.3	26.7
1981	19.4	17.2	26.0	15.9	3.6	3.4	35.4	20.8	29.4
1982	21.3	13.7	24.9	26.3	3.0	2.8	47.5	16.7	27.7
1983	18.4	11.1	22.2	21.0	3.0	2.8	39.5	14.1	25.0
1984	19.2	12.2	22.8	18.8	3.3	2.9	38.0	15.5	25.7
1985	16.7	10.3	19.8	22.1	3.7	2.8	38.7	14.0	22.6
1986	22.2	10.2	21.0	31.5	4.3	2.9	53.7	14.5	24.0
1987	22.2	10.3	20.6	33.5	4.2	3.1	55.7	14.6	23.7
1988	15.1	8.4	5.8	18.1	3.6	2.2	33.3	12.0	8.0
1989	19.1	13.2	12.5	14.9	3.4	0.9	34.1	16.6	13.4
1990	21.9	16.3	18.1	11.6	3.7	1.2	33.5	20.1	19.3
1991	26.9	20.4	21.5	10.4	4.3	1.3	37.3	24.7	22.8
1992	29.8	27.3	23.7	10.8	5.3	1.2	40.6	32.6	24.9
1993	32.0	30.9	24.9	12.5	7.4	1.7	44.5	38.3	26.5
1994	39.2	37.6	26.5	18.5	10.2	2.0	57.8	47.8	28.5
1995	32.4	27.6	27.4	19.7	9.3	2.5	52.1	36.8	29.9
1996	24.9	16.7	25.5	14.2	6.3	2.8	39.1	23.0	28.2
1997	41.8	20.7	32.3	14.4	6.0	2.8	56.2	26.8	35.1
1998	39.4	19.0	30.9	13.2	5.1	2.6	52.6	24.1	33.5
1999	39.4	16.6	30.2	11.5	4.3	3.0	50.9	21.0	33.2
2000	34.4	13.4	23.6	9.7	3.4	2.4	44.2	16.9	26.0
2001	32.7	12.0	25.4	9.7	3.8	2.5	42.3	15.9	28.0
2002	32.7	12.3	25.4	11.0	4.1	3.0	43.7	16.3	28.4
2003[c]	34.0	14.0	25.7	11.4	4.2	2.3	45.4	18.2	28.0

Sources: IMF, *International Financial Statistics Yearbook* (2001, 2004).

a. Claims on private sector (IFS lines 22d, 22f, 22g for commercial banks; 42d, 42e, 42g for development banks); includes nonperforming loans, Fobaproa securities, and other items related to bank rescue programs.

b. Demand, time, savings, and foreign currency deposits (IFS lines 24–25 for commercial banks, 44–45 for development banks).

c. Estimate based on CNBV data.

by the inclusion of overdue loans, as well as a substantial volume of securities that are the counterpart of the nonperforming loans eliminated from the banks' balance sheets and other forms of debt restructuring. Loans to the private sector show the same pattern, but the shifts are of an even greater magnitude; private sector credit has fallen by almost two-thirds since the crisis, amounting to only 14 percent of GDP in 2003.

The sources of funding for commercial bank activities also changed over time. Demand and time deposits increased from 60 percent of liabilities in 1980 to 66 percent in 1995. By 2003, the situation had changed direction, and the deposit share had fallen to only 45 percent. This change was partially due to the diversification of financial instruments. For example, money market funds now account for 18 percent of bank funding. As with assets, however, it is difficult to get an accurate picture of bank liabilities because of the restructured items that were added to the balance sheets.

A group of government-owned development banks operates parallel to Mexico's commercial banks. During the 1980s, total loans of the development banks were as large as or sometimes larger than those of the commercial banks; their volume fluctuated according to government financial needs. Under the Salinas administration, however, they shrank in line with the new market-oriented philosophy. The crisis led to a brief recovery, but they soon began to fall again and currently total around 11 percent of GDP. The single most important source of funding for the development banks has been international credits, reflecting their continuing role in intermediating between international creditors, the government, and selected private borrowers.

While the combined loans of the commercial and development banks are currently 45 percent of GDP, loans to the private sector are only 18 percent; both figures include the remainder of the Fobaproa debt and other rescue operations. This figure is extraordinarily low in comparison with other Latin American countries, as well as those in other developing regions. For example, private sector credit in Chile is four times as high, and in East Asia it is six times as high. Moreover, as mentioned above, credit as a share of GDP has been falling in Mexico since the crisis.

Table 7-2 shows additional characteristics of the commercial banks as of 2003. A first message of the table is that the number of banks in Mexico is relatively low. It declined sharply in the years after the bank nationalization, falling from sixty in 1982 to only twenty in 1991, when the reprivatization began. The twenty included the eighteen institutions that survived the period of government control, plus two that had not been nationalized—Citibank, the only foreign-owned bank in the country, and Banco Obrero, affiliated with the trade unions. Shortly before the crisis, new banks were authorized to begin operations; this process continued for several years before consolidation was reinitiated, resulting in the current thirty commercial banks plus six development banks.[25]

More important than the declining number of banking institutions was the change in ownership. Not only did shifts occur between public and private owners of Mexican nationality, but bank ownership was opened to foreign institutions. Not since the 1880s had foreigners been allowed to own banks, except for representative offices that could not engage in retail operations.[26] Initially, the

---

25. Gruben and McComb (2003).

26. The exception was Citibank, which has been in Mexico since 1929. Since the bank had been helpful to the country in difficult periods, it was allowed special privileges unavailable to other institutions. See Stallings (1987).

Table 7-2. *Mexico: Characteristics of the Banking System, 2003*

Indicator	Domestic private banks		Foreign banks		Commercial banks		Development banks		Total banks	
	Absolute	*Percent*	*Absolute*	*Percent*	*Absolute*	*Percent*	*Absolute*	*Percent*	*Absolute*	*Percent*
No. of institutions	13	36.1	17	47.2	30	83.3	6	16.6	36	100
No. of employees	27,950	23.1	87,091	95.3	115,041	95.3	5,665	4.7	120,706	100
No. of branches	2,051	24.1	5,689	67.0	7,740	91.1	754	8.9	8,494	100
Total assets[a]	339	13.6	1,518	60.8	1,857	74.4	639	25.6	2,496	100
Total loans[a]	234	16.1	754	52.0	988	68.1	462	31.9	1,450	100
Loans/assets	69.0	n.a.	49.7	n.a.	53.2	n.a.	67.6	n.a.	58.1	n.a.
Nonperforming loans/ total loans[b,c]	5.7	n.a.	4.1	n.a.	4.4	n.a.	7.1	n.a.	5.1	n.a.
Return on equity[c]	−19.7	n.a.	11.3	n.a.	5.6	n.a.	−44.3	n.a.	−5.4	n.a.

Sources: Calculated from World Bank (2002) for nonperforming loans and return on equity; CNBV website (www.cnbv.gob.mx) for all other data.

n.a. Not available.

a. Assets and loans in billion of pesos (including Fobaproa/Ipab notes).

b. Declared nonperforming loans as share of loans outstanding (including Fobaproa/Ipab notes).

c. Bital is still included as a domestic bank. Data for 2002.

regulations exempted the three largest banks, but by 1997 they, too, could be acquired. Mexico's two NAFTA partners led the way as Citibank and Bank of Nova Scotia purchased two mid-sized institutions in 1996. At about the same time, the two largest Spanish banks—BBVA and Santander, which had already begun what would be a broad-based entry into Latin America—also entered the market. These initial investments accelerated over the next several years, as BBVA, Santander, and Citibank bought the three largest Mexican banks and HSBC acquired the fourth-ranking local institution. By the end of 2002, only one of the five largest commercial banks in the country remained in local hands. Foreigners owned over 80 percent of commercial bank assets—by far the largest share in any major Latin American country.

As would be expected, the concentration index increased as a result of the decline in the number of banks, but the more important factor was the particular pattern of mergers that added capacity to the banks already at the top of the league table. Thus, in 1997, before the foreign purchases began, the top five banks already represented 72 percent of total assets; this figure rose to 81 percent by 2003.[27]

Table 7-2 also provides data on the development banks. During most of the 1980–2003 period, there were six banks. By far the most important was Nafin, which was a crucial player in Mexico's postwar industrialization drive. About the size of the third-largest commercial bank in Mexico, it was the key intermediary in obtaining foreign exchange from international banks and on-lending it to several local clienteles: the Mexican government and state-owned firms, local financial institutions, and some private sector enterprises with good connections. In the new environment, it has been transformed into a second-tier bank with special responsibility for SMEs. Five other development banks carried out more specific mandates: Bancomext (foreign trade, especially export finance), Banobras (infrastructure), Banrural (agriculture), Fina (sugar), and Banejercito (banking services for military personnel).[28]

Table 7-2 reveals some important differences among the three types of banks. The first concerns the deployment of assets: foreign banks have been especially prone to curtail lending in comparison with either type of domestic bank; the counterpart is a greater share of assets dedicated to holding securities.[29] Second, the development banks are much leaner than either type of commercial bank. Productivity, as measured by the number of personnel and branches as a ratio to assets or loans, is high. This perhaps surprising finding stems from the fact that

27. Calculated from CNBV data. The 2003 figure considers Banco Serfín and Santander Mexicano to be a single institution, since they were already under the same ownership.

28. There are also a number of development trusts, whose functions overlap those of the development banks. They differ in their source of funding and the fact that the latter are regulated by CNBV, while the former are under the direct control of the ministry of finance.

29. See Haber and Musacchio (2005) for an econometric analysis, which demonstrates that foreign banks have a lower propensity to lend than do domestic banks. A similar trend is also found in Chile, although the loan-to-asset ratios are much higher for all banks in Chile than in Mexico.

the development banks now lack large retail operations as a result of their restructuring as second-tier institutions.[30] Third, the painful cleanup process after the 1994–95 crisis, encompassing both the restructuring and the entry of foreign institutions, returned the foreign and most of the domestic commercial banks to a healthy situation with respect to profits and nonperforming loans. The same cannot be said of the development banks, which suffered from their broad mandates and the need to cater to various government needs.

At the urging of the IMF and World Bank, the government recently launched a process of revamping the development banking system: closing some banks, adding others, and redesigning their mandates and methods of operation. The main problem is that the banks have been expected to follow two contradictory logics: a social logic and a profit-making one. The goal, then, is to separate the two, with the former served by development agencies that will be funded by the government budget in a transparent way. Fina and Banrural have been closed, but several new banks have been created. Bansefi supports the new Popular Savings Associations, geared to providing banking services to the low-income population; SHF is a second-tier bank that is supposed to help develop the mortgage market; and Financiera Rural will assume the banking and other functions of Banrural. The aim is not to remove the government from the financial sector, but to make it operate more efficiently and transparently. Public banks are also being encouraged to help develop markets in various sectors of the economy.[31]

Capital Markets

The capital markets in Mexico have never been very robust, although some analysts posit that they are on the verge of significant expansion and improvement in performance.[32] Table 7-3 shows the main components of the markets since the late 1980s. They include the outstanding value of government and corporate bonds and the capitalization of the Mexican Stock Exchange (BMV, by its Spanish acronym). The two markets displayed opposite trends in terms of size over the last two decades. Stock market capitalization rose steadily from 7 percent of GDP in 1986—as financial liberalization began—to a peak of 50 percent just before the crisis; it then plunged to only 20 percent at the end of the sample period. The volume of bonds outstanding was larger than stock market capitalization in the late 1980s (22 percent of GDP), but fell to only 8 percent by the mid-1990s. Bonds then underwent a slow recovery, coming to represent slightly over 20 percent of GDP in 2003. The stock and bond markets combined grew

30. Banrural, now closed, was the most bloated of the development banks, with over 25,000 employees, 500 branches, and responsibility for some 40 percent of finance in agriculture; see World Bank (2002).

31. For a general critique of the operation of the development banks, see OECD (2002) and World Bank (2002). The revamping of the system is being financed by World Bank loans.

32. Personal interviews with bankers and capital market officials in Mexico.

Table 7-3. *Mexico: Stock and Bond Markets, 1986–2003*
Percent of GDP

Year	Stock market[a]	Bonds[b]	Government	Corporate[c]	Total
1986	7.0	n.a.	n.a.	n.a.	n.a.
1987	9.5	n.a.	n.a.	n.a.	n.a.
1988	12.3	n.a.	n.a.	n.a.	n.a.
1989	11.8	22.4	21.2	1.2	34.2
1990	13.9	22.6	21.2	1.4	36.5
1991	34.6	20.0	17.9	2.1	54.6
1992	41.9	14.4	12.0	2.4	56.3
1993	49.7	13.8	11.1	2.7	63.5
1994	45.1	9.7	7.7	2.0	54.8
1995	38.0	8.4	6.3	2.2	46.4
1996	33.2	8.1	5.7	2.4	41.3
1997	39.8	10.2	8.1	2.1	50.0
1998	23.6	9.6	7.5	2.1	33.2
1999	31.8	12.3	10.2	2.1	44.1
2000	21.9	15.0	12.6	2.4	36.9
2001	19.9	20.8	18.2	2.6	40.7
2002	16.8	20.6	18.4	2.2	37.4
2003	20.0	23.6	20.9	2.7	43.6

Sources: Banco de México website (www.banxico.org.mx) for stock market; BIS website (www.bis.org/statistics/qcsv/anx16a.csv) for total and government bonds, (www.bis.org/statistics/qcsv/anx16b.csv) for corporate bonds.
   a. Market capitalization.
   b. Bonds outstanding.
   c. Corporate and financial sector bonds.

from the late 1980s to 1993; afterward they experienced a gradual, fluctuating decline. As of the end of 2003, the combined markets represented around 44 percent of GDP, again a very low figure in comparison with other emerging market economies.

The Mexican Stock Exchange saw its nominal capitalization in pesos rise spectacularly after 1990: a more than twentyfold increase occurred from January 1990 through December 2003. The vast majority of the increase, however, came from price rises in the secondary market, rather than new issues in the primary market. Deflating by the stock market price index shows real growth from 1990 through 1994 (76 percent), but a contraction thereafter (–42 percent). Indeed, the real value of market capitalization at the end of 2003 was almost exactly the same as it was at the end of 1990. In nominal dollar terms, as shown in table 7-4, the market more than tripled in value (although the majority of the increase came in 1990–91). New issues dropped off, however, both in number and in value. The stock market's relative lack of importance is reflected in the low level of participation. Only 159 firms were listed on the BMV at the end of 2003, down from over 200 just before the crisis. Not surprisingly given the

Table 7-4. *Mexico: Characteristics of Stock and Bond Markets, 1990–2003*

	Stock market					Corporate bonds	
Year	Market capitalization[a]	Turnover ratio[b]	No. of listed firms	No. of new issues	Value of new issues[a]	Amount outstanding[a]	No. of issuers
1990	32.7	44	199	11	0.14	3.5	n.a.
1991	98.2	48	209	24	0.87	5.3	n.a.
1992	139.1	37	195	17	0.19	7.7	n.a.
1993	200.7	37	190	19	4.50	9.6	n.a.
1994	130.2	45	206	24	1.79	5.3	n.a.
1995	90.7	33	185	1	0.01	3.0	n.a.
1996	106.5	43	193	14	0.79	2.6	n.a.
1997	156.6	43	198	18	1.33	4.4	15
1998	91.7	29	194	0	0.01	5.3	19
1999	154.0	29	188	4	0.44	5.5	30
2000	125.2	32	179	4	0.10	8.2	67
2001	126.3	32	168	4	n.a.	10.2	66
2002	103.1	24	166	6	n.a.	9.3	70
2003	122.5	20	159	5	0.03	12.9	82

Sources: Standard and Poor's (2000, 2005) for stock market capitalization, turnover ratio, and number of listed firms; BIS website (www.bis.org/statistics/qcsv/anx16b.csv) for amount outstanding of corporate bonds; Bank of México (2001, 2003) for number of new stock issues and number of bond issuers; BMV, *Anuario Bursátil* (various years) for value of new stock issues.

n.a. Not available.

a. Billions of dollars.

b. Amount traded as a share of market capitalization (percent).

characteristics of the market, there is little liquidity. The turnover ratio (value traded as a share of capitalization) averaged about 30 percent in recent years, well below international averages.

The bond market has been and remains dominated by government debt. At the end of 2003, only about 11 percent of the market consisted of private sector paper—not much different from the early 1990s, although the absolute volume increased significantly in the last few years of the period. The main issuers are the central government, state and local governments, and the remaining public sector enterprises. Within the private sector, the banks have been the major participants. Only eighty-two private firms—financial and nonfinancial—issued debt in 2003. The instrument of choice was a new medium-term bond (*certificado bursátil*) that has breathed some new life into the market.[33] Liquidity is low in the long-term segment, especially the private segment. There is virtually no secondary market for corporate debt, which means that investors who want to get out of the market must find their own buyers.[34]

A brief comparison of the Mexican experience with the relatively successful history of the Chilean capital markets reveals two important differences in the

33. Bank of Mexico (2003).
34. Navarrete (2001).

Table 7-5. *Mexico: Size and Allocation of Pension Fund Portfolios, 1998–2003*

Year	Total[a]	Percent of GDP	Investment allocation (percent)				
			Government[b]	Corporate[c]	Banks[d]	Other[e]	Total
1998	5.7	1.5	96.8	3.1	0.2	0.0	100
1999	11.4	2.4	97.4	2.5	0.1	0.0	100
2000	17.1	3.0	91.1	5.4	2.0	1.5	100
2001	27.1	4.3	87.8	7.8	2.4	2.0	100
2002	31.4	5.3	83.1	12.3	2.1	2.4	100
2003	35.7	6.2	82.3	11.0	4.5	2.2	100

Source: CONSAR website (www.consar.gob.mx).

a. Obligatory and voluntary contribution to retirement funds managed by Afores; billions of dollars.

b. Government notes and bonds.

c. Corporate bonds.

d. Financial sector paper.

e. Repurchase agreements (repos) and municipal/state securities.

domestic environment in Mexico. The first is the lack of government effort to develop the markets, which seems to have become a priority only in the last few years. While admitting that there is a long way to go, the central bank emphasizes new steps to provide proper macroeconomic and legal frameworks to encourage capital markets. Most important for the former is a low single-digit inflation rate, while the latter includes better regulation, greater transparency, and the modernization of financial infrastructure. The government has also been trying to increase private access to the bond market by creating a long-term yield curve, equalizing tax treatment, and reducing bureaucratic requirements.[35]

The second distinction with respect to Chile is the relative lack of institutional investors in Mexico. Securities are generally held by a small number of commercial banks, rather than individuals or institutional investors, although this factor is also changing. As noted earlier, Mexico has a new private pension system that went into effect in 1997. The individual accounts are managed by a small number of fund administrators (Afores). Table 7-5 indicates that the Afores grew rapidly, increasing from 1.5 percent of GDP in 1998 to 6.2 percent in 2003. At the end of the period, they held about 22 percent of all government debt and 27 percent of private debt.[36] While they have slowly been shifting away from investment in government paper, such holdings still accounted for over 80 percent of total pension fund assets in 2003. The restrictions on the holding of private sector assets have now been eliminated, but such holdings must be investment grade, and only a small number of Mexican firms are so rated. Nonetheless, the presence and strong growth of the pension funds and other institutional investors (such as insurance companies and mutual funds) prompts

35. Bank of Mexico (2002, 2003).

36. Bank of Mexico (2003).

Table 7-6. *Mexico: International Finance, 1990–2003*
Percent of GDP

Year	Banks[a]	Bonds[b]	ADRs[c]	Stock market[d]	Total
1990	19.6	2.2	0.8	0.8	23.4
1991	18.1	2.7	4.4	1.5	26.7
1992	15.4	3.5	5.8	2.1	26.8
1993	15.1	6.1	8.4	5.1	34.8
1994	15.8	7.4	5.0	3.1	31.3
1995	21.5	10.2	5.3	3.2	40.3
1996	20.5	12.6	4.5	4.8	42.4
1997	20.9	12.3	5.8	6.5	45.5
1998	20.5	12.6	4.4	3.5	41.0
1999	18.2	13.0	8.6	5.2	45.0
2000	24.8	11.4	5.5	3.4	45.1
2001	34.6	10.5	5.4	3.4	53.9
2002	33.2	10.1	4.3	2.6	50.3
2003	34.0	11.8	5.5	3.5	54.8

Sources: BIS website (www.bis.org/statistics/qcsv/anx12a.csv) for bank loans, (www.bis.org/statistics/hcsv/hanx9a_for.csv) for bonds; BMV website (www.bmv.com.mx) for ADRs and stock market investment.
a. Loans from international banks.
b. Outstanding bonds and notes issued in international markets.
c. American depository receipts.
d. Investment in Mexican Stock Exchange by foreigners.

analysts, the government, and the private sector to expect better performance by the capital markets in coming years.[37]

International Finance

Because of its geographical proximity to the United States, Mexico has a much longer and deeper relationship to international financial markets (especially U.S. markets) than its counterparts in South America. Several channels are relevant: international bank loans, international bond issues, American depository receipts (ADRs), and foreign investment in the Mexican stock market. The number of borrowers with access to these sources is extremely small, however, being limited to the central and local governments, the remaining state-owned enterprises, and a small number of large private sector firms.

Although data are hard to obtain and to put into a comparable format, table 7-6 provides a rough idea of the relative magnitudes of the four sources in terms of amounts outstanding. The most important message from the table is that international finance for Mexican borrowers with access followed a very differ-

37. Mutual funds are slightly larger than pension funds in Mexico, while they are much smaller in Chile. The difference is important because pension funds tend to create liquidity problems with their buy-and-hold strategies, whereas mutual funds trade more actively.

ent trajectory than domestic loans, bonds, or stock market capitalization. While domestic sources peaked just preceding the crisis and stagnated or declined thereafter, international finance increased on a relatively continuous basis from 1990 to 2003; the nominal dollar value rose by over 5.5 times in the same period.

At the beginning of the 1990s, the largest source of foreign financial investment was long-term loans from international banks. Although negatively affected by the 1980s debt crisis in Mexico and elsewhere in Latin America, international loans nonetheless amounted to around $50 billion (20 percent of GDP) in 1990. By contrast, international bond issues were only $6 billion, while ADRs and foreign investment in the local stock market were about $2 billion each. In total, international finance amounted to 23 percent of GDP in 1990.

This share increased steadily until 1993, but it fell somewhat as the crisis struck. Unlike domestic finance, however, international finance exceeded its previous peak in 1995 and continued advancing. Mexico's investors were affected by the climate in 1998, as stock market prices plunged around the globe. Nonetheless, by 2003, international finance as a share of GDP stood at 55 percent, its highest level ever. The weight of bank loans in total international finance has declined, but they remain the dominant source, accounting for 34 percent of GDP, followed by bonds with 12 percent, ADRs with 5 percent, and stock market investment with 3 percent. The latter two components fluctuate substantially, while the former are more stable.

When we consider Mexico's combined financial structure—as represented by domestic bank credit, domestic capital markets, and international finance—the third component stands out as unusually important in comparison with other Latin American countries. In addition, international finance has been the most dynamic type of finance, together with domestic bonds. We discuss the implications of this pattern for growth and equality in the next two sections.

Finance, Investment, and Growth

To understand the relationship between finance and growth in recent times in Mexico requires two separate logics. In the first half of the 1990s, the close positive relationship portrayed in most of the literature held true in the Mexican case, as domestic finance and the economy expanded simultaneously. In the second half of the decade, by contrast, GDP growth rates were among the highest in Latin America, but traditional sources of finance contracted year after year. After 2000, the earlier relationship reappeared in a negative way: as the economy stagnated, credit was not made available to support a recovery.

We are particularly concerned in this book about investment as a key component of economic growth and the role of the formal financial system in providing firms with the necessary financial resources. As discussed in the previous section, Mexico in recent decades had three main sources of corporate finance external to the firms themselves: the private and public banking system, the domestic capital markets, and international finance. Table 7-7 provides an overview of the shifts that have taken place in their relative importance. At the end of the financial boom in 1994, domestic commercial banks and the stock market were the dominant sources; international finance accounted for less than 15 percent of total corporate finance. Eight years later, the picture had changed significantly. As domestic sources shrank, international finance came to represent nearly 35 percent of the total.[38] Since relatively few large firms have access to international finance, this pattern has major implications for the growth of smaller enterprises.

Bank Credit

Bank credit has traditionally been the dominant source of finance in Mexico as in the rest of Latin America, so we begin there. Figure 7-2 plots the relationship between GDP growth, investment, and bank credit from both commercial and development banks between 1991 and 2003. The subperiods mentioned above can be identified. From 1991 through 1995, all three variables rose in a synchronized way. In the second half of the decade, a substantial gap opened up between credit and investment. After 2000, the link became closer again.

To go beyond this description, we need to refine the indicator used for domestic credit. Two main clarifications are important. First, while the public sector did not borrow much from the commercial banks in the early 1990s—as budget deficits were slashed and state-owned enterprises were sold—such borrowing increased after 1995. Most of the new credit went to the central government. In addition to the increase in commercial bank credit, the large majority of development bank credit continued to go to the public sector. Second, from 1995 on and especially after 1997, large additional items began to inflate the balance sheets of the commercial banks. These involved the complicated handling of the rescue programs for the banks and their customers. Each of the four programs developed to help the banks—the short-term liquidity facility, capitalization funds, swaps for nonperforming loans, and subsidies for debtors—led to increases in bank assets and liabilities. While some were originally recorded off the books, in 1997 new accounting rules required them to be incorporated. This explains the large jump in "credit" in that year, as shown in figure 7-2.[39]

Figure 7-3, then, reveals the underlying relationship between investment and credit to the private sector from the commercial banks by eliminating both public sector loans and the counterpart items related to the rescue packages. With these simplifications, we find credit growing more rapidly than investment in

38. Comparable figures for Brazil and Chile are 12 percent and 16 percent, respectively.

39. Haber (2005) provides an excellent discussion of the accounting issues. A crucial point is that Fobaproa/Ipab bonds are included as part of banks' credit portfolios, since they are the counterpart of loans passed to the deposit insurance agency.

Table 7-7. *Mexico: Finance for the Corporate Sector, 1994–2002*
Percent of GDP

Year	Domestic banks[a]		Domestic capital markets[b]		International finance[c]			Total
	Commercial	Development	Stock market	Bonds	Loans	Bonds	Equity	
1994	30.8	3.7	45.1	2.0	5.4	3.3	5.0	95.3
1995	20.9	3.5	38.0	2.2	7.8	4.4	5.3	82.1
1996	14.6	3.8	33.2	2.4	7.9	3.7	4.5	70.1
1997	12.1	3.0	39.8	2.1	7.3	4.2	5.8	74.5
1998	11.3	2.9	23.6	2.1	8.2	4.8	4.4	57.3
1999	9.3	3.0	31.8	2.1	7.5	4.6	8.6	66.9
2000	8.5	1.7	21.9	2.4	6.6	3.8	5.5	50.4
2001	7.4	1.7	19.9	2.6	7.5	3.7	5.4	48.2
2002	7.4	1.9	16.8	2.2	7.1	3.1	4.3	42.8

Sources: World Bank (2002) for domestic banks; table 7-3 for domestic capital markets; BIS website (www.bis.org/statistics/hcsv/hanx9a_priv.csv) for international bank loans, (www.bis.org/statistics/qcsv/anx12c.csv) for international bonds; table 7-6 for international equity (ADRs only).

a. Direct lending to corporate sector (excluding nonperforming loans and Fobaproa/Ipab notes) by commercial and development banks.

b. Capitalization of Mexican Stock Exchange and corporate bonds outstanding.

c. International bank loans to nonbank private sector, corporate bonds outstanding, and ADRs.

Figure 7-2. *Mexico: Growth Rates of GDP, Investment, and Total Credit, 1991–2003*[a]

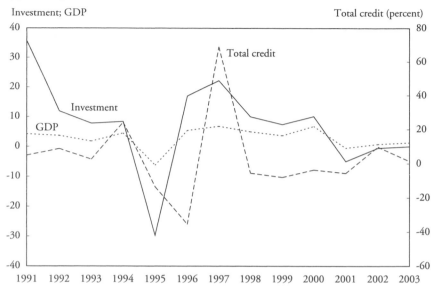

Sources: ECLAC website (www.eclac.cl) for GDP and investment; IMF, *International Financial Statistics Yearbook* (2000 and 2004) for total credit.

a. Total credit includes credit to government and private sector, nonperforming loans, Fobaproa/Ipab notes.

the early 1990s, but contracting from 1995 through 2000, despite the continuing growth in investment. From 2001, both variables tended to stagnate.

All three of the subperiods shown in figures 7-2 and 7-3 represent problematic relationships between credit and investment, although the nature of the problems changed over time. The simultaneous expansion of credit and investment in 1990–94—typical of the postliberalization credit booms in most countries—was faster than the banks (and probably the owners of the firms doing the investment) could manage. Annual rates of increase on the order of 20–30 percent precluded adequate credit analysis, especially by institutions with little experience in this activity; nonperforming assets rose rapidly as a result. An important reason for the expansion was that the new owners had to increase their revenues to compensate for the very high prices they had paid for the banks in the reprivatization process. Ex post analysis indicates that the banking system was in serious trouble well before the devaluation of December 1994. The latter was merely the detonator of the crisis.[40]

The situation changed dramatically in 1995–2000. Bank credit began to contract, making an ever smaller contribution to the financing of still-buoyant investment. This new phase was clearly related to the crisis and its aftermath,

40. Haber (2005).

Figure 7-3. *Mexico: Growth Rates of Investment and Credit to the Private Sector,
1992–2003*[a]

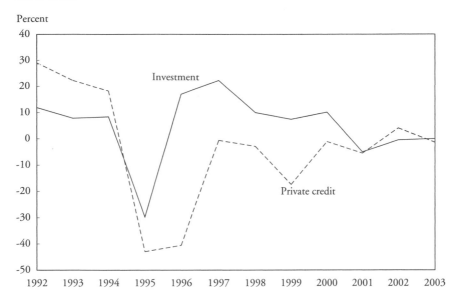

Percent

Sources: ECLAC website (www.eclac.cl) for investment; Haber (2005) for credit to private sector.
a. Credit to private sector excludes nonperforming loans and Fobaproa/Ipab notes.

but at least three hypotheses have been suggested to explain the negative correlation. Although frequently presented as mutually exclusive, they are actually complementary. A first hypothesis is that the banks were so undercapitalized that they could not make new loans; rather, they had to reduce assets to restore their capital ratios, especially since they faced stringent new regulatory requirements.[41] This explanation was undoubtedly true in the immediate aftermath of the crisis, and one of the government programs to aid the banks was focused precisely on recapitalization. Later, however, capital adequacy was no longer a significant issue for most banks, especially after the foreign banks entered the market.

A second hypothesis concerns the defective legal framework within which the banks operate. In general, the legal system has been weak in enforcing contracts. In particular, the difficulty in repossessing collateral when a borrower cannot or will not service its loans makes the banks reluctant to lend. While these problems have always existed in Mexico, they became more serious after the crisis since prime borrowers shifted to the international capital markets, and those seeking loans domestically presented a more risky profile than they had earlier on.[42] The authorities also recognized this second problem, and a new bankruptcy law was

41. Thorne (1998).
42. Krueger and Tornell (1999). The banks themselves emphasize this explanation.

approved in April 2000, but it only partially resolved the underlying issues. The more general problem is one of contract enforcement, which may account for the fact that consumer lending—where enforcement is relatively easy—is the main area where credit has increased.[43]

The third hypothesis is a Mexican variant of a more general problem in emerging market economies: the crowding out of private firms by the public sector. While crowding out is usually thought of as a flow problem—in which governments absorb most of the available credit in any given period—the Mexican case involved crowding out based on the stock of assets. The mechanism by which the nonperforming loans were removed from the banks' books left them with competitively remunerated assets that tempered the need to deal with the costs and risks of making loans. Indeed, the Mexican banks have become quite profitable, despite their lack of lending.[44] In the more traditional sense of crowding out, government debt with relatively high interest rates floods the market, despite low deficits, because authorities are trying to replace external debt by internal debt.[45] Holding government securities, together with charging high fees for financial services, continues to dampen enthusiasm for lending.

The most recent period for which we have complete data—2001 to 2003—witnessed the stagnation of GDP, investment, and credit. The decline in growth rates was largely due to the recession in the United States, which buys some 90 percent of Mexican exports and which had provided the basis for the rapid post-crisis recovery. The lack of credit, however, eliminated the possibility of an off-setting increase in the domestic economy. The issue became much more urgent when growth began to pick up in 2004–05. While credit started to recover in 2004, it was mainly to finance consumption. Commercial lending remains far below its earlier levels.[46]

In addition to these structural arguments about why credit is so low, other relevant factors include interest rates, spreads, and profitability. In our analysis of Chile, these links were positive: lending and profitability grew while interest rates and spreads were low or falling. Competition was an important factor, since it promoted increased bank efficiency and enabled the virtuous circle to continue. In Mexico, this set of relationships has been much more complex and problematic.

We have already described how lending did not increase continuously as it did in Chile; rather, it rose initially and then fell. Table 7-8 shows the relation-

43. Haber and colleagues have produced several papers analyzing the impact of poor contract enforcement; see Haber (2004, 2005); Haber and Musacchio (2005).

44. See González-Anaya (2003) for an elaboration of this hypothesis and a critique of the other two.

45. John Authers, "Staying the Course." *Latin Finance*, September 2004, p. 74.

46. Mexico's president, central bank governor, and other officials have been highly critical of the banks' failure to lend; see Jennifer Galloway, "Another Wake Up Call," *Latin Finance*, April–May 2004, pp. 30–32.

Table 7-8. *Mexico: Performance Indicators for Commercial Banks, 1990–2003*

Year	Loans ratio[a]	Nominal loan rate[b]	Real loan rate[c]	Spread[d]	Efficiency ratio[e]	Return on equity[f]	Non-performing loans[g]
1990	n.a.	42.4	15.3	5.3	n.a.	n.a.	2.3
1991	20.0	28.6	5.3	6.0	n.a.	n.a.	4.1
1992	24.0	23.9	8.5	5.1	n.a.	n.a.	5.7
1993	28.0	22.0	12.2	3.4	n.a.	n.a.	7.4
1994	30.0	20.4	13.4	4.9	n.a.	n.a.	7.4
1995	24.0	58.6	23.6	13.5	n.a.	n.a.	7.7
1996	16.0	36.9	2.4	6.2	n.a.	n.a.	7.8
1997	8.0	24.6	4.0	5.5	n.a.	n.a.	11.3
1998	8.0	28.7	12.8	7.6	64.0	25.6	11.3
1999	6.0	25.9	9.3	6.2	83.2	10.9	8.9
2000	7.0	18.2	8.7	4.5	85.6	6.8	5.8
2001	7.0	13.9	7.5	3.8	64.0	8.6	5.1
2002	7.0	9.4	4.4	4.0	87.0	−10.2	4.6
2003	8.0	6.9	2.4	1.8	74.2	14.2	3.2

Sources: Haber (2005) for loans ratio; IMF, *International Financial Statistics Yearbook* (2004) for loan rate, deposit rate, and CPI; CNBV website (www.cnbv.gob.mx) for nonperforming loans, efficiency ratio, and return on equity.

n.a. Not available.

a. Loans to private sector as share of GDP; excludes nonperforming loans and restructuring credits.

b. Rate for loans to medium-sized firms; this is proxied for 1990–92 by money market rate plus 5 percentage points (average premium).

c. Deflated by consumer price index.

d. Difference between nominal loan rate and deposit rate.

e. Operating expenses as a share of gross operational margin.

f. Profits as a share of equity.

g. Officially declared nonperforming loans as share of total loans outstanding.

ship between lending and other variables. Nominal interest rates fell in the early 1990s, perhaps stimulating demand for credit. After spiking in 1995 because of the crisis, however, they also generally fell in the period of credit contraction. Real rates did not show a clear trend earlier, but they too have been falling after a temporary increase during the worldwide crisis of 1998. Spreads ranged from 4 to 8 percent during the period since 1990 (with the exception of a spike in 1995), and they recently fell to a new low of only 2 percent. Profits became negative in the immediate aftermath of the crisis, but then increased substantially—although in a volatile fashion. A review of the data in table 7-8 thus highlights several variables that might have predicted an increase in credit in the late 1990s and early 2000s, but this did not occur, in part for the reasons discussed earlier. In addition, however, neither competition nor efficiency rose in the recent period; their absence may be another explanation for the lack of lending.

Figure 7-4. *Mexico: Composition of Commercial and Development Bank Loans, 1994 and 2002*

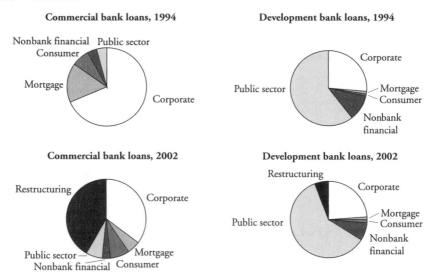

Source: CNBV website (www.cnbv.gob.mx).

Although credit contracted in the aggregate, some credit was provided, and its allocation is central for understanding the process. Figure 7-4 compares the composition of the performing loan portfolios of the commercial and development banks in 1994 and 2002. For the commercial banks, the most dramatic change was the increase in restructuring credits at the clear expense of corporate loans (which fell from 69 to 35 percent of total finance) and housing finance (from 16 to 5 percent). Consumer credit accounted for about the same share in the two years (7–8 percent), but the 2002 figure actually represented a substantial increase from a low of less than 3 percent in 1997–99. Indeed, the upswing in credit shown in figure 7-3 was almost entirely explained by increased consumer credit. Public sector loans also rose slightly in the aftermath of the crisis (from 4 to 7 percent). Development banks, by contrast, saw very little change in their portfolios. The public sector continued to receive the majority of credit (around 60 percent), while corporate borrowers accounted for the next largest share (around 25 percent), and the remaining 15 percent was allocated to smaller users. The loan restructuring of the development banks was less transparent than that of commercial banks, being implemented off the books. Thus only a small share of their portfolios appears as restructured credits.[47]

47. An institution similar to Fobaproa was created to handle nonperforming loans in the development banks (Fideliq, in Spanish). Fideliq exchanged nonperforming loans for promissory notes, but the treasury was more directly liable since the government guaranteed development bank loans. Fideliq was unable to recover much from the nonperforming loans and was paying high rates of interest on them, so in late 2000 the government paid off many of the notes held by the banks.

Table 7-9. *Mexico: Credit as a Share of GDP, by Sector, 1990–2003*

Sector	Average 1990–94[a]	Average 1996–2000[a]	Average 2001–03[a]	Average 1990–2003[a]	Sectoral growth rate 1990–2003
Agriculture	50.8	35.4	16.6	38.5	–0.8
Mining	27.6	11.4	6.5	16.4	–0.5
Manufacturing	37.1	25.2	15.0	28.5	1.8
Electricity and gas	28.1	27.2	46.5	32.1	3.5
Construction	53.3	52.5	11.5	47.2	6.2
Commerce	29.9	16.9	7.1	21.1	1.8
Other services	39.9	21.4	13.2	27.7	5.9
Total	37.9	23.5	12.7	27.8	3.4

Source: ECLAC (unpublished data).

a. Credit to a sector from commercial and development banks, divided by GDP in that sector.

Finally, disaggregating the corporate sector loans may provide additional insights into the relationship between growth and credit. As table 7-9 demonstrates, sectoral trends with respect to credit generally followed those for the economy as a whole: highest across the board in the early 1990s, falling in the second half of the decade, and reaching the lowest levels after 2000. With one exception, every sector's credit-to-GDP ratio fell by large amounts. The exception was electricity and gas, which maintained its credit ratio in the first two periods and saw a big increase in the third. The explanation most probably lies in the ownership characteristics of the sector: some of the most important firms that remain under government ownership are in gas and electricity.

Table 7-9 also presents sectoral growth rates, but they show no close relationship with the credit-to-GDP ratios. Whether levels or growth rates of credit are more likely to affect sectoral growth rates is an empirical question. Growth rates of credit did seem to have some correlation with sectoral growth rates in the early 1990s. For example, agriculture and industry had lower growth rates of both credit and output, while construction and the services were higher with respect to both. During the period when credit was falling, it is hard to identify any relationships, nor is it clear whether credit falling at a slower rate in one sector than another has the same effect as credit growing faster.

Capital Markets and International Finance

In principle, bank credit is available to all kinds of borrowers (large firms, small firms, exporters, importers, consumers, mortgage holders, and so on), but the capital markets and international finance are the purview of a select few. This situation is not unique to Mexico, although the latter group may be especially small in relative terms in the Mexican case. Despite the small number of borrowers with access to the capital markets and international finance, these sources help to explain the unusual pattern found in the second half of the 1990s—

Figure 7-5. *Mexico: Growth Rates of Investment, Stocks, and Bonds, 1990–2003*[a]

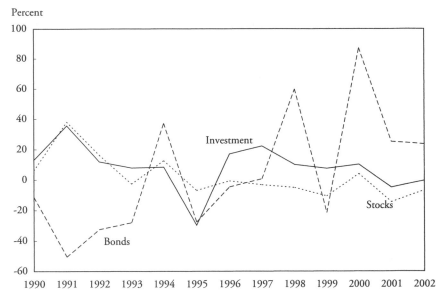

Sources: ECLAC website (www.eclac.cl) for investment; BIS website (www.bis.org) for bonds; Bank of Mexico website (www.banxico.org.mx) for stocks and deflator.

a. Stock market capitalization and total bonds outstanding, deflated by stock market price index.

buoyant investment and GDP growth, together with rapidly shrinking bank credit for the private sector.[48]

Figure 7-5 plots real growth rates of investment against growth of finance from the domestic capital markets, showing bonds and stocks separately. Stock market capitalization—when stripped of the value added by price increases—is fairly closely correlated with investment.[49] The now-expected pattern of finance exceeding investment before the crisis and trailing afterward continues, but it is not as pronounced as with bank credit. The relationship between bonds and investment, by contrast, was quite different. Here, for the first time, we find a finance source lagging in the early part of the decade and rising in the later part. The reason is not hard to discover: the vast majority of long-term bonds were issued by the public sector, especially the central government. Consequently, this type of finance was more closely linked to the public sector borrowing requirement than to investment. As mentioned, the budget was in surplus in the early 1990s, but fell into deficit after the crisis.

48. The role of nonbank finance was very significant for smaller firms. We discuss this source of credit in the next section.

49. This conclusion is similar to that of Gallego and Loayza (2001) in their analysis of Chile. They find no relationship between growth (in that case, of revenues of large firms) and stock market capitalization unless the portion explained by price increases is eliminated.

A more precise way of analyzing the link between investment and the capital markets is to focus on the primary markets, that is, the contribution of new issues of debt and equity. The pattern is similar to that of bank finance: high growth in the early 1990s was followed by a sharp falloff. In the case of the markets, the peak came in 1993, when they contributed 2.5 percent of GDP. The average contribution thereafter was nearer to 0.5 percent through 2000.[50] In other words, the capital markets have been an extremely small source of new finance, even compared with the poor performance of the banks. Between 1998 and 2003, there were twenty-one new public offerings on the Mexican Stock Exchange (BMV), or an average of three and a half per year. This compares with 128 new offerings between 1990 and 1997, or an average of sixteen per year. The long-term debt market has been more active. While the main participants have been public sector actors—namely, states, municipalities, the remaining public sector enterprises, and the central government—corporate issues have become more dynamic in the last few years (see table 7-4). Between shares and bonds, the contribution of the capital markets is now around 1.5 percent of GDP, still below its precrisis peak.[51]

The sectoral composition of the firms with shares listed on the stock exchange was quite different than those relying on bank credit, although comparisons are complicated because of the different categories in which data are available in the two cases. As of year-end 2003, the largest share of stock market capitalization was in the communications and transportation area, which accounted for 36 percent of the total. In descending order, the others were commerce (17 percent), manufacturing (14 percent), construction (12 percent), other services (11 percent), "other" (7 percent), and extractive industries (3 percent). This pattern has changed dramatically in the last two decades. In 1986, for example, manufacturing represented by far the largest share (nearly 39 percent), while communications and transportation played a minuscule role (less than 3 percent). Commerce has increased its share, while the others have declined in importance.[52]

Trying to correlate these data with sectoral growth produces only a few clear links. Transportation and communications was the largest beneficiary of the stock market, and it was the fastest-growing sector until the recent slowdown. At the other extreme, agriculture was the laggard in growth and has had little or no access to the stock market (there may be some agricultural finance included in "other"). In between, the situation is more difficult to disentangle. Manufacturing is the most problematic sector on this dimension. While its growth rate has been strong in relative terms, especially since the crisis, it is one of the few cases in which market capitalization as a share of GDP was lower in 2003 than in 1990. This is probably because the *maquila* (assembly) plants, the fastest

---

50. BMV (2003) and website (www.bmv.com.mx).
51. BMV (2003) and website (www.bmv.com.mx).
52. Bank of Mexico website (www.banxico.org.mx).

growing part of the manufacturing sector, get most of their finance through intrafirm channels.

The relationship between the domestic capital markets and international finance is a close one, with many areas of overlap. One such area is foreign investment in Mexican firms. The BMV reports that 43 percent of market capitalization was held by foreigners at the end of 2003, although less than 10 percent of bonds were foreign owned.[53] Other foreign investment sources include international bank loans, international bond issues, and participation in international equity markets through the placement of ADRs. Figure 7-6 provides relevant data for assessing how international finance correlates with investment in Mexico. This is by far the closest relationship we have found. Investment and international finance track each other with few deviations throughout the period—in the buoyant years of the early 1990s, the crash in 1995, the recovery in the late 1990s, and the lagging performance in the last few years of the period. The graph provides a clear demonstration of the role of the small group of large corporations who do the majority of the investing in Mexico and obtain a substantial amount of their finance from international markets.

While complete data are not available on recipients of international finance, we do have some information on bond issues and ADRs.[54] Of the 36 percent of Mexico's international bonds that were issued by private sector firms, nearly half were in the telecoms sector. Manufacturing (especially construction materials) accounted for a similar share, and services for the remainder. With respect to ADRs, the telecommunications and broadcasting industries were even more dominant, representing 70 percent of the total. Construction and commerce also participated, as did manufacturing and services. Although partial, this information suggests additional reasons for the communications and transportation sectors' leading economic growth in Mexico. The ADRs were also concentrated in terms of number of firms with access. A mere thirty-seven firms were responsible for Mexico's forty-eight main public offerings in the U.S. market between 1990 and 2003. Moreover, two firms (Telmex and Grupo Televisa) represented 62 percent. This finding leads directly to the issue of access to finance, the topic of the next section.

Access to Finance for Small Firms

A number of the points already made about market segmentation in Mexico have implications for unequal access to finance between large firms and their small and medium-sized counterparts (SMEs). To address this question further, we analyze a unique data set on sources of finance by size of firm, based on a quarterly survey carried out by the Bank of Mexico since 1998. Next, we exam-

---

53. BMV (2002) and personal interviews at the BMV. This percentage is two to three times the amount held by foreigners in the Brazilian and Chilean stock markets; see chapters 6 and 8.

54. ADR information is from the Universal Issuance Guide on the Citibank website (wwss.citissb.com/adr/www/brokers/mn_uni.htm).

Figure 7-6. *Mexico: Growth Rates of Investment and International Finance, 1991–2003*

Percent

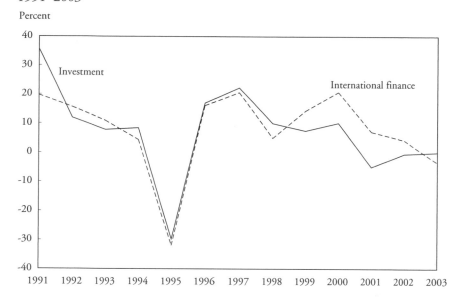

Sources: ECLAC website (www.eclac.cl) for investment; BIS website (www.bis.org), Standard and Poor's (2000, 2005), IMF (unpublished) for international finance.

ine the scope of finance from nonbank sources, which have become increasingly important in Mexico in the past decade as banks have curtailed credit. Finally, we consider attempts by the government itself to support SMEs and assess their potential to narrow the gap between large and small firms.

The starting point for understanding differential access to finance in Mexico is the small number of world-class firms that stand apart from all others—not only small and medium-sized firms, but other large firms, as well. For example, of the fifty largest locally owned private firms in Latin America, twenty-nine are from Mexico (versus sixteen from Brazil and three from Chile); their average sales in 2003 were over $7 billion. Likewise, seven of the top ten multinational operations in Latin America are located in Mexico, as are six of the ten largest state-owned enterprises.[55] Leaving aside ownership characteristics, 116 of the 200 firms in Latin America with sales over $1 billion are from Mexico.[56]

The Bank of Mexico survey recognizes this situation when it divides firms into four categories: small, medium, large, and AAA.[57] Table 7-10 compares the

55. "Las mayores empresas de América Latina en 2003," *América Economía*, July 9–29, 2004.
56. "Las mayores empresas de América Latina en 2002," *América Economía*, July 9–31, 2003.
57. Data from the survey are found on the Bank of Mexico website; see www.banxico.org.mx/eInfoFinanciera/FSinfoFinanciera.html. Size definitions are based on volume of sales in 1997: small (less than about $12.5 million in sales), medium ($12.5 to $65 million), large ($65 to $650 million), and AAA (more than $650 million). The survey is based on a national random, stratified sample of around 1,500 firms, including branches of multinational corporations but not state-

Table 7-10. *Mexico: Sources of Finance, by Size of Firm, 1998 and 2003*
Percent

Source	Small firms[a] 1998	Small firms[a] 2003	Medium firms[b] 1998	Medium firms[b] 2003	Large firms[c] 1998	Large firms[c] 2003	AAA firms[d] 1998	AAA firms[d] 2003
Suppliers	50.0	64.4	42.0	58.2	28.5	49.5	17.8	28.5
Commercial banks	23.9	16.0	26.6	18.5	31.6	22.4	32.1	39.8
Foreign banks	3.7	1.1	8.4	2.8	15.4	6.1	34.2	13.1
Development banks	5.2	2.2	4.1	2.1	3.6	3.0	3.4	2.6
Intra-firm credit	15.8	15.7	17.7	17.5	16.5	16.7	5.7	8.9
Other	1.4	2.6	1.3	1.0	4.4	2.5	6.9	7.2
Total	100.0	100.0	100.0	100.0	100.0	100.0	100.0	100.0

Source: Bank of Mexico website (www.banxico.org.mx).
a. Sales in 1997 less than U.S.$12.5 million.
b. Sales in 1997 between U.S.$12.5 million and U.S.$65 million.
c. Sales in 1997 between U.S.$65 million and U.S.$650 million.
d. Sales in 1997 over U.S.$650 million.

four groups' financial sources in 1998 and 2003. The AAA group stands out as different from all the others. Moreover, the differences between AAA and other large firms widened during the period. In 1998, the AAA firms got about two-thirds of their finance from foreign and local commercial banks. The remainder was mostly from suppliers, although the "other" category, which includes domestic bond issues, represented about 7 percent. Five years later, finance from international banks had fallen sharply, to be replaced mainly by increased amounts from suppliers and local banks—at a time when the latter were cutting loans drastically. Thus, the behavior of the AAA group in Mexico is consistent with the findings of Caballero in his analysis of Chile.[58] Caballero identified a pattern in which the largest firms, in the presence of external shocks, withdraw (or are driven) from international markets. They then displace smaller firms in local credit markets, leaving the displaced firms in precarious straits.

The data for large firms in the table suggest this is exactly what happened in Mexico. In 1998, the large firms' financing pattern was more similar to the AAA firms than to the SMEs. Both large and AAA firms received about the same share of their finance from local commercial banks, and both got significant amounts from international banks. At the same time, large firms differed from AAA firms in their greater use of suppliers' credits and support from other firms in their corporate groups. By 2003, however, the large firms had moved toward the SME pattern. Not only had their international loans fallen, but their local bank financing had also declined. Suppliers provided half their funds.

---

owned enterprises. While serious problems exist with the survey, especially the sample based on 1997 sales data, its conclusions seem to be corroborated by qualitative evidence.
    58. Caballero (2002).

Small and medium firms, despite minor differences between them, shared a financing pattern that relied mainly on suppliers, together with some loans from local banks.[59] They had virtually no access to the international markets, especially by 2003, but they could draw on their corporate groups. The development banks accounted for only a small, and falling, share of finance—even for the smallest firms in the sample.[60]

The survey also provides information on the reasons for seeking bank credit and why it was frequently not used. The main use of funds was for working capital, reflecting the short-term nature of bank credit in Mexico and elsewhere; investment and restructuring of liabilities were a distant second. The explanation for not using bank credit varied over time and by size of firm. For example, high interest rates were cited by large and small firms alike in 1999 and 2000, but less so in recent years.[61] Uncertainty about the economic situation was also mentioned by all kinds of firms, while rejection by banks was an important reason for SMEs but much less important for larger firms. The former reasons suggest a lack of loan demand, while the latter clearly implies a supply constraint or credit rationing.

If firms and households cannot get access to domestic bank credit—the usual way to finance current as well as some capital expenditures—then other sources should appear to fill the gap. This has indeed been the case in Mexico. Nonbank finance refers to different institutions and instruments among different categories of borrowers, but it increased in all cases after the crisis. For the largest firms, nonbank finance typically means foreign finance and—to a lesser extent—the domestic capital markets. For SMEs and households, by contrast, nonbank financing refers to a growing panoply of institutions, ranging from finance companies (known in Mexico as *sofoles*) to the consumer finance divisions of retail stores to investment companies. Consumer finance is relevant to the analysis because owners of small firms frequently seek credit as individuals, thus blurring the distinction between consumer and commercial credit.

The *sofoles*, which can lend but not take deposits, fund themselves mainly from bank loans, including loans from the development banks. They have been extremely agile in moving into the space vacated by the banks with respect to credit for households and micro, small, and medium-sized enterprises. The total

---

59. The definition of small firms varies enormously across countries. In the Mexican survey, for example, small is defined as sales of less than $12.5 million, while in Chile small means sales of less than $650,000. These kinds of differences make comparisons across countries very difficult.

60. Unfortunately, the published information from the survey does not provide absolute figures on the amount of finance provided to each category of firm, nor does it reveal information on the share of finance from internal versus external sources. Based on its detailed study of the Mexican financial sector in 2001, the IMF believes that internal resources (retained earnings) were an increasing share of finance and key to the survival of many firms; see IMF (2002b, p.36).

61. In reality, the highest interest rates were in 1998, so respondents may have been thinking of the past when they answered that question.

number of credits granted by *sofoles* rose from virtually zero in 1995 to 7.3 million in December 2003, while the volume of their credits reached 2.2 percent of GDP in the same period. Most of these funds went for mortgages and auto finance. SMEs accounted for 17 percent of the total number of credits in 2003, but only 1 percent of the loan portfolio. They have been the fastest growing category of loans from *sofoles*, however, because of the entry into the market of a large new provider of credits to micro firms.[62]

The success of retail store credit is best illustrated by the Mexico-based electronics multinational, Grupo Elektra, whose consumer credit division was transformed into the first new bank to receive a license after 1994. Banco Azteca has the specific aim of providing financial services to the estimated 70–80 percent of the Mexican population not currently served by banks. One year after beginning operations in October 2002, it had some 4 million clients and a credit portfolio of $500 million. This ranked Banco Azteca ninth out of the thirty Mexican commercial banks in terms of loan portfolio, but only seventeenth in assets—reflecting the bias against lending at most banks.[63]

A third group of nonbank institutions that could be important for SME finance in the future are mutual funds (*sociedades de inversión*). They operate in three forms: equity trading, bond trading, and venture capital. Firms operating in the third area (*sincas*) were created to promote new projects that would later be brought to the stock market, much as venture firms do in other countries. To date, however, the only funds that have been significant in quantitative terms are those trading in debt, especially government paper. Together, the assets of the mutual funds represent around 5 percent of GDP, but over 85 percent is investment in bonds.[64]

The behavior of the private banks in Mexico since 1994 represents a clear case of market failure with respect to finance for SMEs and households. The government has tried to fill the gap. The key actor continues to be Nafin, but its approach underwent several changes before its current mode of operation was established. In the prereform period, Nafin borrowed money abroad at privileged rates and passed it directly on to firms—mainly large firms in both the public and private sectors. In the 1990s, Nafin became a second-tier bank, still obtaining funds in the international (and domestic) capital markets, but disbursing them through a network of private intermediaries, such as firms

62. Asociación Mexicana de Sociedades Financieras de Objeto Limitado website (www.amsfol.com.mx); AMSFOL is the national association of *sofoles*. The new microcredit institution is Financiera Compartamos (www.compartamos.com).

63. For a summary of Banco Azteca's brief history, see Lucy Conger, "A Bold Experiment at Banco Azteca," *Outlook Journal*, May 2003. Comparative data are from CNBV website (www.cnbv.gob.mx). The bank is still very closely connected to the Elektra department stores and is frequently criticized for charging extremely high interest rates on its loans.

64. Calculated from CNBV website (www.cnbv.gob.mx). Other types of nonbank finance include suppliers' credit, leasing, factoring, and credit unions. The CNBV website describes and provides statistics on those sources that it regulates.

engaged in leasing and factoring, credit unions, and saving and loan associations. This network grew very rapidly, as did the number of firms served. Inefficiency and corruption resulted from the rapid growth—similar to what occurred among the private banks in the same period—and eventually led to a $5 billion charge to the public treasury.[65]

A third epoch began with the inauguration in 2000 of the Fox government, which had a special interest in the private sector in general and SMEs in particular. The administration drew up a national plan for entrepreneurial development, and the new ministry of the economy included a vice minister for SMEs. An attempt was also made to coordinate the many programs to aid SMEs though the interdepartmental committee on industrial policy. In this context, three main programs were developed by a recovering Nafin: (1) a "production chains" program, which operates through the Internet and links factoring companies to large firms and their SME suppliers; (2) lending programs, which mainly provide working capital for SMEs; and (3) a loan guarantee program. In 2003, these programs disbursed over $9 billion, 85 percent of which went to the private sector. Of the private sector portion, 90 percent operated through second-tier procedures, while the remainder was guarantees (9 percent) and a small amount of first-tier lending (1 percent). Extensive technical assistance was also provided to small firms.[66]

While the programs are too recent to evaluate, several points can be raised. First, Nafin engages in a large number of activities that may divert energy and resources from its SME programs. For example, it operates as the government's financial agent, makes first-tier loans to the public sector, helps to develop the capital market through various kinds of intervention, acts as an investment bank, promotes venture capital, and engages in consulting. Second, as of 2003, only about 90,000 firms had received credits or guarantees under the second-tier programs. (A larger group received other benefits, such as training programs and help through Nafin's Internet site.) Third, a significant amount of the funds appear to go to larger firms. The average loan was about $100,000, and the average guarantee was about $60,000 in 2003. While the large majority of credits go to micro, small, and medium-sized enterprises, medium-sized firms are defined as having up to 250 employees and $50 million of sales.[67] Fourth, on the positive side, the number of firms receiving credit rose rapidly in recent years, while the average size of loan decreased. Nafin also scaled down its large

65. As discussed in note 47, the rescue of the development and commercial banks was carried out by separate institutions. Fideliq, the fund set up to handle the problem loans of the former, was under financial pressure, and the government decided to cut its losses and pay off the notes before they matured. This was the source of the $5 billion charge, which was described in the press as the bankruptcy of Nafin. See interview with the then-president of the CNBV, in Israel Rodríguez, "Rechazan que el traspaso de las pérdidas de Nafin al gobierno haya sido un acto ilegal," *La Jornada*, October 28, 2001.

66. Nafin (2003).

67. Nafin (2003) and personal interviews.

loans to the government and public sector firms; on a net basis, these flows were negative in 2003. Finally, Nafin's financial situation improved dramatically as a result of the restructuring following the crisis. Nonetheless, the Nafin programs need to be thoroughly evaluated as soon as possible to determine what groups they are reaching and what impact they are having.

Conclusions

The Mexican financial system clearly has serious problems. Bank loans to the private sector, especially those to enterprises, remain extraordinarily low a decade after the financial crisis of 1994–95. In addition, the capital markets are very small in absolute terms. The stock market is thin and extremely volatile, with market capitalization that is only 40 percent of its previous peak. The bond markets are also small, although they have been expanding in the last few years. Both markets are limited to a small number of large firms, and bonds are dominated by government agencies.

As a consequence, the traditional domestic sources of finance have not been providing much support for investment and growth. A quick rebound from the crisis did occur. Indeed, the Mexican economy was even more dynamic in the five years from 1996 to 2000 than it had been during the financial boom of 1990–94. This recovery, however, was partially based on idle capacity; in addition, new investment was financed by nontraditional sources. For the largest firms, this mainly meant international financial markets. Their smaller counterparts found support in new private sector institutions and the government itself, and they also drew on internal funds and money available from not paying full service on their debts.

While these alternatives provided some temporary relief, they have at least two important shortcomings. First, they have not been sufficiently broad and deep to stimulate a robust expansion of the domestic market. Second, they have been extremely biased in favor of the largest firms and have thus exacerbated an already serious problem of inequality in Mexican society. The banking system urgently needs to resume its lending to private borrowers in the near future. Not only do firms need credit, but households must also gain access—for consumption and mortgages—if the economy is not to rely so heavily on exports. The problem with such dependence was clearly manifested when production stagnated in the face of the recession in Mexico's largest export market.

So what is to be done? One answer—perhaps based on the Chilean experience in the 1980s—is simply to wait. The situation seems to be improving. The banks are stronger, well capitalized, and profitable. Institutional investors are growing rapidly. Moreover, interest rates are falling, which has two advantages: it lowers the cost of credit, and it improves the banks' incentive to lend since holding securities becomes less attractive.

This answer, however, is insufficient in the current circumstances in Mexico. Rapid growth is necessary for both social and political reasons, but it cannot take place if the financial system is not pulling its full weight. Wages are still below their precrisis level, and inequality is rising—although poverty may be falling.[68] The newly invigorated democracy is endangered by a situation in which only a few very privileged actors have access to finance and growth.

The government should take a number of steps; seven seem particularly relevant. First, the Ipab bonds should not be rolled over as they mature. Eliminating them from bank balance sheets would increase the banks' willingness (and need) to lend. Second, competition for consumer credit and loans to SMEs should be stimulated by providing more bank licenses to firms whose main goal is to increase the supply of credit to lower income groups. Third, more should be done to encourage the domestic capital markets to provide a source of funds for large and medium-sized firms (those below the AAA category). Fourth, the development banks should be managed in a way that is efficient and transparent enough so they can help small and micro enterprises, but the private sector should also be encouraged to enter this market. Fifth, dealing with the legal impediments to lending should be a high priority. Several specific steps have been taken, but they are not sufficient to overcome the general problems of a deficient judiciary and a lack of contract enforcement. Sixth, the financial regulatory agencies need greater autonomy and more resources. Relationships with foreign regulators should also be strengthened and clarified, given the overwhelming role of foreign banks in Mexico. Seventh, interest rates should be kept as low as possible to reinforce the other measures. Maintaining macroeconomic stability in general is a prerequisite for further financial deepening.

The details of these measures are obviously crucial and must be carefully thought out by experts who are familiar with local institutional arrangements. Nonetheless, the overall direction is clear, and most of these policy recommendations point in the same direction that Mexican authorities have been moving. The main message here is that much more needs to be done. A rapid—and broad-based—recovery of finance is essential to the other goals the government is trying to achieve.

---

68. See the recent World Bank (2004b) study on this topic.

8

Brazil:
Public Banks Continue
to Play a Key Role

B razil's economic reforms date to the late 1980s and early 1990s, making the country part of the third reform wave in Latin America. Even then, however, the reform process in Brazil was moderate and pragmatic in comparison with the more abrupt and ideologically based changes of some of its neighbors. At the same time, the government had to deal with growing macroeconomic disequilibria that included large fiscal deficits, a growing public sector debt, and price rises that threatened to reach hyperinflationary levels. The combined structural and macroeconomic changes were intended to reorient the economy so as to stimulate a return to rapid growth.

Brazil's financial landscape had been shaped by fifty years of a relatively closed, state-led development strategy. The main features included an important role for public sector banks in financing large development projects and public and private corporations; a limited role for foreign portfolio investment, owing to strict capital controls and minimal access to international financial markets until the 1970s; private intermediaries that provided mainly short-term financing, a significant portion of which was directed to the government; domestic capital markets that, despite their sophistication, played only a small role in the funding of productive activities; and the tradition of using inflation as an important source of financing.[1]

---

1. A historical analysis of the financial sector is found in Lees, Botts, and Cysne (1990). On the role of the financial sector in Brazil's industrialization process, see Studart (1995).

Doubts about the appropriateness of this structure in an increasingly global-ized world led the government to embark on a significant process of change. A successful stabilization program (the *Plano Real*) was introduced in 1994, and inflation fell abruptly from four- to one-digit levels. The very success of the *Plano Real,* however, contributed to serious banking problems in 1995, which triggered a government-sponsored restructuring that deepened privatization and financial opening by allowing foreign financial institutions to enter the domes-tic credit and capital markets. In addition, the monetary authorities promoted a significant improvement in regulation and supervision.

As a result of these reforms, the financial sector evolved in many ways. Com-petition and the competitiveness of national financial institutions increased, leading to improvements in microeconomic efficiency. Foreign banks entered the financial sector (although to a lesser extent than in most of Latin America), while the share of public sector banks was reduced but remained substantial. Capital markets expanded through the growth of institutional investors and the development of myriad new financial instruments. Private investment funds also flourished in the 1990s and became an important industry. Paradoxically, however, credit grew much less than expected, and primary issues of bonds and securities remained very small. In comparison with developed economies and some in the developing world, Brazil's private financial sector remained a rela-tively poor source of funds to firms and households alike. Long-term financing and small and medium-sized firms' access continued to be scarce; most was pro-vided by public banks.

While some of these trends and characteristics are similar to those we have described for Chile and Mexico, they also represent some major differences. The most obvious is the difference in ownership structure. The continuing impor-tance of public banks, combined with extremely competitive private domestic institutions, has limited opportunities for foreign banks in Brazil. Another cru-cial difference is the lack of a systemic banking crisis. Serious problems arose after the stabilization program in 1994, but the authorities took preventive actions and avoided the decade-long trauma experienced by Chile and Mexico. At the same time, Brazil confronts problems that are not as relevant in the other two cases. In particular, macroeconomic disequilibria are more significant in Brazil, manifesting themselves in large budget deficits, high debt ratios, high interest rates, and slow and volatile growth. Similarities are found mainly with respect to Mexico in terms of the small size of the financial sector (as a share of GDP), its orientation toward government finance, and the institutional prob-lems that inhibit its growth.

We discuss all of these issues in the chapter. In the first section, we review the financial reforms implemented in the 1990s (namely, liberalization and the new regulations) and what was expected from them. The second section examines the changes in the structure of the financial sector, including both banks and capital markets. The third analyzes the effects of the reforms and the macroeconomic context on the supply of finance for growth, while the fourth looks at who has had access to finance. The final section concludes with a discussion of the challenges facing Brazil today in the attempt to broaden and deepen the financial sector.

Liberalization, Crisis, and Response

Financial policies in Brazil in the late 1980s and the 1990s were motivated by three evolving goals. From 1988 to 1995, they aimed at deregulating domestic markets and opening them to foreign investors. In 1995, the banks faced severe difficulties, which led to a second round of changes motivated by the need to strengthen the financial sector and promote its stability. Policies included the restructuring of the banking system, further privatization of public banks, a new welcome for foreign banks, and a significant improvement of regulation and supervision. In 1999, a foreign exchange crisis erupted, but the earlier reforms helped the country avoid a twin crisis. The government then began to introduce microeconomic reforms, aimed at increasing the supply of credit and of capital in general.

From Liberalization to Severe Banking Problems

The financial reforms in the late 1980s and early 1990s were strongly motivated by the liberal wave that permeated policymaking in different parts of the developing world, particularly Latin America.[2] These changes were implemented together with other policies, such as the loosening of capital controls, privatization, and market liberalization. The simultaneous changes in the macroeconomic and regulatory environments had important consequences for the financial sector that Brazil inherited from the 1980s.

The 1980s macroeconomic environment was very detrimental to the lending process, since high inflation and volatile growth increased credit risk substantially. This was, however, a period of expansion and concentration in the banking sector, which was by far the most profitable industry in the country during the decade. The explanation for this paradox lies in the fact that Brazilian banks adapted well to the seemingly adverse macroeconomic environment. They did so by specializing in treasury operations and earning substantial profits from inflationary gains associated with the intermediation of the public debt, as was typical of Brazilian banks during the long period of high inflation and indexation.[3]

2. On this process in the Latin American region, see Stallings and Peres (2000). On the reforms in Brazil, see Baumann (2002); Pinheiro, Bonelli, and Schneider (2004).

3. See Studart and Hermann (2001). The "addiction" to inflationary gains is well explained by the OECD (2001, p. 117): "In the inflationary environment, which from the 1950s had become a feature of the Brazilian economy, banks were able to collect substantial intermediation margins. At the same time, borrowers' default rates were kept low by the reduction of their repayment obliga-

By 1988, the sector was already dominated by large de facto financial conglomerates that flourished as a result of high inflation. As an official recognition of the consolidation trend, a banking reform was implemented and a universal banking system was established. This reform transformed commercial banks, investment banks, and finance companies into universal banks, institutions that continue to dominate Brazil's financial system today. Bank credit was not only rationed, but also had very short maturities and was very costly. Policymakers naturally associated such rationing with the lack of competition. Thus, the early reforms significantly reduced entry barriers, which stimulated a rapid growth in the number of institutions. Between 1988 and 1994, the number of banks more than doubled from 106 to 242. Lending expanded in 1990–94, particularly to consumers and businesses. The expansion accelerated in the first months of the *Plano Real*, as the abrupt decline of inflationary gains led banks to search for new sources of income.

The 1988 reforms increased competition substantially, which in turn increased lending, but this otherwise positive result had unexpected perverse consequences for at least two reasons. First, competition in the banking sector in the 1990s was based on the physical expansion of the banks—that is, the number of branches, ATMs, and personnel—which allowed the banks greater access to deposits. Such deposits, in turn, could be allocated with significant profits to the refinancing of the large public debt and other short-term operations. The banks thus had high fixed costs when their inflation gains fell dramatically. Second, after launching the *Plano Real*, the monetary authorities tried to restrict credit expansion by setting very high levels of reserve requirements. The combination created an increasingly dangerous mix of credit expansion and high lending rates, provoking a rise of nonperforming loans and arrears. During this period, significant structural weaknesses in some major private banks became apparent. Serious problems of governance, transparency, and risk management emerged at Banco Econômico and Banco Nacional, for example, which had pivotal roles in triggering government action. Some of these problems could have been spotted with good surveillance. Indeed, these cases clearly reflect the prevailing low standards of banking supervision and regulation, which were the main inspiration of the policy changes from 1995 onwards.

---

tions in real terms. The lucrative float, from revenues earned on temporary reinvestment of low-cost liabilities (such as tax receipts, demand deposits, collateral against loans) in highly remunerated short-term securities, led to an explosive expansion in the number of commercial banks and bank branches. Substantial profits were also earned from treasury operations based on arbitrage of interest rates and currencies. An additional source of earnings was the significant share of current account balances generated via wage payments or maintained for transaction purposes, which did not earn any compensation for inflation. In short, inflation provided multiple sources of windfall gains to the banks. Encouraged by widespread indexation, the public continued to maintain funds in the domestic banking system. As a result, in contrast to other countries experiencing high inflation, currency substitution never developed in Brazil."

Public banks faced additional problems. They were by far the largest suppliers of loans in the system, with around two-thirds of the total in the early 1990s. In addition, their ability to adjust to smaller margins was constrained by their high operational costs (in view of the job stability of a significant share of their employees) and their limited capacity to restructure their portfolios (which were dominated by state government debt). The interest rate hikes of the early 1990s and the expansion of primary deficits increased state and municipal debts substantially after 1992, and public banks became the main financiers of such debts in Brazil.

The Mexican crisis of 1994–95 was the last straw in a process of accelerating bank problems, since the monetary authorities responded to the reversal of capital flows with an additional increase in interest rates and monetary tightening, particularly through high levels of reserve requirements. This policy led to a further deterioration of the payment capacity of the government, the corporate sector, and individual borrowers. Nonperforming loans, for example, rose to 17 percent in late 1995.[4] The increase in bad assets of several institutions caused a rise in the demand for liquidity in the banking sector as a whole, leading to shrinkage in the interbank market. Brazil was on the cusp of a banking crisis, but that crisis—especially the dangerous twin crises discussed in chapter 2—was averted by swift government action. This experience indicates that policy response can make a difference in avoiding the costly crises that many countries have suffered.

Response to a Near-Crisis in the Banking Sector

To avert a full-scale banking crisis, the Brazilian authorities followed steps similar to those we have already discussed in dealing with banking crises, but they took them at a relatively early stage. The first measure was direct intervention through liquidation and the placing of banks under new administration. This was followed by the restructuring of the banking system and then by the introduction of more restrictive regulation and supervision.

During the first three years of the *Plano Real*, forty banks, out of a total of 242, were intervened by the central bank. Of these, twenty-nine were liquidated, four failed, six were placed under temporary administration, and one continued to operate. Two of the largest banks in Brazil, Banco Econômico and Banco Nacional, were liquidated in 1995, requiring cash disbursements by the government of $5 billion and $7 billion, respectively.[5] Banco do Brasil, the largest public sector bank, had to be recapitalized with almost $8 billion in April 1996.[6]

---

4. Baer and Nazmi (2000, p.11).
5. All monetary figures cited in this chapter are in U.S. dollars.
6. Central Bank of Brazil website (www.bcb.gov.br).

Restructuring was carried out through two separate programs, one for private banks (PROER) and one for public banks (PROES). PROER was introduced by decree in November 1995. Its main goals were to protect depositors while helping banks to clean up their balance sheets and reducing the number of institutions. The key instrument was central bank credit lines to provide liquidity to troubled banks and help finance mergers with healthier institutions. The banks had to pledge collateral of 120 percent of a loan's value and to obtain permission for any proposed merger. At the same time, the government provided incentives for healthy banks to acquire troubled institutions. To avoid moral hazard problems in the future, a change of ownership was instituted, and managers and shareholders of institutions that were sold remained legally liable for previous actions. Thirty-two banks went through restructuring that resulted in mergers and acquisitions, some of them with the federal government support mentioned above.[7]

PROES, introduced in 1997, focused on restructuring the state-owned financial institutions; federally owned banks were not included. Credit lines were again provided by the central bank, but more explicit incentives were provided to the bank owners—the state governments—to reduce the number of institutions. The central bank provided 100 percent of the necessary funds for states that opted to liquidate, privatize, or turn the banks into development agencies; those that chose to keep the banks functioning received only 50 percent. Since 1997, ten public banks have been privatized (seven by the states themselves and three by the federal government), six have been liquidated, and three have had their operating authorizations cancelled. Between 1995 and 2003, the number of public banks was reduced from thirty-two to fourteen, while the number of banks with foreign control increased from twenty-one to fifty-three.[8]

This thorough restructuring of ownership in the banking sector was complemented by regulatory measures introduced in late 1995, which were motivated by the search for greater financial stability. These included the establishment of a deposit insurance fund, increased capital requirements for setting up new banks, and new regulations that promoted accountability. Further effort was made to comply with the recommendations of the 1988 Basel Accord and its 1995 revisions. This led to an increase in minimum capital requirements, a tightening of operational limits, and the introduction of comprehensive consolidated supervision of financial conglomerates, including branches and subsidiaries abroad and nonfinancial firms linked to bank conglomerates.

7. On PROER, see Baer and Nazmi (2000); McQuerry (2001); Goldfajn, Hennings, and Mori (2003).
8. On PROES, see Baer and Nazmi (2000); Ness (2000b); Goldfajn, Hennings, and Mori (2003); Beck, Crivelli, and Summerhill (2005).

With respect to supervision, perhaps the most significant of the new measures was the law authorizing the central bank to initiate preventative restructuring in financial institutions that were not meeting system requirements or were demonstrating financial problems. An earlier version of this law authorized the central bank to place banks under one of three forms of special regime—specifically, a temporary system of special administration, intervention, or extrajudicial liquidation—but the law lacked a preventative character. The new rules empowered the central bank to prescribe preventative remedies for faltering banks (for example, increased capitalization, transfer of stockholder control, or mergers and acquisitions), and certain assets of failing banks could be confiscated.

Response to a Foreign Exchange Crisis

Despite the successful stabilization program and the important changes in the banking system, Brazil's macroeconomic difficulties continued in the second half of the 1990s. Inflation was lowered to single digits by 1997, but the depreciation built into the crawling peg exchange rate regime was insufficient to prevent overvaluation. Moreover, the deficit problem had not been resolved fully. Although primary deficits were small, the public sector borrowing requirement added to an already substantial public sector debt. In the context of the Asian crisis of 1997 and the Russian crisis of 1998, Brazil's currency came under attack. A new fiscal package and a large IMF loan in late 1998 did not limit the outflows, and the currency was floated in January 1999.

The crucial point for our purposes is that the strengthening of the banking sector in 1995–97 meant that the banks were not involved to any great extent in the 1999 foreign exchange crisis. Their increasing efficiency, together with the loan retrenchment following stabilization and the drawn-out period before the devaluation (which gave borrowers time to hedge their foreign exchange exposure), protected the banks from the full effects of the devaluation. Thanks to the strong banking sector, the government could pursue a tight monetary policy to avoid an inflationary surge after the devaluation. The lack of high inflation, and the $41 billion international assistance package negotiated in late 1998, helped to maintain investor and consumer confidence and so prevent a steep fall in output.[9] In several ways, then, Brazil was different from Chile, Mexico, and the East Asian cases we have studied. Nonetheless, growth needed to be stimulated, and the financial sector was a key instrument.

Further support thus followed. It included a third government restructuring program, this one for the federally owned banks (PROEF). This process began de facto with the recapitalization of Banco do Brasil in 1996, and the second phase involved an especially rigorous supervision of the banks in 1999 and 2000. The additional weaknesses uncovered led to the creation of PROEF in

---

9. Gruben and Welch (2001). They make an argument very similar to ours with respect to the banks and the 1999 crisis in Brazil.

June 2001 to increase the capital adequacy of four public banks, including Banco do Brasil and Caixa Econômica Federal (CEF), the government mortgage bank. The program resulted in three measures: the transfer of credit risks to a special-purpose company (EMGEA), the exchange of assets with low liquidity and low return for more liquid instruments paying market interest rates, and a capital increase for three of the four banks.[10]

Beyond the Banking Sector

Although most attention was focused on the banks, the capital markets were also seen as a potentially important source of finance in Brazil. Indeed, Brazil's capital markets stand out among emerging markets for both their size and their long history. The stock market dates back to the mid-nineteenth century, but it stagnated in the years of high inflation after 1930. Only after the military coup of 1964 was interest renewed, as the new government sought to quell inflation and revive the markets as a source of finance. While less was accomplished than proposed, the markets picked up substantially over the ensuing fifteen years, partly in response to the indexation scheme that aimed to counter inflation. Important legal changes included the law that created the Securities Commission (CVM, by its Portuguese acronym) and an updating of the 1940 company law.[11]

Three important developments in the last two decades fed the growth of the markets. First, institutional investors came to play a significant role. Although Brazil has not privatized its social security system, as have Chile and Mexico, two sets of funds that represent voluntary private retirement saving are quite large.[12] More important in the Brazilian case are mutual funds, which were about twice the size of the pension funds as of 2002. The institutional investors together accounted for 35 percent of GDP.

A second element behind the growth of capital markets involved recent attempts to modernize the legal context in which they operate. Further revisions of the company law in 1989 and 1997 limited minority shareholder rights as part of the privatization process. In 2001, the Brazilian congress approved two key changes: one made the CVM independent of the finance ministry, with board members serving fixed terms; the second revised the company law yet again to restore the rights of minority shareholders to receive at least 80 percent of the value per share received by controlling interests in the event of an outside takeover. More generally, Brazil has witnessed an on-and-off battle to improve

10. According to Goldfajn, Hennings, and Mori (2003, p. 16), PROEF added $4 billion to the treasury debt, and $20 billion in bonds were issued. They estimate total costs for the three bank restructuring programs to be 8–9 percent of GDP, substantially less than in the twin crisis countries (see chapter 2 in this volume).

11. On the history of the capital markets, see Welch (1993).

12. The two sets are closed company funds and open private funds, which anyone can join. Both are managed by private firms; the assets of the former are many times the size of the latter.

corporate governance procedures. A potentially important achievement was the founding of the so-called New Market (*Novo Mercado* in Portuguese), a section of the São Paulo Stock Exchange (Bovespa) that is open only to companies that enforce international standards of governance.[13]

A third change that promoted the capital markets was Brazil's opening to foreign portfolio investment. While the country had long been a major recipient of foreign direct investment, portfolio investment had been more restricted. The first important easing occurred in 1987, which allowed foreigners to purchase shares in mutual funds administered by Brazilian financial institutions. In 1991, foreign institutional investors were permitted to administer their own portfolios of Brazilian securities. The most important change came shortly thereafter, when Brazilian firms were allowed to list their shares on foreign stock exchanges through global or American depository receipts (GDRs and ADRs).[14] As discussed in chapter 5, this change raised a major competitive challenge for Brazil's own equity markets.

Changes in Structure

Of the three countries studied in this book, Brazil has the largest capital markets in relation to the rest of its financial sector. Stock market capitalization and bonds outstanding far exceed claims by the private and public banks combined, as illustrated in figure 8-1. This pattern emerged in the poststabilization period, when capital markets grew rapidly with the termination of hyperinflation and banks failed to keep pace in terms of credit supply. Bank assets tell a different story, however. Within the Latin American region, Brazilian banks are second only to Chile's in terms of assets (as a share of GDP), but only about one-third of assets are deployed as loans, versus two-thirds in Chile. As we discuss later, the two main reasons for the low share of loans are both connected to the fiscal deficit in Brazil. On the one hand, the government offers large amounts of well-remunerated bonds to finance its deficits. These attract the banks to buy securities rather than make loans, thus feeding capital market growth. On the other hand, the deficits also lead to price increases and the need for high interest rates, which discourages loan demand by households and firms.

The Banking Sector

The Brazilian banking sector underwent significant transformations in the last fifteen years. Some of the changes are shown in table 8-1, from which we extract three important conclusions. First, the banking system today, when measured by loans as a share of GDP, is very small; in 2003 the figure was only around 25

13. See Armijo and Ness (2002, 2004) on attempts to introduce corporate governance in Brazil.

14. Armijo and Ness (2002, 2004).

Figure 8-1. *Brazil: Composition of Financial Markets, 1990–2003*

Percent of GDP

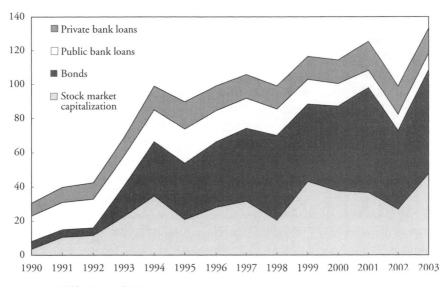

Sources: Tables 8-1 and 8-3.

Table 8-1. *Brazil: Loans and Deposits from the Banking System, 1988–2003*
Percent of GDP

| Year | All banks | | | Private banks | Public banks |
	Total loans[a]	Loans to private sector	Deposits	Total loans[a]	Total loans[a]
1988	33.0	23.6	11.4	11.4	21.6
1989	29.1	21.1	16.1	9.4	19.7
1990	22.6	16.1	12.8	7.5	15.0
1991	24.7	17.8	13.1	8.8	16.0
1992	26.4	20.0	17.9	9.6	16.8
1993	28.3	21.9	21.5	10.8	17.5
1994	32.6	26.6	23.3	13.9	18.7
1995	35.9	30.6	24.0	15.9	20.1
1996	32.8	27.3	23.6	14.5	18.3
1997	31.5	25.7	24.3	13.9	17.6
1998	29.1	26.4	26.8	13.6	15.5
1999	28.1	25.9	27.3	13.5	14.6
2000	27.2	25.9	25.5	13.9	13.3
2001	27.4	26.5	25.2	17.1	10.3
2002	26.0	25.2	25.9	16.5	9.5
2003	24.5	23.6	26.1	14.8	9.8

Sources: Central Bank of Brazil website (www.bcb.gov.br/?timeseriesen) for loans; World Bank website (siteresources.worldbank.org/DEC/DEC%20Data%20and%20Statistics/20487517/FinStructure_Database_60_03.xls) for deposits.

a. Loans to public and private sector.

percent. While the loan ratio has fallen somewhat since 1988, it was only about ten percentage points higher at its peak during this period. As noted above, the sector appears much larger when measured by assets. Bank assets are currently about 90 percent of GDP. Deposits also grew in the 1988–95 period; unlike loans, however, they increased slightly from their 1995 level. In 2003, deposits represented 26 percent of GDP, exceeding the loan share by a small amount.

A second conclusion concerns the relative importance of public and private banks. By public banks, we are referring here to the two large federally owned commercial banks (Banco do Brasil and Caixa Econômica Federal), as well as the National Bank for Economic and Social Development (BNDES) and the remaining state-owned banks. The public banks traditionally dominated the financial system in Brazil, but in 2000 private banks (including foreign institutions) overtook their rivals in terms of loans by a significant amount. The third point has to do with loan recipients. While the private sector received the majority of loans throughout the period, its share increased significantly in the last years of the sample period. In 1995, for example, private sector borrowers accounted for 85 percent of total loans; their share rose to 96 percent in 2003. The privatization process, both of the banks themselves and of the nonfinancial sector, profoundly affected trends among lenders and borrowers alike.

Table 8-2 provides additional information on changes among public and private banks. Two major shifts occurred in ownership of capital. First, while the total number of banks fell from 242 to 164 between 1995 and 2003, the number of public banks shrank more than proportionally, as some were privatized and others were closed. The change in ownership also affected the distribution of deposits held and loans advanced by the banking sector. With the November 2000 sale of Banespa, the bank owned by the state of São Paulo, the public share of loans and deposits fell below 50 percent for the first time in the postwar period.

Second, among private banks, foreign-controlled institutions substantially increased their access to both loans and deposits. European banks (particularly those from Spain) were the largest buyers of domestic banks in Brazil in the 1990s. They aimed at expanding their market share to obtain the economies of scale required to compete at the international level. This was the case of Spain's Santander, which acquired private domestic banks such as Noroeste, Bozano Simonsen, Meridional, and, more recently, Banespa, one of the largest of the formerly government-owned banks. Spain's other major bank, BBVA, acquired Excel-Econômico; the Dutch ABN-Amro bought Banco Real and Banepe, a former government bank; and two Portuguese banks acquired Banco Bandeirantes and Banco Boavista.[15] The U.S. banks that already participated in the retail market (namely, Citibank, J. P. Morgan, BankBoston, and Chase Manhattan)

15. Carvalho (2001).

Table 8-2. *Brazil: Characteristics of the Banking System, 1995–2003*
Percent

Indicator and year	Public banks	Private banks	Foreign banks	Total
Number of institutions				
1995	32	172	38	242
1998	22	123	59	204
2000	17	105	70	192
2003	14	88	62	164
Assets (percent)				
1995	52.3	39.3	8.4	100.0
1998	46.0	35.5	18.5	100.0
2000	36.9	35.5	27.6	100.0
2003	37.7	41.4	21.0	100.0
Deposits (percent)				
1995	58.1	36.5	5.4	100.0
1998	51.5	33.3	15.2	100.0
2000	44.4	34.3	21.4	100.0
2003	43.2	38.9	17.9	100.0
Loans (percent)				
1995	62.3	31.9	5.7	100.0
1998	53.7	31.3	15.0	100.0
2000	39.6	35.0	25.5	100.0
2003	33.4	42.3	24.3	100.0

Source: Central Bank of Brazil website (www.bcb.gov.br/?timeseriesen).

adopted the strategy of strengthening their role as niche banks by acquiring investment banks and securities brokers.

The share of public banks in assets, deposits, and loans was reduced, but they continue to occupy a central role in the financing of investment and growth in the economy. The largest bank continues to be the federally owned Banco do Brasil (with over 16 percent of total assets of the system), which is currently a conglomerate with a vast number of specialized intermediaries. The second largest is the public mortgage bank, Caixa Econômica Federal (with over 10 percent of total assets). BNDES is not a deposit-taking institution, but it is by far the main provider of investment finance in the country. These three public financial institutions alone represent 38 percent of the total assets of the consolidated banking system. In terms of size among commercial banks, Banco do Brasil and CEF are followed by three large domestically owned banks (Bradesco, Itaú, and Unibanco); the largest foreign-owned bank (Santander Banespa) ranks sixth.[16]

This situation represents an interesting puzzle. Despite the significant restructuring, internationalization, and privatization of Brazil's banks, the largest

16. Calculated from the central bank's website (www.bcb.gov.br). For a political-economic analysis of Brazil's federally owned banks, see von Mettenheim (2005).

institutions continue to be either government-owned or private domestic banks. This is very different from the situation in Chile and Mexico, where public banks have a much lower profile and foreign banks are more dominant. The reason lies in the competitive dynamics triggered by the reforms. The rapid expansion of foreign banks forced the large private banks to play an active role in the privatization process from 1998 on and to increase their competitive position vis-à-vis U.S. and European banks in the securities markets. Their size and strength allowed them to compete in ways that Chilean and Mexican banks could not.

The increased competition and differentiated strategies are two of the main determinants of the recent results on the efficiency of Brazil's banking system. Several indicators show that efficiency increased after the successful stabilization program. For instance, the ratios of assets per branch and of assets per employee both rose as branches were closed in the restructuring process. Likewise, operating costs as a share of net income fell for the banking system as a whole, although the private banks (particularly the private domestic banks) made the greatest strides.[17] The increase in microeconomic efficiency, however, did not increase credit or lower interest rates; that is, micro- and macroeconomic efficiency can move in different directions.[18]

Capital Markets

Capital markets are much more fragile institutions than banks. A sustainable expansion and development of capital markets requires at least four main macroeconomic and institutional conditions: relative price stability to stimulate long-term holding of assets and the issuing of securities; the existence of long-term savers in the form of both individual and, particularly, institutional investors; liquidity of secondary markets, which requires the existence of a large number of market makers or speculators; and the protection of property rights, in this case shareholder rights. Some of these features were in place in Brazil in the early 1990s. Price stability was achieved after 1994, and growth rates were positive. Financial opening stimulated interest in Brazil's capital markets—in particular, the stock markets—and the number of investment funds increased significantly. Thus, the assets under the management of institutional investors, especially the pension and mutual funds, rose substantially, as did the liquidity in the secondary markets.

In most cases, the expansion of primary markets (the source of new finance) follows a sustained expansion of secondary markets. Secondary markets did grow significantly until 1998, and this growth stimulated an increase in the size

17. Calculated from "Latin Banking Guide and Directory," *Latin Finance,* August issues (1997–2003).
18. Carvalho, Studart, and Alves (2002). Belaisch (2003) provides a more pessimistic view of the efficiency of Brazilian banks.

Table 8 3. *Brazil: Stock and Bond Markets, 1992–2003*
Percent of GDP

Year	Stock market[a]	Bonds[b]	Government	Corporate[c]	Total
1992	11.6	4.5	1.9	2.6	16.0
1993	22.7	17.7	13.2	4.4	40.4
1994	34.7	31.7	18.6	13.1	66.4
1995	21.0	32.8	21.3	11.5	53.8
1996	28.0	38.3	28.1	10.2	66.3
1997	31.6	42.6	32.7	9.9	74.3
1998	20.4	49.6	36.3	13.3	70.0
1999	43.1	55.6	45.1	10.5	98.7
2000	37.6	49.6	41.3	8.2	87.1
2001	36.6	61.3	51.5	9.9	97.9
2002	26.9	45.9	37.0	8.9	72.8
2003	47.6	61.0	50.1	10.8	108.6

Sources: Standard and Poor's (2000, 2005) for stock market; BIS website (www.bis.org/statistics/qcsv/anx16a.csv) for total and government bonds, (www.bis.org/statistics/qcsv/anx16b.csv) for corporate bonds.

a. Market capitalization.
b. Public and private bonds outstanding.
c. Corporate and financial sector bonds outstanding.

of the primary markets. From the 1998 Russian crisis through 2002, however, the trend was reversed. Although the capitalization of the stock market recovered in 1999, the issues and even the number of listed companies fell, as large firms, including some of the newly privatized ones, began to issue abroad. The volatile performance of the secondary markets, in turn, was one of the key determinants of the shrinking number of listed companies in domestic stock markets.

Table 8-3 provides data on the size of the stock and bond markets between 1992 and 2003. In sharp contrast to the banking sector, both equities and bonds grew tremendously starting in the early 1990s, although they contracted in 1999–2002. Stock market capitalization quadrupled in nominal dollar terms in the eleven years after 1992, while bonds outstanding grew even faster—an impressive thirteenfold increase in the same period. The two markets now represent 48 percent and 61 percent of GDP, respectively, versus only 25 percent for bank claims. The strong performance of bonds, however, was concentrated mainly on government securities issued to finance large deficits. In 1992, government securities accounted for 42 percent of the total, but the share had reached 82 percent by 2003. This pattern is reminiscent of Mexico, but substantially different from Chile, where government surpluses left space for the private sector to raise money from both banks and the bond markets.

Table 8-4 highlights other characteristics of the two markets. The number of listed firms on the Brazilian stock exchange followed patterns similar to those

Table 8-4. *Brazil: Characteristics of Stock and Bond Markets, 1995–2003*

Year	Stock market					Bond market[c]		
	Number of listed firms	Number of new issues	Value of new issues[a]	Market capitalization[a]	Turnover ratio[b]	Number of new issues	Value of new issues[a]	Bonds outstanding[a]
1995	543	31	2.1	147.6	47.9	93	7.5	81.2
1996	551	24	9.2	217.0	61.1	99	8.3	78.0
1997	536	23	3.7	255.5	85.5	57	7.0	75.8
1998	527	20	3.5	160.9	71.0	62	8.4	102.1
1999	478	10	1.5	228.0	53.0	38	3.6	53.1
2000	459	6	0.7	226.2	43.5	42	4.8	46.2
2001	428	6	0.6	186.2	34.5	41	6.6	47.3
2002	399	4	0.4	123.8	32.0	25	4.7	39.5
2003	367	2	0.2	234.6	32.4	17	1.8	50.6

Sources: Standard and Poor's (2000, 2005) for number of listed firms, market capitalization, and turnover ratio; CVM website (www.cvm.gov.br) for new issues; BIS website (www.bis.org/ statistics/qcsv/anx16b.csv) for bonds outstanding.

a. Billions of dollars.

b. Volume traded divided by market capitalization (percent).

c. Corporate bonds only.

identified previously. Delistings substantially exceeded new entrants, so that the number of listed firms fell sharply from 543 in 1995 to only 367 in 2003. Some of this was due to the new law granting firms permission to list abroad, but most was probably the result of hard times in the economy. At the same time, market capitalization rose from $148 billion in 1995 to $235 billion in 2003, making Bovespa the twentieth largest stock exchange in the world and the seventh largest among emerging market economies.[19] The turnover ratio—the usual measure of liquidity in the markets—fluctuated greatly but generally fell after the late 1990s. As in the rest of Latin America, the Brazilian turnover ratio was low in comparison with other regions of the world.

Market capitalization and bonds outstanding are the result of cumulative changes over time. Market capitalization is a combination of new issues and price changes; the latter were substantially more important than the former. New issues were quite robust in the mid-1990s, averaging $4.6 billion and twenty-five new issues a year between 1995 and 1998, but they fell thereafter. The picture for bonds was quite similar, as both the number and volume of new issues fell between 1995–98 and 1999–2003.[20] The Bovespa's price rise in 2003 and the national and international factors behind it, however, appear to have stimulated new issues, as the 2004 performance in both markets showed substantial recovery.[21]

One of the main factors in stimulating the capital markets is the growth of institutional investors, as illustrated by the cases of Chile and, increasingly, Mexico. Brazil differs from the other two countries in that it has not privatized its social security system. Nonetheless, it does have complementary pension funds that have accumulated a fairly large volume of assets, and these have played an important role in the capital markets in recent years. Mutual funds are even more important than pension funds in Brazil. The estimates presented in table 8-5 indicate that these institutional funds exceeded 35 percent of GDP ($160 billion) by 2002. Mutual funds accounted for 62 percent of the total, pension funds for 30 percent, and insurance reserves for the remainder.

In July 1995, Brazil's securities commission introduced several regulatory changes related to mutual funds, establishing high reserve requirements for short-term asset holdings and stimulating longer-term operations with low or no reserve requirements. At the same time, fixed-income financial investment funds were created under four distinct maturity structures—three with minimum terms of thirty, sixty, and ninety days and one with no minimum term. The recent expansion of these mutual funds was extraordinary: their share of total institutional investors' assets was only 5 percent in 1990, but it steadily

19. Standard and Poor's (2005). Emerging market economies with larger stock exchanges include China, Hong Kong, India, Korea, South Africa, and Taiwan.

20. New issues include corporate bonds (debentures) only.

21. There were nine new stock issues in 2004 for a total of $2.1 billion and thirty-seven new bonds for $3.3 billion; calculated from the CVM website (www.cvm.gov.br).

Table 8-5. *Brazil: Assets of Institutional Investors, 1980–2002*
Percent of GDP

Year	Mutual funds	Company pension funds	Private insurance funds	Total
1980	0.3	0.6	0.2	1.1
1985	1.7	2.6	0.5	4.8
1990	0.2	2.8	0.0	3.0
1995	11.1	8.4	1.2	20.7
2000	25.2	11.1	2.5	38.8
2002	21.7	10.4	3.0	35.1

Source: Armijo and Ness (2004).

rose to 62 percent in 2002. Their ability to support private sector investment has been undermined, however, by the short-term orientation of the funds. Their holdings of private securities, which had risen from 6 percent of their total portfolio in 1994 to 13 percent in 1997, fell to 5 percent in 2002. In contrast, their holdings of federal public debt grew from 21 to 55 percent between 1994 and 2002 (see table 8-6).

Private pension funds also grew significantly in the 1990s. These funds were formally established in 1977, when the legislation allowed for the constitution of complementary pension schemes.[22] Two types of pension funds were then legally defined: open and closed. The open funds operate as administrators of individual savings, obtaining funds through the issuance of fully funded pension policies. Closed pension funds are provided by corporations, which administer contributions made by both employers and employees in order to provide pensions in addition to those of the social security fund (INSS). Some are defined benefit funds, while others are defined contribution funds.

A significant change in regulation took place in 1994, when the central bank established upper (rather than lower) limits for the allocation of pension fund investments. The intention behind this regulatory change was to increase flexibility and especially to stimulate a shift from investments in traditional assets, such as government bonds and real estate, toward private securities.

By the end of 2000, pension funds held assets totaling $66.5 billion, which fell to $48 billion in 2002. In addition to their volume, which represented 10 percent of GDP, the allocation of the investments is very important. More information is available for closed funds than for open funds. The closed funds' allocations to fixed income securities—mostly government bonds—rose from 16

22. The basic idea behind this regulatory change was to promote a smooth shift from a public pay-as-you-go system to a fully funded private pension system. This transition implied that the employees who joined the private pension schemes would obtain two pensions when they retired: one provided by the public sector (the Instituto Nacional de Seguridade Social, INSS) and one provided by a private pension fund. On Brazilian pension funds in general, see Studart (2000).

Table 8-6. *Brazil: Size and Allocation of Mutual Fund Portfolios, 1991–2002*
Percent

Year	Government debt	Certificates of deposit	Short-term notes	Stocks and corporate bonds	Other	Total
1991	17	21	6	0	56	100
1992	24	17	2	0	57	100
1993	31	47	2	11	10	100
1994	21	43	2	6	29	100
1995	29	26	16	6	23	100
1996	36	12	28	5	19	100
1997	37	12	23	13	15	100
1998	63	7	11	10	9	100
1999	70	6	9	10	5	100
2000	68	5	12	3	11	100
2001	62	7	13	4	13	100
2002	55	6	21	5	14	100

Source: Central Bank of Brazil website (www.bcb.gov.br/?timeseriesen).

percent of their total investments in 1994 to 57 percent in 2002. Equity fell from 39 to 29 percent in the same period, and other items (such as real estate and time deposits) also shrank considerably. Insurance company reserves and open pension funds were even more concentrated in government securities.[23] The main reason for these changes is the difference in return on these assets. While the government paid high interest rates on its bonds, returns in the stock market were mediocre, especially after 1999.

International Finance

Closely related to domestic capital markets are the international financial markets, which include bank loans, bonds, and equity. As in other countries, many of the same actors—a very small portion of the total number of firms in Brazil—have access to both. Brazilian firms have traditionally been less open to involvement with the international markets than their counterparts in Chile and Mexico, but that pattern began to change over the past decade. The legal changes mentioned earlier, which allowed foreign investors greater entry into Brazilian markets, were a necessary, but not sufficient, condition for greater participation. Other prerequisites included macroeconomic stability, better institutions, and above all the potential for high returns.

The four main channels through which foreign capital entered Brazil were bank loans to Brazilian borrowers (either from the banks' home offices or from local subsidiaries), the purchase of bond issues floated in foreign or international markets, the purchase of global or American depository receipts, and investment

23. OECD (2005, pp. 71–75). Pension funds in Brazil are not allowed to invest abroad.

Table 8-7. *Brazil: International Finance, 1990–2003*
Percent of GDP

Year	Banks[a]	Bonds[b]	ADRs[c]	Total
1990	12.0	0.1	0.0	12.1
1991	12.0	0.2	0.0	12.2
1992	13.1	1.1	0.0	14.2
1993	12.4	2.2	0.0	14.6
1994	9.2	2.3	0.2	11.7
1995	8.2	2.4	0.2	10.8
1996	8.8	3.5	0.2	12.5
1997	9.4	4.5	0.5	14.4
1998	9.0	5.1	0.5	14.6
1999	12.0	8.4	0.8	21.2
2000	11.2	9.3	1.2	21.7
2001	13.5	12.4	1.7	27.6
2002	11.5	15.2	2.1	28.8
2003	11.5	17.9	2.0	31.4

Sources: BIS website (www.bis.org/statistics/hcsv/hanx9a_int.csv) for bank loans, (www.bis.org/statistics/qcsv/anx12a.csv) for bonds; IMF, unpublished data and *Global Financial Stability Report* (September 2004) for ADRs.
a. Claims outstanding by international banks.
b. Bonds outstanding issued in foreign and international markets.
c. Cumulative ADR emissions since 1991.

in Brazil's stock market. Table 8-7 shows the first three; time-series data on the fourth are insufficient to include it in the table.

The earliest form of entering the international markets in the postwar period was through syndicated bank loans, which became important in Brazil in the 1970s and eventually led to the debt crisis of the 1980s. In the period between 1990 and 2003, however, international bank loans stagnated; they represented only 11.5 percent of GDP at the end of the period. Bonds grew much more rapidly, but from a very low starting point. They surpassed loans in 2003, accounting for 18 percent of GDP. The majority of bonds and some of the loans were issued by the government, again as part of deficit financing strategies. In 2003, 18 percent of international loans and 52 percent of international bonds were accounted for by government debt.[24] Private and public firms alike issued ADRs, which also increased in recent years. The biggest single issuer was the state-owned oil company, Petrobras, which accounted for more than one-third of the total. Foreign investment in the stock exchange averaged about one-quarter of total trading in recent years. In 2003, a net inflow of approximately $2.5 billion was recorded, the largest amount in Bovespa's history.[25]

24. Calculated from the BIS website. For international bond issues, see www.bis.org/statistics/qcsv/anx12.csv; for international bank loans, see www.bis.org/statistics/hcsv/panx9a.csv.
25. Bovespa (2004, p. 19).

Table 8-8. *Brazil: Finance for the Corporate Sector, 1992–2003*
Percent of GDP

Year	Domestic finance			International finance			Total
	Banks loans[a]	Corporate bonds[a]	Stock market capitalization	Loans[a]	Bonds[a]	Equity[b]	
1992	20.0	2.6	11.6	3.7	n.a.	0.0	37.9
1993	21.9	4.4	22.7	3.9	0.9	0.0	53.8
1994	26.6	13.1	34.7	3.5	0.8	0.2	78.8
1995	30.6	11.5	21.0	3.3	0.7	0.2	67.2
1996	27.3	10.2	28.0	3.7	1.3	0.2	70.8
1997	25.7	9.9	31.6	4.3	1.7	0.5	73.7
1998	26.4	13.3	20.4	4.5	1.7	0.5	66.8
1999	25.9	10.5	43.1	6.5	2.3	0.8	89.0
2000	25.9	8.2	37.6	6.2	2.1	1.2	81.2
2001	26.5	9.9	36.6	8.0	2.4	1.7	85.1
2002	25.2	8.9	26.9	7.7	2.3	2.1	73.1
2003	23.6	10.8	47.6	6.7	2.8	2.0	93.5

Sources: Table 8-1 for bank loans; table 8-3 for corporate bonds and stock market capitalization; BIS website (www.bis.org/statistics/hcsv/hanx9a_priv.csv) for international loans, (www.bis.org/statistics/qcsv/anx12c.csv) for international bonds, table 8-7 for international equity.
a. For private sector only.
b. ADRs.

Finance, Investment, and Growth

Brazil's vaunted economy, which grew fast enough in the early postwar years to become the eighth largest in the world, has slowed substantially since the early 1980s. Many factors contributed to the slowdown; one was an anemic investment rate. Our argument is that problematic incentives for the financial system played an important role in the decline of investment, thus contributing to the decline in growth rates. Overall, finance for the corporate sector is low, accounting for around 94 percent of GDP in 2003 (see table 8-8). This is larger than in Mexico (43 percent), but much smaller than in Chile (207 percent). The characteristics of corporate finance also differ from the other two countries. Bank finance contributes only a small share, and the public banks continue to play an unusually significant role. Capital markets are relatively large overall, although most of the bond segment serves to finance government deficits. International finance, in turn, trails domestic sources in terms of finance for the private sector.

Bank Credit

In assessing the relationship between finance and growth in Brazil, we first have to emphasize the very small amount of credit that is provided to the private sector. At least three factors contribute to an explanation for the scarcity of credit in the Brazilian case. The first is the context in which lending took place over the last fifteen years. Macroeconomic instability—including large government deficits, high inflation rates, and volatile growth—was at the core of the problems. These problems did not end with the successful stabilization program of 1994. Uncertainty continued, albeit in a different form. Major political and economic shocks occurred during the 1995–2005 period. Growth remained volatile, and economic agents were not sure about what kind of policies would be followed. A deficient institutional framework created additional uncertainty regarding the protection of property rights and judicial enforcement. As a consequence, credit was not only low, but it declined steadily from its peak in 1995. Only since mid-2003 has it begun to rise again, and it remains to be seen if the new trend is sustainable.

A second reason for the low volume of finance has to do with a particular aspect of the macroeconomic context: namely, high interest rates and spreads. Kumar develops a subjective measure of this problem and then draws on a World Bank database on credit conditions to assess it. While she reports that Brazilian firms perceive overall credit conditions to be no worse than in most developing economies, complaints about high interest rates do distinguish the Brazilian environment.[26] This perception is a perfectly accurate reflection of reality, since interest rates and spreads have been and remain extraordinarily high in Brazil. Table 8-9 provides data on nominal and real rates for loans to the private sector and for the spread between lending and deposit rates from 1997 to 2003. Real rates on such loans hovered around 50 percent a year from 2000 to 2003, while spreads exceeded 40 percentage points.[27] Data in the table also confirm the increased efficiency and profitability of the banks in the last few years, which partly reflects the high interest spreads. In this light, credit from public banks provides a major advantage to clients since they lend at heavily subsidized rates. For example, BNDES's nominal long-term lending rate in 2003 was 11 percent.[28]

A third reason for low credit parallels an explanation for a similar problem in Mexico. In that country, a devastating crisis left most of the financial institutions in bankruptcy. The particular way the crisis was resolved—providing the banks with well-remunerated government securities in exchange for their non-performing loans—limited their incentive to lend. In Brazil, despite the absence of a major crisis, the need to finance government deficits led to a similar phenomenon. When deficits could no longer be financed through inflationary

26. Kumar (2005, chap. 1).
27. Great effort has been devoted to trying to account for high spreads. Different studies identify administrative costs, compensation for credit and other types of risk, high reserve requirements, taxes, and bank profits as parts of the explanation. See, for example, Central Bank of Brazil (2003). The high tax on financial transactions is particularly notable; see Albuquerque (2001); Coelho, Erbril, and Summers (2001); Koyama and Nakane (2001).
28. See BNDES website (www.bndes.gov.br). This rate is known as the TJLP (*taxa de juros de longo prazo*).

Table 8-9. *Brazil: Performance Indicators for the Banking System, 1997–2003*
Percent

Year	Loan ratio[a]	Nominal loan rate[b]	Real loan rate[c]	Spread[d]	Efficiency ratio[e]	Return on equity[f]	Return on assets[g]	Non-performing loans[h]
1997	31.5	78.2	73.5	53.8	88.5	n.a.	n.a.	n.a.
1998	29.1	86.4	83.2	55.4	83.2	7.4	0.6	10.2
1999	28.1	80.4	75.5	54.4	83.5	18.9	1.6	8.7
2000	27.2	56.8	49.8	39.6	85.9	11.3	1.0	8.4
2001	27.4	57.6	50.8	39.8	86.9	2.4	0.2	5.7
2002	26.0	62.9	54.4	43.7	76.1	20.8	1.9	5.3
2003	24.5	67.1	52.4	45.1	59.7	21.0	1.9	5.7

Sources: Table 8-1 for total loans as share of GDP; IMF, *Global Financial Stability Report* (September 2004) for ROE, ROA, and NPLs; IMF, *International Financial Statistics Yearbook* (2004) for nominal and real loan rates, deposit rates, and spreads; *Latin Finance* (August issues) for efficiency ratio.

n.a. Not available.

a. Total loans as share of GDP.

b. Average rate for short- and medium-term loans to the private sector.

c. Nominal loan rate deflated by consumer price index.

d. Difference between nominal loan rate and deposit rate.

e. Operating expenses as a share of gross operational margin.

f. Profits as a share of equity.

g. Profits as a share of assets.

h. Nonperforming loans as a share of total loans.

means, the authorities began to issue large amounts of well-remunerated bonds that limited banks' incentive to lend. This pattern was especially true for the private domestic and foreign banks; the public banks followed a different logic, at least to a certain extent.[29]

The volume of credit to the private sector behaved very erratically. The expansion of credit was significant in the high-inflation period of 1990–94, stimulated by the relatively high economic growth after the lost decade of the 1980s. From 1994 to 1997, following the successful stabilization, the supply of private credit fell almost symmetrically to the growth of the four preceding years. From 1997 onwards, the trend fluctuated strongly, owing to the increasing uncertainties surrounding the Brazilian economy. Only since mid-2003 has the private credit supply begun to increase again, as seen in figure 8-2.

We now turn to the issues of who was supplying credit to the private sector, the characteristics of the credit, and its relationship to investment. Table 8-10 begins by disaggregating the data on bank loans in table 8-8 to identify the relative contributions of the private and public banks since 1995. The ten-year period breaks down into two clear subperiods: 1995–2000 and 2001–04. In

29. Gottschalk and Sodré (2005) suggest that the Basel rules may also have played a role in the decline in credit since 1994. In particular, the 0 percent risk weighting of public sector loans has made them attractive to the banks above and beyond the high interest rates on government debt.

Figure 8-2. *Brazil: Credit to Public and Private Sectors, 1988–2004*

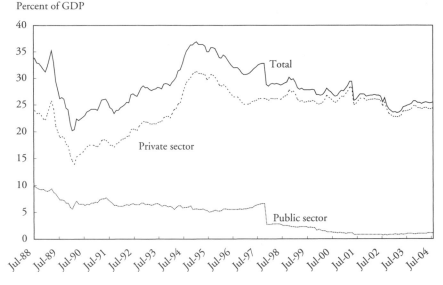

Source: Central Bank of Brazil website (www.bcb.gov.br/?timeseriesen).

both cases, the private banks accounted for the majority of the available credit, but their share increased sharply after 2000, rising from an average of 53 percent to 64 percent. Moreover, credit from the private banks increased slightly as a percentage of GDP, from 14 percent in the first subperiod to 16 percent in the second. The public banks, by contrast, saw their share of total private sector credit fall from 47 to 36 percent, at the same time that the volume fell from nearly 13 percent of GDP to only 9 percent.[30] Total credit fell by two percentage points between the two periods.[31]

The private and public banks display qualitative, as well as quantitative, differences. In particular, the private banks mainly provide short-term working capital, while the public banks provide longer-term investment funds. The interest rates are also quite distinct, as the private banks charge the very high rates just discussed, while the public banks lend at much lower, subsidized rates. The segmentation of the market is notable.

Brazil has a powerful private banking sector, although it differs from the two countries examined previously. Specifically, the foreign component is much weaker than in other major countries in the region. Foreign banks were

30. One of the reasons for the fall in public sector credit had to do with the restructuring of the federally owned banks, which took dubious credits off the banks' books and transferred them to an asset management company.

31. These data are still highly aggregated, since they represent all credit to the private sector, including credit for consumption and mortgages. The IMF estimates that corporate credit constitutes 65 percent of total private sector credit.

Table 8-10. *Brazil: Private-Sector Credit from Private and Public Banks,*
1995–2004
Percent of GDP and percent

	Credit from private banks		Credit from public banks		Total credit	
Year	*Percent GDP*	*Percent*	*Percent GDP*	*Percent*	*Percent GDP*	*Percent*
1995	15.9	52	14.7	48	30.6	100
1996	14.5	53	12.8	47	27.3	100
1997	13.9	54	11.8	46	25.7	100
1998	13.6	52	12.8	48	26.4	100
1999	13.5	52	12.4	48	25.9	100
2000	13.9	54	12.0	46	25.9	100
2001	17.1	65	9.4	35	26.5	100
2002	16.5	65	8.7	35	25.2	100
2003	14.8	63	8.8	37	23.6	100
2004	15.4	63	9.1	37	24.5	100

Source: Banco Central do Brasil website (www.bcb.gov.br/?timeseriesen).

attracted to Brazil by the possibility of exploiting niches that the domestic banks traditionally did not want to pursue—such as small and medium-sized enterprises (SMEs), mortgages, and some long-term investment financing—in the hopes that they would have advantages stemming from their alleged higher efficiency and competitiveness. Domestic private banks, however, proved to have a significant competitive advantage in treasury operations, technology, and access to privileged customers. Because of these hidden barriers to entry, some important foreign banks left the Brazilian market after the Argentine crisis. Moreover, even though the foreign bank share of assets increased, this was basically due to the acquisition of banks with high loan leverage.[32] Overall, the foreign banks tended to mimic their domestic counterparts in making limited amounts of short-term loans, while earning high profits by holding government securities.

The public banks continue to play a vital role in Brazil, contrary to expectations. Both the government and those supporting the reforms in the 1990s believed the changes would revolutionize the credit market. In particular, they expected the entry of foreign banks to expand credit significantly and broaden access for those normally excluded, such as SMEs and poorer households. They further assumed that the public banking sector would continue to shrink because it was less competitive than private, especially foreign, banks. The results turned out differently than anticipated, however, and the public banks continue to play a key role.

At least two factors can be singled out to explain this unexpected trend. First, the remaining public commercial banks went through substantial internal reforms that allowed them to increase their competitiveness rapidly, thereby lev-

32. See Carvalho, Studart, and Alves (2002).

Figure 8-3. *Brazil: Directed versus Free Credit, 1996–2004*

Percent

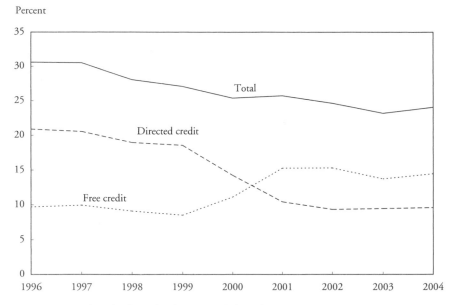

Source: Central Bank of Brazil website (www.bcb.gov.br/?timeseriesen).

eling the playing field between them and their private counterparts.[33] Second, macroeconomic conditions still make short-term operations (particularly treasury operations, but also credit) highly profitable. Private financial institutions never had the appropriate incentives to move into riskier markets, which created a protected niche for the specialized public banks. Public banks continue to be the principal intermediaries of long-term financing in the country: CEF finances mortgages; Banco do Brasil finances agribusiness investment and crops; and BNDES finances a variety of long-term undertakings, from industrial and infrastructure investment to SME programs and social projects.

Public intervention in the Brazilian credit system has worked in two interrelated ways. On the one hand, the public banks themselves made loans to various constituencies that they were assigned to finance. On the other hand, the private banks were also expected to serve certain national or social goals. While these amounts were initially large, directed credit has consistently fallen, although it was only recently replaced by "free" credit. The requirement that the private sector allocate part of its funding to specific sectors is now limited to rural credit and represents a very small share of total loans. Most selective credit is provided through the transfer of special funds, either directly through the main public banks or intermediated by private institutions.[34] As shown in figure 8-3, free

33. For an analysis of the competitiveness of Banco do Brasil, see John Barham, "Lean, Mean Banking Machine," *Latin Finance*, March 2003, pp. 59–61; Fitch Ratings (2004).

34. Morais (2005, pp. 23–24).

Figure 8-4. *Brazil. Growth Rates of Investment, Bank Loans, and BNDES Credit, 1992–2004*

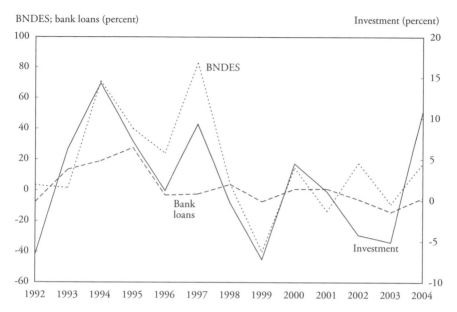

Sources: ECLAC website (www.eclac.cl) for investment; Central Bank of Brazil website (www.bcb.gov.br/?timeseriesen) for bank loans and BNDES credit.

credit supplanted directed credit in 2000, while the total combined credit declined until mid-2003.

BNDES has played an especially pivotal role in directed credit since its founding in 1951. It currently provides around 60 percent of the country's long-term finance, according to the bank's president.[35] The amounts involved are very large in absolute terms. BNDES lent nearly $14 billion in 2004, which is far more than the Inter-American Development Bank lent in all of Latin America and approaches the amount that the World Bank lent in the entire world. BNDES focuses on priority sectors (currently defined to include infrastructure, industrial competitiveness, exports, technology, and support for SMEs), providing about half of its credit directly and the rest through second-tier operations. The vast majority (94 percent in 2004) goes to the private sector, including some foreign firms. BNDES is funded by government sources and lends at a heavily subsidized rate, thus lowering costs for borrowers and giving those with access an important competitive advantage.[36]

Figure 8-4 illustrates the relative importance of BNDES in the investment process by plotting the relationship between investment, total bank credit to the

35. Alana Gandra, "Chief of BNDES Bank Guarantees Hot Economy for Brazil in Coming Months." *Brazzil Magazine,* July 11, 2005 (available at www.BrazzilMag.com).
36. On BNDES, see Teixeira Torres Filho (2005); von Mettenheim (2005, chap. 6).

private sector, and BNDES credit. Although investment and total credit move in a fairly synchronized pattern, an especially close link is found between investment and BNDES credit.[37]

Capital Markets and International Finance

Capital markets in Brazil are still shallow and underdeveloped by international standards, but they have grown rapidly since the successful stabilization program in 1994. Moreover, they have good potential to become a more important source of investment finance. Looking forward to this prospect, José Luis Osorio, chairman of Brazil's securities commission, made the following statement in 2002: "Today there are only two ways that a Brazilian can become a big businessman. He can be born rich, or he can gain access to BNDES financing. We want to create a third way—through the capital markets."[38]

A reexamination of tables 8-3 and 8-4 shows both the advantages and disadvantages that the markets face. Stock market capitalization is fairly small as a share of GDP, although it is large in absolute terms. New issues have fallen off since 1999; it remains to be seen whether the upswing in 2004 will be sustained. Liquidity has also fallen off. One of the problems was the erratic performance of the secondary markets throughout the 1990s, while the primary markets shrank through the delisting of a number of companies. The reasons were interrelated and stemmed from the loss of competitiveness of domestic capital markets in the process of financial opening, which in turn resulted from the initial shallowness of the markets, high volatility, and the high cost of issuing securities domestically vis-à-vis the international markets. At the same time, the markets' potential is demonstrated by a number of different instruments, both relating to the intermediation of resources and risk management instruments, such as derivative contracts.

Bond markets have a different set of problems. Bonds outstanding are larger than the capitalization of the stock market, but the large majority of new issues and amounts outstanding corresponds to the federal and state governments. (Public enterprises are usually classified with the private corporations.) Only about one-sixth of bonds outstanding have been issued by private nonfinancial corporations, and the share has shrunk since stabilization. Crowding out by the government has had clear negative implications for private sector investment and growth. The number and volume of new issues has fallen in the bond market just as it has in the stock market—although, again, a tentative recovery began in 2004.

In addition to macroeconomic volatility, poor institutional conditions have slowed the growth of Brazil's capital markets. Chapter 3 discussed Brazil's rela-

---

37. The discrepancy in 2002 was a result of market instability during the presidential election of that year. BNDES tried to be supportive of growth, despite the fall in investment.
38. Armijo and Ness (2002, p. 18).

tively low scores on commonly used measures of institutions, especially with respect to rule of law and control of corruption. Pinheiro and Cabral focus on the problems that a weak judiciary has in enforcing the rule of law. Using the variation in the size of financial markets across Brazilian states, they find that the enforcement of existing rules is positively related to the volume of credit, even after they take into account the size of state GDP.[39] Armijo and Ness document problems with corporate governance and look at actors pushing for improvements, although, as they point out, the meaning of the term is contested. They cite two reasons that reform has taken place. First, the perception that a country has good corporate governance may increase foreign investment. Second, traditional family-owned firms, which fear loss of control through greater rights for minority shareholders and greater transparency, are nonetheless using a version of corporate governance to defend their own interests. Institutional investors have yet to play a major role in promoting corporate governance in Brazil.[40]

The approval in 2001 of the new company law, which amended the company and securities laws of 1976, was a significant advance in improving the legal environment in Brazil. The law modernized the framework for publicly held companies by augmenting minority shareholders' rights and improving corporate governance, accountability, and transparency. It also created an independent regulatory body to supervise capital market activities. Finally, it defined illegal activities with respect to the stock market, setting severe penalties for wrongdoers.[41] Another important measure was to create incentives for compliance with the new law and the adoption of best practices. This was done through the inauguration of the *Novo Mercado*, based on the German *Neuer Markt* experience. The new market is a listing segment designed for the trading of shares issued by companies that voluntarily agree to adopt corporate governance practices and disclosure requirements beyond those stipulated in Brazilian legislation.[42]

39. Pinheiro and Cabral (2001).
40. Armijo and Ness (2002, 2004).
41. A detailed description of the law can be found in the central bank's newsletter (*Focus*, May 10, 2001).
42. To take part in the Novo Mercado, a company should follow good practices of corporate governance, such as (i) prohibiting the issue of nonvoting shares; (ii) holding public share offerings through mechanisms that favor capital dispersion and broad retail access; (iii) maintaining a minimum free float equivalent to 25 percent of capital; (iv) extending to all shareholders the same conditions provided to majority shareholders in the transfer of the controlling stake in the firm (so-called tag along rights); (v) establishing a single one-year term for the entire board of directors; (vi) using international accounting standards to prepare annual financial statements; (vii) improving quarterly financial statements through the use of consolidated financial statements and special audit review; (viii) accepting the obligation to hold a tender offer by economic value criteria should a decision be taken to delist from the Novo Mercado; and (ix) adhering to disclosure rules on the negotiation of assets issued by the company in the name of the controlling shareholders or the company management (*Focus*, May 10, 2001).

Figure 8-5. *Brazil: Growth Rates of Investment, Stocks, and Bonds, 1994–2003*

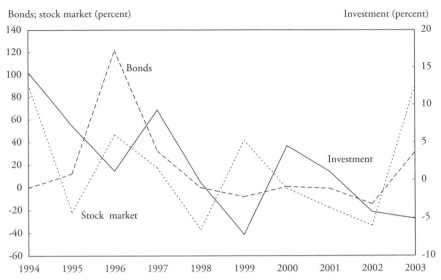

Sources: ECLAC website (www.eclac.cl) for investment; BIS website (www.bis.org) for bonds; Standard and Poor's (2000, 2005) for stock market capitalization.

Despite the complications of macroeconomic instability and poor governance that hindered capital market development, a relationship does seem to exist among equities, private bonds, and investment. As shown in figure 8-5, both bonds and stock market capitalization appear to lead investment by a year. The implication is that the fairly large amounts involved make it necessary for firms to ensure financing before undertaking a project. This situation contrasts with bank credit (including that of BNDES), where no lag was found. Perhaps bank finance can be taken more for granted, thus eliminating the lag with respect to investment.

The largest private firms that participate in the domestic capital markets, together with the federal government and public sector enterprises, are also able to raise money internationally. Syndicated bank loans, foreign and international bond issues, and equity offerings via global or American depository receipts are all part of the menu from which a small privileged group can choose. Although Brazil has a shorter history in these markets than some Latin American countries, especially Mexico, it has become a major player. Over thirty Brazilian firms, for example, are currently listed on the New York Stock Exchange, more than any other Latin American country. They include major private firms in banking, utilities, telecommunications, and industry, but some of the state firms have also listed a portion of their shares, including Petrobras, Telebras, and some of the regional utilities companies. Others are listed in Europe, most notably in

Figure 8-6. *Brazil: Growth Rates of Investment and International Finance, 1991–2003*

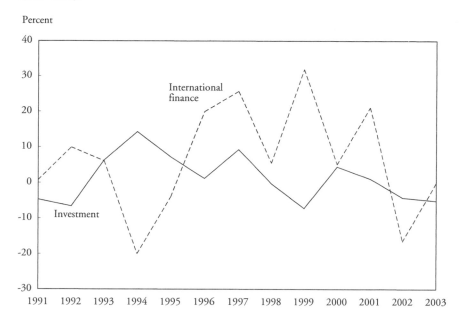

Percent

Sources: ECLAC website (www.eclac.cl) for investment; BIS website (www.bis.org), Standard and Poor's (2000, 2005), IMF (unpublished) for international finance.

Spain. These Brazilian firms have not left Bovespa, but rather have more than one listing.[43]

Private firms in Brazil are important recipients of international loans. In the five years from 2000 to 2004, they accounted for nearly 60 percent of all such loans to Brazil, receiving an amount equal to 6.9 percent of GDP. By contrast, the international bond markets are mainly the purview of the public sector and the banks. Only 17 percent of total bond issues (2.4 percent of GDP) were made by private Brazilian companies (namely, Ambev, CVRD, Telemar, and Vorantim). With respect to foreign investment on the Bovespa, cumulative net investment from 1995 to 2004 amounted to only $5.5 billion; this was 1.7 percent of 2004 market capitalization and 0.8 percent of GDP.[44] A Brazilian financial expert

43. See websites of the New York Stock Exchange (www.nyse.com) and Bovespa (www.bovespa.com.br).

44. Figures on loans and bonds were calculated from data on the BIS website. For international bonds, see www.bis.org/statistics/qcsv/anx12.csv; for international bank loans, see www.bis.org/statistics/hcsv/panx9a.csv. Individual company information was calculated from *Latin Finance* (2003 issues). Total bond issues that could be identified amounted to $15.2 billion, of which $7.0 billion was issued by the federal government or public sector firms and $8.2 billion by the private sector ($6.5 billion by banks and $1.8 billion by nonfinancial corporations). Data on foreign investment on the Brazilian stock exchange are from the CVM website: www.cvm.gov.br/ingl/public/Base_Financiera_English/Bovespa.xls.

claims that foreign portfolio investors play a much larger role in Brazilian firms. He calculates that in 1999, foreign investors in the local stock market held 15 percent of the shares in listed companies.[45] This would imply foreign investment equivalent to over 5 percent of GDP; more research is clearly needed.

When we compare investment trends with foreign sources of finance for the private sector, as shown in figure 8-6, the relationship is not at all close. While foreign capital may have been a precursor of investment spending in Brazil—as suggested with respect to local capital market finance—the weak relationship between the two variables in Brazil contrasts with the much stronger one in Mexico (compare figures 7-6 and 8-6).

Access to Credit for Small Firms

Brazil has the same problems as other Latin American countries in terms of limited access to credit by small firms. We have already described how access is a major issue in both Chile and Mexico. An important difference in the Brazilian case is the role played by public sector banks. In Mexico, Nafin operates almost exclusively through second-tier processes. The National Development Corporation (Corfo) does the same in Chile, although it has partnered with BancoEstado in several programs to help SMEs. BancoEstado itself is prominent in the small loan segment, but it only accounts for about 11 percent of the overall market. In Brazil, the public banks, including both commercial and development banks, play a much larger role and have targeted SMEs as a priority. While some evidence suggests they have had a positive impact, the paucity of information makes drawing conclusions extremely difficult.

Table 8-11 provides estimates of loans to micro and small enterprises by the main public and private commercial banks and BNDES. The table reports that slightly over 20 percent of total loans by value went to small and micro firms in 2003. The largest share was by the public commercial banks (32 percent); the private banks devoted a much smaller share to these firms (14 percent). BNDES (24 percent) is listed separately since a large portion of its loans is channeled through the other institutions, which implies some degree of double counting. To be meaningful, these loan shares must be compared with other characteristics of the firms. The usual comparison is with sales, but size categories are not defined in this way in Brazil. We therefore use volume of salaries paid as the best proxy. By this measure, micro enterprises account for 10 percent of salaries and small firms for 16 percent. The combined total of 26 percent is only slightly larger than the share of credit received by micro and small firms. In terms of employment, the difference is much greater: micro firms employ 36 percent of the total workforce, and small firms account for another 21 percent.[46]

45. Ness (2000a), cited in Armijo and Ness (2002).
46. Data on salaries and employment are from Sebrae (2005, tables 6 and 7).

Table 8-11. *Brazil: Credit to Micro and Small Enterprises, 2003*
Millions of reais and percent

Institution	Total loans	Loans to micro and small firms	Share of micro and small firms
Banco do Brasil	29,900	9,800	32.8
CEF	3,439	3,301	95.6
Nossa Caixa	1,088	782	71.8
Total public	34,427	13,883	40.3
Total private[a]	108,243	14,775	13.6
Subtotal	142,670	28,658	20.1
BNDES	39,836	9,585	24.1
Total[b]	182,506	38,243	21.0

Sources: Morais (2005, p. 46); BNDES website (www.bndes.gov.br) for BNDES data.
a. Bradesco, Itaú, Unibanco, ABN Amro, HSBC.
b. Includes some double counting.

Table 8-12. *Brazil: Loan Portfolios of Public and Private Banks, 2003*
Percent

Size of loan[a]	Commercial banks			Development banks	Credit cooperatives
	Government	Private	Foreign		
Less than U.S.$15,000	15.1	15.1	16.0	7.5	17.5
U.S.$15,000–30,000	41.3	21.4	26.5	6.9	61.7
U.S.$30,000–300,000	16.3	12.4	10.1	5.7	17.3
U.S.$300,000–15,000,000	16.9	33.2	34.6	15.9	3.5
More than U.S.$15,000,000	10.4	17.9	12.8	64.0	0.0
Total	100.0	100.0	100.0	100.0	100.0

Source: Central Bank of Brazil, *Financial Stability Report* (November 2004, p. 59).
a. Converted into dollars at exchange rate of 3.33.

A second type of information that is potentially relevant for studying access to credit in Brazil is the allocation of credit by size of loan. Most analysts assume—for lack of better information—that small loans are more or less equivalent to loans for small firms or individuals.[47] Table 8-12 provides information on size of loan and ownership characteristics of financial institutions for Brazil in 2003. Different ownership types have very different lending patterns. Credit cooperatives and government-owned commercial banks specialize in small loans: 79 percent of the loan portfolio of the former is composed of loans of less than $30,000, while 56 percent of the latter is in this category. Both private and foreign-owned commercial banks concentrate on the very broad $300,000 to $15,000,000 segment. Development banks, among which BNDES accounts for about 80 percent, have a heavy concentration in the largest loan category. About

47. Kumar (2005, pp. 187–88) questions this assumption, saying that many small loans in Brazil go to middle-class consumers and mid-sized firms.

64 percent of their loans are for more than $15 million, but BNDES is also a large supplier of loans to SMEs, as we discuss below.

A third comparison is with our other two case studies, although we can only make very rough estimates given the different types of data involved. The available, albeit very partial, evidence suggests that the share of micro and small firms with some access to bank credit was fairly similar in Brazil and Mexico. For Brazil, data for São Paulo indicate that 19 percent of small and micro firms have access to bank loans (9 percent from public banks and 10 percent from private banks).[48] In Mexico, the central bank survey reports that 18 percent of small firms have access to bank loans.[49] The figure for Chile is much higher, however, at 44 percent.[50] An important lesson, to which we return in the conclusion, is that the share of existing credit going to SMEs needs to rise at the same time that overall credit is increased.

We now turn to the sources and instruments through which credit is provided to small firms in Brazil. As indicated above, the public banks are extremely important, but the private banks and other bank and nonbank sources also participate. The largest sources of SME finance are BNDES and Banco do Brasil (see table 8-10), but much of the funding for the latter comes from the former, so we begin there.

BNDES cannot take deposits. It receives its funding from various government and international sources, and it allocates its smaller loans (those under about $3.5 million) through second-tier operations.[51] This obviously includes loans for SMEs. In 2004, over $4 billion of the $14 billion BNDES budget went to SMEs, with $3 billion going to micro and small firms and the remainder to medium-sized companies. The lead financial agents were Banco do Brasil and Bradesco, the largest private bank, each of which was responsible for about $650 million. Dozens of other banks and financial institutions, including foreign firms, also serve as financial agents. The agents are charged with evaluating proposals and distributing resources as they think best, since they are closer to the final users of the small loans than is BNDES itself. The main sectors supported are industry, agriculture and ranching, services, infrastructure, and trading.

BNDES also supports SMEs in many other ways. It has its own direct credit lines, as well as a guarantee program created by Congress in 1997, which protects financial institutions from the higher credit risk involved in SME loans. It runs a program to promote new small companies and underwrites microfinance institutions. In 2003, the bank launched the BNDES card, which provides SMEs with a preapproved credit line of up to 50,000 reais (about $17,000) with

48. Sebrae (2004, p. 50). These data are surely an overestimation for the country as a whole, so they can be considered an upper limit on access. Data are for 2003.

49. Bank of Mexico website (www.banxico.org.mx); see also chapter 7. Again these data are an upper limit since the definition of small firms has a high cutoff. Data are for 2003.

50. Román (2003, p. 30); see also chapter 6. Data are for 2000.

51. Information in the next two paragraphs is from the BNDES website (www.bndes.gov.br).

terms of up to two years. The cards are issued through financial institutions. By the end of 2004, 25,000 cards had been issued; not surprisingly given the low ceiling, most of the cards have gone to micro enterprises.

A substantial part of BNDES funds for micro, small, and medium-sized enterprises is managed by Banco do Brasil, the largest bank in Latin America, which also uses its own funds for these purposes. The main sector supported by Banco do Brasil is agriculture, including both large-scale operations and small rural holdings. The bank also has several working capital lines for small industrial and services companies. For example, BB Giro Rápido provides working capital for 660,000 companies with annual sales up to about $1.5 million, while the newer BB Giro Automático serves firms with sales up to $150,000. Additional financing is provided for foreign trade transactions for SMEs, and a new program has been developed to help small firms begin to sell abroad.[52]

Despite their currently smaller role with respect to SMEs, the major national and foreign private banks are also beginning to move into this area. Several reasons seem to be behind their new interest: the banks can charge higher interest rates and spreads on loans to small firms; smaller firms tend to be loyal clients and to be open to the purchase of other financial products; the low level of bank access among small firms provides a market to be exploited; and loans to small firms can result in accounts from the firms' employees. In addition, new credit scoring techniques, better credit bureaus, and increased use of the Internet have made it more economical to service smaller clients. Among the banks that have established special arrangements to attract small firms are the local giants Bradesco, Itaú, and Unibanco, as well as BankBoston, Santander, and HSBC.[53]

In addition to the commercial and development banks, other financial institutions that are important for SMEs in Brazil include credit cooperatives, leasing companies, and factoring firms—although the latter are designated as nonfinancial by Brazilian law. The 1,000 credit cooperatives are grouped into three large networks and provide mostly small loans to their one million or so members. Credit cooperative are now allowed to own banks. The leasing companies are substantially larger than the cooperatives in terms of assets, representing 3.3 percent of total financial system assets versus only 0.75 percent for cooperatives. Factoring is outside the system, but the 700 companies were estimated to have a portfolio of about $1 billion and to handle deals representing 2.3 percent of GDP, much of it serving smaller firms that have difficulty obtaining bank finance. Leasing, by contrast, tends to be associated with larger firms (for technology purposes) and middle- or upper-class individuals (for automobiles).[54]

52. Banco do Brasil website (www.bb.com.br).
53. Based on interviews with bankers as reported in Morais (2004). Banks vary substantially in how they define small firms and how they approach the challenge of responding to their needs. Some emphasize small and medium-sized firms, while others focus on micro and small businesses. One common approach is to set up special units to deal with smaller clients.
54. Kumar (2005, chap. 4).

Conclusions

The Brazilian financial system continues to be bank-based and dominated by public financial institutions, despite the large size of its capital markets. This structure represents the inheritance of the import-substitution policies of the early postwar years and the macroeconomic uncertainties of the 1980s, which made the private banks very conservative in terms of seeking alternative mechanisms of intermediation and expanding the maturity of their operations. At the same time, the capital markets were limited to equity and short-term bonds and notes issued by a small number of companies, most of which were government owned. Institutional investors were dominated by pension funds associated with public enterprises, insurance companies, and investment funds dealing almost exclusively with short-term securities, particularly inflation-indexed public bonds.

In the 1990s Brazil's financial system faced many challenges, posed by changes in regulation, external opening, and a macroeconomic environment that was substantially different from that of the previous decade. A bank reform was introduced in 1988, which permitted the formal consolidation of existing financial institutions into universal banks. The process of privatization initiated in the 1990s changed the structure of the pension funds (a significant number of which became private entities), while creating profitable opportunities for dealing with stocks and corporate bonds. The rise of external portfolio flows into the economy gave an additional boost to capital markets. Finally, the achievement of price stability in 1994 changed both the operating environment for banks and the portfolio allocation strategy of institutional investors. Financial opening and increased competition accelerated the consolidation process of financial institutions, the introduction of technological improvements, the rising importance of institutional investors, the growth of securities and derivatives markets, and the consolidation and internationalization of the financial business.

In 1994–95, the near-crisis in the banking sector heightened the demand for greater stability. This resulted in important changes in regulation and supervision, particularly related to the initiatives encompassed by the Basel Accord. The process of restructuring the private banking sector, which began in 1995, generated significant changes in the pattern of ownership in the sector, including an increase in foreign participation and a further consolidation within large financial conglomerates. In 1997, a deep reform of the public banking sector was initiated, leading to the privatization or restructuring of most of the state banks and financial institutions.

Increasing macroeconomic and market uncertainties in 1997–98 triggered significant changes in the strategies of financial institutions. The growing domestic public debt and the high interest rate policy again led private institutions to gear their portfolio allocation toward short-term public assets. At the same time, the reduced access of Brazilian firms to international markets renewed the search for alternative mechanisms to finance economic activity, thereby reinforcing the domestic bond markets to some extent.

As of the mid-2000s, the Brazilian financial system is profitable and stable, but it still does not fulfill its main function—namely, to provide adequate resources for the productive sector so as to support the effort to return to a high-growth path. A large part of the problem derived from the series of shocks that hit the economy: the currency crisis in 1999; the energy crisis in 2001, exacerbated by the economic and political problems in neighboring Argentina; and the instability around the presidential elections in 2002. Nevertheless, difficulties also remain inherent in the financial system itself and its relationship to the macroeconomic context in Brazil.

Expanding the financial sector and transforming it into a more functional instrument for sustained economic development continues to be one of the greatest challenges facing policymakers in Brazil. With regard to the banking sector, a key endeavor is to reduce spreads in order to increase the demand for credit. The central bank set out an agenda in this area in 1999. It includes several measures to increase competition among banks (by introducing more transparency and flexibility for bank account holders), reduce the tax burden on loans, and lower compulsory reserve levels. In 2004, the government defined rules for simplified bank accounts and for lower interest rates on loans when payments are withheld from wages. These changes per se are among the main factors responsible for the country's recent credit expansion, but their effect on bank spreads has been limited. At the same time, interest rates remain high, and they will only come down when inflation has been brought under control.

In the area of long-term financing, particularly the capital markets, the government agenda has been centered on institutional issues, such as reforming the bankruptcy laws and strengthening property rights. The effects of such microeconomic reforms are long term, however, and developing capital markets takes more than an adequate institutional setting. Other requirements include macroeconomic stability, active secondary markets, and the prospect of strong profits. Another factor is the presence a sufficient group of actors to participate—firms that want to seek resources and are able to meet the necessary prerequisites, as well as institutional and other investors.

In the meantime, the rising demand for long-term financing has increased the burden on the public banks. BNDES, in particular, has the capacity to expand loans based on the existing funding mechanisms, but this capacity will be seriously challenged if growth is sustained and the demand for investment financing rises accordingly. Under those circumstances, the public banks will need to find innovative ways to leverage their financing capacity, probably by tapping private markets for cofinancing, project financing, securitization, and so on. This scenario may present a window of opportunity for the government to move from direct resource allocation toward the greater challenge of market enhancement and market development.

Another serious challenge facing Brazil is finance for SMEs. Authorities will need to consider both a medium-term and a long-term strategy for addressing this issue. The medium-term strategy involves designing risk-mitigating policies (such as improving the quality and transparency of SME accounting information, expanding the use of credit bureaus, and training SME administrators in account and financial disclosure methods), establishing tax and other incentives to increase the participation of SMEs in the formal economy, building collateral-substitution mechanisms (such as credit guarantee schemes), and supporting venture capital for eligible firms. The long-term strategy should include policies to reduce macroeconomic instability so as to create a more stable business environment for SMEs; institution building and marketing enhancements to foster the development of financial markets in general, as well as financial intermediaries specialized in granting credit to SMEs; and the introduction of markets specialized in dealing with smaller firms. The development of an appropriate regulatory framework, clear and transparent rules of the game, and adequate supervision is a sine qua non for any market to flourish, but it is not sufficient.

All of these policies to increase finance and provide greater access are meant to stimulate the private sector, not substitute for it. The proper role for public policy must continuously be addressed, so that government intervention does not displace the market and scarce fiscal resources are used in the most socially efficient way. A long-term way to deal with these problems is to introduce market-enhancing policies, that is, policies that are meant to improve the conditions for finance and to increase the size and depth of financial markets.

PART III

Policy Recommendations for a Stronger Financial System

9

A Policy Agenda for the Financial Sector

This book has analyzed the domestic financial system in Latin America and how it has changed since the early 1990s. Expanding finance is one of the major challenges facing governments of developing countries, as they try to speed up economic growth and reduce poverty to improve the welfare of their citizens. A large body of literature now provides evidence that access to finance, through domestic banking systems and local capital markets, is an essential element for promoting growth. Our evidence indicates that the relationship runs in the other direction as well, but finance and growth are clearly intertwined. A smaller body of research suggests that there is also a positive relationship between finance and poverty reduction. Financial stability plays an important role in both relationships, since financial crises are highly damaging to growth prospects, and they are particularly harmful to the most vulnerable groups in society.

We focus on the domestic financial sector, but we make it clear throughout the book that it is necessary to take account of the multiple links between domestic and international finance. First, increased financial liberalization allows a greater volume of foreign portfolio investment to enter developing economies, through both domestic banking systems and capital markets. Second, foreign banks and capital markets provide an alternative source of finance for some borrowers from developing countries, especially governments and large corporations. Third, foreign ownership of banks and other financial institutions in developing countries has increased substantially. Fourth, international rules and regulations are having a growing impact on the operation of domestic financial systems. One of the crucial tasks of our analysis is to assess these relationships and suggest ways to take advantage of the positive aspects of financial globalization while avoiding the negative ones.

In addition to domestic-international links, we also highlight connections between the public and private sectors. We agree with the general thrust of financial liberalization. The economies of Latin America, and most other developing countries, have become far too complex for governments to micromanage their financial systems, but this does not mean that governments no longer have any role to play. While particular circumstances vary from country to country, we can suggest a minimal list of required government functions. Governments need to provide a stable macroeconomic environment; they must provide a strong institutional framework, including prudential regulation and supervision; and they should engage in market-enhancing policies to deal with problems of missing or incomplete financial markets. We discuss the precise meanings of these various roles more fully below.

This concluding chapter has two goals. One is to summarize the main findings of the book. The summary is divided into three parts. The first two review Latin America's lagging behavior with respect to banking and capital markets. The third compares the country experiences we have presented—the three Latin American case studies and some of the material on East Asia. We want to explain the reasons for Latin America's disappointing performance, but we are also interested in identifying lessons from the successes of the different countries and the problems they have encountered. The other goal is to outline a set of policy recommendations, based on the results of our research. They are organized according to five policy areas: macroeconomic environment, institutional development, regional and international context, finance for investment, and access to finance for small firms.

Banks and Capital Markets since 1990

Banks and capital markets are the main components of domestic financial systems in Latin America. They share a number of features, especially the context in which they operate. The main contextual factors in which we are interested include macroeconomics, institutions, and international financial linkages. Nonetheless, banks and markets are also different enough in their operations and their prerequisites that we need to discuss them separately. We concentrate first on Latin America and then bring in our analysis of East Asia when we compare our country-level findings on an intra- and interregional basis.

The Weakness of Latin American Banks

Financial liberalization began in Chile in the 1970s and was widely adopted throughout the region in the 1980s and 1990s. Government control of interest rates, high reserve requirements, and directed credit are largely—though not completely—a thing of the past. These changes transformed the operation of Latin America's banking systems, establishing new rules for their operation, new ownership patterns, and new roles for governments. Some of the changes were inherent in the liberalization process itself, while others stemmed from the crises that frequently followed liberalization.

We defined financial liberalization as the deregulation of the domestic financial sector. Our main hypothesis, which was supported by various types of evidence, suggested that whether liberalization resulted in crisis was determined mainly by the policies that accompanied it. We focused on three kinds of policies. First was macroeconomic policy. Far too many countries instituted financial liberalization under very adverse macroeconomic conditions: low and volatile growth; high inflation and significant budget deficits; and exchange rate regimes that led to trade deficits, large capital inflows, and increased financial fragility. A second policy that often accompanied reforms was capital account opening before domestic banking systems were strong enough to deal with the new challenges arising from international integration. This increased vulnerability and created channels for contagion. A third policy, whose absence frequently contributed to crises, was adequate prudential regulation and supervision. The tendency among the cases studied was to implement minimal regulation after the initial liberalization, which often resulted in lending booms, lack of proper risk management, and ever larger volumes of nonperforming loans.

Successful policies with respect to macroeconomic performance, capital account management, and regulation and supervision depended on the existence of strong institutions. Without good institutions in place, good policies could not be carried out, and crises were likely to be the outcome. By institutions, we refer throughout the book to the broad definition of the term: the formal and informal rules that shape the behavior of individuals and organizations by reducing uncertainty. Institutions in the more concrete sense—such as capable finance ministries and central banks, together with strong regulatory agencies and well-paid and skilled supervisors—were also essential for good performance.

One of our major findings was the tremendous cost of financial crises. Analysts usually focus on the fiscal costs, but crises also result in lost GDP, high interest rates, and falling asset prices. While it is difficult to sum these amounts, the fiscal cost and lost GDP in the first year alone averaged nearly 40 percent of GDP across the countries we studied. Moreover, these costs linger for a very long time. Our evidence, for example, suggests that it may take at least a decade for countries to return to the credit-to-GDP ratios that prevailed in the precrisis period.

Partially because of the lingering effects of crises, the domestic financial systems in Latin America are not working well today. With the exception of Chile, most standard indicators are weak in comparison with other emerging market countries, to say nothing of industrial economies. For example, the average ratio of credit to GDP in Latin America was only 41 percent in 2003, while it was 96 percent in East Asia and 94 percent in the G-7 countries. A much smaller share of available credit goes to the private sector in Latin America than in East Asia (just over 50 percent versus 85 percent, respectively), and nonperforming loans and financial inefficiency are high. Margins between active and passive interest rates are therefore high to cover the cost of these inefficiencies, which limits demand for credit while still providing the high returns that make banking a lucrative business.

Many experts argue in recent literature that the main reason for the poor performance is the continuing presence of state-controlled banks, even after liberalization. While we found evidence that supports this argument in many cases, we also found exceptions—most notably where strong institutions are present. Regulation and supervision are very important, but so are control of corruption, strong judiciaries, transparency, and general support for the rule of law. Type of ownership becomes less important when public sector banks are treated the same as their private sector counterparts, without regulatory forbearance. Likewise, if the institutional context is weak, even foreign banks will be hobbled.

In addition to bank performance, we have also addressed two economywide problems that result from the incentive structure that banks face in Latin America: the lack of long-term finance for investment, which constrains growth, and the lack of access to any kind of finance for smaller enterprises. The two are closely related. The long-term finance problem is typical of economies that are heavily reliant on commercial banks, which normally restrict themselves to providing short-term loans as a means of controlling credit risk. It also enables them to monitor their clients more closely. At the same time, however, it means that firms must finance long-term projects by rolling over short-term credit, using retained earnings, or entering the capital markets if they can obtain access. This problem led development banks in both Latin America and East Asia to provide long-term credit in the early postwar years. As a result of poor management, however, most of those banks have since been closed or turned into second-tier institutions. Brazil is the main example in Latin America where development banks continue to play an important role in the financial sector.

The problem of access for small and medium-sized firms is the other challenge that we highlight with respect to the region's financial systems. Large firms are not financially constrained. Research shows that they move from one type of finance to another, depending on the state of global markets. When access to international finance is limited, they move into domestic markets—including credit markets—thereby displacing smaller firms from the latter. Small firms, by contrast, do not have access to either international finance or domestic capital markets. The (very) partial exception may be a few medium-sized firms in domestic stock markets. This means that small firms are limited to bank credit, retained earnings, family resources, and suppliers' credit. Given this panorama, the gap between large and small firms continues to widen. The reasons that banks are reluctant to finance small firms are well known—namely, lack of information and high transaction costs. Public sector banks in some countries have helped to tackle both problems through first- and, especially, second-tier operations. Nonetheless, survey evidence demonstrates that small firms continue to lack credit, which prevents their growth and hinders employment expansion.

The Underdevelopment of Latin American Capital Markets

Financial liberalization focused mainly on the banking sector, but spillover effects also helped the capital markets since liberalization signaled that a country wished to attract private funds, both domestic and foreign. The privatization process was important as well. Newly privatized enterprises no longer had access to government funding, so they began to seek private sources that included domestic capital markets. At the same time, newly privatized pension funds needed assets to match the maturity of their liabilities and thus became a source of demand in those cases where they were not restricted to holding government debt. Over time, reforms took place in the financial sector itself as regulation and supervision were modernized, corporate governance was improved, and transparency was increased.

Nonetheless, these changes have had a limited impact, and Latin American economies remain bank based. Only a small number of countries have active stock and bond markets. Among the seven largest economies, the average ratio of bonds outstanding to GDP was 37 percent in 2003, while stock market capitalization averaged 34 percent. This compared with 60 percent and 80 percent, respectively, in East Asia, and 141 percent and 100 percent among G-7 countries. Chile and Brazil are the leaders in Latin America with respect to both bonds and equities, but their markets are much smaller than those of their Asian counterparts. As with the banking sector, most of the Latin American bond markets consist of government issues; only 22 percent of bonds outstanding were issued by the private sector in Latin America, compared with 63 percent in East Asia.

Bonds outstanding and stock market capitalization both increased substantially after 1990 in Latin America, but they peaked late in the decade. The number of firms listed on local stock markets declined significantly, therefore, as delisting exceeded new entrants. Delisting occurred for two main reasons: the reluctance of firms to provide the information required by new corporate governance standards, and the preference of new foreign owners to list in their home markets. The process exacerbated already existing problems of illiquidity in the markets, which, in turn, made investors more hesitant to participate.

In assessing whether capital markets will flourish in the future, we found support for several hypotheses that have much in common with our analysis of banks. First, poor macroeconomic performance (that is, low savings rates, low and volatile growth rates, and high inflation) made investors in Latin America reluctant to put money into domestic capital markets. Second, structural reforms (such as financial liberalization, privatization, and pension reform) helped promote capital markets, but many were carried out in ways that undermined the intentions of their supporters. The cases in which financial liberalization resulted in crises were dramatic examples. Third, generally low-quality institutions, both at the societal level (rule of law and adequate judicial systems to enforce it) and the market level (good corporate governance), hindered the development of stock and bond markets. Fourth, the availability of international financial opportunities frequently diminished the urgency with which government and private sector actors pursued the development of capital markets. In addition, the delistings noted above have had negative implications for the already low levels of liquidity in Latin American markets.

Our discussion of banks identified two problems that their weakness poses for economic growth in Latin America: lack of long-term finance for investment and lack of access to finance for small firms. The capital markets present similar instances of market failure. Although the stock and bond markets, by definition, provide long-term finance, the indicators typically used to measure their size focus on market capitalization and bonds outstanding, rather than on new issues that provide investment financing. (For lack of alternative data, we use these measures as well.) In all developing countries, especially in Latin America, new issues on stock markets have largely dried up since the late 1990s. Bond markets have been more active, but most new issues have been for government borrowers. While some changes are beginning to occur, most notably in Chile and Mexico, private sector issues remain a small minority throughout the region. Access, of course, is more restricted in the capital markets than in the banking system. Only a few private firms, together with governments and state-owned enterprises, are large enough to participate.

Explaining Latin America's Poor Performance

The diagnoses featured in the literature to explain poor performance emphasize inefficient public sector banks, overly burdensome regulation of both banks and capital markets, and the limitations that small economies pose for capital market development. These arguments certainly have merit. We argue, however, that they need to be expanded to include the context in which financial systems operate.

FINANCE AND CONTEXTUAL FACTORS. Three contextual factors are especially important for finance: the macroeconomic framework, the institutional
environment, and the international setting. The case study materials we have
used in the book provide the basis for exploring this argument and searching for
lessons that can be useful for Latin America in the future. Table 9-1 presents a
comparison of six countries, three in Latin America (Chile, Brazil, and Mexico)
and three in East Asia (Korea, Singapore, and Thailand). As indicated previously, the three Latin American examples represent the best-functioning financial systems in the region. The three from Asia include a range: one of the best
and two that have had problems in recent years.

The table is divided into three sections: level of financial development, the
three contextual factors just mentioned, and income data as a control factor. All
of the indicators are highly simplified representations. For financial development, they are the volume of total finance and finance provided to the private
sector. To represent the macroeconomic context, we use savings, inflation, and
growth rates; for institutions, we use the World Bank indicators discussed in
chapter 3; and for the international environment, we use the ratio of international finance to domestic finance. The control factors are aggregate and per
capita GDP, which are often argued to be strongly correlated with financial
structure.

Three overall points can be extracted from the table. First, the countries fall
into three groups with respect to volume of finance: Singapore, with total
finance over 300 percent of GDP; Chile, Korea, and Thailand, with between
200 and 300 percent; and Brazil and Mexico, with less than 200 percent. The
same groupings hold with respect to finance to the private sector, although
Brazil and Mexico are even further behind. Second, while two of the three Latin
American countries perform poorly in comparison with their Asian counterparts, this is not a simple case of East Asia outperforming Latin America. Nor is
it a case of richer countries or larger economies enjoying greater financial development than poorer, smaller ones. Third, the contextual variables are closely
correlated with financial development. The countries with the strongest macroeconomic and institutional scores also register the best financial performance.
The international variable suggests that international finance provided a possible alternative to domestic finance in the cases of Latin America; it was also
important for Singapore, as an international financial center.

In addition to examining overall patterns in table 9-1, we provide a brief look
at the six cases. Singapore, a small economy with a high per capita income, is
interesting for our purposes mainly insofar as it provides an exemplary case. It is
possible for a country to do everything well. High growth, high savings, low
inflation, strong institutions, and an open economy dominated by foreign banks
are associated with a deep financial sector, which, in turn, supports more
growth, more savings, and so on. While Singapore has fluid access to international

Table 9-1. *Latin America and East Asia: Determinants of Financial Depth, 2003*

	Domestic financial system				Contextual factors			Control variables	
Country	Total[a]	Loans[b]	Bonds[c]	Equity[d]	Macro[e]	Institutions[f]	International[g]	GDP[h]	Per capita GDP[i]
Singapore	364	141	64	159	5.2	2.05	50	93	21,941
	294	112	23	159	0.5				
					46.7				
Chile	240	64	57	119	4.6	1.39	36	82	5,196
	209	62	28	119	2.8				
					27.3				
Korea	227	99	74	54	5.4	0.73	13	586	12,232
	204	95	55	54	3.6				
					31.9				
Thailand	214	91	40	83	3.5	0.19	18	141	2,276
	180	79	18	83	1.8				
					32.0				
Brazil	155	46	61	48	2.4	−0.08	26	620	3,510
	88	29	11	48	14.7				
					21.5				
Mexico	86	42	24	20	2.8	0.06	56	592	5,792
	39	16	3	20	4.5				
					18.2				

Sources: Table 5-2 for loans; table 5-3 for bonds; table 5-4 for equity; table 3-7 for institutions; table 5-6 for international; World Bank, *World Development Indicators* (online) for macro, GDP, and per capita GDP.
a. Sum of credit, bonds, and equity; first line is total finance, second line is finance to private sector.
b. Claims outstanding by deposit money banks as share of GDP.
c. Bonds outstanding as share of GDP.
d. Market capitalization as share of GDP.
e. First line is average GDP growth rate, 1994–2003; second line is consumer price change, 2003; third line is gross domestic savings as percent of GDP, 2003.
f. World Bank indicators of governance, 2002.
g. Ratio of total international finance (loans, bonds, and equity) to total domestic finance (loans, bonds, and equity).
h. Gross domestic product in billions of constant 2000 dollars.
i. Per capita gross domestic product in constant 2000 dollars.

financial markets, the government still promotes local capital markets. Singapore's political system, however, provides little space for contestation and accountability. Indeed, its score on that factor in the World Bank's governance index is negative.

Korea, a large economy with high per capita income, and Thailand, a medium-sized economy with mid-level income, are examples of more partial success. A superficial lesson from these cases is that if macroeconomic performance is strong enough, institutions become less important. In both cases (especially Thailand), institutions leave much to be desired, but this did not seem to hinder financial development overall. Nonetheless, while banks provide large amounts of finance in both countries, capital markets are less developed than in other cases presented in the table, with only around half of total finance coming from the markets. Institutional deficiencies may well be a drag in this respect.

It is Chile, however, that offers the most important lessons for Latin America. First, it is part of the region and so shares a number of characteristics with its neighbors that the Asian countries do not. Second, it is a small economy with only a mid-level per capita income. Third, Chile has not always had a good performance on the various indicators we are studying. Rather, it made very significant improvements in both its macroeconomic management and its institutions over the last two decades. These have enabled the country to support capital markets that are large in comparison to its bank claims, which is unusual in emerging market economies. Moreover, the availability of international finance has not stood in the way of the development of domestic capital markets. Finally, given its lack of fiscal deficits, the bond market has space for private sector initiative, rather than serving merely to finance government shortfalls. Latin American countries would do well to study the steps taken by the Chilean government and the financial sector to achieve such a strong performance.

Brazil and Mexico, the two largest economies in Latin America, are the laggards among the six in all aspects under consideration. They have the smallest financial sectors, matched by higher inflation, lower growth, and lower savings than the other four, and they also have lower-quality institutions. At the same time, the two countries display significant differences. Most important is the fact that Brazil's capital markets are nearly as large as those of Korea and Thailand. The vast majority of bonds outstanding consist of government debt, however, as the private sector is crowded out. Both countries need to consider ways to improve macroeconomic management and strengthen their institutions. In addition, international options for obtaining finance may be hindering domestic financial market performance, especially in Mexico with its close proximity to the United States.

LONG-TERM FINANCE. Having identified potential sources of lessons for Latin America in terms of finance in general, we now turn to our two particular concerns: long-term finance and access for small firms. Table 9-2 provides rele-

Table 9-2. *Latin America and East Asia: Long-Term Finance and Access, 2003*

Country	Investment ratio[a]	Long-term credit constraint[b]	Capital markets[c]	Government activities[d]	SME credit constraint[e]	Government activities[f]
Singapore	32.5	15.9	182	Medium/high	12.8	Medium
Chile	23.0	41.7	147	Low	31.1	Medium
Korea	32.2	n.a.	109	High	n.a.	High
Thailand	27.9	76.1	101	Medium	43.9	Low/medium
Brazil	20.7	63.8	59	High	30.0	High
Mexico	19.5	87.6	23	Low	64.7	Medium/high

Sources: World Bank, *World Development Indicators* (online) for investment ratio; tables 5-3 and 5-4 for capital markets; World Bank website (info.worldbank.org/governance/wbes) for scores on credit constraints; authors' estimations, based on country materials, for government activities.

n.a. Not available.

a. Gross domestic capital formation as share of GDP, average of 1995–2003.

b. Percentage of all firms who report lack of long-term finance as "major or moderate obstacle" in business environment.

c. Market capitalization and private sector domestic bonds outstanding as share of GDP.

d. Government support programs for investment financing.

e. Percentage of small firms who report financing as "major obstacle" in business environment.

f. Government support programs for SMEs.

vant data. The first column presents the ratio of investment to GDP. The second shows survey data on the extent to which lack of long-term finance is a major or moderate obstacle to business operations and growth. The third and fourth indicate two ways to satisfy the need for long-term finance: capital markets and government programs. The fifth column turns to SME credit, also presenting survey data about whether lack of finance is a major obstacle to the operations of small firms. The final column estimates government efforts in this area.

The World Business Environment Survey (WBES) provides a source of data on whether long-term finance is a "major or moderate problem" in individual countries. A large majority of firms in Brazil (64 percent), Thailand (76 percent), and Mexico (88 percent) said it was. Very few firms in Singapore agreed (16 percent). Chile fell in the middle (42 percent). Comparing these responses to the availability of long-term finance from the domestic bond and stock markets yields interesting results. In Singapore, which has the most finance available through bonds and equity (nearly 200 percent of GDP), few firms complain about finance. In Mexico and Brazil, by contrast, where capital market finance is scarce (between 20 and 60 percent of GDP), entrepreneurs predictably see great difficulties. Chile lies in the middle, as would be expected. The surprise is that long-term finance is also cited as an obstacle in Thailand, despite what appears to be an ample supply. (Korea is not included in the survey.)

In the face of a perceived market failure, some governments have tried to supplement private sector finance through long-term loans from public sector development banks. Brazil's National Bank for Economic and Social Development (BNDES) is the most prominent example. The bank currently lends nearly $14 billion a year, which is nearly 15 percent of Brazil's annual gross domestic investment.[1] The vast majority of the funds go to the private sector, including foreign firms; priority areas include infrastructure, basic inputs, exports, national technology development, and SMEs. The survey data, however, suggest that the BNDES loans are not sufficient to meet the demand, and investment rates are extremely low despite the availability of finance.[2]

Korea also has powerful public sector banks. Korea Development Bank (KDB) is the largest and, like BNDES, specializes in long-term finance for investment purposes. The biggest share of its loans goes to the industrial sector, followed by gas, electricity, and water and then by transportation and communications. In 2003, loans totaled around $10 billion (6 percent of the country's investment that year). The Export-Import Bank complements KDB by financing exports; it lent nearly $8 billion in 2003. Unfortunately, Korea is not included in the WBES, so we do not know the opinion of Korean entrepreneurs. Nonetheless, Korea has long had a high investment rate, and some experts argue that government finance has been a significant factor.[3]

Singapore and Thailand focus more on public-private partnerships to support investment, but they do so in rather opaque ways. Singapore's government accounts for a large share of the country's very high investment rate, operating through the Government Investment Corporation and Temasek, which together manage assets representing more than 150 percent of GDP. Much of this investment, however, is carried out overseas. One of the sources of funds is the Central Provident Fund, the government-controlled pension system, whose assets are about 65 percent of GDP.[4] Thailand has a number of so-called specialized financial institutions. The joint public-private Industrial Finance Corporation of Thailand (IFCT) appears to have been most analogous to BNDES and KDB, although on a much smaller scale. Its loan book, as of early 2003, was nearly $4 billion, although annual flows were much lower. In 2004, IFTC merged with the Thai Military Bank and DBS-Thai Danu Bank, a subsidiary of the large Singapore bank. It is not yet clear what the role of the new institution will be.[5]

Unlike the other cases, Chile and Mexico rely mainly on the private sector to finance business investment today, although both had prominent development banks that played an important role in the industrialization of the two coun-

1. See chapter 8. The BNDES annual disbursements are more than the World Bank lends annually on a worldwide basis through the IBRD window.
2. See discussion of Brazil in chapter 8.
3. On finance in Korea, see Hahm (1999); Fitch Ratings (2002a); IMF (2003c); Ahn and Cha (2004). On the development banks in particular, see KDB (2003); KEXIM (2003).
4. On Singapore's financial system, see Montes and Giap (1999); Hew (2002); IMF (2004e); Fitch (2002b).
5. On finance in Thailand, see Vajragupta and Vichyanond (1999); Vichyanond (2002); IMF (2004f); Warr (2004); Fitch Ratings (2005).

tries. Now those two institutions—the National Development Corporation (Corfo) and Nacional Financiera (Nafin), respectively—have become second-tier banks that primarily serve SMEs. Having moved away from public funding of investment, Chilean governments have sought to provide incentives to enlarge both the banking sector and the capital markets. The data in table 9-2 on the investment ratio and the availability of long-term finance reflect their success relative to neighboring countries—although much remains to be done.[6] Mexico still has a development banking sector, but most of it is being phased out or turned toward social goals. At the same time, the private sector has not stepped in to fill the gap in terms of investment finance. Bank credit to firms is very limited and almost exclusively for working capital, while the capital markets remain very small despite recent expansion. These problems are reflected in both the low investment rates and the fact that entrepreneurs signal that long-term finance is a more serious problem than in our other cases.[7]

In summary, table 9-2 suggests that lack of long-term finance is a serious constraint on investment and growth in most of the countries we are following in this chapter. The countries with large capital markets, which specialize in long-term finance for a limited sector of the corporate population, complain less about this problem and have higher investment rates. This includes Singapore and Chile. Chile relies exclusively on private sector finance, but Singapore complements its capital markets with a direct government role in investment. Brazil and Korea have large public banks whose mission is to provide long-term finance. While Brazil's bank is larger than Korea's, it has not had the same impact in terms of increasing the investment rate. Mexico is in the worst position, since it has neither strong capital markets nor an active development bank. Businesses note the lack of finance, which is correlated with low investment. Thailand's situation is unusual since it has had a relatively high investment rate, but there are serious complaints about the lack of finance. This apparent anomaly may have to do with the aftermath of the country's 1997 crisis (the survey was taken in 2000).

ACCESS FOR SMEs.   SME credit displays both similarities and differences with respect to the country responses on long-term credit. That is, in Singapore, owners of small and medium-sized firms indicate little difficulty with access to finance (less than 13 percent report it is a major problem), while in Mexico they report a great deal of trouble (nearly 65 percent see it as a major constraint). The other three countries fall in between; again no information is available for Korea. While private sector institutions have expressed some interest in expanding SME finance in recent years—as a result of both the higher margins in that area and the migration of larger firms to the capital markets and international finance—they have yet to make much of a dent in the existing demand. Governments have

6. See discussion of Chile in chapter 6.
7. See discussion of Mexico in chapter 7.

thus identified this problem as another case of market failure and have given its resolution even higher priority than increasing finance for investment.

Two main approaches have been followed, with the countries divided along regional lines. Brazil, Chile, and Mexico have come to rely heavily on second-tier banking operations, with some support from public sector commercial banks in the first two cases. The key concept is partnerships between the public and private sectors, with the former helping to build markets for an underserved part of the population.

As discussed earlier, the provision of finance for SMEs is one of the priorities of Brazil's BNDES. Some, but not all, of this lending is done through second-tier operations with the government-owned Banco do Brasil, the largest commercial bank in the country, and with various private institutions. Banco do Brasil does some of its own lending in addition to participating in BNDES activities. In both cases, lines of credit for working capital and investment goods are provided together with guarantees, technical assistance, and innovative approaches to SME finance through the use of credit cards. Between the two, some $5 billion was provided in 2003.[8]

The main government agent for SMEs in Mexico is Nafin, the former development bank, which now targets small firms as one of its principal activities. (It also acts as the government's fiscal agent and makes direct loans to public sector firms.) Nafin provided loan and guarantee disbursements of around $8 billion in 2003, almost all of which was channeled through second-tier operations; its financial support programs thus reached 90,000 companies and its technical assistance efforts another 250,000. One of its most successful techniques is an Internet-based network of private firms that are interested in providing factoring services to SMEs.[9]

Chile has established a partnership between its former development bank, Corfo, and the state-owned commercial bank, BancoEstado, to support SMEs. Working together, they have designed a successful program (Fogape) to offset transaction costs for private sector banks that are willing to finance SMEs. They also engage in direct lending to small firms and provide guarantees so such firms can borrow from private banks. The amounts involved are much smaller than in Brazil and Mexico, with only around $300 million a year from Corfo and Fogape combined in 2003. However, BancoEstado lends another $2–3 billion annually to small firms. If this amount is included, then the public sector in Chile provides far more on a per capita basis than do Brazil and Mexico, but it is done on commercial terms.[10]

Korea and Thailand, by contrast, have state-owned banks that provide direct finance to SMEs. In Korea, the Industrial Bank of Korea (IBK) fulfills this function,

8. See discussion of Brazil in chapter 8.
9. See discussion of Mexico in chapter 7.
10. See discussion of Chile in chapter 6.

while Thailand has an institution specifically called the SME Bank. Korea's Industrial Bank is the leading source of finance for small firms in that country and devotes 85 percent of its $35 billion loan book to SMEs; some $4 billion in new loans were disbursed in 2003. In addition to traditional types of lending, IBK has introduced a factoring system similar to that at Nafin, and it has helped smaller firms enter the international bond market through an issue jointly guaranteed with Japan's Bank for International Cooperation. It also engages in venture-type financing for a select group of SMEs.[11] Thailand's SME Bank carries out similar activities, but on a smaller and less sophisticated level. Total loans in 2003 were around $680 million, involving 6,000 small and medium-sized firms.[12]

As the highest-income country of the six, Singapore's efforts with respect to SMEs are heavily focused on fostering entrepreneurship and innovation. Some programs are directly administered by government agencies, such as the Economic Development Board, and others are carried out in conjunction with private institutions and individual "angels." Many programs are geared for technology start-ups, but opportunities are also available for firms in more traditional sectors. Instruments include fixed- and variable-rate loans, insurance, equity investments, tax incentives, technical assistance through hiring external experts, and support for developing overseas markets.[13]

The problems of SMEs in general, and their financial needs in particular, are a high priority throughout the developing world because of their potential impact on poverty reduction and employment generation. Unfortunately, it is hard to evaluate the two types of experiences that we have reviewed—direct lending by government banks in East Asia versus second-tier finance in Latin America—because of lack of comparable information. It is also unclear whether successful experiences can be replicated, but the area calls out for more comparative research. We need to identify best practices by both public and private sector institutions, and the prerequisites for their implementation, as a first step to providing solutions.[14]

Toward a Policy Agenda on Finance

Latin American governments generally agree that policy initiatives need to be undertaken in the area of finance. Those who regard finance as an important determinant of growth are eager to deepen and improve the sector's perform-

11. Industrial Bank of Korea (2003) and website (www.kiupbank.co.kr). Nugent and Yhee (2002) offer a useful analysis of SME financing in Korea.

12. SME Bank (2003) and website (www.smebank.co.th).

13. See website of Action Community for Entrepreneurship (www.ace.org.sg).

14. Interesting work on SMEs, finance, and poverty has been reported recently by the World Bank. See, for example, Berger and Udell (2004); Beck and others (2004); Cull and others (2004); Honohan (2004, 2005).

ance. Even those who believe that finance is basically a response to growth real-ize that the proper financial infrastructure must be in place for a smooth response to occur. The issue of what should be done, however, is not clear-cut. Moreover, the different characteristics across countries complicate the policy dis-cussion enormously. Initial conditions are obviously central to policy choice. These vary widely, as we have shown throughout the book, which implies that a one-size-fits-all solution is not appropriate.

Our aim in these final pages is to suggest a set of mid-level policy recommen-dations. We identify areas that require reform and suggest some general approaches, based on best practices found in our research. Aligning them with specific policy instruments must be the task of public and private sector actors in each individual country. We argue that five areas constitute the central core of a policy agenda to promote a robust financial system that will promote growth and equity. They include good macroeconomic management, development of strong institutions, cautious integration into the international economy, support for a long-term segment of the financial markets, and a major thrust toward expanding finance for small firms.

Macroeconomic Management

A first policy area that we have identified as crucial for the development of both banks and capital markets is sound macroeconomic management. It is virtually impossible to foster healthy banks and especially robust capital markets in the midst of high inflation and volatile growth. Brazil in the late 1980s and early 1990s shows that banks can adjust so as to be highly profitable under such cir-cumstances, but they will do so through speculative activities rather than lend-ing to support private sector investment or consumption. Argentina provides a different kind of example, in which a strong regulatory environment proved no match for serious macroeconomic failure. Bond markets are much more fragile than banks. Under poor macroeconomic conditions they will—at best—provide finance for governments, while corporate issues dwindle and stock markets remain thin and volatile.

Many aspects of macroeconomic policy are important, and they are closely interrelated among themselves and with finance. Stable growth, low inflation, fiscal discipline, and high savings are all essential components of an environ-ment in which financial markets can flourish. Of these elements, Latin Ameri-can countries have made the most progress in controlling inflation. Brazil's *Plano Real* was the final step that returned the region to single-digit levels in the mid-1990s. In many cases, these inflation gains were purchased through fixed exchange rates that ultimately fed into financial crises. Now a new approach seems to have taken hold, involving flexible exchange rates and the slow, but steady, use of monetary and fiscal policy to bring inflation down further in those cases where it is necessary. Chile, throughout the 1990s, was an example of this

276 Policy Recommendations for a Stronger Financial System

kind of approach, in contrast to the Argentine, Mexican, or Brazilian style of stabilization. These hard-won gains must be protected and, in some cases, extended, but within a context of substantial exchange rate flexibility.

A key aspect of stabilization must be fiscal discipline, despite political pressures to the contrary. Fiscal discipline is important because deficits must be financed—whether through printing money, issuing domestic bonds, or tapping the international markets. Each mechanism has its costs for financial development. Inflation and the resulting uncertainty are one cost, together with the need to compensate with tight monetary policy and high interest rates. Crowding out in local bond markets is another, as can be seen in many Latin American countries where the large majority of bonds consist of government debt. Finally, careless use of international finance, with mismatches of various kinds, has proved to be a powerful element underlying financial crisis. While fiscal deficits declined sharply in the early 1990s, they have been creeping up again, which constitutes an obvious area of concern throughout the region. They must be controlled, but the target level of deficit (or surplus) has to be decided according to political and economic circumstances in individual countries.

Growth, savings, and finance are an interrelated triad in the macroeconomic sphere. Econometric evidence suggests that finance is the independent variable in the relationship with growth, but the latter will always generate some type of finance when necessary. The question is how stable and robust the finance will be. The situation in Mexico since 1995 is an interesting example. Despite a continuous decline in bank lending and minuscule domestic capital markets, growth and investment were buoyant in the second part of the decade, supported by international finance for large firms and nonbank finance for SMEs. While the steep fall in Mexico's growth rate in the early 2000s was mainly due to the drop in U.S. economic growth, the lack of finance for the majority of firms meant that the domestic economy was not able to buffer the external slowdown.

Savings are also primarily a result of the growth process, although tax and other policy measures can have a positive effect on saving propensities. Some portion of available savings will then be recycled through the domestic financial system. The deep financial systems in East Asia are clearly a reflection of the high savings rates in that region. The situation in Latin America is weaker than that in Asia for two main reasons: the savings rates are lower per se, and skewed income distribution and macroeconomic instability create incentives for capital flight, moving existing savings out of the country rather than channeling them into domestic capital markets to finance investment. Each individual country needs to design instruments and incentives to help channel savings into the financial system and into productive use, but this must take place within a context of stable growth.

Institutional Development

Institution building constitutes a second policy area that is crucial for strengthening the financial sector. Political stability is a prerequisite for any program to develop societywide or sector-specific institutions. In particular, continuity of political-economic approach is a sine qua non. Too often in the past, Latin America has gone through large pendular swings in policy orientation, which has the effect of undermining any kind of institution building. One of the most positive aspects of recent years is the increased tendency toward economic policy continuity, even when governments of different political persuasions replace each other. Governments and the private sector alike are coming to realize that institutions take a long time to create, but can be destroyed very rapidly.

Given an appropriate political context, institution building must take place in two distinct areas. The first is the area we have emphasized in the book: the rules and norms that govern societal interactions by controlling uncertainty. We have focused on two types of rules and norms, both of which are essential for fostering financial development. At the societal level, the World Bank has helped to define and measure a set of governance institutions. Of their six elements, we worked with four: government effectiveness, regulatory quality, rule of law, and control of corruption. We found a strong relationship between these indicators and both bank performance and capital market size, which suggests a fruitful—if difficult—area where governments should try to make progress in the near future. At the financial sector level, a more specific set of institutions is important. Both corporate governance in firms that are potential borrowers and governance of the financial sector itself must be strengthened. Examples that we and others have found to be related to capital market development include disclosure of financial information, general transparency, contract enforcement, protection of minority shareholders, bans on insider trading, and simple and expeditious bankruptcy procedures. These practices have a strong impact on whether bankers are willing to make loans and investors are willing to put money into capital markets. The relationship is especially important with respect to finance for the private sector. Governments may be able to get resources for themselves through various means, but private sector finance is much more fragile.

A second area for developing institutions is more concrete, involving specialized agents and markets. With respect to banking, perhaps the most important is the regulatory and supervisory system. Opinions differ on the best type of regulation and supervision for both banks and capital markets. The prevailing view is that a strong government role is essential, but a few experts have recently begun to argue that private sector monitoring is preferable. Our view is that it would be a mistake to rely exclusively on the latter, given the problems of macroeconomic shocks, contagion, and procyclicality that characterize today's open economies. Nonetheless, activities such as increasing information disclosure and transparency and introducing external ratings and audits can be useful supplements to government regulation and supervision. Government-based supervision and private monitoring should be viewed not as substitutes, but as complements. Important attributes of supervisors must include high skill levels, pay scales that prevent them from being bribed or hired away, and adequate training. Training can usefully be carried out in connection with regulatory agencies of industrial countries, which is especially important when foreign banks control the dominant share of local markets (as in Mexico). Information sharing and perhaps joint supervision are additional topics that need much more attention than they have received to date.

With respect to capital markets, the key requirements include fostering the development of new actors and strengthening market infrastructure. On the demand side, we have described the importance of institutional investors, including pension funds and insurance companies. At the same time, we found a degree of contradiction between institutional investors and the liquidity that is necessary to attract other participants to the stock and bond markets. One answer is to promote another kind of institutional investor—mutual funds—that tends to specialize in short- to medium-term investments because of client requirements. On the supply side, a central issue is attracting enough firms to list on local exchanges. Among others, two interrelated problems need government attention. On the one hand, strong corporate governance must be promoted if markets are to flourish. On the other hand, some firms are unwilling to engage in the disclosure and transparency that are the essence of corporate governance. Convincing them that it is in their long-run interest to do so is an ongoing task of financial authorities in all emerging market economies.

International and Regional Context

While the international context in which Latin American banks and capital markets operate is clearly important to their performance, policy in this area is complicated. Some experts emphasize the need to reform the international financial architecture. Developing countries do not have much leverage, however. Moreover, the interests of developing countries do not always coincide, which hinders the creation of alliances that could increase their influence. For example, the richer countries are more concerned with access to private flows, whereas the poorer ones are more interested in aid. Those with access to private capital are concerned about measures to enhance the stability of international debt instruments; those who rely on public sector flows tend to be more interested in conditions for debt relief.

Given this panorama, we recommend that Latin American countries devote their main efforts to decreasing their own vulnerability, yet without abandoning the discussion of international financial policy.[15] In large measure, this means

15. Williamson (2005) has recently suggested some interesting ideas for a policy agenda that emphasizes both the creditor and debtor sides.

pursuing sound macroeconomic policy, as discussed earlier. For example, higher savings rates and lower fiscal deficits both decrease the need for external finance. Similarly, conservative debt management strategies can help countries avoid being caught out when conditions change in international financial markets. Within the context of sound macroeconomic management, judicious use of controls on capital inflows may help to prevent capital surges from undermining domestic stability. Maturity, currency, and interest rate mismatches should be avoided when engaging in international transactions. Finally, decreasing a country's international vulnerability is a strong reason for developing local capital markets.

A powerful argument against the last point involves the relatively small size of most Latin American economies, with the exception of Brazil and Mexico. Small market size does indeed affect the ability of local capital markets to provide for the financial needs of governments and large firms. Some World Bank economists, among others, have recently argued that because of size constraints, the best approach is to push forward with international financial integration and forget about local markets. We do not believe this recommendation is helpful except, perhaps, for the largest borrowers. Medium-sized firms will not be able to tap international markets, but they could participate locally. In addition, local markets could supplement international offerings by larger borrowers. We suggest that governments continue their efforts to expand domestic markets through market-enhancing policies, such as promoting improved corporate governance and expanding the types of actors who can participate. The latter might include the introduction of equity markets for new or small firms, as has been done in Brazil, Chile, and Korea.

An alternative that the World Bank rejects, but that we think deserves more exploration, is the creation of regional capital markets. East Asian governments have taken the lead in this area and have already set up some relevant institutions. For example, a small regional bond market has been established, and central banks have negotiated swaps. On the private sector side, banks have begun investing across borders, increasing the demand for regionally based brokerages, investment banks, and other such institutions. Latin American countries would do well to follow the results with care to see what can be accomplished. Within Latin America itself, harmonization of macroeconomic policies is a first step, but others could be taken as well. Regional and subregional development banks should take a leading role in these activities.

Long-Term Finance for Investment

The lack of long-term finance for investment is one of two market failures that we highlight in the book. The lack of such finance is arguably one cause of the low investment ratios found in Latin America, although some approaches have been more successful than others in addressing the problem. For example, Brazil has large amounts of long-term finance available through BNDES, yet it has one of the lowest investment rates in the region. Chile, by contrast, offers no long-term government finance, but it has promoted capital markets with greater success as measured by investment ratios. Mexico has little finance of either kind, relying instead on nonbank and international finance together with retained earnings. Again, however, the investment ratio is very low. Market-enhancing policies could play a useful role in stimulating the development of both public and private institutions.

Three forms of market enhancement offer the potential to increase long-term finance. A first approach centers on banks, since they are the single largest source of finance in the region—despite the poor performance in recent years. The maturities of bank loans that are to be used for investment need to be extended. One possibility would be to establish carefully designed guarantees from national or regional public sector banks. Another would be to encourage a system for the securitization of long-term loans for investment, along the lines of the mortgage market in a number of countries. While the U.S. system is the best known, Chile has long securitized its mortgage debt, and Mexico and Brazil have also begun to use this approach. In the U.S. case, the institutions involved are quasi-public, but regional development banks could play this role, as could private firms with sufficient resources. This would allow banks to make long-term loans, but then get them off their books so as to continue making new finance available.[16]

A second approach is to promote capital markets in countries where the market is large enough to support them. Brazil and Mexico are clearly candidates, and the Chilean markets are already active in a relatively small economy. A key factor is fiscal restraint, so that available funds are not monopolized by the public sector. Based on our review of various experiences, we identify three additional requirements: namely, good corporate governance, the presence of institutional investors, and sufficient liquidity in the secondary markets to give investors confidence. While some conflict may arise between the second and third items, it is most likely to occur with pension funds and insurance companies, given their long time horizons. Other institutional investors, such as mutual funds, are more active traders. As mentioned above, the possibility of regional capital markets should also be explored as a way to resolve the size problem.

A third approach involves a direct government role in providing long-term finance. The negative experience with government development banks in many countries has frequently led to the closure of these banks or their conversion into second-tier institutions. It is worth studying the relatively successful cases, however, to see if any mechanisms could be adapted to other locations. Korea's

16. Securitization is easier for mortgages than for investment loans because of the standardization of the underlying assets and the ability to repossess in case of default. Greater institutional creativity would be required for investment loans.

KDB is a case in point, as is Brazil's BNDES, although the issue of why BNDES has been unable to raise investment rates needs to be thoroughly explored. A number of regional and subregional development banks have also played a positive role in financing investment. The Inter-American Development Bank, the Andean Development Corporation, and the Central American Bank for Economic Integration are all important examples within Latin America. The World Bank provides an example on a global scale. These regional and global institutions could also usefully be examined for lessons on how well-managed development banks can contribute to long-term finance for investment. The poor experience with public sector banks in the past should not be grounds for automatic elimination of this option.

Access to Finance for Small Firms

The other market failure that we have been following is the lack of finance for small firms. The two most important reasons that SMEs have difficulties obtaining finance are lack of information about the firms (because of poor record-keeping or insufficient history) and high bank transaction costs (the unit administrative costs of making small loans are much higher than for large ones). The challenge, then, is to design instruments to deal with these problems. The solution must take into account some important differences between two types of small firms, since they may require different solutions to their financing problems. Small firms in traditional sectors can be supported by existing institutions (banks and nonbank intermediaries), but high-tech start-ups may need finance more akin to venture capital in developed countries. Again, market-enhancing policies are required.

The countries we have studied have tried four approaches to increase finance for small firms, with differing degrees of success. Governments in other countries can gain useful insights from their successes and failures. The first approach is the traditional way of providing finance to small firms: direct loans from government-owned commercial or development banks. These experiences have generally been quite negative, in terms of both managing the banks and getting the money to the intended recipients. Nonetheless, some relatively successful cases are worth reviewing, such as Chile's BancoEstado, Brazil's BNDES and Banco do Brasil, and Costa Rica's public banks. Several banks in East Asia, such as Korea's Industrial Bank, may also offer some useful experiences. After suffering serious problems in the past, these institutions have restructured operations and improved internal bank management. Tough regulation, which put the public banks on the same level playing field as their private competitors, has also been essential in turning around performance and making the banks potentially useful instruments for supplying finance to SMEs.

The second approach involves second-tier banks. These have been much more common than direct lending in recent years in Latin America. These are government-owned institutions that provide funds to (usually private) commercial banks to on-lend to small and medium-sized firms. Two of the most successful instruments used by second-tier banks have been guarantees for loans that private banks make to small firms and subsidies for transaction costs. Chile's BancoEstado, in collaboration with Corfo, has used both methods with fairly good results. Mexico's Nafin has a large program that offers guarantees to banks for the loans they make to small and medium-sized firms. Brazil's BNDES also does much of its lending to SMEs via second-tier operations with both public and private commercial banks, which are responsible for the analysis and approval of both credits and guarantees. BNDES officials argue that the latter are closer to the customers and thus can make better-informed decisions than the large development banks themselves.

Third, new institutions and techniques to support lending are being introduced in Latin America. Credit bureaus have lowered the information costs for SME lending, while credit scoring has lowered transaction costs. Leasing and factoring have also become important sources of finance for small firms. Leasing enables them to obtain equipment without having to make a large initial outlay, while factoring makes it possible for them to get access to funds before they are paid for the products they produce. Indeed, factoring has become the technique of preference at Mexico's Nafin, where a second-tier arrangement has been devised to link large purchasers and private factoring firms with small subcontractors. Likewise, studies show that a substantial amount of investment by small firms in Chile is carried out through factoring and leasing. In Brazil, both BNDES and Banco do Brasil have introduced credit cards for SMEs, which provide preapproved medium-term credit for working capital and investment, and BNDES administers a lending and technical assistance program for SME exporters. New actors have also appeared to support SMEs. In Mexico, the absence of lending from commercial banks led to the formation of a group of nonbank institutions (*sofoles*). Since they cannot take deposits, the *sofoles* get money from the banks and the capital markets. They have lent mainly for consumer and housing purposes, but they have also made loans to SMEs. A mark of their success is the fact that several have been purchased by the large banks.

Finally, a select group of small firms needs large amounts of money to undertake substantial investments in high-technology areas. Such firms have gained access to venture capital funds in developed countries and in some Asian countries. Taiwan has perhaps the most developed set of venture capital firms, but Korea and Singapore are also moving in this direction. Mexico has incipient venture capital firms (Sincas, a type of mutual fund), although they have not yet taken off, while the latest capital market reform in Chile contains provisions to stimulate venture capital. This is clearly an area for future activity, probably though a partnership between public and private sectors. It may also involve a special stock exchange for new firms so as to provide an exit for venture partners and an ongoing source of finance for the firms at a later stage. A study of the Asian experiences would be a useful first step.

Final Comments

To close our analysis of Latin America's financial systems at both the regional and national levels, a few simple messages are worth emphasizing. First, finance is an important determinant of growth and welfare. It thus merits receiving the highest priority on the policy agenda of the region. Second, the financial systems in most Latin American countries work poorly, including both the banking systems and the capital markets. They are not providing either the support needed for higher growth or the access required to expand opportunities to less privileged groups in society. Most Latin American governments have declared growth with equity to be their overarching goal; finance is a key instrument— one that can assist them or undermine them. Third, changes must be made. Financial liberalization resolved some problems, but it created many others. It is now time to push forward with a new reform agenda that will address existing deficiencies. We have put forward one set of proposals; others have made their own suggestions. Ultimately, individual governments and private sector actors in each country must choose broad strategies and select specific policies that will work in their particular case. Even with a clear and coherent agenda, however, strengthening the region's financial systems will be a long-term process full of difficulties. It is urgent to start now.

References

Acemoglu, Daron, Simon Johnson, and James Robinson. 2001. "Colonial Origins of Comparative Development: An Empirical Investigation." *American Economic Review* 91(5): 1369–401.

———. 2002. "Reversal of Fortune: Geography and Institutions in the Making of the Modern World Income Distribution." *Quarterly Journal of Economics* 117(4): 1231–94.

——— . 2004. "Institutions as the Fundamental Cause of Long-Run Growth." Working paper 10481. Cambridge, Mass.: National Bureau of Economic Research.

ADB (Asian Development Bank). 2004. *Asian Development Outlook.* Oxford University Press.

Agosín, Manuel R., and Ricardo Ffrench-Davis. 2001. "Managing Capital Inflows in Chile." In *Short-Term Capital Flows and Economic Crisis,* edited by Stephany Griffith-Jones, Manuel F. Montes, and Anwar Nasution, 199–225. Oxford University Press.

Agosín, Manuel R., and Ernesto Pastén. 2003. "Corporate Governance in Chile." Working paper 209. Santiago: Central Bank of Chile.

Ahn, Choong Young, and Baekin Cha. 2004. "Financial Sector Restructuring in South Korea: Accomplishments and Unfinished Agenda." *Asian Economic Papers* 3(1): 1–21.

Alba, Pedro, Leonardo Hernández, and Daniela Klingebiel. 2001. "Financial Liberalization and the Capital Account: Thailand 1988–1997." In *The Political Economy of the East Asian Crisis and Its Aftermath: Tigers in Distress,* edited by Arvid Lukauskas and Francisco Rivera-Batiz, 110–64. Cheltenham: Edward Elgar.

Albuquerque, Pedro H. 2001. "Impactos econômicos da CPMF." Discussion paper 21. Brasília: Central Bank of Brazil.

Allen, Franklin, and Douglas Gale. 2000. *Comparing Economic Systems.* MIT Press.

Amsden, Alice H. 1989. *Asia's Next Giant: South Korea and Late Industrialization.* Oxford University Press.

————, ed. 1994. "The World Bank's 'The East Asian Miracle': Economic Growth and Public Policy." *World Development* 22(4): 615–70 (special section).

Amyx, Jennifer. 2004. "A Regional Bond Market for East Asia? The Evolving Political Dynamics of Regional Financial Cooperation." Pacific economic paper 342. Canberra: Australian National University, Australia-Japan Research Center.

Aoki, Masahiko, Hyung-Ki Kim, and Masahiro Okuno-Fujiwara, eds. 1997. *The Role of Government in East Asian Development: Comparative Institutional Analysis.* Oxford: Clarendon Press.

Armijo, Leslie, and Walter L. Ness. 2002. "Modernizing Brazil's Capital Markets, 1985–2001: Pragmatism and Democratic Adjustment." Paper prepared for the Annual Meeting of the International Studies Association. New Orleans, 25–28 March.

————. 2004. "Contested Meanings of 'Corporate Governance Reform': The Case of Democratic Brazil, 1985–2003." Paper prepared for the Annual Meeting of the Western Political Science Association. Portland, Ore., 11–13 March.

Asher, Mukul G. 2002. "Southeast Asia's Social Security Systems: Need for a System-Wide Perspective and Professionalism." *International Social Security Review* 55(4): 71–88.

Baer, Werner, and Nader Nazmi. 2000. "Privatization and Restructuring of Banks in Brazil." *Quarterly Review of Economic and Finance* 40(1): 3–24.

Baldacci, Emanuele, Luiz R. de Mello, and María G. Inchauste. 2004. "Financial Crises, Poverty, and Income Distribution." Working paper 02/4. Washington: International Monetary Fund.

Bank of Mexico. 2001. "Los mercados de capitales." Mexico City. Available at www.banxico.org.mx.

————. 2002. "Mercado de valores de renta fija: el caso mexicano." Mexico City. Available at www.banxico.org.mx.

————. 2003. "El desarrollo de los mercados de capitales." Presentation prepared for the XIV Convención del Mercado de Valores. Bank of Mexico, Mexico City, 26 November.

Barth, James R., Gerard Caprio Jr., and Ross Levine. 2001a. "Bank Regulation and Supervision: What Works Best?" Policy research working paper 2725. Washington: World Bank.

————. 2001b. "The Regulation and Supervision of Banks around the World: A New Database." Policy research working paper 2588. Washington: World Bank.

————. 2005. *Rethinking Bank Regulation: Till Angels Govern.* Cambridge University Press.

Batra, Geeta, Daniel Kaufmann, and Andrew H. W. Stone. 2003. *Investment Climate around the World: Voices of Firms from the World Business Environmental Survey.* Washington: World Bank.

Baumann, Renato, ed. 2002. *Brazil in the 1990s: An Economy in Transition.* New York: Palgrave Macmillan.

Beck, Thorsten, Juan Miguel Crivelli, and William Summerhill. 2005. "State Bank Transformation in Brazil: Choices and Consequences." *Journal of Banking and Finance* 29(8–9): 2223–57.

Beck, Thorsten, Asli Demirgüç-Kunt, and Ross Levine. 2003. "Law and Finance: Why Does Legal Origin Matter?" *Journal of Comparative Economics* 31(4): 653–75.

Beck, Thorsten, and others. 2004. "Finance, Firm Size, and Growth." Paper prepared for the Conference on Small and Medium Enterprises: Overcoming Growth Constraints. World Bank, Washington, 14–15 October.

Belaisch, Agnès. 2003. "Do Brazilian Banks Compete?" Working paper 03/113. Washington: International Monetary Fund.

Berger, Allen, and Greg Udell. 2004. "A More Complete Conceptual Framework for SME Financing." Paper prepared for the Conference on Small and Medium Enterprises: Overcoming Growth Constraints. World Bank, Washington, 14–15 October.

BIS (Bank for International Settlements). 2000. "Cycles and the Financial System." *Annual Report*. Basel.

———. 2002. "The Development of Bond Markets in Emerging Economies." BIS paper 11. Basel.

———. 2004. "Foreign Direct Investment in the Financial Sector of Emerging Market Economies." Basel: Bank for International Settlements, Committee on the Global Financial System.

Blum, Jürg. 1999. "Do Capital Adequacy Requirements Reduce Risk in Banking?" *Journal of Banking and Finance* 23(5): 755–71.

BMV (Bolsa Mexicana de Valores). 2003. *Informe anual, 2003*. Mexico City.

BNDES (Banco Nacional de Desenvolvimento Econômico e Social). 2002. *BNDES—Fifty Years of Development*. Brasília.

Bonin, John P., and Istvan Abel. 2000. "Retail Banking in Hungary: A Foreign Affair?" Working paper 356. Ann Arbor, Mich.: University of Michigan, William Davidson Institute.

Borio, Claudio. 2003. "Toward a Macroprudential Framework for Financial Regulation and Supervision?" Working paper 128. Basel: Bank for International Settlements.

Borio, Claudio, Craig Furfine, and Philip Lowe. 2001. "Procyclicality of the Financial System and Financial Stability: Issues and Policy Options." BIS paper 1. Basel: Bank for International Settlements.

Bortolotti, Bernardo, and Domenico Siniscalco. 2004. *The Challenges of Privatization: An International Analysis*. Oxford University Press.

Bovespa (Bolsa de Valores de São Paulo). 2004. *Annual Report*. São Paulo.

Boyd, John H., Ross Levine, and Bruce D. Smith. 2001. "The Impact of Inflation on Financial Sector Performance." *Journal of Monetary Economics* 47(2): 221–48.

Brothers, Dwight S., and Leopoldo M. Solís. 1966. *Mexican Financial Development*. University of Texas Press.

Budnevich, Carlos. 2000. "El sistema financiero chileno y su institucionalidad regulatoria: las políticas bancarias en los noventa." In *El estado y el sector privado: construyendo una nueva economía en los años 90,* edited by Oscar Muñoz Gomá, 199–245. Santiago: FLACSO/Dolmen.

Bulmer-Thomas, Victor. 2003. *The Economic History of Latin America since Independence*. 2nd ed. Cambridge University Press.

Burki, Shahid Javed, and Guillermo E. Perry. 1997. *The Long March: A Reform Agenda for Latin America and the Caribbean in the Next Decade*. Washington: World Bank, Latin American and Caribbean Studies.

———. 1998. *Beyond the Washington Consensus: Institutions Matter*. Washington: World Bank, Latin American and Caribbean Studies.

Caballero, Ricardo J. 2002. "Coping with Chile's External Vulnerability: A Financial Problem." Working paper 154. Santiago: Central Bank of Chile.

Calderón, Alvaro, and Ramón Casilda. 2000. "The Spanish Banks' Strategies in Latin America." *CEPAL Review* 70: 73–92.

Calderón, Alvaro, and Stephany Griffith-Jones. 1995. "Los flujos de capital extranjero en la economía chilena: renovado acceso y nuevos usos." Productive development series 24. Santiago: Economic Commission for Latin America and the Caribbean.

Calomiris, Charles, Daniela Klingebiel, and Luc Laeven. 2004. "A Taxonomy of Financial Crisis Resolution Mechanisms: Cross-Country Experience." Policy research working paper 3379. Washington: World Bank.

Calvo, Guillermo A. 1998. "Capital Flows and Capital-Market Crises: The Simple Economics of Sudden Stops." *Journal of Applied Economics* 1(1): 35–55.

Camdessus, Michel. 1995. "Address by the Managing Director of the IMF at the UN World Summit for Social Development." Copenhagen.

Capaul, Mierta. 2003. "Corporate Governance in Latin America." Background paper for *Whither Latin American Capital Markets?* Washington: World Bank, Office of the Chief Economist, Latin American and Caribbean Region.

Caprio, Gerard, Patrick Honohan, and Joseph Stiglitz, eds. 2001. *Financial Liberalization: How Far, How Fast?* Cambridge University Press.

Caprio, Gerard, and others, eds. 2004. *The Future of State-Owned Financial Institutions.* Brookings.

Cárdenas, Enrique, José Antonio Ocampo, and Rosemary Thorp, eds. 2000. *An Economic History of Twentieth-Century Latin America,* vol. 3: *Industrialization and the State in Latin America: The Postwar Years.* New York: Palgrave Macmillan.

Carkovic, María, and Ross Levine. 2002. "Finance and Growth: New Evidence and Policy Analyses for Chile." In *Economic Growth: Sources, Trends and Cycles*, edited by Norman Loayza and Raimundo Soto, 343–75. Santiago: Central Bank of Chile.

Carvalho, Carlos Eduardo, Rogerio Studart, and Antônio José Alves Jr. 2002. "Desnacionalizacão do setor bancário e financiamento das empresas: a experiência brasileira recente." Discussion paper 882. Brasília: Instituto de Pesquisa Econômica Aplicada.

Carvalho, Fernando J. 2001. "The Recent Expansion of Foreign Banks in Brazil: First Results." Working paper CBS-18-01. Oxford: University of Oxford, Center for Brazilian Studies.

Central Bank of Brazil. 2003. *Avaliação de 4 anos do projeto juros e spread bancário.* Brasília.

Central Bank of Chile. 2000. "Indicadores económicos y sociales de Chile, 1960–2000." CD Rom. Santiago.

Chin, Kok-Fay, and K. S. Jomo. 2003. "From Financial Liberalization to Crisis in Malaysia." In *Financial Liberalization and Crisis in Asia,* edited by Chung H. Lee, 104–32. London: Routledge.

Cho, Yoon Je. 2002. "Financial Repression, Liberalization, Crisis, and Restructuring: Lessons of Korea's Financial Sector Policies." Research paper 47. Tokyo: Asian Development Bank Institute.

Chong, Alberto, and Florencio López-de-Silanes, eds. 2005. *Privatization in Latin America: Myths and Realities.* Stanford University Press.

Chow, Peter C. Y., and Bates Gill, eds. 2000. *Weathering the Storm: Taiwan, Its Neighbors, and the Asian Financial Crisis.* Brookings.

Cifuentes, Rodrigo, Jorge Desormeaux, and Claudio González. 2002. "Capital Markets in Chile: From Financial Repression to Financial Deepening." Economic policy paper 4. Santiago: Central Bank of Chile.

Claessens, Stijn, Asli Demirgüç-Kunt, and Harry Huizinga. 2001. "How Does Foreign Entry Affect Domestic Banking Markets?" *Journal of Banking and Finance* 25(5): 891–911.

Claessens, Stijn, and Daniela Klingebiel. 2001. "Competition and Scope of Activities in Financial Services." *World Bank Research Observer* 16(1): 19–40.

Claessens, Stijn, Daniela Klingebiel, and Luc Laeven. 2003. "Financial Restructuring in Banking and Corporate Sector Crises: What Policies to Pursue?" In *Managing Currency*

Crises in Emerging Markets, edited by Michael P. Dooley and Jeffrey A. Frankel, 147–85. University of Chicago Press.

———. 2004. "Resolving Systemic Financial Crises: Policies and Institutions." Policy research working paper 3377. Washington: World Bank.

Claessens, Stijn, Daniela Klingebiel, and Sergio L. Schmukler. 2002. "The Future of Stock Exchanges in Emerging Economies: Evolution and Prospects." In *Brookings-Wharton Papers on Financial Services: 2002*, edited by Robert E. Litan and Richard Herring, 167–212. Brookings.

———. 2004. "Stock Market Development and Internationalization: Do Economic Fundamentals Spur Both Similarly?" Background paper for *Whither Latin American Capital Markets?* Washington: World Bank, Office of the Chief Economist, Latin American and Caribbean Region.

Clarke, George, Robert Cull, and María Soledad Martínez Peria. 2001. "Does Foreign Bank Penetration Reduce Access to Credit in Developing Countries? Evidence from Asking Borrowers." Policy research working paper 2716. Washington: World Bank.

Clarke, George, and others. 2002. "Bank Lending to Small Businesses in Latin America: Does Bank Origin Matter?" Policy research working paper 2760. Washington: World Bank.

———. 2003. "Foreign Bank Entry: Experience, Implications for Developing Economies, and Agenda for Further Research." *World Bank Research Observer* 18(1): 25–59.

Cline, William. 2002. "Financial Crises and Poverty in Emerging Market Economies." Working paper 8. Washington: Center for Global Development.

Coe, David T., and Se-Jik Kim, eds. 2002. *Korean Crisis and Recovery*. Seoul: International Monetary Fund and Korea Institute for International Economic Policy.

Coelho, Isaias, Liam P. Ebril, and Victoria P. Summers. 2001. "Bank Debit Taxes in Latin America: An Analysis of Recent Trends." Working paper 01/67. Washington: International Monetary Fund.

Collyns, Charles V., and G. Russell Kincaid, eds. 2003. *Managing Financial Crises: Recent Experiences and Lessons for Latin America*. Occasional paper 217. Washington: International Monetary Fund.

Copelman, Martina. 2000. "Financial Structure and Economic Activity in Mexico." Paper prepared for the Conference on Financial Structure and Economic Development. World Bank, Washington, 10–11 February.

Corbo, Vittorio, and Klaus Schmidt-Hebbel. 2003. "Efectos macroeconómicos de la reforma de pensiones en Chile." Paper prepared for the Conference on Reformas a los Sistemas de Pensiones: Sus Efectos y Retos. International Federation of Pension Fund Administrators, Panama City, 10–11 July.

Corsetti, Giancarlo, Paolo Pesenti, and Nouriel Roubini. 1998a. "What Caused the Asian Currency and Financial Crisis? Part I: A Macroeconomic Overview." Working paper 6833. Cambridge, Mass.: National Bureau of Economic Research.

———. 1998b. "What Caused the Asian Currency and Financial Crisis? Part II: The Policy Debate." Working paper 6834. Cambridge, Mass.: National Bureau of Economic Research.

Cristini, Marcela, Ramiro A. Moya, and Andrew Powell. 2001. "The Importance of an Effective Legal System for Credit Markets: The Case of Argentina." In *Defusing Default: Incentives and Institutions*, edited by Marco Pagano, 119–56. Washington: Organization for Economic Cooperation and Development, Development Center and Inter-American Development Bank.

Crockett, Andrew. 2000. "Marrying the Micro- and Macroprudential Dimensions of Financial Stability." *BIS Speeches*. Basel: Bank for International Settlements.

————. 2001. "Market Discipline and Financial Stability." *BIS Speeches*. Basel: Bank for International Settlements.

Crystal, Jennifer S., B. Gerard Dages, and Linda S. Goldberg. 2001. "Does Foreign Ownership Contribute to Sounder Banks in Emerging Markets? The Latin American Experience." In *Open Doors: Foreign Participation in Financial Systems in Developing Countries*, edited by Robert E. Litan, Paul Masson, and Michael Pomerleano, 217–66. Brookings.

Cull, Robert, and others. 2004. "Historical Financing of Small and Medium Size Enterprises." Paper prepared for the Conference on Small and Medium Enterprises: Overcoming Growth Constraints. World Bank, Washington, 14–15 October.

Dages, B. Gerard, Linda Goldberg, and Daniel Kinney. 2000. "Foreign and Domestic Bank Participation in Emerging Markets: Lessons from Mexico and Argentina." *Federal Reserve Bank of New York Economic Policy Review* 6(3): 17–36.

Daseking, Christina, and others. 2004. *Lessons from the Crisis in Argentina*. Occasional paper 236. Washington: International Monetary Fund.

De Gregorio, José, Sebastian Edwards, and Rodrigo O. Valdés. 2000. "Controls on Capital Inflows: Do They Work?" *Journal of Development Economics* 63(1): 59–83.

De Krivoy, Ruth. 2000. *Collapse: The Venezuelan Banking Crisis of '94*. Washington: The Group of Thirty.

De la Torre, Augusto. 2002. "Reforming Development Banks: A Framework." Presentation prepared for the Seminar on Public-Sector Banks and Privatization. World Bank, Washington, 10 December.

De la Torre, Augusto, Eduardo Levy-Yeyati, and Sergio L. Schmukler. 2003. "Living and Dying with Hard Pegs: The Rise and Fall of Argentina's Currency Board." *Economía* 3(2): 43–99.

Del Angel-Mobarak, Gustavo A. 2005. "La banca mexicana antes de 1982." In *Cuando el estado se hizo banquero: consequencias de la nacionalización bancaria en México*, edited by Gustavo Del Angel-Mobarak, Carlos Bazdresch, and Francisco Suárez Dávila, 43–56. Mexico City: El Trimestre Económico.

Del Angel-Mobarak, Gustavo A., Carlos Bazdresch, and Francisco Suárez Dávila, eds. 2005. *Cuando el estado se hizo banquero: consequencias de la nacionalización bancaria en México*. Mexico City: El Trimestre Económico.

Dell'Ariccia, Giovanni, Enrica Detragiache, and Raghuram Rajan. 2005. "The Real Effect of Banking Crisis." Working paper 05/63. Washington: International Monetary Fund.

Demetriades, Panicos, and Svetlana Andrianova. 2004. "Finance and Growth: What We Know and What We Need to Know." In *Financial Development and Economic Growth: Explaining the Links*, edited by C. A. E. Goodhart, 38–65. New York: Palgrave Macmillan.

Demirgüç-Kunt, Asli, and Enrica Detragiache. 1998a. "Financial Liberalization and Financial Fragility." Working paper 98/83. Washington: International Monetary Fund.

————. 1998b. "The Determinants of Banking Crisis in Developing and Developed Countries." *IMF Staff Papers* 45(1): 81–109.

————. 2002. "Does Deposit Insurance Increase Banking System Stability? An Empirical Investigation." *Journal of Monetary Economics* 49(7): 1373–406.

————. 2005. "Cross-Country Empirical Studies of System Bank Distress: A Survey." *National Institute Economic Review* 192(1): 68–83.

Demirgüç-Kunt, Asli, Enrica Detragiache, and Poonam Gupta. 2000. "Inside the Crisis: An Empirical Analysis of Banking Systems in Distress." Working paper 00/156. Washington: International Monetary Fund.

Demirgüç-Kunt, Asli, and Harry Huizinga. 1999. "Determinants of Commercial Bank Interest Margins and Profitability: Some International Evidence." *World Bank Economic Review* 13(2): 379–408.

Demirgüç-Kunt, Asli, and Ross Levine, eds. 2001. *Financial Structure and Economic Growth.* MIT Press.

Demirgüç-Kunt, Asli, Ross Levine, and Hong-Ghi Min. 1998. "Opening to Foreign Banks: Issues of Stability, Efficiency, and Growth." In *The Implications of Globalization of World Financial Markets,* edited by Seongtae Lee, 83–115. Seoul: Bank of Korea.

Díaz-Alejandro, Carlos. 1985. "Good-bye Financial Repression, Hello Financial Crash." *Journal of Development Economics* 19(1–2): 1–24.

Díaz-Bonilla, Carolina, and others. 2004. "El plan de la convertibilidad, apertura de la economía y empleo en Argentina: una simulación macro-micro de pobreza y desigualdad." In *¿Quién se beneficia del libre comercio? Promoción de exportaciones en América Latina y el Caribe en los 90,* edited by Enrique Ganuza and others, 107–31. Bogotá, Colombia: United Nations Development Program and Alfaomega.

Dini, Marco, and Giovanni Stumpo. 2002. "Análisis de la política de fomento a las pequeñas y medianas empresas en Chile." Productive development series 136. Santiago: Economic Commission for Latin America and the Caribbean.

Dooley, Michael P., and Jeffrey A. Frankel, eds. 2002. *Managing Currency Crises in Emerging Markets.* University of Chicago Press.

Dornbusch, Rudi. 2002. "Malaysia's Crisis: Was It Different?" In *Preventing Currency Crises in Emerging Markets,* edited by Sebastian Edwards and Jeffrey A. Frankel, 441–60. University of Chicago Press.

Dowers, Kenroy, and Pietro Masci, eds. 2003. *Focus on Capital: New Approaches to Developing Latin American Capital Markets.* Washington: Inter-American Development Bank.

Easterly, William, and Ross Levine. 2003. "Tropics, Germs, and Crops: How Endowments Influence Economic Development." *Journal of Monetary Economics* 50(1): 3–39.

Eckert, Carter J. 1991. *Offspring of Empire: The Koch'ang Kims and the Colonial Origins of Korean Capitalism, 1876–1945.* Seattle: University of Washington Press.

ECLAC (Economic Commission for Latin America and the Caribbean). 2001. *Economic Survey of Latin America and the Caribbean, 2000–2001.* Santiago.

———. 2002. *Growth with Stability: Financing for Development in the New International Context.* Libros de la CEPAL 67. Santiago.

———. 2003. *Foreign Investment in Latin America and the Caribbean, 2002 Report.* Santiago.

Edwards, Sebastian. 1996. "A Tale of Two Crises: Chile and Mexico." Working paper 5794. Cambridge, Mass.: National Bureau of Economic Research.

EIU (Economist Intelligence Unit). 2001. *Country Finance: Mexico.* London.

Engerman, Stanley, and Kenneth Sokoloff. 1997. "Factor Endowments, Institutions, and Differential Paths of Growth among New World Economies: A View from Economic Historians of the United States." In *How Latin America Fell Behind,* edited by Stephen Haber, 260–304. Stanford University Press.

———. 2002. "Factor Endowments, Inequality, and Paths of Development among New World Economies." *Economía* 3(1): 41–109.

ESCAP (Economic and Social Commission for Asia and the Pacific). 1998. *Financial Sector Reform, Liberalization, and Management for Growth and Stability in the Asian and the Pacific Region: Issues and Experiences.* Bangkok.

Eyzaguirre, Nicolás, and Osvaldo J. Larrañaga. 1991. "Macroeconomía de las operaciones cuasifiscales en Chile." Fiscal policy series 21. Santiago: Economic Commission for Latin America and the Caribbean.

Fanelli, José María. 2003. "Growth, Instability, and the Crisis of Convertibility in Argentina." In *The Crisis That Was Not Prevented: Lessons for Argentina, the IMF, and Globalisation*, edited by Jan Joost Teunissen and Age Akkerman, 32–67. The Hague: Forum on Debt and Development.

Fernández de Lis, Santiago, Jorge Martínez, and Jesús Saurina. 2001. "Credit Growth, Problem Loans and Credit Risk Provisioning in Spain." BIS paper 1. Basel: Bank for International Settlements.

Ffrench-Davis, Ricardo, ed. 2001. *Financial Crises in "Successful" Emerging Economies*. Brookings.

———. 2002. *Economic Reforms in Chile: From Dictatorship to Democracy*. University of Michigan Press.

———. 2005. *Reforming Latin America's Economies: After Market Fundamentalism*. New York: Palgrave Macmillan.

Ffrench-Davis, Ricardo, and Stephany Griffith-Jones, eds. 2003. *From Capital Surges to Drought: Seeking Stability for Emerging Economies*. New York: Palgrave Macmillan.

Ffrench-Davis, Ricardo, and Barbara Stallings, eds. 2001. *Reformas, crecimiento y políticas sociales en Chile desde 1973*. Santiago: Economic Commission for Latin America and the Caribbean and LOM Ediciones.

Fishlow, Albert, and others, eds. 1994. *Miracle or Design? Lessons from the East Asian Experience*. Washington: Overseas Development Council.

Fitch Ratings. 2002a. "Country Report: The Korean Banking System." New York.

———. 2002b. "Country Report: The Singapore Banking System." New York.

———. 2003. "Country Report: Vietnam Banking System Update." New York.

———. 2004. "Credit Analysis: Banco do Brasil." New York.

———. 2005. "Credit Analysis: Thai Military Bank." New York.

FitzGerald, E. V. K. 1978. "The State and Capital Accumulation in Mexico." *Journal of Latin American Studies* 10(2): 263–82.

Fontaine, Juan Andrés. 1996. *La construcción de un mercado de capitales: el caso de Chile*. Washington: World Bank.

Foxley, Juan. 1998. "Reformas a la institucionalidad del crédito y el financiamiento a empresas de menor tamaño: la experiencia chilena con sistemas de 'segundo piso' 1990–1998." Financing development series 74. Santiago: Economic Commission for Latin America and the Caribbean.

Fry, Maxwell J. 1995. *Money, Interest, and Banking in Economic Development*. 2nd ed. Johns Hopkins University Press.

Fuentes, Rodrigo J., and Carlos P. Maquieira. 2001. "Why Borrowers Repay: Understanding High Performance in Chile's Financial Market." In *Defusing Default: Incentives and Institutions*, edited by Marco Pagano, 189–223. Washington: Organization for Economic Cooperation and Development, Development Center and Inter-American Development Bank.

Galindo, Arturo, and Alejandro Micco. 2003. "Do State-Owned Banks Promote Growth? Cross-Country Evidence for Manufacturing Industries." Working paper 483. Washington: Inter-American Development Bank, Research Department.

Gallego, Francisco A., and Norman Loayza. 2001. "Financial Structure in Chile: Macroeconomic Developments and Microeconomic Effects." In *Financial Structure and Economic Growth*, edited by Asli Demirgüç-Kunt and Ross Levine, 299–346. MIT Press.

García-Herrero, Alicia. 1997. "Banking Crises in Latin America in the 1990s: Lessons from Argentina, Paraguay, and Venezuela." Working paper 97/40. Washington: International Monetary Fund.

García-Herrero, Alicia, and María Soledad Martínez Perla. 2005. "What Determines the Mix of Foreign Bank Claims and Does It Matter?" Paper prepared for the Conference on Globalization and Financial Services in Emerging Economies. World Bank, Washington, 20–21 June.

García-Herrero, Alicia, and others. 2002. "Latin American Financial Development in Perspective." Working paper 216. Madrid: Banco de España, Servicio de Estudios.

Garrido, Celso. 2005. *Desarrollo económico y procesos de financiamiento en México: tranformaciones contemporáneas y dilemas actuales.* Mexico City: Siglo XXI.

Gerschenkron, Alexander. 1962. *Economic Backwardness in Historical Perspective: A Book of Essays.* Cambridge, Mass.: Belknap Press of Harvard University Press.

Ghosh, Swati, and Mari Pangestu. 1999. "Indonesia: Macro-Financial Linkages and Buildup of Vulnerabilities." Background paper for the Asian Development Bank and World Bank study on Managing Global Financial Integration in Asia. Washington.

Gill, Indermit Singh, Truman Packard, and Juan Yermo. 2004. *Keeping the Promise of Social Security in Latin America.* World Bank and Stanford University Press.

Glaeser, Edward L., and others. 2004. "Do Institutions Cause Growth?" *Journal of Economic Growth* 9(3): 271–303.

Glick, Reuven, and Michael Hutchinson. 2001. "Banking and Currency Crises: How Common Are Twins?" In *Financial Crises in Emerging Markets,* edited by Reuven Glick, Ramón Moreno, and Mark Spiegel, 35–69. Cambridge University Press.

Gochoco-Bautista, María Socorro. 2003. "Financial Liberalization and Economic Reform: The Philippine Experience." In *Financial Liberalization and Crisis in Asia,* edited by Chung H. Lee, 133–50. London: Routledge.

Goldfajn, Ilan, Katherine Hennings, and Hélio Mori. 2003. "Brazil's Financial System: Resilience to Shocks, No Currency Substitution, but Struggling to Promote Growth." Working paper 75. Brasília: Central Bank of Brazil.

Goldsmith, Raymond William. 1966. *The Financial Development of Mexico.* Paris: Organization for Economic Cooperation and Development, Development Center.

———. 1969. *Financial Structure and Development.* Yale University Press.

González-Anaya, José Antonio. 2003. "Why Have Banks Stopped Lending in Mexico since the Peso Crisis?" Working paper 118. Stanford, Calif.: Stanford Center for International Development.

Goodhart, Charles A. E. 2004. "Some New Directions for Financial Stability?" Per Jacobsson Lecture. Basel: Bank for International Settlements.

Gottschalk, Ricardo, and Cecilia Azevedo Sodré. 2005. "International Codes and Standards (C&S) and Development Finance: A Case Study of Brazil." Brighton, U.K.: Institute of Development Studies.

Graf, Pablo. 1999. "Policy Responses to the Banking Crisis in Mexico." Policy paper 6. Basel: Bank for International Settlements.

Graham, Carol, and Moisés Naím. 1998. "The Political Economy of Institution Building." In *Beyond Trade-offs,* edited by Nancy Birdsall, Carol Graham, and Richard Sabot, 321–61. Washington: Brookings and Inter-American Development Bank.

Gregoire, Jorge, and Hugo Ovando. 1974. "El mercado de capitales en Chile." *Estudios Monetarios III,* 245–328. Santiago: Central Bank of Chile.

Griffith-Jones, Stephany. 2003. "How to Prevent the New Basle Capital Accord from Harming Developing Countries." Paper prepared for the International Monetary Fund–World Bank Annual Meeting. Dubai, September.

Griffith-Jones, Stephany, and Avinash Persaud. 2005. "The Pro-cyclical Impact of Basle II on Emerging Markets and Its Political Economy." Brighton, U.K.: Institute of Development Studies.

Gruben, William C., and Robert McComb. 1997. "Liberalization, Privatization, and Crash: Mexico's Banking System in the 1990s." *Federal Reserve Bank of Dallas Economic Review* (1st quarter): 21–30.

———. 2003. "Privatization, Competition, and Supercompetition in the Mexican Commercial Banking System." *Journal of Banking and Finance* 27(2): 229–49.

Gruben, William C., and John H. Welch. 2001. "Banking and Currency Crisis Recovery: Brazil's Turnaround of 1999." *Economic and Financial Review* (4th quarter): 12–23.

Gupta, Asha. 2000. *Beyond Privatization.* London: Palgrave Macmillan.

Haber, Stephen, ed. 2002. *Crony Capitalism and Economic Growth in Latin America: Theory and Evidence.* Stanford University, Hoover Institution Press.

———. 2004. "Why Institutions Matter: Banking and Economic Growth in Mexico." Working paper 234. Stanford, Calif.: Stanford Center for International Development.

———. 2005. "Mexico's Experiments with Bank Privatization and Liberalization, 1991–2003." *Journal of Banking and Finance* 29(8–9): 2325–53.

Haber, Stephen, and Aldo Musacchio. 2005. "Contract Rights and Risk Aversion: Foreign Banks and the Mexican Economy, 1997–2004." Paper prepared for the Conference on Globalization and Financial Services in Emerging Economies. World Bank, Washington, 20–21 June.

Hahm, Joon Ho. 1999. "Financial System Restructuring in Korea: The Crisis and Its Resolution." In *East Asia's Financial System: Evolution and Crisis*, edited by Seiichi Masuyama, Donna Vanderbrink, and Chia Siow Yue, 109–43. Tokyo: Nomura Research Institute and Institute of Southeast Asian Studies.

Hanson, James A. 2004. "The Transformation of State-Owned Banks." In *The Future of State-Owned Financial Institutions*, edited by Gerard Caprio and others, 13–49. Brookings.

Hausler, Gerd, Donald J. Mathieson, and Jorge Roldós. 2003. "Trends in Developing Country Capital Markets around the World." In *The Future of Domestic Capital Markets in Developing Countries*, edited by Robert Litan, Michael Pomerleano, and Vasudevan Sundararajan, 21–44. Brookings.

Hausmann, Ricardo, and Michael Gavin. 1996. "The Roots of Banking Crises: The Macroeconomic Context." In *Banking Crises in Latin America*, edited by Ricardo Hausmann and Liliana Rojas-Suárez, 27–79. Washington: Inter-American Development Bank.

Hawkins, John. 2002. "Bond Markets and Banks in Emerging Economies." BIS paper 11. Basel: Bank for International Settlements.

Held, Gunther, and Luis Felipe Jiménez. 2001. "Liberalización, crisis y reforma del sistema bancario: 1974–99." In *Reformas, crecimiento y políticas sociales en Chile desde 1973*, edited by Ricardo Ffrench-Davis and Barbara Stallings, 133–71. Santiago: Economic Commission for Latin America and the Caribbean and LOM Ediciones.

Hellmann, Thomas, Kevin Murdock, and Joseph Stiglitz. 1997. "Financial Restraint and the Market Enhancing View." In *The Role of Government in East Asian Development: Comparative Institutional Analysis*, edited by Masahiko Aoki, Hyung-Ki Kim, and Masahiro Okuno-Fujiwara, 163–207. Oxford: Clarendon Press.

Hernández, Leonardo, and Fernando Parro. 2004. "Sistema financiero y crecimiento económico en Chile." Working paper 291. Santiago: Central Bank of Chile.

———. 2005. "Economic Reforms, Financial Development, and Growth: Lessons from the Chilean Experience." Working paper 238. Stanford, Calif.: Stanford Center for International Development.

Herring, Richard J., and Nathporn Chatusripitak. 2000. "The Case of the Missing Market: The Bond Market and Why It Matters for Financial Development." Working paper 11. Tokyo: Asian Development Bank Institute.

Hew, Denis. 2002. "Singapore as a Regional Financial Centre." Paper prepared for the Conference on the Role of Capital Markets in Asian Economic Development. Nomura Research Institute and the Institute for Southeast Asian Studies, Tokyo, 7–8 March. Available at www.tcf.or.jp/documents/index.html.

Ho, Khai Leong, ed. 2005. *Reforming Corporate Governance in Southeast Asia: Economics, Politics, and Regulations.* Singapore: Institute of Southeast Asian Studies.

Hoelscher, David S., and Marc Quintyn. 2003. *Managing Systemic Banking Crises.* Occasional paper 224. Washington: International Monetary Fund.

Holzmann, Robert, and Richard Hinz. 2005. *Old-Age Income Support in the Twenty-First Century: An International Perspective on Pension Systems and Reform.* Washington: World Bank.

Honohan, Patrick. 2004. *Financial Sector Policy and the Poor: Selected Findings and Issues.* Working paper 43. Washington: World Bank.

———. 2005. "Banking Sector Crises and Inequality." Policy research working paper 3659. Washington: World Bank.

Honohan, Patrick, and Daniela Klingebel. 2003. "The Fiscal Cost Implications of an Accommodating Approach to Banking Crises." *Journal of Banking and Finance* 27(8): 1539–60.

Hutchcroft, Paul D. 1999. "Neither Dynamo nor Domino: Reforms and Crises in the Philippine Political Economy." In *The Politics of the Asian Economic Crisis,* edited by T. J. Pempel, 163–83. Cornell University Press.

IDB (Inter-American Development Bank). 1995. *Economic and Social Progress in Latin America, 1995 Report.* Washington.

———. 2001. *Economic and Social Progress in Latin America, 2001 Report.* Washington.

———. 2004. *Economic and Social Progress in Latin America, 2005 Report.* Washington.

IFC (International Finance Corporation). 1990. *Emerging Stock Market Factbook.* Washington.

———. 1995. *Emerging Stock Market Factbook.* Washington.

IMF (International Monetary Fund). 1997. *World Economic Outlook, Interim Assessment: Crisis in Asia: Regional and Global Implications.* Washington.

———. 1998a. "Financial Crises: Characteristics and Indicators of Vulnerability." *World Economic Outlook, 1998,* 74–97. Washington.

———. 1998b. "Peru: Selected Issues." Country report 98/97. Washington.

———. 2001. "Mexico: Financial System Stability Assessment." Country report 01/192. Washington.

———. 2002a. "Chile: Selected Issues." Country report 02/163. Washington.

———. 2002b. "Mexico: Selected Issues." Country report 02/238. Washington.

———. 2003a. "Chile: Selected Issues." Country report 03/312. Washington.

———. 2003b. "Costa Rica: Financial System Stability Assessment." Country report 03/103. Washington.

———. 2003c. "Republic of Korea: Financial System Stability Assessment." Country report 03/81. Washington.

———. 2003d. "Vietnam: Selected Issues." Country report 03/381. Washington.

———. 2004a. "Chile: Financial Sector Assessment Program." Country report 04/236. Washington.

———. 2004b. "Compilation Guide on Financial Soundness Indicators." Washington.

———. 2004c. "Costa Rica: 2004 Article IV Consultation." Country report 04/298. Washington.

———. 2004d. "Peru: Selected Issues." Country report 04/156. Washington.

————. 2004e. "Singapore: Financial System Stability Assessment." Country report 04/104. Washington.

————. 2004f. "Thailand: Selected Issues." Country report 04/1. Washington.

————. 2005a. "Financial Sector Assessment Program—Background Paper." Document for the International Monetary Fund and World Bank Boards, prepared by the Staff of the Monetary and Financial Systems Department. Washington.

————. 2005b. "Republic of Korea: 2004 Article IV Consultation." Country report 05/49. Washington.

IMF (International Monetary Fund) and World Bank. 2005. "Financial Sector Assessment Program: Review, Lessons, and Issues Going Forward." Document for the International Monetary Fund and World Bank Boards, prepared by the Staff of the International Monetary Fund and World Bank. Washington.

Jenkins, Hatice. 2000. "Commercial Bank Behavior in Micro and Small Enterprise Finance." Development discussion paper 741. Harvard University, Institute for International Development.

Jomo, K. S., ed. 2001. *Malaysian Eclipse: Economic Crisis and Recovery*. London: Zed Books.

Kagami, Mitsuhiro, and Masatsuga Tsuji, eds. 2000. *Privatization, Deregulation, and Economic Efficiency*. Cheltenham: Edward Elgar.

Kaminsky, Graciela L., and Carmen M. Reinhart. 1998. "Financial Crises in Asia and Latin America: Then and Now." *American Economic Review* 88(2): 444–48.

————. 1999. "The Twin Crises: The Causes of Banking and Balance-of-Payments Problems." *American Economic Review* 89(3): 473–500.

Kaminsky, Graciela L., and Sergio Schmukler. 2003. "Short-Run Pain, Long-Run Gain: The Effects of Financial Liberalization." Working paper 9787. Cambridge, Mass.: National Bureau of Economic Research.

Kang, David C., ed. 2001. *Crony Capitalism: Corruption and Development in South Korea and the Philippines*. Cambridge University Press.

Kantis, Hugo, Masahiko Ishida, and Masahiko Komori. 2001. *Entrepreneurship in Emerging Economies: The Creation and Development of New Firms in Latin America and East Asia*. Washington: Inter-American Development Bank.

Kaplan, Ethan, and Dani Rodrik. 2002. "Did the Malaysian Capital Controls Work?" In *Preventing Currency Crises in Emerging Markets,* edited by Sebastian Edwards and Jeffrey A. Frankel, 393–440. University of Chicago Press.

Kaufmann, Daniel, and Aart Kraay. 2002. "Growth without Governance." *Economía* 3(1): 169–229.

Kaufmann, Daniel, Aart Kraay, and Massimo Mastruzzi. 2004. "Governance Matters III: Governance Indicators for 1996, 1998, 2000, and 2002." *World Bank Economic Review* 18(2): 253–87.

Kiguel, Miguel A. 2001. "The Argentine Financial System in the Nineties." Paper prepared for the Conference on Domestic Finance and Global Capital in Latin America. Federal Reserve Bank of Atlanta, Atlanta, 1–2 November.

Kim, Yun-Hwan, ed. 2001. *Government Bond Market Development in Asia*. Manila: Asian Development Bank.

KDB (Korea Development Bank). 2003. *Annual Report*. Seoul.

KEXIM (Korea Export-Import Bank). 2003. *Annual Report*. Seoul.

Koyama, Sérgio Mikio, and Márcio I. Nakane. 2001. "Os efeitos da CPMF sobre a intermediação financeira." Discussion paper 23. Brasília: Central Bank of Brazil.

Krueger, Anne, and Aaron Tornell. 1999. "The Role of Bank Restructuring in Recovering from Crises: Mexico 1995–98." Working paper 7042. Cambridge, Mass.: National Bureau of Economic Research.

Krugman, Paul. 1979. "A Model of Balance-of-Payments Crises." *Journal of Money, Credit, and Banking* 11(3): 311–25.

Kuczynski, Pedro Pablo, and John Williamson, eds. 2003. *After the Washington Consensus: Restarting Growth and Reform in Latin America*. Washington: Institute for International Economics.

Kumar, Anjali. 2005. *Access to Financial Services in Brazil*. Washington: World Bank.

La Porta, Rafael, Florencio López-de-Silanes, and Andrei Shleifer. 2000. "Government Ownership of Banks." Working paper 7620. Cambridge, Mass.: National Bureau of Economic Research.

———. 2002. "Government Ownership of Banks." *Journal of Finance* 57(1): 265–301.

———. 2003. "What Works in Securities Laws?" Working paper 9882. Cambridge, Mass.: National Bureau of Economic Research.

La Porta, Rafael, Florencio López-de-Silanes, and Guillermo Zamarripa. 2002. "Related Lending." Working paper 8848. Cambridge, Mass.: National Bureau of Economic Research.

La Porta, Rafael, and others. 1997. "Legal Determinants of External Finance." *Journal of Finance* 52(3): 1131–50.

———. 1998. "Law and Finance." *Journal of Political Economy* 106(6): 1113–55.

Lardy, Nicholas. 2001. "Foreign Financial Firms in Asia." In *Open Doors: Foreign Participation in Financial Systems in Developing Countries*, edited by Robert Litan, Paul Masson, and Michael Pomerleano, 267–86. Brookings.

Larraín, Felipe, and Marcelo Selowsky, eds. 1991. *The Public Sector and the Latin American Crisis*. San Francisco: ICS Press.

Lee, Chung H., ed. 2003. *Financial Liberalization and the Economic Crisis in Asia*. London: Routledge.

Lees, Francis A., James M. Botts, and Rubens Penha Cysne. 1990. *Banking and Financial Deepening in Brazil*. New York: St. Martin's Press.

Lensink, Robert, and Niels Hermes. 2004. "The Short-Term Effects of Foreign Bank Entry on Domestic Bank Behaviour: Does Economic Development Matter?" *Journal of Banking and Finance* 28(3): 553–68.

Levine, Ross. 1998. "The Legal Environment, Banks, and Long-Run Economic Growth." *Journal of Money, Credit, and Banking* 30(3): 596–613.

———. 1999. "Law, Finance, and Economic Growth." *Journal of Financial Intermediation* 8(1–2): 8–35.

———. 2004. "Finance and Growth: Theory and Evidence." Working paper 10766. Cambridge, Mass.: National Bureau of Economic Research.

Levine, Ross, and Sergio L. Schmukler. 2004. "Migration, Spillovers, and Trade Diversion: The Impact of Internationalization on Domestic Stock Market Activity." Background paper for *Whither Latin American Capital Markets?* Washington: World Bank, Office of the Chief Economist, Latin American and Caribbean Region.

Levine, Ross, and Sara Zervos. 1998. "Stock Markets, Banks, and Economic Growth." *American Economic Review* 88(3): 537–58.

Levy-Yeyati, Eduardo, Alejandro Micco, and Ugo Panizza. 2004. "Should the Government Be in the Banking Business? The Role of State-Owned and Development Banks." Working paper 517. Washington: Inter-American Development Bank, Research Department.

Lewis, W. Arthur. 1950. *The Principles of Economic Planning*. London: Dennis Dobson Ltd.

Lindgren, Carl-Johan, Gillian García, and Matthew I. Saal. 1996. *Bank Soundness and Macro-economic Policy*. Washington: International Monetary Fund.

————. 1999. *Financial Sector Crisis and Restructuring: Lessons from Asia*. Occasional paper 188. Washington: International Monetary Fund.

Liso, Josep M., and others. 2002. "La banca en Latinoamérica: reformas recientes y perspectivas." Colección de Estudios Económicos 30. Barcelona: Caja De Ahorros y Pensiones de Barcelona, Servicio de Estudios.

Litan, Robert E., Paul Masson, and Michael Pomerleano, eds. 2001. *Open Doors: Foreign Participation in Financial Systems in Developing Countries*. Brookings.

Litan, Robert E., Michael Pomerleano, and Vasudevan Sundararajan, eds. 2002. *Financial Sector Governance: The Roles of the Public and Private Sectors*. Brookings.

————, eds. 2003. *The Future of Domestic Capital Markets in Developing Countries*. Brookings.

Lizano, Eduardo. 2003. *Visión desde el banco central, 1998–2002*. San José, Costa Rica: Academia de Centroamérica.

————. 2005. "Veinte años sin crisis financieras (1984–2004): el caso de Costa Rica." *Revista FLAR* 1: 103–66.

Lora, Eduardo. 2002. Comment on "Growth without Governance," by Daniel Kaufmann and Aart Kraay. *Economía* 3(1): 216–24.

Lora, Eduardo, and Ugo Panizza. 2002. "Structural Reforms in Latin America under Scrutiny." Working paper 470. Washington: Inter-American Development Bank, Research Department.

Ma, Guonan, and Eli M. Remolona. 2005. "Opening Markets through a Regional Bond Fund: Lessons from ABF2." *BIS Quarterly Review* (June): 81–92.

Mackey, Michael W. 1999. "Report on the Comprehensive Evaluation of the Operations and Functions of the Fund for the Protection of Bank Savings 'FOBAPROA' and Quality of Supervision of the FOBAPROA Program, 1995–1998." Mexico City: Congress of Mexico.

Makler, Harry M., and Walter L. Ness Jr. 2002. "How Financial Intermediation Challenges National Sovereignty in Emerging Markets." *Quarterly Review of Economics and Finance* 42(5): 827–51.

Marcos Yacamán, Jesús. 2001. "Competition and Consolidation in the Mexican Banking Industry after the 1995 Crisis." Policy paper 4. Basel: Bank for International Settlements.

Marshall, Enrique. 2004a. "El acceso de las PYMEs a los servicios financieros." Presentation prepared for the Club Monetario. Universidad Finis Térrea, Santiago, December.

————. 2004b. "Una vision moderna de la regulación y supervisión bancaria." Presentation prepared for the IV Encuentro Internacional de Finanzas, Santiago, 7–9 January.

Martínez, Lorenza, and Alejandro Werner. 2002. "Capital Markets in Mexico: Recent Development and Future Challenges." Paper prepared for the Seminar on Estabilidad Macro-económica, Mercados Financieros, y Desarrollo Económico. Bank of Mexico, Mexico City, 12–13 November.

Masson, Paul Robert. 1999. "Contagion: Monsoonal Effects, Spillovers, and Jumps between Multiple Equilibria." In *The Asian Financial Crisis: Causes, Contagion, and Consequences*, edited by Pierre Richard Agénor and others, 265–83. Cambridge University Press.

Masuyama, Seiichi. 2002. "Development of Capital Markets and the Reform of Corporate Governance in Asia." Presentation prepared for the Conference on the Role of Capital Markets in Asian Economic Development. Nomura Research Institute and the Institute for Southeast Asian Studies, Tokyo, 7–8 March. Available at www.tcf.or.jp/documents/index.html.

Mathieson, Donald J., and Jorge Roldós. 2001. "How Important Is Financial Sector FDI and What Are Its Impacts?" In *Open Doors: Foreign Participation in Financial Systems in Devel-*

oping Countries, edited by Robert E. Litan, Paul Masson, and Michael Pomerleano, 15–55. Brookings.

Mathieson, Donald J., and others. 2004. *Emerging Local Securities and Derivatives Markets.* Washington: International Monetary Fund.

McKinnon, Ronald I. 1973. *Money and Capital in Economic Development.* Brookings.

McQuerry, Elizabeth. 1999. "The Banking Sector Rescue in Mexico." *Federal Reserve Bank of Atlanta Economic Review* 84(3): 14–29.

———. 2001. "Managed Care for Brazil's Banks." *Federal Reserve Bank of Atlanta Economic Review* 86(2): 27–44.

Mehrez, Gil, and Daniel Kaufmann. 2000. "Transparency, Liberalization, and Banking Crises." Policy research working paper 2286. Washington: World Bank.

Mena, José V. 2005. "BancoEstado: A Successful Public Bank in Latin America." Presentation prepared for the Conference on Public Banks in Latin America. Inter-American Development Bank, Washington, 25 February.

Mian, Atif. 2005. "Foreign, Private, and Government Banks: New Evidence from Emerging Markets." Paper prepared for the Conference on Globalization and Financial Services in Emerging Economies. World Bank, Washington, 20–21 June.

Micco, Alejandro, and Ugo Panizza. 2004. "Bank Ownership and Lending Behavior." Working paper 520. Washington: Inter-American Development Bank, Research Department.

Mishkin, Frederick. 2001. *The Economics of Money, Banking, and Financial Markets.* 6th ed. Boston: Addison Wesley.

Monge-Naranjo, Alexander, Javier Cascante, and Luis J. Hall. 2001. "Enforcement, Contract Design and Default: Exploring the Financial Markets of Costa Rica." In *Defusing Default: Incentives and Institutions*, edited by Marco Pagano, 225–69. Washington: Organization for Economic Cooperation and Development, Development Center and Inter-American Development Bank.

Montes, Manuel F. 1999. "The Philippines as an Unwitting Participant in the Asian Economic Crisis." In *Asian Contagion: Causes and Consequences of a Financial Crisis*, edited by Karl D. Jackson, 241–68. Boulder, Colo: Westview Press.

Montes, Manuel, and Tan Khee Giap. 1999. "Developing the Financial Services Industry in Singapore." In *East Asia's Financial Systems: Evolution and Crisis*, edited by Seiichi Masuyama, Donna Vanderbrink, and Chia Siow Yue, 231–59. Tokyo: Nomura Research Institute and Institute of Southeast Asian Studies.

Montgomery, Heather. 2002. "Taipei, China's Banking Problems: Lessons from the Japanese Experience." Research paper 42. Tokyo: Asian Development Bank Institute.

———. 2003. "Taiwan's Looming Banking Crisis." *Journal of Asian Economics* 14(4): 645–67.

Morais, José Mauro. 2005. "Crédito bancário no Brasil: participação das pequenas empresas e condições de acesso." Productive development series 168. Santiago: Economic Commission for Latin America and the Caribbean.

Morales, Juan Antonio. 2005. "Bolivia: An Economy (Almost) without State-Owned Banks." Presentation prepared for the Conference on Public Bank in Latin America. Inter-American Development Bank, Washington, 25 February.

Morley, Samuel A., Roberto Machado, and Stefano Pettinato. 1999. "Indexes of Structural Reform in Latin America." Economic reform series 12. Santiago: Economic Commission for Latin America and the Caribbean.

Myrdal, Gunnar. 1968. *Asian Drama: An Inquiry into the Poverty of Nations*, 3 vols. New York: Twentieth Century Fund.

Nafin (Nacional Financiera). 2003. *Informe anual, 2003.* Mexico City.

Nasution, Anwar. 1998. "'Big Bang' versus 'Go Slow': Indonesia and Malaysia." In *Financial Reform in Developing Countries*, edited by José M. Fanelli and Rohinton Medhora, 245–95. London: Macmillan.

—. 1999. "The Financial Crisis in Indonesia." In *East Asia's Financial System: Evolution and Crisis*, edited by Seiichi Masuyama, Donna Vanderbrink, and Chia Siow Yue, 74–108. Tokyo: Nomura Research Institute and Institute of Southeast Asian Studies.

—. 2002. "The Indonesian Economic Recovery from the Crisis in 1997–1998." *Journal of Asian Economics* 13(2): 157–80.

Navarrete, Alfredo F. 2001. "The Role of the Corporate Bond Market in Mexico as a Source of Finance." Paper prepared for the Conference on Financial Markets in Mexico. Center for Research on Economic Development and Policy Reform, Stanford, Calif., 5–6 October.

Nellis, John, and Nancy Birdsall, eds. 2005. *Reality Check: The Distributional Impact of Privatization in Developing Countries*. Washington: Center for Global Development.

Ness, Walter L. 2000a. "Financing Brazilian Firms through Domestic Capital Markets." Buenos Aires: Universidad Argentina de Empresas.

—. 2000b. "Reducing Government Bank Presence in the Brazilian Financial System: Why and How?" *Quarterly Review of Economics and Finance* 40(1): 71–84.

Nidhiprabha, Bhanupong. 2003. "Premature Liberalization and Economic Crisis in Thailand." In *Financial Liberalization and Crisis in Asia*, edited by Chung H. Lee, 27–46. London: Routledge.

North, Douglass C. 1961. *The Economic Growth of the United States, 1790–1860*. Upper Saddle River, N.J.: Prentice-Hall.

—. 1990. *Institutions, Institutional Change, and Economic Performance*. Cambridge University Press.

Nugent, Jeffrey B., and Seung-Jae Yhee. 2002. "Small and Medium Enterprises in Korea: Achievements, Constraints, and Policy Issues." *Small Business Economics* 18 (1–3): 85–119.

Obstfeld, Maurice. 1986. "Rational and Self-Fulfilling Balance-of-Payment Crises." *American Economic Review* 76(1): 72–81.

Ocampo, José Antonio. 2003. "Capital-Account and Counter-Cyclical Prudential Regulation in Developing Countries." In *From Capital Surges to Drought: Seeking Stability for Emerging Economies*, edited by Ricardo Ffrench-Davis and Stephany Griffith-Jones, 217–44. New York: Palgrave Macmillan.

O'Dougherty, Pascual, and Moisés J. Schwartz. 2001. "Prudential Regulation of Foreign Exchange: The Mexican Experience." Policy paper 1. Basel: Bank for International Settlements.

OECD (Organization for Economic Cooperation and Development). 2001. *OECD Economic Surveys: Brazil, 2000–2001*. Paris.

—. 2002. *OECD Economic Surveys: Mexico, 2001–2002*. Paris.

—. 2005. *OECD Economics Surveys: Brazil, 2005*. Paris.

Oman, Charles. 2001. "Corporate Governance and National Development." Technical paper 180. Paris: Organization for Economic Cooperation and Development, Development Center.

Oman, Charles, Steven Fries, and Willem Buiter. 2003. "Corporate Governance in Developing, Transition, and Emerging-Market Economies." Policy brief 23. Paris: Organization for Economic Cooperation and Development, Development Center.

Pangestu, Mari, and Manggi Habir. 2002. "The Boom, Bust, and Restructuring of Indonesian Banks." Working paper 02/66. Washington: International Monetary Fund.

Park, Daekeun, and Yung Chul Park. 2005. "Toward Developing Regional Bonds Markets in East Asia." *Asian Economic Papers* 3(2): 183–209.

Peck, Joseph, and Eric S. Rosengren. 2000. "Implications of the Globalization of the Banking Sector: The Latin American Experience." *Federal Reserve Bank of Boston New England Economic Review* (September–October): 45–62.

Pinheiro, Armando Castelar, and Célia Cabral. 2001. "Credit Markets in Brazil: The Role of the Judiciary and Other Institutions." In *Defusing Default: Incentives and Institutions*, edited by Marco Pagano, 157–88. Washington: Organization for Economic Cooperation and Development, Development Center and Inter-American Development Bank.

Pinheiro, Armando Castelar, Regis Bonelli, and Ben Ross Schneider. 2004. "Pragmatic Policy in Brazil: The Political Economy of Incomplete Market Reform." Discussion paper 1035. Brasília: Instituto de Pesquisa Econômica Aplicada.

Pollack, Molly, and Alvaro García. 2004. "Crecimiento, competitividad y equidad: rol del sectorfinanciero." Financing development series 147. Santiago: Economic Commission for Latin America and the Caribbean.

Powell, Andrew. 2005. "On the Real Dangers That Lurk Behind Basel II for Emerging Economies." Buenos Aires: Universidad Torcuato Di Tella.

Pritchett, Lant. 2002. Comment on "Growth without Governance," by Daniel Kaufmann and Aart Kraay. *Economía* 3(1): 224–27.

Przeworski, Adam. 2004a. "Institutions Matter?" *Government and Opposition* 39(4): 527–40.

———. 2004b. "The Last Instance: Are Institutions a Deeper Cause of Economic Development?" *European Archives of Sociology* 45(2): 168–88.

Puga, Fernando Pimentel. 1999. "Sistema financeiro brasileiro: reestruturação recente, comparações internacionais e vulnerabilidade à crise cambial." Discussion paper 68. Brasília: Banco Nacional de Desenvolvimento Econômico e Social.

Radelet, Steven, and Jeffrey Sachs. 1998. "The East Asian Financial Crisis: Diagnosis, Remedies, Prospects." *Brookings Papers on Economic Activity* 8(1): 1–74.

Reisen, Helmut. 2000. "Revisions to the Basel Accord and Sovereign Ratings." In *Global Finance from a Latin American Viewpoint*, edited by Ricardo Hausmann and Ulrich Hiemenz, 71–80. Paris: Inter-American Development Bank and Organization for Economic Cooperation and Development, Development Center.

Republic of China. 2004. *Taiwan Statistical Data Book, 2004*. Taipei: Council for Economic Planning and Development, Executive Yuan.

Reynoso, Alejandro. 2004. "Opening up a Securities Market: Mexico's New Push for Liberalization, 2003–2004." Paper prepared for the Conference on Latin American Financial Systems and the Challenges of Economic Growth. Stanford Center for International Development, Stanford, Calif., 11–13 November.

Rioja, Felix, and Neven Valev. 2004a. "Does One Size Fit All? A Reexamination of the Finance and Growth Relationship." *Journal of Development Economics* 74(2): 429–47.

———. 2004b. "Finance and the Source of Growth at Various Stages of Economic Development." *Economic Inquiry* 42(1): 127–40.

Rivas, Gonzalo. 2004. "Opciones de la banca de desarrollo en Chile: el 'convivado de piedra' del sistema financiero chileno." Financing development series 148. Santiago: Economic Commission for Latin America and the Caribbean.

Rodrik, Dani, Arvind Subramanian, and Francesco Trebbi. 2002. "Institutions Rule: The Primacy of Institutions over Geography and Integration in Economic Development." Working paper 9305. Cambridge, Mass.: National Bureau of Economic Research.

Rojas-Suárez, Liliana, and Steven R. Weisbrod. 1996. "The Do's and Don'ts of Banking Crisis Management." In *Banking Crises in Latin America*, edited by Ricardo Hausmann and Liliana Rojas-Suárez, 119–68. Washington: Inter-American Development Bank.

Román, Enrique. 2003. "Acceso al crédito bancario de las microempresas chilenas: lecciones de la década de los noventa." Financing development series 138. Santiago: Economic Commission for Latin America and the Caribbean.

Salomon Smith Barney. 2001. "Foreign Financial Institutions in Latin America, 2001 Update." New York.

Sanhueza, Gonzalo. 1999. "La crisis financiera de los años ochenta en Chile: análisis de sus soluciones y su costo." *Economía Chilena* 2(1): 43–68.

———. 2001. "Chilean Banking Crisis of the 1980s: Solutions and Estimation of the Costs." Working paper 104. Santiago: Central Bank of Chile.

Sebrae (Serviço Brasileiro de Apoio as Micro e Pequenas Empresas). 2004. *Sistema financiero e as pequenas empresas: diagnósticos e perspectivas.* Brasília.

———. 2005. *Boletim estatístico de micro e pequenas empresas.* Brasília.

Shaw, Edward S. 1973. *Financial Deepening in Economic Development.* Oxford University Press.

Shleifer, Andrei, and Robert W. Vishny. 1997. "A Survey of Corporate Governance." *Journal of Finance* 52(2): 737–83.

———. 1998. *The Grabbing Hand: Government Pathologies and Their Cures.* Harvard University Press.

SME Bank. 2003. *Annual Report.* Bangkok.

Snyder, Richard. 2001. *Politics after Neoliberalism: Reregulation in Mexico.* Cambridge University Press.

Stallings, Barbara. 1987. *Banker to the Third World: U.S. Portfolio Investment in Latin America, 1900–1987.* University of California Press.

————, ed. 1995. *Global Change, Regional Response: The New International Context of Development.* Cambridge University Press.

———. 2005. "Financial Sector Development in Latin America and East Asia: A Comparison of Chile and South Korea." In *Managing Development: Globalization, Economic Restructuring, and Social Policy,* edited by Junji Nakagawa, 139–61. London: Routledge.

Stallings, Barbara, and Wilson Peres. 2000. *Growth, Employment, and Equity: The Impact of the Economic Reforms in Latin America and the Caribbean.* Brookings.

Stallings, Barbara, and Rogerio Studart. 2003. "Financial Regulation and Supervision in Emerging Markets: The Experience of Latin America after the Tequila Crisis." In *From Capital Surges to Drought: Seeking Stability for Emerging Economies,* edited by Ricardo Ffrench-Davis and Stephany Griffith-Jones, 292–316. New York: Palgrave Macmillan.

Standard and Poor's. 2000. *Emerging Stock Market Factbook, 2000.* New York.

———. 2005. *Global Stock Markets Factbook, 2005.* New York.

Stiglitz, Joseph E. 1994. "The Role of the State in Financial Markets." In *Proceedings of the Annual Bank Conference on Economic Development 1993,* edited by Michael Bruno and Boris Pleskovic, 19–52. Washington: World Bank.

———. 2002. *Globalization and Its Discontents.* W. W. Norton.

Stiglitz, Joseph E., and Shahid Yusuf, eds. 2001. *Rethinking the East Asian Miracle.* Washington: World Bank.

Studart, Rogerio. 1995. *Investment Finance in Economic Development.* London: Routledge.

———. 2000. "Pension Funds and the Financing of Productive Investment: An Analysis Based on Brazil's Recent Experience." Financing development series 102. Santiago: Economic Commission for Latin America and the Caribbean.

———. 2003. "Changing Expectations, Capital Surges and the Banking Sector: Argentina, Brazil, Chile and Mexico in the 1990s." In *Financial Stability and Growth in Emerging Economies,* edited by Jan Joost Teunissen and Mark Teunissen, 15–44. The Hague: Fondad.

Studart, Rogerio, and Jennifer Hermann. 2001. "Sistemas financeiros no mercosul: perspectivas a partir das reformas dos anos 1990." Discussion paper 799. Brasília: Instituto de Pesquisa Econômica Aplicada.

Taylor, Lance. 1983. *Structuralist Macroeconomics: Applicable Models for the Third World*. New York: Basic Books.

Teichman, Judith A. 2001. *The Politics of Freeing Markets in Latin America: Chile, Argentina, and Mexico*. University of North Carolina Press.

Teixeira Torres Filho, Ernani. 2005. "Financiación de la inversión: el caso del banco de desarrollo de Brasil (BNDES)." Presentation prepared for the Seminar on Financial Sector in Latin America. Economic Commission for Latin America and the Caribbean, Santiago, 28–29 April.

Thorne, Alfredo. 1998. "Mexico's Banks Still Undercapitalized." *J. P. Morgan Economic Research Note* (November 13).

Titelman, Daniel. 2003. "La banca de desarrollo y el financiamiento productivo." Financing development series 137. Santiago: Economic Commission for Latin America and the Caribbean.

Turner, Philip. 2002. "Procyclicality of Regulatory Ratios." In *International Capital Markets: Systems in Transition*, edited by John Eatwell and Lance Taylor, 475–84. Oxford University Press.

Underhill, Geoffrey. 2001. "The Public Good versus Private Interests and the Global Financial and Monetary Systems." In *The Market or the Public Domain? Global Governance and the Asymmetry of Power*, edited by Daniel Drache, 274–95. London: Routledge.

United Nations. 1999. *World Economic and Social Survey, 1999*. New York.

Uribe, José Darío and Hernando Vargas. 2002. "Financial Reform, Crisis, and Consolidation in Colombia." Paper prepared for the Preparatory Workshop for Madrid Seminar of the Eurosystem and Latin American Central Banks. Central Bank of Colombia, Bogotá, 21–22 March.

Uthoff, Andras. 2001. "La reforma del sistema de pensiones y su impacto en el mercado de capitales." In *Reformas, crecimiento y políticas sociales en Chile desde 1973*, edited by Ricardo Ffrench-Davis and Barbara Stallings, 231–61. Santiago: Economic Commission for Latin America and the Caribbean and LOM Ediciones.

Vajragupta, Yos, and Pakorn Vichyanond. 1999. "Thailand's Financial Evolution and the 1997 Crisis." In *East Asia's Financial System: Evolution and Crisis*, edited by Seiichi Masuyama, Donna Vanderbrink, and Chia Siow Yue, 34–73. Tokyo: Nomura Research Institute and Institute of Southeast Asian Studies.

Valdés Prieto, Salvador. 1992. "Ajuste estructural en el mercado de capitals: la evidencia chilena." In *El modelo económico chileno*, edited by Daniel L. Wisecarver, 401–44. Santiago: Centro Internacional para el Desarrollo Económico (CINDE).

Vichyanond, Pakorn. 2002. "Capital Market Development in Thailand." Paper prepared for the Conference on the Role of Capital Markets in Asian Economic Development. Nomura Research Institute and Institute of Southeast Asian Studies, Tokyo, March 7–8. Available at www.tcf.or.jp/documents/index.html.

Von Mettenheim, Kurt. 2005. "Commanding Heights: The Politics of Brazilian Federal Government Banking." Oxford: Center for Brazilian Studies.

Wade, Robert. 1990. *Governing the Market: Economic Theory and the Role of Government in East Asian Industrialization*. Princeton University Press.

Walker, Eduardo H., and Fernando Lefort. 2002. "Pension Reform and Capital Markets: Are There Any (Hard) Links?" Social protection discussion paper series 0201. Washington: World Bank.

Warr, Peter, ed. 2004. *Thailand beyond the Crisis*. London: Routledge.

Welch, John H. 1993. *Capital Markets in the Development Process: The Case of Brazil*. University of Pittsburgh Press.

Weyland, Kurt. 2002. *The Politics of Market Reform in Fragile Democracies: Argentina, Brazil, Peru, and Venezuela*. Princeton University Press.

Williamson, John. 2005. *Curbing the Boom-Bust Cycle: Stabilizing Capital Flows to Emerging Markets*. Policy Analyses in International Economics 75. Washington: Institute for International Economics.

Woo, Jung-en. 1991. *Race to the Swift: State and Finance in Korean Industrialization*. Columbia University Press.

World Bank. 1992. *World Development Report, 1992*. Oxford University Press.

———. 1993. *The East Asian Miracle: Economic Growth and Public Policy*. Oxford University Press.

———. 1999. *Global Economic Prospects, 1998/99*. Washington.

———. 2001. *Finance for Growth: Policy Choices in a Volatile World*. Oxford University Press.

———. 2002. "Mexico: Financial Sector Assessment." Washington.

———. 2004a. *Global Development Finance, 2004*. Washington.

———. 2004b. *Poverty in Mexico: An Assessment of Conditions, Trends, and Government Policies*. Washington.

———. 2004c. *Whither Latin American Capital Markets?* Washington: World Bank, Office of the Chief Economist, Latin American and Caribbean Region.

World Economic Forum. 1999. *The Global Competitiveness Report, 1999*. Oxford University Press.

Yang, Ya-Hwei, and Jia-Dong Shea. 1999. "Evolution of Taiwan's Financial System." In *East Asia's Financial System: Evolution and Crisis*, edited by Seiichi Masuyama, Donna Vanderbrink, and Chia Siow Yue, 260–90. Tokyo: Nomura Research Institute and Institute of Southeast Asian Studies.

Yermo, Juan. 2004. "Pension Reform and Capital Market Development." Background paper for *Keeping the Promise of Social Security in Latin America*. Washington: World Bank, Office of the Chief Economist, Latin American and Caribbean Region.

Yoshitomi, Masaru, and Sayuri Shirai. 2001. "Designing a Financial Market Structure in Post-Crisis Asia: How to Develop Corporate Bond Markets." Working paper 15. Tokyo: Asian Development Bank Institute.

Zervos, Sara. 2004. "The Transaction Costs of Primary Market Issuance: The Case of Brazil, Chile, and Mexico." Background paper for *Whither Latin American Capital Markets?* Washington: World Bank, Office of the Chief Economist, Latin American and Caribbean Region.

Zhuang, Juzhong. 2000. *Corporate Governance and Finance in East Asia*. 2 vols. Manila: Asian Development Bank.

Zysman, John. 1983. *Governments, Markets, and Growth: Financial Systems and the Politics of Industrial Change*. Cornell University Press.

Index